The Essential
Greek Historians

The Essential Greek Historians

Edited, with Introductions and Notes, by
STANLEY M. BURSTEIN

Hackett Publishing Company, Inc.
Indianapolis/Cambridge

For further information, please address
   Hackett Publishing Company, Inc.
   P.O. Box 44937
   Indianapolis, Indiana 46244-0937

   www.hackettpublishing.com

Cover and interior design by E. L. Wilson
Composition by Aptara, Inc.

Library of Congress Control Number: 2021944430

ISBN-13: 978-1-64792-040-1 (pbk.)
ISBN-13: 978-1-64792-050-0 (cloth)
ISBN-13: 978-1-64792-051-7 (PDF ebook)

The paper used in this publication meets the minimum requirements of American
National Standard for Information Sciences—Permanence of Paper for Printed
Library Materials, ANSI Z39.48–1984.

∞

Contents

Chapter 3: Xenophon, *The Hellenica*

Chapter 4: Aristotle, *The Constitution of Athens*

Chapter 5: *The Parian Marble*

Chapter 6: Polybius, *The Histories*

Chapter 7: Memnon, *History of Heracleia*

Chapter 8: Plutarch, *Life of Alexander*

To the memory of
Dr. Mortimer H. Chambers Jr. (1927–2020)
Distinguished scholar, teacher, mentor, colleague, and friend

PREFACE

Greek historians frequently complain that most of ancient Greek literature has been lost. So, for example, of the almost 1,000 Greek writers who wrote histories, the works of less than a dozen have been preserved, and not all of those completely. As the familiar cliché goes, however, a glass can be viewed as half empty or half full, and in the case of Greek historical literature, the glass is definitely half full. The works that have been preserved include those of some of the most distinguished prose authors in Greek literature and some of the most interesting narrative literature to survive from antiquity. For over half a century, the most popular introduction to Greek historiography for students has been M. I. Finley's *The Portable Greek Historians*.

The Portable Greek Historians has served students well, but its weaknesses have become more and more apparent with time. Three are particularly noteworthy. First, although no anthology can be truly comprehensive, Finley did not provide students with a true picture of the range and variety of Greek historiography by limiting his selections to the works of only four authors. Second, the translations he used were archaic—the latest was published in 1889—and are increasingly difficult to read by contemporary students. Third, and finally, the supporting material—introduction, notes, and bibliography—were all limited. The present anthology aims to remedy these flaws and to provide contemporary students with an introduction to the riches of ancient Greek historiography that will serve them as well as *The Portable Greek Historians* did. To that end, more readable translations have been used and provided with the necessary supporting materials, including contextual summaries and footnotes and a list of suggested readings.

Every author acquires debts to other scholars in the course of research and writing, and I would like to take this opportunity to acknowledge mine. First, and foremost, is to a great historian and teacher, Professor Mortimer H. Chambers Jr. of UCLA, who kindly agreed to review and revise Sir Frederick G. Kenyon's translation of Aristotle's *The Constitution of Athens*. I would also like to express my gratitude to Dr. Andrew Smith, who generously granted permission to reprint selections from his excellent translation of Memnon's *History of Heracleia Pontica*. Thanks also are due to Professors Frank Holt of the University of Houston, Jennifer T. Roberts of the City University of New York, and Raimund Schulz of the University of Bielefeld, who read and commented on earlier drafts of the Introduction. Finally, I particularly would like to thank Rick Todhunter of Hackett Publishing Company, who suggested this project and has supported it throughout.

NOTE ON TRANSLATIONS

There have been literally dozens of English translations of the major Greek historians since the Renaissance, some of which, for example, the philosopher Thomas Hobbes's translation of Thucydides's *History of the Peloponnesian War*, are themselves literary classics. At the same time, the archaic language of even the best of the many available translations makes them increasingly difficult for contemporary students to read and appreciate. For that reason, the translations used in this book, which are listed below, have been selected for both their accuracy and their readability:

Aristotle, *The Athenian Constitution*, trans. by Sir Frederick Kenyon (London: G. Bell, 1914) with corrections and revisions by Mortimer H. Chambers.

Herodotus, *On the War for Greek Freedom: Selections from the Histories*, trans. by Samuel Shirley with Introduction and Notes by James Romm (Indianapolis: Hackett Publishing Company, 2003).

Memnon, *History of Heracleia*, trans. by Andrew Smith (Attalus.org [www.attalus .org/info/memnon.html]).

Plutarch, *Lives That Made Greek History*, trans. by Pamela Mensch with Introductions and Notes by James Romm (Indianapolis: Hackett Publishing Company, 2012).

Polybius, *The Histories*, trans. by W. R. Paton, 6 vols. (Cambridge, MA: Harvard University Press, 1922–1927).

Thucydides, *On Justice, Power, and Human Nature*, trans. by Paul Woodruff (Indianapolis: Hackett Publishing Company, 1993).

Xenophon, *Hellenica*, trans. by Carleton L. Brownson, 2 vols. (Cambridge, MA: Harvard University Press, 1918–1921).

The *Parian Marble* has been translated specially for this volume by the editor, Stanley M. Burstein. Unless otherwise noted, he has also created anew all introductions and notes.

For consistency's sake, the spelling of some terms and names in the translations of Xenophon (Chapter 3), Aristotle (Chapter 4), Polybius (Chapter 6), and Memnon (Chapter 7) have been Americanized.

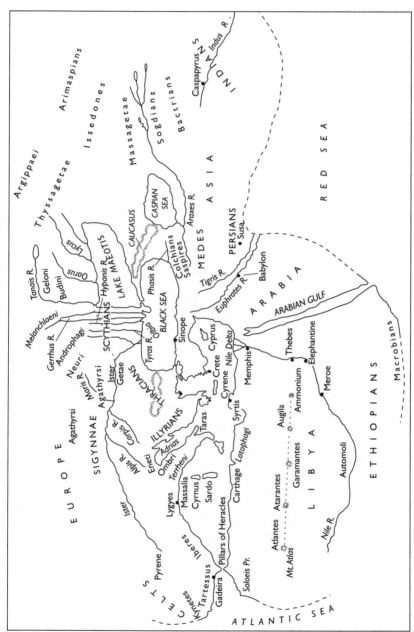

Herodotus's View of the World. From Herodotus, *On the War for Greek Freedom*. Edited by James Romm. Hackett Publishing Company, 2003. Reprinted by permission.

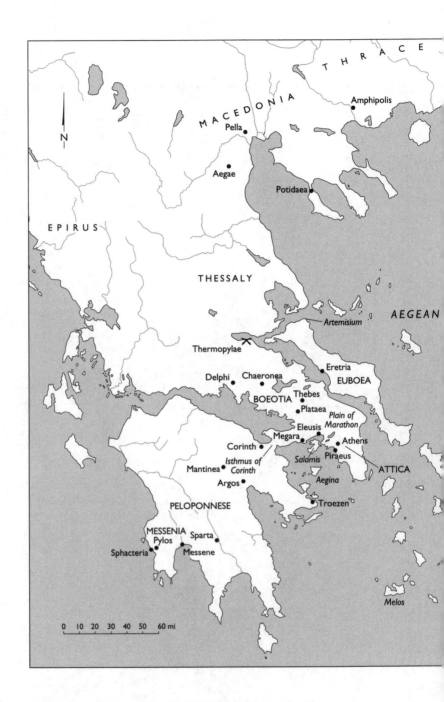

The Greek World. From Plutarch, *Lives That Made Greek History*. Edited by James Romm. Hackett Publishing Company, 2012. Reprinted by permission.

BLACK SEA

Perinthus

Byzantium

Bosporus

Chersonese

Hellespont

SEA

Lesbos

Mytilene

A N A T O L I A

L Y D I A

Sardis

Ephesus

Samos

Delos

Miletus

CARIA

Naxos

Halicarnassus

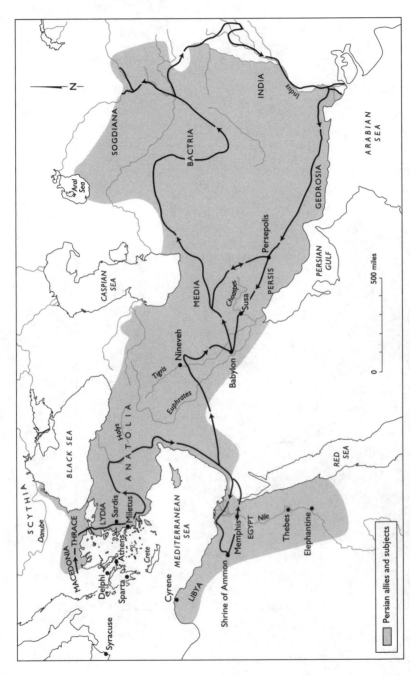

The Persian Empire and the Route of Alexander's Campaigns. From Plutarch, *Lives That Made Greek History*. Edited by James Romm. Hackett Publishing Company, 2012. Reprinted by permission.

INTRODUCTION

Historians working in the second half of the nineteenth century CE considered the founding of the Olympic Games in 776 BCE the earliest verifiable event in Greek history. To these scholars, the history of Greece—and its Egyptian and Near Eastern neighbors—before that date was largely a blank. Now the situation is dramatically different. Textbooks of ancient history routinely begin their narrative histories of Greece (and Egypt and Mesopotamia) thousands of years earlier. Modern historians are able to do this thanks to two triumphs of modern scholarship: the decipherment of the written records of ancient Egypt and Mesopotamia and archaeologists' discovery and excavation of many of the principal sites of these ancient civilizations.

Yet students of ancient-history textbooks cannot miss the difference between their textbooks' accounts of Egyptian and ancient Near Eastern history, and of Greek and Roman history. Names of kings and references to battles abound in the former. Missing, however, are the accounts of political and military history and the kinds of fine-grained, personal details that characterize Greek and Roman history. The reason for this disparity is straightforward: the Egyptians and the peoples of the ancient Near East did not write history and the Greeks and Romans did. But what is history?

That is a deceptively simple question to which, since antiquity, innumerable answers have been given. Before we attempt to define the term, however, we must make a necessary distinction. *History* is what historians study and try to reconstruct—the events and developments that unfolded, in real time, in the past. But the syntheses, narratives, and critical examinations created by historians based on their study of these past events constitute *historiography*, and it is to this term we refer when we say that the Greeks and Romans "wrote history." According to a recent brief and lucid definition, historiography is "the elaborated, secular, prose narrative . . . of public events, based on inquiry."[1] While not all historiography is secular—church history is an obvious exception—this definition highlights two distinctive elements that have characterized European historiography from its Greek origins to the present: it is a form of literature, and it is based on evidence discovered by inquiry. Historical thinking, as implied by this definition, is, in the striking phrase of a recent scholar, an "unnatural act."[2] It is not surprising, therefore, that while virtually all peoples are interested in their past and tell stories about it, only two ancient peoples—the

---

1. John Burrow, *A History of Histories: Epics, Chronicles, Romances and Inquiries from Herodotus and Thucydides to the Twentieth Century* (New York: Alfred A. Knopf, 2008), 3.
2. Sam Wineburg, *Historical Thinking and Other Unnatural Acts: Charting the Future of Teaching the Past* (Philadelphia: Temple University Press, 2001).

Greeks and the Chinese—developed and maintained historiographic traditions throughout antiquity.[3] As it is not possible to treat both Greek and Chinese historiography in one small book, the selections collected in this volume are intended to introduce students to representative examples of Greek historiography from its origin in the fifth century BCE to its change of primary focus—from the history of Greece to that of Rome—in the second century CE.

Greek historiography was a rich and varied tradition. Although the works of fewer than a dozen Greek historians survive today, we know the names of almost a thousand authors who wrote historical works during the period covered by this book. The subjects they tackled ranged widely and included mythology, ethnography, the history of Greece, and universal history. Despite the broad range and variety of Greek historiography, most ancient Greek historians shared three characteristics. First, unlike Chinese historians, who tended to be government officials, they were private individuals. Second, Greek historians' preferred subjects were war and politics. Third, and finally, most had actively participated in the political life of their cities. Ancient literary critics generally agreed that the father of Greek historiography was Herodotus of Halicarnassus and that his *Histories*, the book we now refer to as the *History of the Persian Wars*, was the first historical work written in Greek.

Unfortunately, we know little more than the barest details of Herodotus's life. He was born in Halicarnassus to a mixed Greek and Carian family and died in the Athenian colony of Thurii in South Italy. References in the *Histories* to events of the 420s BCE indicate that he was still alive at that time and therefore suggest that he was born in the early fifth century BCE, perhaps in the 480s BCE. Of his life between those two dates, we know only that he may have been exiled from Halicarnassus because of his opposition to the city's tyranny and that he settled in Thurii sometime after its foundation by Athens in 444 BCE. Allusions in the *Histories* also indicate that he traveled widely in the Greek world during his exile, visiting, at a minimum, Samos, Delphi, Athens, South Italy, and the Black Sea, and probably also giving public readings based on his researches. In addition, he visited several non-Greek countries, including Phoenicia and Egypt. This brief sketch gives some idea of the breadth of experience that Herodotus brought to writing the *Histories*. But for more about the origin of his *Histories*, and of Greek historiography generally, we must turn to the book itself.

The *Histories* is a remarkable book. In the fifth century BCE, when prose works were short, intended to be read aloud in one brief meeting, Herodotus produced a work almost as long as Homer's *Iliad* and *Odyssey* combined. The *Histories* is not only the longest prose work to survive from the fifth century BCE, but it was

---

3. The Jews developed a form of historiography but had ceased to write history by the first century BCE, while Roman historiography was clearly developed under Greek influence and cannot be considered an independent development.

probably also the longest prose work written to that date in Greek. Its content was as remarkable as its length. In nine books, Herodotus traces the rise of the Persian Empire from its foundation in the mid-sixth century BCE to the epic confrontation between the Persian Empire and the Greek alliance led by Athens and Sparta in the 490s and 480s BCE. His detailed ethnographies[4] of the peoples conquered by Persia during its rise to power highlight the empire's power and the magnitude of the ultimate Greek victory. Why Herodotus wrote such an extraordinary work, which could not easily be read aloud, is one of the great questions of classical scholarship.

Attempts to answer that question have dominated the last 150 years of Herodotean studies. The reason most commonly offered is that the apparent division of the *Histories* into two halves—the first four books, which emphasize ethnography, and the last five books, which essentially comprise a monograph on the Persian Wars—reflects Herodotus's intellectual development. Although they differ in details, most such interpretations agree in maintaining that Herodotus began his career as an ethnographer. It was only later that he would have become a historian, when he decided to refocus his book on the theme of the confrontation between Persia and Greece and to integrate the ethnographic material he had collected during his travels into the big story of the rise of the Persian Empire and the failure of its invasion of Greece in 480/79 BCE. Accepting such theories would mean, ironically, that the founding father of Greek historiography wrote a history of the Persian Empire, not of Greece. Equally important, scholars recognize that Herodotus did not write in a vacuum; he was influenced by the late sixth-century BCE mythographer and geographer Hecataeus of Miletus, one of the major figures of Ionian natural philosophy.

Hecataeus wrote two books, the first of which was the *Periodos Ges*, or *Journey Around the Earth*. The *Periodos Ges* was a geography of the world known to the Greeks in two books; it took readers on an imaginary voyage around the Mediterranean and Black Seas and was intended to accompany a world map. Hecataeus's other work was the *Genealogies*, a systematic account of Greek mythology and legend from the origin of the gods to the last of the heroes of Greek legend. Of Hecataeus's works, only fragments survive, found in brief quotations and allusions made by later authors. But these little bits and pieces suffice to show that the *Periodos Ges* included ethnographic information on non-Greek peoples living from Iberia to India and Central Asia to Egypt, while in the *Genealogies*, he subjected Greek mythology and legend to a rationalistic critique intended to eliminate elements that couldn't exist in nature because (as he said in his preface) the stories of the Greeks were "many and foolish." A particularly good example of Hecataeus's method was his rationalization of stories about Cerberus, the three-headed hound who guarded the entrance to Hades. Hecataeus claimed that such stories actually referred not to

---

4. Ethnographies are descriptions of foreign peoples, usually including accounts of their environment, history, society, customs, and religion.

a mythical three-headed dog but rather to a real, and exceptionally venomous, snake who had killed numerous men.

It's clear that Herodotus was familiar with and made use of Hecataeus's works. Hecataeus is the only prose author to which Herodotus refers by name in the *Histories*, and numerous passages in that work show Hecataeus's influence. So, for example, at the beginning of the *Histories*, Herodotus provided a rationalized version of the story of Io. According to Greek myth, Zeus slept with Io; Hera, Zeus's jealous wife, then took her revenge on Io by changing her into a cow and driving her—via an annoying gadfly—into Egypt. In Herodotus's version of the story, however, Io's unnatural transformation into a cow is eliminated. She is instead depicted as an Argive princess kidnapped by Phoenician merchants and transported to Egypt to be sold as a slave. Herodotus's knowledge of Hecataeus's works is also revealed in other passages of the *Histories*, including his critique of maps in which the world is portrayed as encircled by Ocean despite the lack of proof that Ocean existed, and Herodotus's refutation of the Hecataean theory that Ocean is the source of the Nile. Nevertheless, the theory that Herodotus began his career as an ethnographer in the manner of Hecataeus—and that traces of his career as an ethnographer can be found in the early sections of the *Histories*—is overly simplistic.

Though some scholars have attempted to show that the *Histories* is a composite work, one that illustrates different stages of Herodotus's intellectual development, a detailed study of the *Histories* clearly reveals that it is a carefully organized and unified work that reflects intellectual trends of the mid-fifth century BCE. Thus, for example, Herodotus's unprejudiced descriptions of the cultures of "barbarians" (which caused the second-century CE essayist and biographer Plutarch to denounce him as a "barbarian lover") reflected the sophists' cultural relativism. Likewise, while epic works such as the *Iliad* and *Odyssey*, among others, attest to the Greeks' long-standing interest in their ancient past, Herodotus wrote about a recent event— the Persian Wars—that was still topical in the late fifth century BCE. Throughout Greece, festivals and monuments commemorated the Greek victory; artists and poets such as the Athenian dramatist Aeschylus and the Theban choral lyric poet Pindar celebrated it in their works; and other prose authors wrote books featuring themes related to the Persian Wars. At the same time, the growth of the Athenian Empire and the increasing hostility between Athens and Sparta encouraged regret over the collapse of the Panhellenic alliance that had defeated Persia and preserved Greek freedom.[5]

Luckily for us, and unlike most ancient Greek historians, Herodotus frequently interrupts his own narrative to comment on the process of research and writing.

---

5. The Greek defense against the Persian invasion in 480/79 BCE was conducted by an alliance known as the Hellenic League, led by Sparta and Athens. The names of the thirty-one cities, mostly from central and southern Greece, are preserved on the so-called Serpent Column, the base of the monument dedicated to Apollo at Delphi, which still exists in Istanbul.

He refers to himself and his opinions on historical questions literally hundreds of times throughout the *Histories*. In his preface, he provides his clearest statement about his goals and methodology:

> Herodotus of Halicarnassus here gives the results of his researches [*historie*], so that the events of human history may not fade with time and the notable achievements of both of Greeks and of foreigners may not lack their due fame; and, among other things, to show why these people came to make war on one another.

Ancient literary critics called Herodotus the most Homeric of historians. That characterization is fully justified by his preface, in which he declares his purpose is to ensure that the "notable achievements" of people not "lack their due fame"; this was also the goal of traditional epic poetry like Homer's. Yet Herodotus clearly distinguishes his project from Homer's poetry in two ways. First, while Homer claimed the authority of the Muses for the validity of his story, Herodotus asserted personal responsibility for the truth of his work, declaring that it represented the giving forth "of the results of the researches" of Herodotus of Halicarnassus. In Herodotus's time, *historie*, the Greek word translated here as "researches"—as in "inquiries"—did not mean "history" as we understand it. Instead, it meant "research" in the sense of a judicial investigation collecting evidence relevant to settling a dispute. Second, unlike Homer—whose only explanation for the cause of the events described in the *Iliad* was that "the will of Zeus was fulfilled"—Herodotus included "why these people came to make war on one another" among the things to be investigated. Herodotus did not deny that the gods could occasionally influence human events. Still, with rare exceptions, he adduced human, not divine, causes for historical events. Moreover, Herodotus's methodology and goals, as outlined in his preface, required that he deal, perhaps for the first time, with two central problems every historian faces: the identification and analysis of relevant sources and the periodization of events.

Over the past half-century, our understanding of the nature of Herodotus's sources has changed radically. Herodotus claimed that his inquiry was based on observation, judgment, and what he heard, and of these methods of collecting evidence, clearly the last—oral testimony—was the most important. While inscriptions and other written texts are cited in the *Histories*, recent scholarship indicates that Herodotus relied primarily on oral sources. He collected these oral accounts from informants, men he called *logioi*, or "men who know traditions," during his travels. Although Herodotus refers to both Greek and non-Greek informants, most were probably Greek-speaking since he seems not to have spoken any other language.

Oral traditions have been studied extensively, particularly in Africa, by anthropologists and historians, and their research has revealed four characteristics that are typical of such sources. First, facts are not isolated but embedded in narratives focused on individuals. Second, such traditions are continually modified to reflect the changing interests of the people who preserve and tell them. Third, chronologically earlier parts of narratives tend to become less detailed over time. Fourth, and finally, oral tradition rarely preserves accurate information concerning events that happened more than a century before the stories were collected and recorded.

As all these features are readily apparent in the *Histories*, it is clear that Herodotus conducted his inquiry by collecting oral narratives, which he called *logoi*.[6] We can tell that in composing the *Histories*, Herodotus scrutinized these narratives for authenticity, then organized them around the theme of the Persian Wars. Fortunately, Herodotus is transparent about the tests to which he subjected the oral traditions he collected. For example, he says he knows four accounts about the early life of Cyrus II, the founder of the Persian Empire, but that he will recount only the one related by Persians "who seem to tell the simple truth about Cyrus's achievements without exaggeration."[7] In other words, Herodotus used a subjective criterion—the potential bias of his informants—to evaluate the reliability of the traditions concerning Cyrus. Other tests he applied were probability and the lack of empirical evidence. So, he rejected the charge that the Athenian family of the Alcmaeonidae tried to betray Athens to the Persians in 490 BCE after the battle of Marathon because of their well-known opposition to tyranny. Likewise, he ridiculed the idea of a universal Ocean because its existence had not been confirmed by observation. Still, Herodotus was aware that he had only limited critical tools at his disposal. Thus, he warned his readers that he was obligated to report what he was told but not necessarily to believe it, and that this is true of his whole book.

Herodotus's choice of subject, and the limitations of the oral sources on which he depended, forced him to grapple with the issue of periodization—the practice of setting historical events into clearly defined chronological periods. Herodotus was aware that Greek mythology included numerous tales of conflict between Greece and Asia, and that a historian could look to such stories (e.g., those told about the Trojan War) to find the ultimate origin of hostility between Persia and Greece. But, as Herodotus notes at the beginning of the *Histories*, Hecataeus already had exposed the limitations of mythology as a historical source. This conclusion was reinforced for Herodotus by his inability to get, from his oral sources, reliable information about centuries-old events. As a result, Herodotus justified the omission of mythological data from his book with the comment, "believe what you please. I will pass no judgment." He states he will begin his account with the reign of the mid-sixth-century BCE Lydian king Croesus, "by indicating the man whom I myself know to have begun the outrages against the Greeks, I shall proceed with my history, which will be no less concerned with unimportant cities than with the

---

6. Singular *logos*.

7. Herodotus, *Histories* 1.95.

great."[8] In doing so, Herodotus created a work that not only unified a century of Greek and Asian history around the theme of the Persian Wars but, for the first time, also distinguished between mythical and historical time. He made this distinction—which would be accepted by most subsequent Greek historians—on the grounds that reliable evidence only exists for the latter.

The fifth century BCE in Greece was a period of intellectual ferment and experimentation in many fields, including historiography. Numerous other authors had published on historical subjects by the time the *Histories* were completed in the 420s BCE. Of these authors, we now have only the names and some fragments from their works. But these fragments provide ample evidence of the experimentation then going on in the composition of various historical forms, including biography, chronicle, the history of individual cities, and ethnography. Fortunately, the most influential of these works, the *History of the Peloponnesian War* by the Athenian historian Thucydides, survives complete. According to a charming story, when he was a boy, Thucydides heard Herodotus read from his work and cried; and Herodotus told his father that "his son's nature impelled him toward study."[9] The story is probably apocryphal, but it reflects ancient critics' recognition that Thucydides was Herodotus's first and most important successor.

As with Herodotus, we know only the outlines of Thucydides's biography. The one certain fact of his career, that he was a *strategos*, a general, in 424 BCE suggests that he was born in the late 460s BCE or early 450s BCE since he had to be at least thirty years of age to hold that office. Also like Herodotus, Thucydides belonged to an ethnically mixed family. His Athenian noble family, called the Philaids, had important contacts in Thrace (as his father's Thracian name, Olorus, indicates). Like Herodotus, Thucydides was very much a man of his time. His work reveals familiarity with the principal intellectual trends of the mid-fifth century BCE, including sophistic thought, natural philosophy, Hippocratic medicine, and rhetoric. Finally, and again like Herodotus, Thucydides spent almost two decades as an exile during which he was able to travel widely to conduct research for his book. He was exiled because, during his time as a *strategos*, he failed to prevent the Spartans from capturing the important Athenian colony of Amphipolis in northern Greece. Though the date of his death is unknown, it probably occurred soon after his return to Athens after the end of the Peloponnesian War in 404 BCE. We can infer this date from the fact that he was unable to finish his book and because his work shows no awareness of events of the early 390s BCE.

At first glance, it is hard to believe that Thucydides was Herodotus's successor. The austere prose style and impersonal third-person narrative of the *History of the Peloponnesian War*, together with its almost total lack of ethnographic material, contrast sharply with the flowing style—what ancient critics called Herodotus's

---

8. Herodotus, *Histories* 1.5.
9. Marcellinus, *Life of Thucydides* 54.

"running style"—personal narrative tone and extended ethnographies that characterize the *Histories*. Though he doesn't mention Herodotus by name, Thucydides warns readers that his work, unlike Herodotus's, "may not be the most delightful to hear."[10] Yet the *Peloponnesian War* contains some of the most vivid passages in all of ancient Greek literature, including the harrowing accounts of the plague at Athens in 430 BCE and the civil war at Corcyra in 427 BCE.

More careful reading, however, reveals significant similarities between the *Histories* and *The Peloponnesian War*, beginning with Thucydides's preface:[11]

> Thucydides, an Athenian, wrote up the war of the Peloponnesians and the Athenians as they fought against each other. He began to write as soon as the war was afoot, with the expectation that it would turn out to be a great one and that, more than all earlier wars, this one would deserve to be recorded. He made this prediction because both sides were at their peak in every sort of preparation for war, and also because he saw the rest of the Greek world taking one side or the other, some right away, others planning to do so.

Because he could not obtain reliable evidence for early Greek history, Thucydides, following Herodotus, took as his subject an event of the recent, not distant, past: a great war that involved all of Greece. His narrative of the war consists of accounts of battles interspersed with speeches delivered by important political and military leaders. Though Thucydides cites inscriptions and other written sources, his primary sources were also oral narratives collected during his exile—an exile that, as he notes, provided him with access to people from both sides of the conflict. Like Herodotus, Thucydides comments on his goals and methodology, and his significant innovations in both areas influenced the development of later Greek historiography. Unlike Herodotus, who wrote at least a generation after the events he described, Thucydides wrote about a war in which he was a participant, and this personal experience is reflected in his approach to both researching and writing its history.

Thucydides's innovations were both conceptual and methodological, and together they redefined the scope and purpose of Greek historiography. In contrast to Herodotus, who maintained in his work the Homeric goal of recording great deeds, Thucydides emphasized the utility of his history to his readers because "what was done in the past . . . given the human condition, will recur in the future, either in the same fashion or nearly so."[12] While Herodotus mingled human and divine causes in explaining historical events, Thucydides eliminated references to divine causation at the same time he introduced a distinction between underlying causes—such as Spartan fear of growing Athenian power, to him, the "truest"

---

10. Thucydides, *Peloponnesian War* 1.22.
11. Thucydides, *Peloponnesian War* 1.1.
12. Thucydides, *Peloponnesian War* 1.22.

cause of the Peloponnesian War—and the superficial pretexts discussed by politicians at the time the war broke out. Finally, his emphasis on the utility of his history to future readers forced him to narrow his focus to the war itself and the decision-making of the men who conducted it.

In two ways, Thucydides also significantly refined the methodology he inherited from Herodotus. First, he insisted on the need for a precise chronology for his account; he organized his narrative around the passing of summers and winters instead of employing Herodotus's loose relative chronology. Second, while Thucydides and Herodotus both relied on oral tradition as the basis for their histories, the former rejected the latter's principle that he was bound to repeat what he was told even though he might not necessarily believe it. Thucydides believed that "people take in reports about the past from each other all alike, without testing them—even reports about their own country."[13] Instead, he insisted on a stricter standard, claiming that, with regard to events, "I did not think it right to set down either what I heard from people I happened to meet or I merely believed to be true," but "even for events at which I was present myself, I tracked down detailed information from other sources as far as I could."

Thucydides was equally critical of another Homeric tradition adopted by Herodotus in his *Histories*: the practice of using speeches by characters to highlight the major issues involved in his narrative. Aware, however, that Herodotus couldn't possibly have overheard Croesus's conversations with the Athenian statesman Solon or Cyrus of Persia, Thucydides claimed to treat such speeches with the same critical skepticism he applied to oral reports.[14] Scholars still debate the exact nature of that critical approach. Specifically, it has not been possible for scholars to agree on how to resolve the tension between Thucydides's statement[15] that he "made each speaker say what I thought the situation demanded" and his claim that he kept "as near as possible to the general sense of what was actually said." Nevertheless, Thucydides's innovations—his emphasis on the history of the immediate past, based on reliable oral reports; his strict focus on war and politics; and his interest in providing a useful work instead of one celebrating great deeds—had an immediate, and lasting, effect on the numerous historians who followed him. (Whether or not they were willing to admit to his influence is a different story.)

By the fourth century BCE, history had become recognized as a literary genre with its own rules. The word *historie*, whose traditional meaning of "research" was still standard in the fifth century BCE, had come to mean "history" in our sense a century later. It was in the fourth century that Aristotle notoriously claimed history was less philosophical than poetry because the former dealt with particulars and the latter with universals. Most ancient critics, however, didn't agree with

---

13. Thucydides, *Peloponnesian War* 1.20.
14. Thucydides, *Peloponnesian War* 1.22.
15. Thucydides, *Peloponnesian War* 1.22.

Aristotle's low opinion of history, viewing the fourth century BCE as the golden age of Greek historiography. Of the six historians whose works constituted the canon of Greek historical literature, four—Philistus of Syracuse in Sicily, Ephorus of Cyme and Theopompus of Chios from Anatolia, and Xenophon of Athens—wrote in the fourth century BCE. Unfortunately, of the numerous historical works written in this period, only *The Constitution of Athens* by Aristotle (or one of his colleagues) and the works of Xenophon survive. Nevertheless, what we know of these canonical works and authors is enough for us to point to three defining characteristics of fourth-century historiography. First, the historians came from all over the Greek world. Second, new historical forms—including regional and city histories, universal histories,[16] memoirs, and period studies—continued to appear. Third, and most important, while historians continued to rely primarily on oral sources, they also began to draw on the works being produced by their contemporaries and predecessors, and to justify their own works by criticizing those of their rivals.

Xenophon, the only one of the four canonical fourth-century BCE historians whose works survive, was born c. 430 BCE and died in the early 350s BCE. His life was a dramatic one. Growing up during the turbulent years of the late fifth century BCE, he witnessed Athens's defeat in the Peloponnesian War and the rise and fall of Spartan hegemony in Greece during the early fourth century BCE. Though ancient critics considered him a philosopher because of his association with Socrates,[17] Xenophon was first and foremost a soldier. He probably served in the cavalry during the Tyranny of the Thirty in Athens,[18] as well as in numerous campaigns in Europe and Asia, including the revolt of the Persian prince Cyrus against his brother Artaxerxes II in 400 BCE. He was exiled, most likely because he fought for the Spartans against Athens in the Corinthian War of the mid-390s BCE. The limited surviving evidence suggests he never returned to Athens, instead living for two decades on an estate given to him by the Spartans at Scillus in Elis, and finally dying at Corinth. Like Herodotus, Thucydides, and so many other Greek historians, therefore, the defining experience of Xenophon's life was his exile, which gave him a unique breadth of experience of both the Greek and non-Greek world. The Panhellenism found in his work—the dream that a united Greece could finally end the threat of a resurgent Persia bent on regaining all it had lost in the Persian Wars of the previous century—likely stems from his wide-ranging travels.

---

16. Universal histories were works that attempted to cover the history of the world known to the Greeks.

17. Xenophon portrayed himself as a friend of, not a student of, Socrates, but, like the philosopher Plato, he wrote several important works defending Socrates's reputation after his death, including an *Apology*, a version of the speech Socrates delivered in his own defense at his trial.

18. This is the dictatorship set up at Athens by the Spartans after the end of the Peloponnesian War. A full account of it is provided in the selections from Xenophon's *Hellenica*.

Xenophon was a famous man by the time he died in the 350s BCE, having written numerous books, all of which survive, on a wide variety of subjects including philosophy, history, political theory, and technical topics. Today, his fame largely rests on the *Anabasis*, his memoir of his experiences in the Greek mercenary army recruited by the Persian prince Cyrus for his revolt against his brother Artaxerxes II. But it was Xenophon's other historical work, the *Hellenica*, that earned him a place in the ancient canon of great Greek historians. In form, the *Hellenica* is a continuation of Thucydides's *History of the Peloponnesian War*, picking up the historical narrative from the point at which Thucydides's work breaks off in 411 BCE and carrying it through, in seven books, to the battle of Mantinea in 362 BCE.

The *Hellenica* is a strange book, made up of two parts, reflecting the development of Xenophon's views on the events of his lifetime. The first part, which includes most of the first two books, is a continuation of Thucydides's *History of the Peloponnesian War*, covering the last seven years of the Peloponnesian War from 411 BCE to 404 BCE; this portion of the *Hellenica* was probably written in the 380s BCE. It is so similar in concept and form to Thucydides's work that ancient critics understandably assumed Xenophon was responsible for publishing Thucydides's *History of the Peloponnesian War* after the earlier historian's death. The second part of the *Hellenica* is a history of Greece as a whole in five books organized around the theme of the rise and fall of Spartan hegemony in Greece. This second part was most likely written in the late 360s BCE and early 350s BCE, and it is infused with the Panhellenism so popular in the fourth century BCE.

Few ancient historical works have fallen so far out of scholarly favor as has the *Hellenica*. Unimpressed with Xenophon's carelessness regarding chronology, his numerous omissions from the historical record (including such significant events as the establishment of the Second Athenian League, the liberation of Messenia by the Theban leader Epaminondas, and the foundation of the Arcadian League), and his unconcealed bias against Thebes, twentieth-century scholars dismissed the *Hellenica* as a mere "memoir" and ignored its significance for the development of Greek historiography. This judgment is unfair, and we can point to at least two significant contributions Xenophon made to the development of historical writing. First, Xenophon was the first to interpret the history of post–Peloponnesian War Greece as a struggle between Sparta, Athens, and Thebes for the succession to fifth-century BCE Athenian hegemony; this is the same interpretation given in many modern textbooks. Second, while he followed Thucydides in believing that history was useful, Xenophon redefined the nature of that utility, emphasizing its religious and ethical dimensions. To achieve this redefinition, he repeatedly cited as moral exemplars those military commanders who succeeded by respecting omens and who won the loyalty of their men through the quality of their leadership. Xenophon does not, however, provide much help in understanding his contemporaries' views on how history should be written: unlike Herodotus, Thucydides, and other historians of his era, he did not begin the *Hellenica* with a preface explaining his goals and methodology.

The fragments of the lost works of other fourth-century BCE historians provide some hints about fourth-century BCE historians' ideas about historical method, however. Ephorus, author of the first universal history in Greek historiography, insisted that historical developments can only be understood in their geographical contexts and that detailed accounts of mythical events had to be treated with skepticism because sound evidence for such remote periods could not be obtained. Theopompus of Chios, who wrote a continuation of Thucydides's *History of the Peloponnesian War* as well as a huge, fifty-eight-book history of Greece centered on Philip II of Macedon, understood the potential value of inscriptions as historical sources. Similarly, the historians of Athens—the so-called Atthidographers—drew on the evidence of monuments and archival documents like the list of archons to reconstruct early Athenian history. But the fullest overview of fourth-century BCE Greek historians' methodology is provided by *The Constitution of Athens*, written by Aristotle or one of his colleagues sometime in the 330s BCE or 320s BCE, during the reign of Alexander the Great.

Unlike the works, for example, of Herodotus and Thucydides, manuscripts of *The Constitution of Athens* did not survive the end of antiquity; a copy of the work, written on papyrus, was discovered in Egypt in 1891 and quickly published. Strictly speaking, however, *The Constitution of Athens* is not a history like those works already mentioned. Instead, it is part of a collection, compiled by Aristotle and his students, of descriptions of 158 constitutions of Greek cities. Aristotle intended this collection to serve as a database for the sort of political analysis found in his *Politics*. It has, however, much in common with the local histories of Athens and other Greek cities. In addition to a chronological account of changes in the Athenian constitution from the legendary origin of Athens to the end of the fifth century BCE, it also includes a description of the democratic constitution as it existed in the fourth century BCE. Moreover, because its author was not a historian, *The Constitution of Athens* provides valuable evidence for the view of historiography held by educated Greeks in the fourth century BCE. Two of *The Constitution of Athens*'s qualities are particularly noteworthy. First, its narrative begins with the foundation of Athens by the legendary king Ion; this foundation leads us to believe that contemporary historians, like the Atthidographers, writing histories of their home cities, rejected Herodotus's distinction between mythical and historical time. Second, the wide range of sources used by *The Constitution of Athens*'s author—including the works of such historians as Herodotus and Thucydides, the poems of Solon, political pamphlets, Solon's laws, and other documentary texts and inscriptions—indicates that historians were no longer relying solely on the oral tradition in writing their works, although it clearly remained of great importance.

In modern histories of Greece, the defeat of the combined armies of Athens and Thebes in the battle of Chaeronea in 338 BCE by Philip II of Macedon and the remarkable reign of his successor, Alexander the Great, mark the beginning of the Hellenistic period, conventionally said to extend from Alexander's death in

323 BCE to the death of the last independent Macedonian ruler, Cleopatra VII of Egypt, in 30 BCE. For the ancient Greeks, this critical period of their history was bookended at the beginning by the conquest of the Persian Empire by Alexander and its end by the division of the Near and Middle East between Rome and the new Iranian-ruled empire of the Parthians.[19] For much of the intervening 300 years, the territory of the former Persian Empire was divided into several Macedonian-ruled kingdoms in which Greeks and Greek culture dominated elite society and culture. At the same time, the *polis* or city-state, which had been the focus of Greek politics for almost half a millennium, lost the ability to conduct an independent political life. Not surprisingly, so momentous a change in the Greek world was reflected in their historiography, which flourished on an unprecedented scale; more than half of the Greek historians we know today wrote during the Hellenistic period.

The scope of Hellenistic historiography was wide. Understandably, many of the works from this period treated Alexander the Great's conquests and the wars of his successors. Such works included memoirs of Alexander's officers as well as histories written by scholars. These works tended to have a biographical focus, and the emphasis on biography spilled over into histories of Greece that increasingly highlighted the roles of leading politicians, kings, and tyrants, and their relations with their cities' Macedonian overlords. Not surprisingly, the educated Greek's view of what was important in history also changed. So, for example, the *Parian Marble*, a chronicle of Greek history compiled in 262 BCE, highlighted three major themes in Greek history—the great antiquity of Greece, its cultural achievements, and the importance of monarchy—while almost completely ignoring the political history of archaic and classical Greece.

There was also renewed interest in the world outside Greece. Ethnographies, both of the peoples conquered by Alexander and those encountered by his Macedonian successors, were common, and for the first time, non-Greeks from Babylonia to Rome attempted to use Greek historical forms to tell the story of their own peoples. All of these trends are evident in the work of the second-century BCE historian Polybius, whose huge forty-book history focused not on Greece but on the rise of Rome as the dominant power in the Mediterranean. Not surprisingly, his work is the only Hellenistic-era history preserved by Byzantine scholars, who saw themselves as Romans, not Greeks.

Unlike the historians we have considered up to this point, Polybius's life is comparatively well documented. He was probably born about 200 BCE to one of the leading families in the Achaean League[20] and died shortly after 120 BCE at the age

---

19. The Parthians were nomadic invaders from Central Asia who spoke a language belonging to the Iranian family of Indo-European languages and ruled much of the territory of the old Persian Empire from the second century BCE to the early third century CE.
20. The Achaean League was a confederation of cities centered in the Peloponnesus. For details, see the selections from the second book of Polybius's *Histories*.

of eighty-two. Thus, his life coincided with growing Roman influence in Greece. Lycortas, his father, headed the faction that advocated a pragmatic attitude toward Rome, insisting on the Achaean League's right to pursue its own interests so long as they did not endanger its friendship with Rome. That neutral position became increasingly difficult for Polybius to maintain during the critical years of the Third Macedonian War (170 BCE to 168 BCE). As with the other historians we have considered, exile was the defining experience of Polybius's life. His exile began at the end of the Third Macedonian War in 168 BCE, when Rome followed the advice of the pro-Roman faction in Achaea and deported to Italy 1,000 "fair-weather" friends, including Polybius.

Polybius's exile lasted for seventeen years. During this time, he lived in the household of Scipio Aemilianus, the conqueror of Carthage in the Third Punic War. His connection to the high-profile Scipio gave Polybius access to some of the leading political and intellectual figures of mid-second-century BCE Rome. Equally important for his development as a historian, he was able to travel throughout the western Mediterranean in Scipio's entourage; Polybius even witnessed the destruction of Carthage and led an exploratory expedition down the west coast of Africa. The climax of his political career came after the end of the Achaean War in 146 BCE when he was instrumental in developing the terms of the Roman settlement of Greece. He helped persuade the Greek cities not to resist the Romans. In return for his help, he was honored with statues erected in Greek cities throughout the Peloponnesus.

Polybius's mammoth history was a milestone in Greek historiography, providing for the first time a comprehensive account of events throughout the Mediterranean world during a critical period of its history. Polybius described his work as a "universal history." But unlike his most important predecessor, the fourth-century BCE historian Ephorus—whose work was "universal" because it was a chronological account of the whole Greek world from the Trojan War to his own time—the universality of Polybius's history consisted in his addressing a period in which the whole Hellenistic world was united for the first time by a single process: the expansion of Roman power:[21]

> For who is so worthless or indolent as not to wish to know by what means and under what system of government the Romans in less than fifty-three years have succeeded in subjecting nearly the whole inhabited world to their sole government—a thing unique in history?

Polybius answered this question in the first twenty-nine books of his work, covering in detail the fifty-three years from 220 BCE to 168 BCE. These books are written very much in the historiographic tradition established by Herodotus

---

21. Polybius, *Histories* 1.1.5.

and thus celebrate great deeds. Sometime after the simultaneous end in 146 BCE of the Third Punic War, the Third Macedonian War, and the Achaean War, however, Polybius reconsidered the purpose of his book, transforming it into what he called a "pragmatic history"—that is, a practical work intended to instruct present and future statesmen, both Greek and Roman. To that end, he added ten books dealing with the period from 168 BCE to 146 BCE to make clear the character of Roman policy, their methods of rule, and the reactions of their subjects in order "that contemporaries will thus be able to see clearly whether the Roman rule is acceptable or the reverse, and future generations whether their government should be considered to have been worthy of praise and admiration or rather of blame (3.4.6–7)."[22]

More than any historian we have considered so far, Polybius was interested in letting his readers know his ideas about how to write history, devoting an entire book—unfortunately incompletely preserved—to historiographical questions[23] and frequently interrupting his account to discuss methodological issues. The ideal historian, in his view, did more than just collect written sources. A historian should be widely traveled so he can understand the geographical context of historical events; have political and military experience; and, above all, be able to identify relevant witnesses and critically evaluate their accounts of events. As his criteria indicate, oral testimony remained, in Polybius's opinion, the most important historical source. But his work also reveals a wide use of other sources, including official documents, letters, inscriptions, and the works of other historians. Above all, if his history was to be useful to its readers, it had to be *true*; this included speeches, which should accurately represent, as far as possible, what the speakers actually said. In his understanding of the purposes and methodology of historiography, Polybius most resembles Thucydides, and like that author, he limits the divine element in history to a minimum, adducing as a cause Tyche—Fortune—for the unforeseeable and incalculable element in human affairs such as natural disasters or the forcible unification of the Hellenistic world under the expansion of Roman power.

There were no further significant improvements in Greek historical methodology after the Hellenistic period. There was, however, a new factor in the historians' world: Rome. Although the expansion of Roman power over the Greek world was the underlying theme of Polybius's history, he wrote at the beginning of the process. For the rest of antiquity, Roman domination was the reality all Greek historians had to face. How they dealt with it varied, but none could avoid the question of the relationship of Greece to Rome. One solution, adopted in the early first century CE by a historian named Dionysius of Halicarnassus, was to deny that there was a problem at all by arguing that the ancestors of the Romans were actually

---

22. For an example of his criticism of his predecessors, however, see Polybius, *Histories* 2.56–2.58.
23. Polybius, *Histories* 12.

Greeks and that Latin was a Greek dialect. A different approach was taken by local historians, such as Memnon from the city of Heracleia in the Black Sea.

All that we know of Memnon's life is that he lived sometime after the year 47 BCE and that he wrote a large-scale history of Heracleia in at least sixteen books. His history is lost, but fortunately, a manuscript containing books nine to sixteen dealing with the period from 364 BCE to 47 BCE survived until the ninth century CE, when the Byzantine patriarch Photius summarized it. The fact that Memnon devoted eight books to the period before 364 BCE suggests that, like previous historians of Heracleia, he began his history with the legendary contacts between Heracles and the Argonauts with the Mariandynoi, the Anatolian people who inhabited the site of Heracleia before the Greeks arrived in the mid-sixth century BCE. It is also clear from Photius's summary that Memnon was the sort of library historian Polybius despised, virtually copying his sources such as the third-century BCE history of Heracleia by a historian named Nymphis. Memnon's narrative focuses on two themes: the long and glorious history of Heracleia and its loyalty to Rome. He excuses rare instances of disloyalty (such as the city's support of Rome's last major eastern enemy, the Pontic king Mithridates VI) as aberrations caused by the temporary deception of the Heracleiote people by evil men. For local historians such as Memnon, the purpose of history was to celebrate the great Greek past while affirming the positive role of their cities in the Roman Empire of his day. A less confrontational approach was adopted by the biographer Plutarch of Chaeronea, whose *Parallel Lives* provided his elite Greek and Roman readers with a historical panorama populated equally by great men from both Greece and Rome.

Plutarch was born c. 40 CE and died around 120 CE. His was a quiet life. Born into one of the elite families of Roman Greece at the city of Chaeronea in Boeotia, he received a thorough education, including study at Athens. He spent most of his life serving as a priest at the nearby sanctuary of Delphi. Opportunities for political activity in Greece were limited under the Roman imperial rule. But in an essay addressed to ambitious young men contemplating a political career, Plutarch claimed service as an ambassador was still possible. He followed his own advice, visiting Rome several times, at least once as an ambassador. While in Rome, he lectured on philosophy and made such influential friends in the Roman aristocracy as the senator and former consul Quintus Sosius Senecio. Plutarch later dedicated several of his works, including, most likely, his *Parallel Lives* to Senecio. Plutarch reached the peak of his career shortly before his death when he received from Emperor Trajan the *consularia ornamenta*, the ornaments of a consul, the highest Roman honor available to a non-senator.

In some ways, Plutarch is an unusual figure to include in an anthology of selections from Greek historiography. While today he is best known for his huge series of parallel biographies of major figures of Greek and Roman history—ranging from Theseus and Romulus, the legendary founders of Athens and Rome, to the end of the Roman Republic—Plutarch was famous in his own time, and then in late antiquity, primarily as a philosopher. More importantly, Plutarch repeatedly denied that he was writing history. He claimed he was writing "lives," and therefore omits much that other historians would usually have included in their works:[24]

> For it is not histories I am writing, but lives; and the most glorious deeds do not always reveal the workings of virtue or vice. Frequently, a small thing—a phrase or flash of wit—gives more insight into a man's character than battles where tens of thousands die, or vast arrays of troops, or sieges of cities.

In actuality, however, things are not so simple.

In antiquity, just as now, the boundary between history and biography was fluid. Historians like Xenophon, Polybius, and Plutarch's Roman contemporary Tacitus all wrote biographies, and Plutarch himself wrote one of the few historiographic essays to survive from antiquity: *On Malice in Herodotus*, his study of bias in Herodotus's *Histories*. Despite his disclaimer, political and military history provide the framework for his biographies, and he doesn't hesitate to express his opinions concerning such historical controversies as the historicity of the Spartan lawgiver Lycurgus. He also used the same sources as self-described historians, including the works of historians (in both Greek and Latin), letters of famous men, collections of official documents and inscriptions, literary texts, and, where appropriate, monuments. Moreover, historians since at least Xenophon had shared Plutarch's goal of praising the virtues and blaming the vices of famous men by examining how they were displayed in action. When considered as a whole, his parallel lives provide one of the most comprehensive overviews of the history of Greece and Rome from their earliest days up to Plutarch's lifetime to survive from antiquity. Later ancient and Byzantine historians treated Plutarch's *Lives*—especially the Roman entries—as important historical sources.

Plutarch is an appropriate figure with which to close this anthology of selections from the works of classical Greek historians. Greek historiography did not end, of course, in the second century CE. On the contrary, a continuous line of Greek historians, who modeled their works on those of Herodotus and Thucydides, can be traced as late as the seventh century CE. Still, the fundamental changes in the development of Greek historiography that occurred shortly after Plutarch's death justify ending this survey with the second century CE. New genres—most notably church history and universal chronicles such as Eusebius's *Ecclesiastical History* and *Chronicle*—continued to appear. But there were dramatic changes in the identities of the later historians and the focus of their works.

Like Plutarch, most of these later Greek historians had close contact with the Roman aristocracy. Indeed, the majority of historians writing in Greek in late antiquity were Roman officials. More importantly, they increasingly identified as

---

24. Plutarch, *Life of Alexander* 1.2.

Romans, especially after virtually all inhabitants of the Roman Empire became Roman citizens in 212 CE. It is not surprising, therefore, that their Roman identity was reflected in their texts, which were histories of Rome, not Greece. While the works of Herodotus and Thucydides continued to be valued as literary classics and stylistic models to be imitated, their content ceased to be of interest. This set the agenda for the medieval Byzantine historians, whose works treated in detail the history of the Jews and Romans but ignored almost entirely classical Greek history. Not until the fifteenth century CE would a Greek intellectual—the philosopher George Gemistus Pletho—attempt to return to his ancient roots and try to write a history of classical Greece.

CHAPTER 1

Herodotus, *The Histories*

FROM BOOK I

Preface

Herodotus of Halicarnassus here gives the results of his researches[1] so that the events of human history may not fade with time and the notable achievements both of Greeks and of foreigners may not lack their due fame; and, among other things, to show why these peoples came to make war on one another.

Mythical Confrontations

Herodotus begins the Histories *proper with a brief summary of myths which could be viewed as providing evidence of early conflicts between Greeks and various Asian peoples, but then dismisses these myths on the ground that he cannot find reliable information about them. It is easy to treat this passage as an amusing send-up of Greek mythology and pass over it to get to "real history." That, however, would be a mistake since it illustrates several fundamental aspects of Herodotus's thought that recur throughout the* Histories. *First, he cites as his sources "Persian storytellers," suggesting that Greek mythology was universal, being known not only to Greeks but to non-Greeks as well. Second, while Herodotus never denies that the gods can influence history, they are not historical actors, so any divine causation is absent from these stories. Third, and finally, while legends may have a basis in historical fact,* historiē, *research cannot provide reliable evidence about them.*

[1.1] Persian storytellers place the responsibility for the quarrel on the Phoenicians, a people who came to the Mediterranean from the so-called Red Sea region and settled in the country where they now dwell.[2] They at once began to make long

---

1. For *historiē*, translated here as "researches," see Introduction, p. xix.
2. In early Greek geography, "Red Sea" referred to the Persian Gulf and/or the Indian Ocean. Why Herodotus believed the original home of the Phoenicians was in this region is unknown.

trading voyages with cargoes of Egyptian and Assyrian goods, and one of the places they called at was Argos, at that time the most eminent of the places in what is now called Hellas. Here on one occasion they were displaying their goods, and for five or six days after their arrival, when they had sold almost all their goods, there came down to the shore a considerable number of women. Among these was the king's daughter, whose name was Io, daughter of Inachus (and on this point the Greeks are in agreement). These women were standing about the vessel's stern, buying what they most fancied, when the Phoenicians, at a signal, made a rush at them. The greater number of the women escaped, but Io was seized along with some others. They were thrust on board, after which the ship made off for Egypt.

[1.2] This is the Persian account of how Io came to Egypt—the Greeks have a different account—and how the series of wrongs began. Some time later, they say that certain Greeks—their name is not given, but they were probably Cretans—put into the Phoenician port of Tyre and carried off the king's daughter, Europa. So far it had been a case of an eye for an eye, but the Persians say that the Greeks were responsible for the next outrage. They sailed in a warship to Aea in Colchis on the river Phasis, and then, when they had finished the business for which they had come, they seized the king's daughter, Medea.[3] The king sent an envoy to Greece to demand reparation for the abduction and to request the return of his daughter. The Greeks replied that, since they had received no reparation for the abduction of Io from Argos, they in turn refused to give one.

[1.3] The Persians say that it was two generations later when Paris, son of Priam, influenced by these stories, resolved to use abduction to get a wife from Greece, being confident that he would get away with this unpunished, just as the Greeks had done; so he carried off Helen. The Greeks decided to send messengers to demand the return of Helen, together with reparations for her abduction. But they were answered with a rebuke about the seizure of Medea, for which the Greeks had made no reparations, nor had they returned the woman. So how could they now expect reparations from others?

[1.4] Up to this point there had been nothing worse than the abduction of women on both sides, but thereafter, say the Persians, the Greeks were much to blame; for before the Persians had made any assault on Europe the Greeks mounted a military expedition against Asia.[4] The abduction of women is, of course, quite wrong, but only fools make a great fuss about it, while wise men pay little heed; for it's obvious that women would not be carried off unless they themselves were willing. The Persians say that the peoples of Asia paid little regard to the seizure of their women, whereas the Greeks, merely for the sake of a Spartan woman, gathered a great army, invaded Asia, and destroyed the kingdom of Priam. Thereafter they have always

---

3. Medea was supposedly a princess in Colchis—modern Georgia—kidnapped by Jason and the Argonauts during their quest for the golden fleece.
4. The Trojan War.

regarded Greece as an enemy, for the Persians consider Asia, and the peoples dwelling there, as their concern, while Europe and the Greeks are something apart.[5]

[1.5] Such, then, is the Persian account; the destruction of Troy, they say, was the origin of their hostility to Greece. As to Io, the Phoenicians disagree with the Persian account, and they deny that it was by abduction that they brought her to Egypt. They say that while in Argos she had an affair with the ship's captain, and finding herself pregnant, she voluntarily accompanied the Phoenicians to escape the shame of exposure.

Well, believe what you please; I will pass no judgment. Rather, by indicating the man[6] whom I myself know to have begun the outrages against the Greeks, I shall proceed with my history, which will be no less concerned with unimportant cities than with the great. For those that were formerly great are now diminished, while those which are now great were once small. Being well aware that human prosperity never long endures, I shall deal with both alike.

Lydia (c. 680 BCE to 546 BCE)

> For Herodotus, the real history of the Persian Wars began with aggression by an Asian state against the Greeks, the kingdom of Lydia. Lydia was a successor state of the Hittite Empire, which had dominated Anatolia in the second millennium BCE but had collapsed in the early twelfth century BCE. Like the Hittites, the Lydians were Indo-Europeans, speaking a language belonging to the so-called Luwian family, which was widespread in western and southwestern Anatolia. By the sixth century BCE, they were the dominant power in Anatolia, ruling an empire that extended from the Aegean Sea to somewhere near modern Ancyra. Herodotus's account focuses on the growth of that empire, with particular emphasis on how the Greek cities of the Aegean coast came under Lydian control, a process that was completed during the reign of the last king of Lydia, Croesus.

[1.6] Croesus, king of Lydia, reigned over the peoples west of the river Halys, which flows from the south between the Syrians and the Paphlagonians, and runs northward into the Black Sea.[7] He was the first foreigner, as far as we know, to have contact with the Greeks, subjugating some by forcing payment of tribute and

---

5. Herodotus introduces here a central thesis of the *Histories*, namely, the idea that Asia was the domain of the Persians and Europe of the Greeks.

6. Croesus, king of Lydia, from c. 560 BCE to 546 BCE.

7. "Syrians" refer to the inhabitants of Cappadocia, not present-day Syria. Herodotus described Croesus's kingdom as consisting of Anatolia from approximately modern central Turkey west to the Mediterranean Sea.

forming friendships with others. He subjugated the Ionians, Aeolians, and Dorians who dwell on the Asian seaboard and made a treaty of friendship with the Lacedaemonians. Before the time of Croesus's reign, all the Greeks were free.

[1.7] Now sovereignty over Lydia had once belonged to the descendants of Heracles,[8] and I shall describe how it came to pass into the hands of the Mermnads, the ancestors of Croesus. The Heraclids had held power for 22 generations, or 505 years, each son succeeding his father in turn, until the throne came down to Candaules, son of Myrsus.

[1.8] This Candaules was utterly devoted to his wife, whom he considered to be by far the most beautiful woman on earth. Among his bodyguard was a man named Gyges, who was the king's particular confidant, and Candaules not only discussed state matters with this man but expounded to him many praises of his wife's beauty. One day the king, who was destined to come to a bad end, spoke to Gyges thus: "Gyges, I am not sure that you fully believe me when I speak of my wife's beauty. Well then, since a man is inclined to trust his eyes more than his ears, I will arrange for you to see her naked." Gyges gave a cry of horror. "Master," he said, "what a shocking idea. Do you bid me look on my queen when she is naked? When a woman puts off her clothes, she puts off her modesty. We should obey the rules of morality devised for mankind ages ago, and one of these rules requires us to look only on what is our own. I am convinced that she is the fairest of women, and I beg you not to ask me to do what is wrong."

[1.9] Thus did he try to resist the king, dreading what harm might ensue for himself. But the king replied: "Be of good cheer, Gyges, and have no fear that I am making a trial of you, or that any injury will befall you from my wife. I will surely contrive that she won't know that you have seen her. I will station you in our bedroom behind the door as it opens. When I have entered, my wife too will follow me to bed. Near the door is a chair. On this she will lay her garments one by one as she takes them off. You will have plenty of opportunity to see her. Then, when she walks to the bed with her back to you, take care to slip through the door without her seeing you."

[1.10] Gyges made ready to do what he could not avoid. Candaules brought him into the bedroom and was soon followed by the queen. Gyges watched her enter and place her clothes on the chair, and when she turned her back to him and moved toward the bed, he quietly slipped out. But the queen caught sight of him. Realizing what her husband had done, she neither gave vent to her shame by screaming nor gave any other indication that there was anything amiss, but she resolved to take revenge on Candaules. For with the Lydians, as with almost all foreign peoples, it is reckoned a shameful thing even for a man to be seen naked.

---

8. Note that Herodotus accepted the historicity of Heracles. Tracing the origin of the first Lydian dynasty to Heracles allowed him to connect Lydian history to the chronology of Greek legend established by Hecataeus.

[1.11] For the time being she gave no sign and kept quiet. But as soon as morning came, she made ready those of her servants whom she knew to be most devoted to her and summoned Gyges. Not suspecting that she knew anything of what had happened, he came at her bidding, for it was quite usual for him to be called to attend on the queen. "Gyges," she said, "I offer you the choice of two courses that are open to you, and you may choose whichever you please. Either kill Candaules and take the throne, with me as your wife, or you must die on the spot, so that never again will you give such unquestioning obedience to Candaules as to see what is forbidden. Either he who plotted this must die, or you, who have broken our laws by beholding me naked."

Gyges was at first astounded and fell to begging the queen not to force him to make such a dreadful choice. But his pleadings were in vain, and he realized that he was, in truth, faced with the necessity either of slaying his master or of losing his own life. He chose to live. "Since you compel me against my will to kill the king," he said, "come, tell me how we are to attack him." "The assault will come from the very place where he displayed my nakedness," she said, "and you will strike while he is asleep."

[1.12] There was no escape possible for Gyges; either he or Candaules must perish. When night fell, he followed the queen into the bedroom. She gave him a dagger and concealed him behind the very same door. Then, when Candaules was asleep, Gyges slipped out of his hiding place, struck, and took possession of both queen and kingdom. [1.13] His hold on the throne was confirmed by the oracle at Delphi. For when the Lydians, angered at the fate of Candaules, took up arms, and when civil strife seemed inevitable between Gyges's partisans and the rest of the population, they agreed to consult the oracle and abide by its decision as to whether Gyges should rule or the throne be restored to the Heraclids. The answer favored Gyges, but the Priestess also added this: That the Heraclids would be avenged in the fifth generation from Gyges. This prophecy was disregarded by the Lydians and their kings until it was fulfilled.

[1.17] Alyattes[9] used to make annual inroads into Milesian territory in the following way. He made his invasions when the crops were ripe, accompanied by the sound of pipes, harps, and flutes. He never destroyed the farmhouses or burned them or tore off their doors but left them undamaged, destroying only the trees and crops before withdrawing. It was pointless to lay siege to the city because the Milesians commanded the sea. Now the reason why he refrained from demolishing the dwellings was this, so that the Milesians would be encouraged to sow seed and work the land, thereby providing a source of plunder for his future invasions.

[1.18–19] This went on for eleven years, in the course of which the Milesians were twice defeated in battle. But in the twelfth year the burning of the crops had an unusual sequel. As soon as the crops were set on fire, a strong wind drove the

---

9. King of Lydia from c. 610 BC to 560 BC.

flames onto the temple of Athena at Assesus, which burned down to the ground. At the time this caused little stir, but when the army returned to Sardis, Alyattes fell ill. As his illness continued, he sent messengers to the Delphic oracle to inquire about it, either on somebody's advice or on his own initiative. The Priestess refused to make any reply to the messengers until the Lydians should rebuild the temple of Athena of Assesus in Milesian territory. This is what I myself have gathered from the Delphians, but the Milesians add the following details to the story: They say that Periander of Corinth, a close friend of Thrasybulus who at that time was ruler over Miletus, got to know of the oracle's reply and sent a message giving Thrasybulus prior information, so that he could take appropriate measures.

[1.21] Alyattes, on receiving the oracle's reply, sent a messenger to Miletus, proposing a truce that would last until he could rebuild the temple. Anticipating through his foreknowledge what Alyattes was likely to do, Thrasybulus adopted the following plan: Gathering together in the public square all the grain in the city from both public and private sources, he instructed everyone at a given signal to start drinking and holding parties. His purpose was this, to induce the messenger reporting to Alyattes to make mention of the immense pile of grain and the high spirits of the populace. And this, indeed, was what came about. The messenger marked what was going on, delivered his message, and returned to Sardis. A peace treaty was then signed, and it was for this reason alone, as I judge, that Alyattes, expecting to find the Milesians oppressed by famine and the populace reduced to extreme suffering, was informed by the messenger that the situation was quite the reverse of what he had thought.

Thereafter peace was established, the two sides becoming friends and allies. Alyattes built two temples instead of one to Athena of Assesus and recovered from his illness. This was the way that Alyattes concluded his war with the Milesians and their leader Thrasybulus.

[1.23–24] This Periander, the one who gave information about the oracle to Thrasybulus, was the son of Cypselus and ruler over Corinth. During his lifetime there occurred a very great wonder, as the Corinthians say (and the Lesbians agree with them): Arion of Methymna, by far the foremost lyre-player of his period—the man who first, as far as we know, composed the dithyramb, gave it its name, and taught it at Corinth[10]—was carried on a dolphin's back to Taenarum. Arion, they say, after spending a great part of his life at Periander's court, felt an urge to sail to Italy and Sicily. There he amassed a great fortune and eventually decided to return to Corinth. Having faith in Corinthians above all others, he hired a Corinthian vessel to sail from Tarentum. But when they were at sea, the crew formed a conspiracy to throw Arion overboard and seize his wealth. Realizing what they were about, he gave them his money and begged for his life. But the sailors, unmoved, ordered him to take his own life if he wished to be buried on land, or else to leap overboard forthwith. Faced

---

10. A type of choral song sung in honor of Dionysus.

with this painful dilemma, Arion asked the crew to allow him to stand on the quarterdeck, dressed in his full musician's robes, and to sing for the last time, after which he undertook to do away with himself. The sailors, pleased at the prospect of hearing a performance by the best musician in the world, gathered amidships, and Arion, donning his full attire, took up his lyre, stood on the quarterdeck, sang a stirring air, and then flung himself into the sea, fully robed just as he was.

The sailors continued their voyage to Corinth, but the story goes that a dolphin swam up, took Arion on his back, and carried him to Taenarum. Arion reached land, made his way to Corinth in his musician's attire, and related what had befallen him. The incredulous Periander would not release him but kept him under strict guard while he watched for the crew's arrival. When at last they did arrive, he summoned them and asked them if they had any news of Arion. "Yes," they replied, "he is in Italy; we left him safe and well at Tarentum." Thereupon Arion made his appearance, attired just as he had been when he leaped overboard. The sailors were dumbfounded and could make no further denial. This is the story as told by the people of Corinth and Lesbos, and there is at Taenarum an offering made by Arion, a small bronze figure of a man riding a dolphin.

[1.28–30] Under Croesus's rule, nearly all the peoples west of the river Halys were added to the Lydian empire, except the Cilicians and Lycians. When Croesus had subjugated all these and added them to his empire, there came to his capital, Sardis, then at the height of its wealth, all the most distinguished teachers of that period throughout the length and breadth of Greece, and one of these was Solon of Athens.[11] The Athenians had entrusted to him the task of drawing up a code of laws for them, having bound themselves with mighty oaths to make no change in it for a period of ten years without his permission. Solon carried out this task and then went abroad so as not to be compelled to alter any of his laws—but giving out as a pretext that he wanted to see something of the world. First he visited the court of Amasis, ruler of Egypt, and then the court of Croesus at Sardis.

He was welcomed and hospitably entertained at Croesus's palace, and in three or four days' time, at Croesus's bidding, servants escorted Solon around the royal treasuries to display the magnificence of Croesus's wealth. When Solon had had the opportunity to view and examine all that was there, Croesus said to him, "My Athenian friend, much talk of you has reached us, both in respect of your wisdom and of your extensive travels in search of knowledge. Now I have a great desire to put this question to you: Who is the happiest man you have ever seen?" He was, of course, expecting to be named the happiest of humankind, but Solon was no flatterer. With strict regard for the truth, he replied, "O king, it was Tellus the Athenian." Croesus, amazed at that reply, asked with some sharpness, "And how do you arrive at this

---

11. For Solon, see Aristotle, *The Constitution of Athens* 5–11. Since Solon established his reforms at Athens in 594 BC, his supposed meeting with Croesus is probably fictional.

judgment?" "In the first place," said Solon, "living at a time when his native city was flourishing, he had fine, handsome children and got to see children born to *them*, all of whom survived. Secondly, after enjoying a prosperous life, as we judge of prosperity, he came to a most glorious end. In a battle between the Athenians and their neighbors of Eleusis, he played his part in the battle, put the enemy to flight, and died most nobly. The Athenians granted him a state funeral at the very place where he fell, and paid him great honor."

[1.31] Solon's account of the many blessings of Tellus spurred Croesus on to ask who it was whom Solon judged the happiest of men after Tellus, doubtless expecting that he, Croesus, would at least be placed second. But Solon replied, "Two young men of Argos, Cleobis and Biton. Their means were quite sufficient for their needs, and they were blessed with remarkable physical strength. They were both prizewinners in athletic contests, and the following tale is told of them. When the Argives were holding the festival of Hera, it was an urgent religious duty for the mother of these men to be conveyed to the temple in a special carriage, but the oxen had not returned from the fields in time to pull it. In this emergency the two sons got into the harnesses and pulled the wagon themselves, with their mother aboard, a distance of almost six miles to the temple. After this remarkable feat, witnessed as it was by the entire assembly, their lives came to a most wonderful close, whereby the deity revealed how much better for humankind is death than life. The Argives were crowding around the two young men, congratulating them on their strength, and the women were rejoicing with their mother on having such sons. Overjoyed at the public recognition of their achievement, their mother stood before the statue of the goddess and prayed to her to grant Cleobis and Biton, the sons who had brought her such honor, the greatest blessing that can befall mortals. After her prayer, when they had sacrificed and feasted, the two sons lay down to sleep in the temple and never rose again. They were finished. The Argives had statues made of them and set them up at Delphi—to show that they honored them first among humankind."

[1.32] To these, then, did Solon award second place for happiness. In his exasperation Croesus said, "My Athenian friend, do you so despise my happy state that you rank me beneath common folk?" To this Solon replied, "Croesus, you are questioning one who understands how the divine power is envious of human good fortune, and never leaves it long undisturbed. Over a lengthy period of time one sees much that one would wish not to see and undergoes much one would wish not to. Let us take 70 years as the space of a man's life. This period, if you disregard the intercalary months, contains 25,200 days. If you add a month every other year so as to make the seasons come around at their due time, you have 35 extra months, that is, 1,050 days. So the full total comes to 26,250 days.[12] Of these days not a single one is like

---

12. Since a year measured according to the lunar calendars used by the Greeks was significantly shorter than a true solar year, the Greeks tried to correct the problem by inserting intercalary—additional—months at irregular intervals.

another in what it brings forth. So you see, Croesus, the extent to which people are at the mercy of chance. I hold you to be exceedingly rich and the ruler over many peoples. But I will not answer your question until I learn that you have reached the end of your life in the same state of happiness. The man who is immensely rich is no better off than the man who just makes ends meet, unless he has the good fortune to reach the end of his life in the same happy state. Many wealthy men are unlucky, while many in moderate circumstances are blessed by fortune. The man who is very rich but unlucky has only two advantages over the man who is merely lucky, but the latter has many advantages over the former: The rich man is better able to fulfill his desires and to cope with disaster when it befalls him, but the poor and lucky trumps him: Though he cannot manage desires and disasters as easily, his good luck dispels the need to do so, for he avoids injury, disease, and calamity and is blessed in children and good-looking. If, beyond these boons, he also comes to a good end of life, then this is the man you are seeking, the man who merits the title 'happy.' But until his death you should withhold the title 'happy'; he is merely temporarily fortunate.

"No human being can possess all blessings, just as no single country can produce all that it needs; it will possess one thing and lack another. Similarly, no man is entirely self-sufficient; he will surely lack something. But whoever possesses the greatest number of blessings and retains them until he reaches the end, and then dies happily, he is the one, in my opinion, who should be awarded the title. In every matter you should look to the ending. To many men the god grants but a glimpse of blessedness, only to bring them to utter ruin."

[1.33] This view found no favor with Croesus, and he contemptuously dismissed Solon, regarding as a fool a man who urged him to look to the ending of every matter and who paid no heed to present prosperity.

[1.34] After Solon's departure, terrible punishment, sent by god, fell upon Croesus, probably because he considered himself the happiest of men. It began with a dream that seemed to indicate that disaster was about to befall his son. Croesus had two sons, of whom one was a cripple, being deaf and mute, while the other, named Atys, surpassed all other young men of his time. Croesus dreamed that Atys would be killed by a blow from an iron weapon. When he awoke and reflected on his terrifying dream, he took action. He arranged a marriage for his son and no longer permitted him to take the field with the Lydian soldiers whom he used to command. He banished all war-like weapons—javelins, spears, and so on—from the men's quarters and had them gathered together in the women's apartments, lest any weapon hanging on the wall should chance to fall on his son.

[1.35] While he was busy with arrangements for the marriage, there came to Sardis a man in the grip of misfortune, with blood on his hands, a Phrygian by birth and of royal lineage. Presenting himself before Croesus, this man begged the king to cleanse him from the blood-guilt according to the laws of the land, and this Croesus did. (The Lydian method of purification is very similar to that of the

Greeks.)[13] After the ceremony, Croesus questioned the man. "Stranger, who are you? From what part of Phrygia do you come to seek my protection? What man or woman have you slain?" "Sire," replied the man, "I am the son of Gordias, whose father was Midas, and my name is Adrastus. I accidentally slew my own brother, and I have been driven into exile, destitute." "You are descended from a family with friendly relations to mine," said Croesus, "and you have come among friends, where you shall lack for nothing. I urge you to bear your misfortune as best you can." Thus did Adrastus come to reside with Croesus.

[1.36] At about this time there was a monstrous wild boar on Mount Olympus in Mysia. Issuing forth from its mountain lair it used to ravage the Mysians' crops. Many an expedition did the Mysians make against it, but inflicted no injury on it while themselves sustaining many injuries. Finally their messengers sought audience with Croesus and spoke as follows: "Sire, a monster of a boar has appeared in our land, destroying our crops. Our efforts to catch it have all been in vain. Now we beg you to send us your son with a chosen band of young men and hunting dogs, so that we may drive it out of our land." Bearing in mind his dream, Croesus answered with these words: "Let there be no more mention of our son. I could not send him because he is newly married and has much to occupy him. However, I will send you a select band of men with hunting equipment, and I will urge them to show the utmost zeal in ridding your land of this beast."

[1.37] The Mysians were all satisfied with this answer, but then Atys, who had heard of the Mysians' request, came in. Seeing that Croesus declined to send him, Atys spoke to him as follows: "Father, it was once thought most noble and most honorable for me to win renown in war and hunting. Now you have cut me off from both these pursuits, although you have seen no cowardice or lack of spirit in me. What will people think of me when I appear in public? How will the citizens regard me, how will my bride regard me? What kind of man will she think she has married? Either let me take part in the hunt or give me reason for your refusal."

[1.38] "My son," said Croesus, "it is not because I have seen cowardice or any other fault in you that I act in this way. It is because of a dream I had that you had not long to live, and that you would perish by an iron weapon. It was that dream that made me hasten your wedding and makes me reluctant to send you off on this enterprise. I am taking these precautions so I may keep you out of death's reach during my lifetime. You are my only son, for I cannot look on that other one, with his defect, as my son."

[1.39–40] "It is understandable, Father," replied Atys, "that you should take precautions after being visited by such a dream. But there is a point in that dream that has escaped your notice, and it is not improper for me to mention it. You say that the dream indicated that I would be killed by an iron weapon. But what sort

---

13. Unfortunately, Herodotus does not explain how the Lydian ritual resembles the Greek ritual for purifying a person of the pollution resulting from the shedding of blood.

of hands does a boar have? How can it use an iron weapon? Had the dream foretold that I would be killed by a boar's tusk or the like, you would be doing your duty. But it is a *weapon* that is in question, and since I shall not be fighting against men, let me go." "My son," replied Croesus, "I own myself vanquished in the matter of the dream's interpretation, and, being vanquished, I change my decision and permit you to go to the hunt." [1.41–43] Thereupon the king sent for Adrastus the Phrygian and said to him, "When you came to me, Adrastus, smitten by dire disaster—for which I do not reproach you—I cleansed you, received you into my household, and provided for all your needs. Now I call upon you to requite good with good. I charge you to be my son's guardian when he goes forth to this hunt, to protect him against robbers or evildoers who may come upon you. Furthermore, you too have the duty of going where you may win distinction by your deeds. That is your heritage, and you do not lack strength." "Sire," replied Adrastus, "I would not normally wish to go on this expedition. It is not proper for one who is smitten with misfortune to seek the company of more fortunate young men, nor do I desire it, and I would hold back on many accounts. But since you ask me to do so and it is my duty to please you—for I owe you a great debt of gratitude—I am ready. Your son, whom you bid me protect, shall be unharmed as far as his protector can ensure it, and you may look for his safe return." Such was Adrastus's answer, after which the party set out with a chosen band of men and dogs. They came to Olympus, sought out the boar, surrounded it, and hurled their spears. It was then that the stranger named Adrastus, the man who had been purified from blood-guilt, hurling his spear missed his mark and hit Croesus's son; struck by an iron blade, Atys fulfilled the prophecy of the dream.

[1.44] A messenger hastened to tell the father of his son's fate. The shock of his son's death was dreadful but was made more horrible by the fact that he had been killed by one whom Croesus himself had purified of blood-guilt. In the excess of his grief Croesus called upon Zeus as the god of purification, asking him to bear witness to his sufferings at the hands of the stranger whom he had purified; he called upon Zeus as the god of the hearth, because in welcoming the stranger into his home he had unwittingly entertained the slayer of his son; he called upon Zeus as the god of comradeship, in that the man whom he had charged to guard his son had been found to be his greatest enemy. [1.45] Soon the Lydians arrived, bearing the body and followed by the slayer. Standing before the body he submitted himself to Croesus, stretching forth his hands and bidding Croesus to slaughter him on top of the corpse. To crown his previous trouble, he said, he had ruined the man who had cleansed him, and he could no longer bear to live.

At these words, in spite of his own domestic sorrow, Croesus took pity on Adrastus. "Since you condemn yourself to death," he said, "justice makes no further demands on you. You are not to blame for this calamity, except that your unwitting hand did the deed. No, it was some god, who long ago gave me warning of what was to be."

So Croesus buried his son with fitting ceremony. But when all was quiet about the grave, Adrastus, son of Gordias, and grandson of Midas, the man who had destroyed his own brother and then had destroyed him who had granted him purification, knowing himself to be the most ill-fated of humankind, slew himself upon the tomb.

[1.46–47] For two years Croesus continued in deep mourning for his son and was roused from grief only by the rapidly increasing power of the Persians on his eastern border, a power founded by Astyages, son of Cyaxares, and greatly increased by Cyrus, son of Cambyses. It occurred to Croesus to take the initiative by attacking the Persians before they could grow even stronger; in pursuit of this plan, Croesus contrived to make trial of the various oracles in both Greece and Libya. To this end, he dispatched messengers to the oracles at Delphi, at Abae in Phocis, at Dodona, to the oracles of Amphiaraus and Trophonius, to the oracle of Branchidae in Milesia, and, not content with Greek oracles, to the oracle of Ammon in Libya. He sent these messengers as a test of the knowledge of the oracles: If one oracle was found to know the truth, then he would send a second time to ask if he should undertake a campaign against the Persians. These messengers were instructed to consult the different oracles on the hundredth day after leaving Sardis and to inquire what Croesus, king of Lydia, was doing at that moment. They were to write down the reply and bring it straight back to Croesus. What the rest of the oracles replied is not told by any of my sources, but at Delphi, as soon as the Lydians arrived in the enclosure and put their question to the god, the Pythia said as follows, speaking in hexameter verse:

> I can count the grains of sand on the beach, and I can measure the sea.
> I understand the speech of the dumb, and I hear the voiceless.
> There has come to my nostrils the odor of the hard-shelled tortoise
> Boiling together with lamb's flesh in a brazen cauldron, With a base of bronze and a
> bronze cover.

[1.48–50] These words the Lydians recorded and carried back to Sardis. At last all the replies came back to Croesus, who opened and read them, and it was the Delphic reply that he accepted with deep reverence, declaring that it was the only true oracle in the world. For after dispatching his messengers Croesus had devised an action least open to guesswork. On the appointed day he had cut up a tortoise and a lamb and boiled them together in a brazen cauldron with a brazen lid. Croesus now proceeded to offer the most sumptuous sacrifices to Apollo of Delphi. [1.53–54][14] The messengers who conveyed these gifts were to put the following question to the oracle: "Croesus, king of Lydia and other nations, convinced that you are the only

---

14. Herodotus's account of Croesus's dedications to Apollo of Delphi, which explains his expectation that the god would favor him, has been omitted.

true oracle in the world, has sent you these gifts and asks you if he should march against the Persians, and also whether he should make allies of some other army." In reply the oracle prophesied that if Croesus marched against the Persians he would destroy a great empire. As to an alliance, he should seek friendship of the most powerful of the Greeks. Croesus was overjoyed at this reply, confident that he would destroy the power of Cyrus. He bestowed further presents on Delphi, two gold staters for every citizen, having first inquired how many there were. In return the Delphians granted to Croesus and to all Lydians, in perpetuity, the right to become citizens of Delphi, exemption from taxes, priority in access to the oracle, and front seats at all state functions.

[1.55–56] Being now eager to extract full value from an oracle of whose genuineness he was firmly convinced, Croesus sent one more question—would his reign be a long one? The Priestess made the following reply:

> When a mule shall sit on the Median throne, then stay not, Tender-footed Lydian, but flee by the many-pebbled stream Of Hermus, and think no shame of being a coward.

This reply gave Croesus more satisfaction than any other. Was it likely that a mule would become king of the Medes?

[1.71] Croesus, having missed the meaning of the oracle, now prepared to invade Cappadocia,[15] confident that he could destroy the power of Cyrus and his Persians. While he was making these preparations a certain Lydian named Sandanis, already renowned for his wisdom, gave him the following advice, thereby greatly increasing his reputation with the Lydians. "Sire," he said, "you are preparing to fight against men who are so poor that they dress in leather, breeches and all. Their country is so rough that they eat what they can manage to get, never as much as they want. They have no wine to drink, only water. They have no luxuries, not even figs for dessert. If you conquer them, what will you take from them, seeing that they have nothing? If they conquer you, think what you will lose. Once they have tasted our good things, they will hold on to them and will not ever let go. Indeed, as it is, I am grateful to the gods for not putting it into the minds of the Persians to attack the Lydians." Croesus rejected this advice, yet Sandanis was right on one point. The Persians had no luxuries of any sort before they conquered Lydia.

[1.73–74] Croesus made the invasion of Cappadocia because he wanted to extend his territories and, more importantly, because he trusted the oracle. But there was this further reason—he wanted to take revenge on Cyrus on behalf of Astyages. Astyages, formerly king of Media, had been conquered and held in subjugation by Cyrus. Astyages was Croesus's brother-in-law, and the marriage connection came

---

15. Herodotus (1.6) earlier defined the boundary between Lydia and Cappadocia as formed by the Halys River.

about in this strange way. A band of Scythians, a nomadic people, left their country as a result of internal strife and emigrated to Media. They were at first welcomed by Cyaxares, at that time ruler over Media, who treated them kindly as suppliants. He even entrusted to them the education of some boys, whom they were to teach their language and the use of the bow. As time went on, the Scythians, who continually went out hunting and returned with game, on one occasion returned empty-handed. Cyaxares, a man of quick temper, received them with harsh words and abuse. Resenting this undeserved ill-treatment, the Scythians resolved to kill one of their pupils, chop him up, prepare the pieces like game, serve them to Cyaxares as a side dish, and then make their escape to the court of Alyattes at Sardis. And that is indeed what happened. Cyaxares and his guests ate some of the meat. The Scythians escaped to Alyattes and sought his protection. Cyaxares demanded their return. Alyattes refused, and war broke out between Lydia and Media. It lasted five years, with victory going first to one side, then to the other. After all this indecisive fighting, in the sixth year, there was a battle during which day suddenly turned into night. (This change from daylight to darkness had been foretold to the Ionian Greeks by Thales of Miletus, who even fixed the year in which it did in fact occur.)[16] When the Lydians and the Medes saw day turn into night, they became awestruck and broke off the engagement, and both sides became anxious to make peace. Certain mediators (Syennesis the Cilician and Labynetus the Babylonian) were responsible for bringing about a reconciliation and for making a peace treaty reinforced by a marriage connection. These men persuaded Alyattes, king of Lydia and father to Croesus, to give his daughter in marriage to Astyages, Cyaxares's son; for agreements do not usually remain strong unless backed up by strong assurances. (These nations have the same form of oathtaking as the Greeks, but in addition they make an incision in the skin of their arms and lick each other's blood.) [1.75] I will explain further on why Cyrus had overthrown, and now was holding prisoner, his grandfather Astyages. But it was this insult that Croesus held against Cyrus, leading him to ask the oracle whether he should attack the Persians; and when he received a double-edged answer, he assumed the oracle was on his side and invaded Persian territory.

When Croesus reached the river Halys, he crossed it, in my opinion, by the existing bridges. But there is a version widespread in Greece that it was Thales of Miletus who took the army across. They say that the bridges did not exist at this time, and that Thales, who was present in Croesus's camp, solved the difficulty by splitting the river into two channels. This he did by digging a deep, crescent-shaped channel from a point above the camp around to the rear of the camp, so that the

---

16. The reference is probably to the total eclipse of the sun that occurred on May 28, 585 BCE, and was visible in Cappadocia. Whether Greek astronomical knowledge in the early sixth century BCE was sufficient for Thales to accurately predict such an eclipse is, however, unclear.

river ran for a space in two channels, each of which could be forded. Some even say that the river was entirely rerouted and the old channel left dry. But this I cannot accept; for how would the army have crossed again on their return journey?

[1.76] Be that as it may, Croesus crossed the river with his army and reached the district called Pteria in Cappadocia. He ravaged the properties of the Syrians who lived there, captured the town of the Pterians, enslaved the inhabitants, seized the outlying settlements, and drove out the Syrians, though they were uninvolved in the quarrel.

Cyrus meanwhile had assembled his army and marched to meet Croesus, recruiting more men on his way. Before marching out he had already sent messages in an attempt to persuade the Ionians to throw off their allegiance to Croesus, but the Ionians had not heeded him. When he had encamped opposite Croesus, the two armies met in a sharp struggle. There were heavy losses on both sides, but the result was indecisive, and night broke off the engagement.

[1.77–78] Croesus's army was somewhat inferior in number to Cyrus's forces, and it was to this that he attributed his lack of success. When Cyrus did not advance to attack on the following day, Croesus decided to withdraw to Sardis. He intended to reinforce his army by calling on his allies, the Egyptians (for he had made an alliance with Amasis, king of Egypt),[17] and also the Babylonians (for he had made an alliance with these too, who were at this time ruled by Labynetus), and the Spartans. These were to join him at an appointed time, and then he proposed to wait until the winter was over and attack Cyrus in the following spring. So he sent out messengers, requesting his allies to assemble at Sardis in four months' time, and meanwhile he disbanded his mercenaries, for he did not imagine that Cyrus would venture to march on Sardis after the even fortunes of the recent battle.

At this time an unusual incident occurred. Snakes swarmed in the suburbs of Sardis, and horses, leaving their customary pastures, came and devoured them. Croesus regarded this as an omen, as indeed it was, and he sent messengers to Telmessus where there were seers skilled in interpretation. These messengers were told the significance of the omen, but they had no opportunity to report back to Croesus, who became a prisoner before they could complete the return voyage to Sardis. The interpretation of the Telmessian seers, which they gave before knowing that Croesus was captured, was as follows: Snakes were natives of the soil, horses were beasts of war and foreigners. Croesus must expect the coming of a foreign army that would subdue the natives of Sardis.

[1.79] When Croesus retired toward Sardis after the battle of Pteria, Cyrus found out that he was going to disband his army. So he took counsel and resolved that his best plan was to march on Sardis as swiftly as possible before the Lydian forces could gather again. No sooner said than done, and Cyrus made such good speed that he reached Sardis as his own messenger. This unexpected development

---

17. King of Egypt from 570 BCE to 526 BCE.

put Croesus in a dilemma, but he nevertheless led out his Lydians to battle, for at this time there were no braver or stouter warriors than the Lydians, or better horsemen.

[1.80] The armies met on a level plain before Sardis. When Cyrus viewed the battle-array, he was very apprehensive of the Lydian cavalry, and he adopted the suggestion made to him by a certain Mede named Harpagus. He gathered together all his camels that were used as pack animals to carry stores and provisions, unloaded them, and mounted men on their backs to act as cavalry. These he ordered to advance against Croesus's cavalry, to be followed by the infantry, while his own cavalry brought up the rear. The reason for this maneuver was the instinctive fear that camels inspire in horses, who cannot endure the sight or smell of them. In this way the Lydians' cavalry, their greatest source of confidence, would be rendered useless. Having made these dispositions, Cyrus gave a general order to his army to kill all the Lydians they encountered except Croesus, whom he wanted taken alive even if he offered resistance.

When battle was joined, as soon as the Lydian horses smelled and saw the camels, they turned and fled, and Croesus found his hopes dashed to the ground. But there was no cowardice on the part of the Lydians. Seeing what was happening, they leaped from the saddle and fought as infantry. There were heavy losses on both sides, but finally the Lydians were forced to give way and retreat within their walls, where they were besieged by the Persians.

[1.81] Thus began the siege of Sardis, and Croesus, believing it would be a lengthy affair, sent messages from the besieged city to his allies, this time begging for assistance, not in four months' time but immediately, to relieve the siege. He applied to all his allies, among them the Spartans.

[1.82] The Spartans were at this time engaged in a quarrel with Argos over some border territory called Thyreae, which had belonged to Argos but had been cut off and seized by the Spartans. The Argives marched out to recover it, and a conference was held at which it was decided that the fighting should be restricted to three hundred men on each side, and Thyreae should belong to the victors. The main body of each army should not stay to watch the fighting, but retire each to its own homeland, so as to avoid the temptation of coming to the assistance of their own men if they were being defeated. On these terms they retired, and the chosen three hundred on either side joined the battle.

So equally balanced was the contest that out of six hundred men only three were left alive—two Argives, Alcenor and Chromius, and one Spartan, Othryades; and these survived only because night fell. The two Argives hastened back to Argos, claiming victory, but the Spartan Othryades remained on the field of battle, stripping the dead and carrying back their spoils to the Spartan camp.

On the following day both sides returned to discuss the outcome. For a while both sides claimed victory, the Argives because they had the greater number of survivors, and the Spartans because, while the Argives had run away, their own man had remained on the battlefield and stripped the dead. The argument led to blows, and then to a general engagement in which both sides suffered heavy losses, with the Spartans finally victorious. From that day onward the Argives, who were previously required to wear their hair long, began cutting it short and made a vow that no Argive man should wear long hair, nor any Argive woman wear gold jewelry, until Thyreae was reclaimed. Meanwhile the Spartans did the opposite: They began wearing their hair long, which had not been their custom before. It is said that the single Spartan survivor of the three hundred, being ashamed to return to Sparta after the death of his companions, killed himself there at Thyreae.

[1.83] Such were the circumstances in which the Spartans found themselves when the messenger from Sardis arrived, seeking assistance for the besieged Croesus. Nevertheless, when the Spartans heard his message, they were eager to send help. But by the time they had completed their preparations and the ships were ready to sail, a second message brought news that the city had fallen and that Croesus was taken prisoner. The Spartans were greatly distressed, but there was nothing they could do.

[1.84] This was how the city of Sardis was taken: On the fourteenth day of the siege, Cyrus sent cavalrymen to ride through his army, proclaiming a rich reward to whomever should be the first to scale the walls. This was followed by a concerted assault, which met with no success. While the others were resting, a Mardian named Hyroeades resolved to make an attempt at a point in the fortifications that was left unguarded because there appeared to be no danger of its ever being scaled. There was a sheer drop there, which made it inaccessible. (Many years before these events a former king of Sardis, named Meles, had a concubine who gave birth to a lion. The seers of Telmessus declared that if the lion were carried around the walls of Sardis, the fortress would be impregnable. Meles followed their advice and carried the lion around the entire circuit of the walls except for this part, which he considered impossible to scale.) This Hyroeades had observed one of the Lydians climbing down the precipice to retrieve a helmet that had rolled down. This put the idea into his head. He made the ascent himself, was followed by many others and finally by a great mass of the Persians. Thus was Sardis taken, and the city was sacked.

[1.85] What was Croesus's fate? I have already mentioned that he had a son, a fine enough young fellow except for being mute from birth. In the days of his prosperity, Croesus had spared no effort to help the lad and had consulted the Delphic oracle. The Priestess replied,

O Lydian, king over many peoples, thou foolish Croesus, Seek not to hear the longed-
　　for sound of thy son's voice In thy palace. Far better were it otherwise,
　For his first words will be spoken on a day of great sorrow.

When the city was taken, a Persian soldier advanced on Croesus to slay him, not knowing who he was. Croesus saw him. But, sunk in misery, he paid no heed, not caring whether he lived or died. But this son, the mute one, was so appalled by the danger that he gained speech and cried, "Fellow, do not kill Croesus." These were the first words that he uttered, and he retained the power of speech for the rest of his life.

[1.86] So Croesus was captured alive after a reign of fourteen years and a siege of fourteen days. He had indeed fulfilled the oracle by destroying a great kingdom—his own. He was brought before Cyrus, who had him put in chains and placed on a pyre which he had constructed, and with him fourteen Lydian boys.[18] Perhaps he intended making an offering to some god, perhaps he was fulfilling some vow, or perhaps he had heard tell that Croesus was a pious man, and he wanted to find out if some divine power would save him from being burned alive. As Croesus stood upon the pyre, in spite of his miserable condition, he remembered the saying of Solon, surely divinely inspired, that no man could be called happy during his lifetime. Remembering this, he sighed bitterly, and breaking a long silence, he uttered a deep groan and thrice called Solon's name: "Solon, Solon, Solon."

On hearing this, Cyrus bade his interpreters ask Croesus upon whom he was calling. For some time Croesus maintained an obstinate silence, but when they forced him to speak, he replied, "One who should speak with every ruler in the world—if only my riches could buy this." As this answer seemed mysterious and they continued to question him, pressing him hard and giving him no rest, he told how Solon the Athenian came to Sardis and was unimpressed by all the magnificence he saw there, and how everything he said, meant generally for all humankind but especially for those who deemed themselves happy, had come true in his case exactly as Solon had said.

While Croesus was still speaking, the fire had been kindled and was burning around the sides. Then Cyrus, listening to the interpreters, had a sudden change of heart. He reflected that he himself, a mere mortal, was burning alive another man who had once been equally as prosperous as he. This thought, and the thought of retribution, and the realization of the instability of the human condition, persuaded him to order his men to extinguish the fire as quickly as possible and to bring Croesus and those with him safely down. But the fire had got a hold, and in vain did his men try to extinguish it.

[1.87] Now the Lydians tell that when Croesus realized that Cyrus had had this change of heart, and when he saw that every man was engaged in a vain attempt to extinguish the fire, he called loudly upon Apollo. "If any of my gifts have found favor in thy sight, come to my aid, rescue me from this present peril." Thus did he, with tears, call upon the god, and although the day had been clear with hardly a breeze,

---

18. Croesus's fate was controversial in antiquity. The so-called Myron Vase of c. 500 BCE portrays Croesus on the pyre with no indication that he survived, while Bacchylides in his third ode, which was performed in 468 BCE, claimed that Apollo saved him from the pyre and transported him to the land of the mythical Hyperboreans, who supposedly lived in the remote north of Europe.

the sky was suddenly darkened with clouds, and a storm broke with such a violent downpour of rain that the flames were extinguished.

In this way Cyrus learned that Croesus was a good man and a friend to the gods, and when he had brought him down from the pyre, he questioned him. "Croesus, who of humankind induced you to march against my country and become my enemy rather than my friend?" Croesus made answer, "O king, what I did has proved to be for your good fortune and for my own ill fortune. The fault lies with the god of the Greeks, who encouraged me to embark on this campaign. No one is so foolish as to choose war instead of peace. In peacetime children bury their fathers, in wartime fathers bury their children. It must be by divine will that this has come upon me." Cyrus set him free, seated him at his side and treated him kindly, gazing at him in wonder, as did all his attendants.

[1.88–89] Croesus sat deep in thought; then, turning around and seeing the Persians sacking the city, "O king," he said, "shall I tell you what is in my mind or ought I to keep silence?" Cyrus bade him speak frankly without fear. "This vast crowd of men," said Croesus, "what are they so busily doing?" "Why, they are plundering your city and carrying off your treasures," said Cyrus. "Not my city, nor my treasures," was the reply. "They are no longer mine. It is you they are robbing." These words gave Cyrus food for thought, and dismissing his attendants, he asked Croesus what was his advice under these circumstances. "Since the gods have made me your slave," said Croesus, "it is right for me to advise you for your good. Persians are proud by nature, and poor. If you suffer them to accumulate great wealth from sacking the city, you can expect that whoever gets the most will rebel against you. If you will be advised by me, you will station men of your personal guard at every gate, and let them take all the valuables as men bring them out, saying that a tenth part of the spoil must be given to Zeus. They will not resent this act of piety and will willingly surrender their spoil."

[1.90] Cyrus was highly pleased at what seemed to him good advice, and after giving the orders Croesus had recommended, he said to Croesus, "I see that you are willing to do me service. Ask me for any gift you please in return." "The greatest boon you can bestow on me," said Croesus, "is to allow me to send these chains to the god of the Greeks whom I have most honored, and to ask him if it is his custom thus to reward those who serve him." And he explained to Cyrus how he had come to trust the oracle, the magnificent gifts he had sent, and the oracle's reply. Cyrus laughed. "This request is granted, and anything else you may ask." So Croesus sent to Delphi, and instructed his messengers to lay the chains on the floor of the temple and ask the god if he was not ashamed of having encouraged Croesus to make war against the Persian empire, in the belief that he would end the power of Cyrus, from which venture had come such "rewards" (here he bid them point to the chains). Was it usual (he bid them ask) for Greek gods to be so ungrateful?

[1.91] It is said that the Priestess replied to these reproaches as follows: "Even the gods cannot escape allotted destiny. In the fifth generation Croesus expiated the crime of his ancestor, a soldier in the bodyguard of the Heraclids, who succumbed to a woman's treachery, slew his master, and seized a throne that was not his.[19] Nevertheless Apollo wanted the fall of Sardis to be postponed to the time of Croesus's son but failed to persuade the Fates. They did, however, make some concession to him: They put off the fall of Sardis for three years, and Croesus should understand that his fate caught up to him three years late. Then again, Apollo came to his rescue when he was on the pyre. As to the oracle, Croesus does wrong to blame it, for Apollo foretold only this, that if he took the field against the Persians, he would destroy a great empire. Croesus should have made a further inquiry as to whether the empire was that of the Persians or his own. But he failed to understand the reply, made no further inquiry, and was himself to blame. Again, when he consulted the oracle on the last occasion and Apollo's answer made reference to a mule, this too Croesus misunderstood. The mule meant Cyrus, for he is the offspring of parents of different races,[20] an aristocratic mother and a baseborn father. His mother was a Mede, daughter of Astyages, king of Media, while his father was a Persian, at that time subject to the rule of the Medes, and in every way inferior to his wife." When the Lydian messengers returned with this reply, Croesus had to admit that the fault was his, not the god's.

[1.93] The country of the Lydians has few remarkable features in comparison with other countries, except for the gold dust carried down by the river from Tmolus. It does, however, show the greatest work of human hands except for those wrought by the Egyptians and Babylonians. I refer to the tomb of Croesus's father, Alyattes, the base of which is built of huge stone blocks surmounted by a huge mound of earth. It was constructed by the joint efforts of three classes: tradesmen, craftsmen, and prostitutes. Five stone pillars stood on the summit even up to my own days, with inscriptions engraved on them showing the contributions of each class; calculations reveal that the prostitutes' share was the largest. The daughters of the common people of Lydia all ply the trade of prostitute to collect money for their dowries, and they continue to do so until they marry, choosing their own husbands. The tomb is nearly three-quarters of a mile in circumference and about a quarter-mile wide; there is a large lake near it called Gyges's Lake, which the Lydians say is never depleted. And that's what the tomb is like.

[1.94] The Lydians' way of life is not unlike our own, except for the prostitution of their daughters. They were the first people we know of to adopt silver and gold coinage[21] and to engage in trade, and they also claim to have invented the games now

---

19. The reference is to Gyges's agreement (1.11) to Candaules's wife's demand that he murder her husband to avenge the shame resulting from her being seen naked by a strange man.
20. A mule is the offspring of two different species, a horse and a donkey, just as Cyrus was the child of a Median mother and a Persian father.
21. Herodotus is correct in ascribing the invention of coinage to the Lydians. The earliest Lydian coins, however, were not of gold and silver but of electrum, a natural alloy of gold and silver, and were issued c. 640/630 BCE.

played by them and the Greeks. This invention they date back to the time when they colonized Tyrrhenia in Italy. In the time of King Atys the whole of Lydia suffered a terrible famine, which they endured as best they could. But as the famine continued, they devised various ways to alleviate their misery, including games of dice, knucklebones, and ball games. In fact, they claim to have invented all games except checkers. On one day they would play all day long, hoping to banish all thought of food, and the next day they would eat and not play. This mode of life continued for eighteen years. Finally, as their sufferings went on unabated and even grew worse, the king divided the population into two groups and decided by lot which group should emigrate and which should remain. He himself took charge of the group chosen to stay where they were, while the emigrants were commanded by his son Tyrrhenus. After the lots had been drawn, the departing group went down to the coast at Smyrna and fashioned boats and, after loading on all the equipment needed for the voyage, sailed away in search of land and livelihood. They passed by many peoples and finally settled in Umbria in northern Italy, where they remain to this day. But they have changed their name from Lydians to Tyrrhenians, after their great leader Tyrrhenus.[22]

The Reign of Cyrus the Great

Herodotus's account of Lydia is a prologue to his main subject, the growth of the Persian Empire and its conflict with the Greeks. That subject begins with the reign of Cyrus the Great, and he states the two issues that dominate his narrative right at the beginning: Cyrus's origin and the rise of Persia. After briefly describing the rise of the Median Empire, whose overthrow was the key to Cyrus's rise to power, he provides a biography of Cyrus allegedly based on Persian sources. The focus then shifts to Cyrus's two great conquests: Lydia and Babylon. Herodotus concludes his biography of Cyrus with his death while attempting to conquer the Massagetae, a Central Asian nomadic people, thereby introducing one of the main themes of the history, the inability of the Persians to expand their empire beyond Asia into Europe.[23]

---

22. Tyrrhenians was the Greek name for the Etruscans of Central Italy. Herodotus's identification of them as Lydian immigrants was already controversial in antiquity, being contested, for example, by the first century BCE historian Dionysius of Halicarnassus, who claimed that they were native to Italy. Most scholars now agree that the Etruscans were native to Italy since there is no archaeological evidence for a break in the cultural development of Italy that could be associated with the arrival of a new people from Anatolia.

23. In Herodotus's geography, Europe was the largest continent, extending across the northern portion of the known world from the Atlantic Ocean to somewhere near India. The Massagetae, therefore, lived in the eastern portion of Europe, not Asia.

[1.95] And now to Cyrus. Who was this man who destroyed the empire of Croesus, and how did the Persians gain the mastery of Asia? I shall base my account on the Persian authorities, who seem to tell the simple truth about Cyrus's achievements without exaggeration, and I shall ignore three other versions.

Going back in history to the time when the Assyrian empire had ruled upper Asia for 520 years, it was the Medes who began the revolt against them, fighting for their freedom with such bravery that they shook off the Assyrian yoke.[24] Other nations followed their example until every nation in that part of the continent had won their freedom. But once again they fell under autocratic rule, in the following manner:

[1.96–97] Among the Medes was a wise man named Deioces, who, in his lust for power, did the following: The Medes at this time dwelled in small villages, and Deioces, already a man of note in his own village, during a period when lawlessness was rampant throughout Media, displayed ever-increasing zeal in the practice of just dealing, understanding that justice and crime are opposing forces. In view of the character he acquired, the men of his own village chose him to judge disputes among themselves. This function he performed with absolute integrity. The considerable reputation he gained among the villagers spread to other villages, the inhabitants of which had suffered much from corrupt judgments. Gladly they submitted their disputes to Deioces for arbitration, and finally they would turn to nobody else. As people came to recognize the impartiality of his judgments, they resorted to him in increasing numbers, and Deioces saw that he was becoming indispensable. Thereupon he refused to sit in the judge's seat any longer. "It is no profit to me," he said, "to neglect my own affairs in order to render judgment all day for my neighbors." Robbery and lawlessness spread among the villages even more than before, and the Medes gathered together in a meeting to discuss this. (I imagine that Deioces's friends spoke loudest.) "We cannot go on like this," they said. "Let us appoint one of our number as king, so that the country can be well governed and we can turn our attention to our own affairs without danger of disorder." Thus they were persuaded to set up a monarchy, and when candidates were nominated, Deioces was by far the most popular choice. They agreed to appoint him king.

[1.98–99] Deioces's first action was to order them to build a palace worthy of a king and to give him a bodyguard. This they did, building him a great strong palace on the site he chose and allowing him to select his bodyguard from all the Medes. When he was first in firm control, he compelled the Medes to build one capital city that would excel in importance all other settlements. His wishes were met, and a mighty fortress was built that they called Ecbatana, fortified with concentric walls, each circle standing above its outer neighbor by the heights of its battlements. There

---

24. This is the first appearance of the idea of world history as organized around a succession of world empires: Assyrian, Median, and Persian. Later historians added the Macedonian and Roman Empires.

are seven circular walls, the innermost containing the palace and the treasury; the outermost and largest is about the size of the walls of Athens. The battlements of the outermost circle are colored white, the next black, the third crimson, the fourth blue, the fifth orange, and the next two silver and gold. In this way Deioces walled in himself and his own palace, while ordering the people to dwell outside the inner wall.

When the work of construction was completed, Deioces introduced for the first time the following protocol. Nobody was admitted to his presence, all business being conducted through messengers. Nobody was allowed to see the king, and it was an offense to laugh or spit in his presence. The purpose of all this pomp was to debar his contemporaries from setting eyes on him, for having been brought up with him, themselves of no inferior stock and as good men as he, they might resent him and plot against him. But if nobody saw him they would regard him as different from ordinary men.

[1.100] These arrangements being established and his power confirmed, he was stern in the administration of justice. All applications for judgments were conveyed to him by written documents and his decisions similarly sent out. He punished arrogant offenders, and his spies and listeners were active throughout his realm.

[1.101–2][25] Deioces unified all the different tribes of Media, but in his reign of fifty-three years he did not extend his empire. (These are the tribes of the Medians: the Bousae, Paretaceni, Strouchates, Anzanti, Budii, Magi.) It was his son Phraortes, succeeding his father, who, not content to rule the Medes alone, carried arms beyond the borders of Media. The first country he conquered and attacked and subdued was Persia. With these two powerful peoples under his control, he reduced one nation after another throughout Asia until he attacked the Assyrians who held Nineveh.[26] This nation had formerly been masters of Asia but were now isolated through the defection of their allies, though still thriving within their own borders. Phraortes was slain, after a reign of twenty-two years, and most of his army was destroyed.

[1.103] With Phraortes dead, Cyaxares, son of Phraortes and grandson of Deioces, succeeded to the throne. He is said to have been a more powerful warrior than his ancestors; he was the first to divide up the Asians into separate contingents according to their weaponry, separating the spearmen, archers, and cavalry that had formerly been mixed together. (It was he who had been battling the Lydians at the time when day turned into night.) He gathered under his rule all the peoples of Asia

---

25. The following two chapters were translated by James Romm.

26. Herodotus's made two errors in his account of the conquest of Assyria. First, he ignored or did not know that the Medes fought the war in alliance with Babylon. Second, he assumed that Cyaxares (625 BCE–585 BCE) came to the throne before the twenty-eight year Scythian domination (653 BCE–625 BCE) instead of at the end of it.

east of the Halys River, and with this coalition of subjects, he attacked Nineveh, avenging his father and hoping to destroy the city.

[1.107] Astyages, son of Cyaxares, then inherited the throne. Astyages had a daughter named Mandane, and one night he had a strange dream about her. He dreamed that she urinated to such an extent as to fill the whole city and flood the whole of Asia. He told his dream to the dream-interpreters of the Magi,[27] and their interpretation filled him with alarm. When Mandane came of age, instead of marrying her to some high-ranking Mede, in fear of the dream he gave to her a Persian named Cambyses, a man of decent family and quiet disposition, whose rank was considered far inferior to that of a Mede even of the middle class.

[1.108] Before Mandane and Cambyses had been married a year, Astyages had another dream. He dreamed that a vine grew from his daughter's genitals and overshadowed the whole of Asia. Again he submitted the dream to the interpreters and then sent to Persia for his daughter, who was now pregnant. When she arrived, he kept her under guard, intending to destroy the child, for the Magi had told him that his daughter's child would displace him from the throne. When the child was born, Astyages summoned his kinsman Harpagus, the most trustworthy of the Medes and controller of all his property. "Harpagus," he said, "the task I am assigning you is one that you must carry out most faithfully. Do not shirk it; if you betray me and cast your lot with others, you will pay for it in the end. Take Mandane's child to your own house, kill it, and bury it as you see fit." "Sire," replied Harpagus, "you have never as yet had reason to reproach me for failing in my duty, and I am on guard against letting you down at some future time. If this be your will, it is my duty to obey." Such was the reply of Harpagus.

[1.109] The baby was dressed in grave-clothes and delivered to Harpagus, who went home in tears. When he had told his wife all that had been said, she asked him what he had in mind to do. "I will not obey Astyages," he said, "even if he grows more insane than he is now. I will not consent to it nor take part in so cruel a murder, and that for many reasons. Firstly, the child is my kinsman. Secondly, Astyages is getting on in years and has no son. If he dies and is succeeded by Mandane, whose son I am to have a hand in murdering, will not a perilous future await me? My present safety demands that the child should die, but one of Astyages's servants must do it, not one of mine."

[1.110] So saying, he immediately sent a messenger to one of the king's herdsmen, Mitradates, whom he knew to have suitable pastureland and mountains infested with wild beasts. With him lived a female servant, his wife, whose name was Cyno ("Bitch") in Greek, or Spaco in the Median language; for the Medes call a female dog a spaca. . . . The herdsmen hastened to answer the summons, and Harpagus spoke to him as follows: "The king orders you to take this baby and

---

27. According to Herodotus, the Magi were the priestly caste of the Medes. The reinterpretation of Magus as meaning magician was a later development.

expose it in the most desolate spot you know of among the mountains, where it may the soonest perish. He bade me add this: If you do not kill the child but find some means of preserving it, you will die most horribly. I am appointed to see that this is done."

[1.111–12] The herdsman took the child and returned to his cottage. As fate would have it, his wife, who had daily been expecting her own child, was that day delivered while her husband was away in the city. They had each had their worries, he over his wife's confinement, she because her husband had so unexpectedly been summoned by Harpagus. When the man returned home with unexpected speed, his wife asked him right away why Harpagus had sent for him so eagerly. "Wife," he said, "would that I had never seen what I saw and heard on my visit to the city, and would that such things not befall our masters! The entire household of Harpagus is a scene of sorrow. I entered in dismay. There was a baby lying there, kicking and howling, dressed in gold and brightly colored garments. On seeing me, Harpagus told me to take the child and carry it off in haste and expose it to the wildest part of the mountains. The king has so ordered, he said, and he uttered terrible threats if I should disobey. I took the child and went off with it, thinking that it belonged to one of the servants. Although I was surprised at the gold and expensive clothes and the wailing in Harpagus's household, I should never have guessed whose it was, had I not learned the whole story from the servant who escorted me out of town. It is the child of Mandane, daughter of Astyages, and Astyages commands that it is to be destroyed. Look, here it is." So saying, the herdsman uncovered the child. When she saw what a fine, strong child he was, his wife burst into tears and, throwing herself at his knees, besought him not to expose the child. "But I have no choice," said he, "Harpagus will send his spies to check on me, and I shall perish horribly if I do not obey." Not being able to persuade him, his wife had an alternative suggestion. "Since I have failed to persuade you, and the dead body of the child has to be seen, do as I say. I, too, have given birth, but my boy-child was stillborn. Take our child and expose it, and let us rear the child of Astyages's daughter as our own. In this way you will not be discovered disobeying our master, and we shall do well out of it. For our dead child will have a royal burial, and the other child will live."

[1.113] The herdsman was well pleased with his wife's suggestion and at once proceeded to carry it out. He handed over to her the child he had brought condemned to death, and his own dead child he placed in the basket in which he had carried the other. Dressing it in all the raiment that the other child had been wearing, he conveyed it to a most desolate place in the mountains and left it there. When the child had lain exposed for two days, the herdsman went to town, leaving one of his assistants to watch over the body, and told Harpagus he was ready to show him the child's corpse. Harpagus dispatched the most trustworthy of his guards, who confirmed this by eyewitness account, and he had the herdsman's child buried. So the child was buried, and the herdsman's wife took over and reared the child who was one day to be Cyrus but was not yet so called.

[1.114–15] When the boy had reached the age of ten, his identity was revealed in the following manner. In the village where the herdsman's oxen were kept, the lad was playing on the road with the other boys of his age. In their game of pretend, they elected the supposed herdsman's son as their king. He appointed them to various tasks, some to build houses, some to be a bodyguard, one to be the "king's eye,"[28] one to be the king's chamberlain, and so on. But one of the players, son of Artembares, a man of some distinction among the Medes, refused to carry out the task Cyrus had assigned him. Cyrus ordered the other boys to seize him and, when they obeyed, he whipped him savagely. The boy was furious at this humiliating treatment, and when he was released, he went home to the city and with loud lamentations related to his father what the herdsman's son had done to him. The indignant Artembares hastened to Astyages with his boy to inform him of his outrageous treatment. "Sire," he said, showing the welts on the lad's shoulders, "see how we have been insulted by your slave, a herdsman's son." Intending to avenge the boy for the sake of his father's honor, Astyages summoned the herdsman and his son and, when they presented themselves, he fixed his gaze on Cyrus and said, "Did you, the son of a man of humble station, have the effrontery to inflict such injuries on the son of one who is my distinguished subject?" "Master," said the boy, "it was with justice that I so treated him. For in our game the boys of the village, of whom he was one, made me their king. They thought me the most suitable for that office. The other boys carried out my orders, but he would not listen and paid no heed until he was punished. If for this I deserve to suffer, I am ready."

[1.116] As he was speaking, Astyages began to recognize him. The boy's features seemed to resemble his own, the boy's answer was not that of a slave, and the date of the exposure seemed to fit with the boy's age. Thunderstruck, Astyages was for a time speechless. With difficulty he recovered and, wishing now to get rid of Artembares so that he could question the herdsman alone, he said, "Artembares, I will deal with this matter so that you and your son shall have no cause for complaint." So he dismissed Artembares and ordered his servants to take Cyrus to an inner room. When the herdsman was left on his own, Astyages questioned him. "Where did you get the boy? Who gave him to you?" "The boy is mine," said the herdsman, "and his mother is still with me." "You are a fool to drive me to extreme measures," said Astyages, signaling to the guards to seize the man. The herdsman was being carried off to be tortured when he revealed the truth. He told all the facts from the beginning and fell to begging the king for mercy.

[1.117] Now that the herdsman had told the truth, the king gave him no further attention, but transferring his anger to Harpagus, he ordered his guards to summon him. When he appeared, Astyages said, "Harpagus, when I gave you my daughter's child, how did you dispose of him?" Seeing the herdsman present, Harpagus realized that it was useless to try to lie his way out. "Sire," he said, "when I took

---

28. The "king's eye" was the Persian king's chief spy.

charge of the child I debated with myself how I might satisfy your wishes and yet avoid becoming a murderer in your daughter's eyes and in your eyes. So I called this herdsman and handed over the child to him, telling him that it was you who commanded me to kill him. In that there was no lie, for those were your orders. I instructed him to expose the child in some remote mountain spot and to remain with it until it died, threatening him with terrible punishment if he disobeyed. When he had carried out these orders and the child was dead, I sent the most trustworthy of my eunuchs to see for me, and had the child buried. That, sire, was what happened, and that was the fate that befell the child."

[1.118] This was the straightforward story told by Harpagus, and Astyages, concealing his anger, repeated to Harpagus the herdsman's account and ended by saying that the child was alive, and this was all to the good. "I was greatly distressed," he said, "by what had been done to the child and much disturbed by my daughter's enmity toward me. And now, to mark this stroke of good fortune, send your own son to visit our newcomer, and come to a banquet, for I intend to celebrate the deliverance of the boy by sacrificing to the gods, to whom the honor belongs."

[1.119] Harpagus made a low bow and went home in high spirits. His failure in strict obedience had turned out so fortunately that he was even invited to a banquet to celebrate this happy occasion. He told his wife, in great joy, all that had happened and sent his son, an only child of thirteen, to Astyages's palace, bidding him do whatever the king commanded.

But when Harpagus's son came to the palace, Astyages had him butchered and cut into joints. Some of the flesh he boiled, some he roasted, making it ready for the table. When the time came for the banquet, the guests assembled, among them Harpagus. Dishes of mutton were served up to the other guests and to Astyages, but to Harpagus was served the flesh of his son, except for the head, hands, and feet, which had been put aside and covered in a dish. When Harpagus had eaten enough, Astyages asked him whether he had enjoyed the feast. "Very much," replied Harpagus. Then, those who were appointed to do so brought in the boy's head, hands, and feet and bade Harpagus lift the lid and take what he would. Harpagus obeyed and saw the remains of his son. He did not collapse or lose his self-control. "Do you know of what animal's flesh you have eaten?" asked the king. "Yes," said Harpagus, "and whatever the king does is to be accepted." With this reply he gathered the remains and went home. He intended, I imagine, to bury it all together. Such was Harpagus's punishment.

[1.120] Astyages now turned his mind to Cyrus. Summoning those of the Magi who had interpreted his dream, he asked them whether they still attached the same significance to it. They remained firmly of the same opinion; the boy had been destined to displace him from the throne, had he lived and not met with an early death. "The boy is alive and well," said Astyages, "and when he was living in the country, the boys of the village elected him their king. He carried out his duties as real kings do, appointing guards and sentries and messengers and all. What do you think this signifies?" "If the boy is alive and well," said the Magi, "and has been 'king' in this unplanned manner, you can rest assured that he will not rule a second time. Sometimes oracles are fulfilled in trivial ways, and the issue of dreams has often been of slight importance." Astyages replied, "My own opinion agrees with yours. As the boy was named king, the dream has been fulfilled, and he no longer presents any danger to me. Still, consider carefully what is the best course for my house and for yourselves."

"We, too," answered the Magi, "are deeply concerned for the prosperity of your reign. If power should pass into the hands of this boy, a Persian, we who are Medes and of different race will become subservient to the Persians, whereas with you on the throne—one of ours—we receive great power and privilege from you. Thus we always watch out for you and your regime. We would tell you if we apprehended any danger arising from this boy. But we are confident that your dream has had a trivial issue, and we invite you to share our confidence. Send the boy to his parents in Persia where he will be out of sight."

[1.121] Satisfied with this reply, Astyages called Cyrus and said, "My boy, I once did you a wrong because of a misleading dream, but you have been saved by your own good fortune. Be off now to Persia; I will provide an escort. There you will find a father and mother of a very different kind than herdsman Mitradates and his wife."

[1.122] It was with boundless joy that his parents welcomed Cyrus, for they had thought him long since dead. He told them the tale of his survival, saying he had learned his history on the journey thither; he had been entirely in the dark before that, believing himself to be the son of Astyages's cowherd. He explained how he was raised by the cowherd's wife, whom he greatly praised; indeed her name, Cyno ("Bitch"), came up over and over throughout the story. His birth parents, taking their cue from the name, began putting out the rumor that Cyrus, when exposed, had been reared by a dog—this so as to make the survival of their son seem more miraculous to the Persians. So began this well-known rumor.

[1.123] Cyrus grew up to be the bravest and the most popular among all his young companions. Then Harpagus began to court his favor, sending him gifts. For Harpagus longed to take revenge on Astyages, but he realized that he was powerless to do this on his own. As Cyrus came of age, he sought him as an ally, likening his own sufferings to those of Cyrus. Already, prior to this, he had secretly approached each of the great Median nobles, urging the advantages of transferring power from Astyages to Cyrus because of the severity of the former's rule. When he thought the time was ripe, Harpagus had to face the difficulty of sending the message to Cyrus, who dwelled far away in Persia, because all the roads were guarded. Finally, he devised the following plan. He split open a hare without removing its fur, inserted a letter, sewed up the hare, gave it to the most trustworthy of the servants, dressed him as a huntsman complete with hunting net, and sent him off to Persia, ordering him to present the hare to Cyrus and tell him by word of mouth to cut it open with his own hands when nobody else was present.

[1.124] His orders were obeyed. Cyrus received the hare, cut it open, and read the following message: "Son of Cambyses, since the gods have you in their care—as your good fortune shows—take revenge on Astyages, your would-be murderer. If he had had his way, you would have died. To the gods and to me you owe your survival. No doubt you have long ago learned what he did to you and how he punished me because I did not kill you but gave you to the herdsman. If you will now be guided by me, you will become master of the whole of Astyages's kingdom. Persuade the Persians to revolt and take the field against the Medes. If I am appointed to lead Astyages's army against you, you will conquer; and the same is true if any other Mede of high rank is so appointed. For they will be the first to desert and to join you in destroying him. All is ready here. Act, and act quickly."

[1.125–26] After reading this letter, Cyrus began to think how best he might persuade the Persians to revolt, and he hit upon the following device as being most effective. He composed a suitable document and, summoning an assembly of Persians, unrolled the parchment and read it out, declaring that Astyages had appointed him commander of the Persians. "And now," he said, "I command each one of you to appear before me with a scythe." (There are many tribes among the Persians, only some of which Cyrus summoned and persuaded to revolt: These are the Pasargadae, the Maraphi, and the Maspii; of them the Pasargadae rank the highest, and the Achaemenidae, from which the Persian kings derive, are a clan of these. The other tribes, which are dependents of those already mentioned, are the Panthialii, Derousiaei, and Germanii—all farming peoples—and the nomadic tribes Dai, Mardi, Dropici, and Sagartii.) When the Persians had dutifully appeared with their scythes, he ordered them to clear an area of land full of thorns, about two miles square, in the space of a day. This task was accomplished, and then he gave them a second command: They were to appear the following day after having bathed. Meanwhile, Cyrus gathered together all his father's goats, sheep, and oxen, slaughtered them, and prepared to entertain the entire Persian host at a banquet, together with the choicest wine and dainties. When the Persians arrived the following day, he seated them in a meadow and feasted them. Then he asked them, "Which do you prefer, yesterday's tasks or today's good cheer?" They replied that there was a vast difference between them. "Men of Persia," said Cyrus, "your situation is this. If you hearken to me, you will have no servile tasks but will enjoy these and a thousand other pleasures. If you pay no heed to me, you must face countless toils like yesterday's. Listen to me and win your freedom. I know that I am divinely appointed to win your liberation, and I am sure that you are in no way inferior to the Medes in war or in any other way. This being so, I urge you to revolt against Astyages this very day." Now, the Persians had long resented the rule of the Medes and, with their newfound leader, they were eager to seek their freedom.

[1.127–28] When Astyages learned what Cyrus was about, he summoned him by messenger but instead received this reply: That Cyrus would be there much sooner than Astyages would like. Thereupon Astyages put all the Medes under arms and was so deluded as to appoint Harpagus to command them, forgetting the injury he had done him. When the two armies met in battle, some of the Medes who were not privy to the plot fought manfully, while others defected to the Persians, and the greater number played the coward and fled. When news of this disgraceful defeat reached Astyages, he uttered threats against Cyrus: "He will pay for this!" He first impaled the Magi dream-interpreters who had persuaded him to let Cyrus go, then he armed all the Medes who had been left in the capital, above and below military age, and led them out to battle. They were defeated with great loss, and Astyages was taken prisoner.

[1.129] Harpagus now came to taunt the captive, hurling the bitterest insults at him and reminding him of the banquet at which the king had feasted him with his son's flesh. "What does it feel like to be a slave instead of a king?" he asked. Astyages only looked at him and then asked in return, "Was it you who urged Cyrus to revolt?" "Yes," said Harpagus, "I wrote the letter. It is my doing." "Then you are the most stupid and wickedest of men," said Astyages, "the most stupid because, if you were indeed the instigator of the revolt, you could have seized the crown for yourself instead of giving it to another. The most wicked because, on account of that banquet, you have enslaved all the Medes. If you had to confer the crown on somebody other than yourself, it would have been most just to give this prize to a Mede rather than a Persian. Now the Medes, guiltless as they are, will be the slaves of Persian masters—these same Persians who were once slaves of the Medes."

[1.130] After a reign of thirty-five years, Astyages lost his throne in the way I have described. And because of his harsh rule, the Medes, who had ruled Asia west of the Halys for 128 years (not counting the period of Scythian power),[29] had to bow before Persian domination. Some time later, under Darius, the Medes had a change of heart and mounted a rebellion, but they were defeated in battle and the rebellion was put down. But to return to the time of Astyages: The Persians, led by Cyrus, rebelled from the Medes and became masters of Asia from that day to this. As for Astyages himself, Cyrus did not ill-treat his former enemy and kept him at his court until he died.

Thus was Cyrus born and raised and made king, and later conquered Croesus (as I have already related) after Croesus had first wronged him. As a result of this conquest, he came to rule all Asia.

[1.131] A word now about Persian customs, of which I have some personal knowledge. It is not the Persians' practice to set up images and temples and altars; they regard it as foolish to do so because, I think, they do not conceive the gods as having human form, as the Greeks do. They regard Zeus as being the whole circle of the sky, and they sacrifice to him on mountaintops. They worship the sun, the moon, the earth, fire, water, and the winds. In addition to this old-established

---

29. The reference is to the twenty-eight years from 653 BCE to 625 BCE when the Scythians dominated western Asia.

religion, they have taken over from the Assyrians and the Arabians the worship of Aphrodite, Queen of Heaven. The Assyrians call Aphrodite Mylitta, the Arabs Alilat, and the Persians Mitra.[30]

[1.133] As regards their deliberations, all important decisions are first discussed when they are drunk. On the next day, the master of the house where they have assembled submits the decision for reconsideration when they are sober. If it is approved, it is ratified; if not, it is abandoned. Conversely, any decision they have reached when they are sober is reconsidered when they are drunk.

[1.134][31] They honor most after themselves those who inhabit the lands nearest to them, they honor slightly less those who dwell next to those, and so on in that fashion; they give the least honor to those dwelling farthest from themselves, since they hold themselves to be by far the best among the races of humankind, while others have a share of virtue that diminishes over distance, so that the basest are those inhabiting lands farthest from themselves.

[1.135] The Persians adopt foreign ways more easily than any other people. Since they deemed Median dress more lovely than their own, they now wear it, and they use Egyptian armor in war. They start practicing all sorts of indulgences as soon as they learn of them; thus from the Greeks they have adopted pederasty.[32]

[1.136–37] Every man has several wives and an even greater number of mistresses. A great proof of manliness, second only to prowess in fighting, is to be the father of many boys. The king sends presents every year to the fathers of the greatest number of boys, for it is his belief that his strength lies therein.

Boys are educated from the age of five to the age of twenty, and they are taught three things only: to ride, to shoot the bow, and to tell the truth. Before the age of five, a boy is reared by women only, and his father never sets eyes on him. The purpose of this custom is to avoid distress to the father if the child should die in infancy, and a good custom it is.[33] Another praiseworthy custom is this, that not even the king is allowed to put a man to death for a single offense, nor is the master allowed to inflict irreparable injury on any of his servants. It is only when, on mature consideration, they find that the wrongdoing outweighs good service that they give vent to anger.

---

30. Herodotus assumed that all peoples worshipped the same gods but under different names. In the case of Mitra, who was actually a male deity, Mithra, he was probably deceived by the fact that the god's name ended in *a*, which in Greek was a feminine marker.

31. Chapters 134 and 135 were translated by James Romm.

32. Herodotus's attitude toward pederasty, literally "love of prepubescent boys," which was a common practice among Greek aristocrats, is not clear, but it is interesting that this should be, in his view, the only aspect of Greek culture that the Persians considered worthy of adoption.

33. This is a rare example of a foreign custom that Herodotus personally considered praiseworthy.

[1.138] What they are forbidden to do, they are also forbidden to speak of. They consider lying to be the most shameful thing, and second to that, being in debt, chiefly because being in debt is frequently a cause of lying.

[1.141] To return to where I left off the story: The Ionians and the Aeolians, hearing of the Persian conquest of Lydia, immediately sent their envoys to Cyrus at Sardis, asking for the same terms as had been granted to them by Croesus. Cyrus replied with the following story. A flute-player who saw some fish in the sea played his flute to them, hoping that this would induce them to come ashore. His hopes were in vain, so he took a net, drew a large catch, and hauled them in. Seeing the fish leaping about, he said to them, "You can stop that. When I played my flute for you, you refused to dance, and now it is too late." Cyrus was referring to the time when, besieging Croesus in Sardis, he had invited the Greeks to revolt and they had refused; they were offering their allegiance only now when he was the conqueror.

When the Ionians received this reply, they began to see to their defenses, all except the Milesians, to whom Cyrus granted the same terms as they had enjoyed under the Lydians. The other cities met in common council and resolved to send a joint embassy to Sparta, seeking assistance.

[1.152–53] They chose a Phocaean named Pythermus as their spokesman, who, dressed in purple so as to attract a larger audience, made a long speech to the Spartans. The Spartans paid him no heed and rejected the idea of helping the Ionians; they sent the envoys away but were sufficiently stirred as to send a penteconter[34] to the Asiatic coast, no doubt to keep an eye on what was happening. The galley put in at Phocaea, and the most eminent of the crew, a man named Lacrines was sent to Sardis to warn Cyrus not to injure any Greek city, for the Spartans would not allow it. Cyrus asked some Greek bystanders, "Who are these Spartans, and how many in number?" When he had received their answer, he said to the Spartan spokesman, "I have never yet been afraid of men who have a place specially appointed in the middle of their city where they gather to cheat one another, swearing false oaths. If my fortunes thrive, they will have their own troubles to chat about, never mind those of the Ionians." Cyrus's jibe was directed against the universal Greek practice of having a marketplace for buying and selling, a practice quite unknown to the Persians.

After this, Cyrus put Tabalus in charge of Sardis as governor and appointed a Lydian named Pactyes to deal with the gold of Croesus and his countrymen; he himself marched off toward Ecbatana, bringing Croesus with him; he paid little heed to the Ionians and delegated one of his generals to subdue them, preferring to lead the assaults on the Bactrians, Sacae, and Egyptians.

[1.154–56] Cyrus had marched no great distance when news was brought to him that the Lydians, encouraged by Pactyes, had revolted. Pactyes, he learned, had taken the gold of Sardis down to the coast and used it to hire mercenaries and

---

34. This was a ship powered by fifty rowers that was the standard Greek warship before the widespread adoption of the trireme in the fifth century BCE.

persuade the coastal peoples to support him; then he had marched on Sardis and was now besieging Tabalus in the stronghold of the city. "How can I bring an end to all of this?" said Cyrus to Croesus, who was accompanying him. "It seems that the Lydians will not cease to bring trouble on me and on themselves. My best course, I fear, is to enslave them all. It appears that I have acted like a man who has slain the father and spared the children. For you, who were more than a father to them, I have taken away prisoner, and have restored their city to the Lydians. After that, is it surprising that they have rebelled against me?"

When Croesus heard Cyrus thus speak his mind, he feared that Sardis would be utterly destroyed. "O king," he said, "what you say is fairly said. Yet do not give full vent to your wrath, nor destroy an ancient city that is guiltless alike of former and current misdoings. For former misdoings I am responsible, and I have paid a heavy price. This time the villain is Pactyes, the man to whom you entrusted Sardis, and who alone should be punished. Forgive the Lydians, but take the following measures to ensure their future loyalty and good conduct. Forbid them to possess weapons of war, order them to wear tunics under their cloaks and soft slippers on their feet, and make them teach their sons to play the lute and the harp and to tend shops for a living. You will soon see them turning into women instead of men, and they will never again be a source of trouble to you." Such was Croesus's advice, for it seemed to him preferable to being sold into slavery, and he realized that he could not persuade Cyrus to change his mind unless some drastic alternative was suggested. As it was, Cyrus was delighted with this suggestion and ceased his anger, saying he would do as Croesus suggested.

[1.177] While Harpagus was subduing the western side of Asia Minor, Cyrus himself marched against the north and east, conquering every people and leaving none untouched. I shall pass over his minor conquests and turn my attention to those that required the most effort and that most deserve retelling.

[1.178] Having brought all the continent under his control, Cyrus turned his army against the Assyrians.[35] Assyria contains many great cities, but the most notable and the strongest is Babylon, which became the seat of government after the fall of Nineveh; a vast city of square formation, its sides are nearly fourteen miles long and its circuit fifty-six miles. It is more splendidly adorned than any other city we know of. It is surrounded by a broad, deep moat full of water and further protected by strong outer and inner walls.

---

35. Herodotus's understanding of the historical geography of Mesopotamia was confused by vague memories of the Assyrian Empire that had included both northern Mesopotamia—Assyria proper—and southern Mesopotamia—Babylonia. As Herodotus viewed the conquest of Nineveh as ending Assyrian imperial power but used the term "Assyria" to designate all of Mesopotamia, he believed that Babylon became the new Assyrian capital instead of the center of a distinct state which historians call the Neo-Babylonian Empire (626 BCE–539 BCE).

[1.183] The great temple of Bel, the Babylonian Zeus,[36] is a square building with gates of bronze, two stades each way, still existing in my time. In the center is a solid tower, a stade in breadth and height; on this is superimposed a second tower, and on this a third, and so on to a total of eight towers. A way of ascent is provided, encircling the towers in spiral form, and about halfway up there is a resting place and seats for those making the ascent. On the summit of the topmost tower is a great shrine containing a magnificent couch with rich coverings and a golden table beside it. No image is to be found there, and no mortal stays the night there except for one native woman all alone, whoever may be chosen by the god—so we are told by the Chaldaeans who are the priests of this god. The Chaldaeans also say—though I do not find this credible—that the god himself comes to the temple and rests on the bed.

[1.184, 187] I shall discuss in my Assyrian account[37] the notable rulers of Babylon who in the past added to its adornment and defenses; among them were two queens, Semiramis and Nitocris, separated by five generations. The latter was responsible for devising a remarkable hoax. Above the main gate of the city she had a tomb built for herself high above the very gates, bearing the following inscription: "If any king of Babylon after me is in need of money, let him open my tomb and take what he wants, but he should in no way do this except in dire need; that would be a bad idea." The tomb remained intact until the time of King Darius. He resented not being able to use this gate, which would have necessitated driving beneath the corpse of Nitocris, and he also considered that the inscription was an invitation to take the money. But when he opened the tomb, he found no money, just the corpse and an inscription reading: "If you were not a greedy scoundrel, you would not have opened the tomb of the dead." Such is the kind of queen Nitocris is said to have been.

[1.188–89] It was against the son of Nitocris, Labynetus, king of Assyria, that Cyrus was now making war. (When a Persian king takes the field, he is abundantly furnished not only with provisions from his homeland and his own cattle but with water from the river Choaspes, which flows past Susa, his capital city. No Persian king will ever drink from any other stream, and wherever he goes, a supply of this water, readily boiled, is conveyed in silver vessels by a long column of four-wheeled mule-wagons.) On his march, Cyrus reached the river Gyndes, which later joins the Tigris and flows into the Persian Gulf. While Cyrus was preparing to cross the river by boat, one of his sacred white horses, a high-spirited animal, plunged into the river in an attempt to cross on his own and was carried away by the current and drowned. In high wrath with the river that had dared to insult him, Cyrus swore

---

36. Baʾal = Bel is not a name but a title meaning "Lord" which was assigned to various Near Eastern storm gods of which the most important was Marduk, the chief god of Babylon and the creator of the world, whom the Greeks identified with their storm god, Zeus.

37. Herodotus does not seem to have fulfilled his promise to write an account of Assyria.

that he would so weaken it that even a woman could cross it with ease without wetting her knees. He suspended his march against Babylon, divided his army into two sections, marked out on either side of the river 180 channels in a straight line in all directions, and ordered his men to dig. Even with this huge labor force, it took the whole summer to complete the task. So Cyrus punished the river Gyndes by dividing it into 360 streams and then resumed his march on Babylon.

[1.190–91] The Babylonians had gone forth in battle-array to await him. Cyrus now arrived and the Babylonians attacked; in the ensuing engagement the Babylonians were defeated and forced to retire within their own walls where they felt secure. They already knew of Cyrus's ceaseless activity and had seen him attacking every nation in turn, and so they had accumulated a vast stock of provisions that would last for several years. The siege became a protracted affair, and Cyrus was beginning to despair of making any impression on the defenses when an ingenious plan was devised, whether by himself or another I do not know. He stationed part of the forces where the Euphrates, flowing under the walls, enters the city, and part where it flows out, with orders to invade through the channel as soon as the waters were shallow enough. When he had given these instructions, he took the nonserviceable part of his army to a point above the city and diverted the river into the adjoining lakes by means of ditches.

When the level of the Euphrates had sunk to thigh level, his forces proceeded silently along the riverbed and entered the town. Had the Babylonians realized what was happening, they could have shut the gates leading to the river, manned the walls on either side of the river, and caught the Persians in a trap. But, as it was, the Persians took them by surprise, and the Babylonians themselves say that their city is so large that the outer suburbs were captured before the people at the center had any idea that there was something amiss. In fact, there was a festival in progress, and they were singing and dancing while the city was being taken.[38]

[1.195] The Babylonian style of dress is as follows: A linen tunic reaches right down to the feet, and over this there is a woolen tunic, with a coverlet on top. Their shoes are of a peculiar native kind, rather like those to be found in Boeotia. They wear their hair long, with a bonnet, and their bodies are perfumed all over. Every man has his own seal and his own staff specially made for him, on top of which is carved an apple or a rose or a lily or an eagle or some other figure. No staff is without some ornament.

[1.196] They used to have a custom that, in my opinion, was most cleverly devised, and that is shared, I believe, with the Eneti of Illyria. Every village practiced it once a year. Girls who had reached marriageable age were gathered together in one place, while the men stood around in a circle. The herald then called upon

---

38. The capture of Babylon took place in 539 BCE. Babylon, thereafter, became one of the four principal royal residences of the Persian kings.

each girl to stand up in turn, starting with the most beautiful, and offered her for sale. When she had been purchased for a considerable sum of money, he passed on to the next fairest. Marriage was the purpose of the bargaining. The wealthy Babylonian bachelors would bid against each other for the most beautiful brides, while the common folk, for whom beauty in a wife was a luxury they could not afford, were actually paid to take the least prepossessing of the maidens. For when the herald had disposed of all the fairest, he would start on the plainest, perhaps a cripple, and ask who would take the least money to marry her, until she was assigned to the one who demanded the smallest sum. In this way the money accruing from the sale of the most beautiful damsels provided dowries for the ill-favored or cripples. A father was not allowed to marry his daughter to whomever he would, and nobody was permitted to take away a maiden he had bought without providing sureties that he would marry her. In case of disagreement between husband and wife, the money would be returned. Men from other villages were also allowed to buy a wife at these sales. This very admirable custom has now fallen into disuse and has been succeeded by a quite different practice. When hardship came to the city after its conquest, the common people resorted to prostituting their daughters as a means of eking out a living.

[1.197] Another of their customs, scarcely less ingenious than their former marriage custom, is concerned with illness. They have no doctors but carry the sufferers out into the marketplace where passersby offer advice and remedies, either having experienced the same sickness themselves or having observed it in other cases. They suggest such remedies as have proved efficacious for themselves or that have been seen to succeed with others. Nobody is allowed to pass by in silence; they must ask the sufferer the nature of his ailment. They bury their dead in honey, and their lamentations are similar to those used in Egypt.

[1.201] After the conquest of Assyria, Cyrus's next ambition was to subjugate the Massagetae. These are said to be a numerous and mighty nation, dwelling eastward beyond the river Araxes; some authorities believe them to be of Scythian descent. It is not clear whether the Araxes is greater or smaller than the Danube. Some say that it contains many large islands as big as Lesbos, and that these are inhabited by men who live on roots that they dig up in the summer, while for their winter supplies they lay in store the fruits of certain trees that they have found to be suitable for food. Other trees they have found to bear fruit of a peculiar kind. Gathering in groups, they sit in a circle around a fire and they cast this fruit into the flames. As it burns, it sends out smoke, the smell of which makes them drunk just as wine does the Greeks. The more fruit they cast into the flames, the more drunk they get, until they jump up and start singing and dancing.[39]

[1.204] There were many motives that impelled Cyrus to make war on the Massagetae. First, there was his belief in his superhuman origin. Secondly, he could

---

39. The reference is to cannabis, that is, marijuana.

reflect on his uninterrupted success in the past; for wherever he campaigned, no nation could withstand his assault.

[1.205–6] At this time the Massagetae were ruled by a queen, Tomyris, who had succeeded to the throne on her husband's death. Cyrus sent a messenger to her on the pretext of asking for her hand in marriage, but Tomyris rejected his overture, knowing well that it was her kingdom, not herself, that he was wooing. Failing in this stratagem, Cyrus now openly embarked on a campaign against the Massagetae. He advanced to the river Araxes and prepared bridges for his army to cross and fortified his ferryboats to force a landing. While he was thus busily engaged, Tomyris sent him this message: "King of the Medes, abandon what you are about. You cannot know if it will turn out as you would like it. Rule over your own people and endure to see me rule over mine. But of course you will not hearken to me, for you cannot bear to live at peace. Well, then, if you are so eager to try the strength of the Massagetae, you need not engage in the toil of bridge-building. We will retire a three days' march from the river, and you may cross over to our territory. But if you prefer to engage us on your own territory, go and withdraw some distance, and we will cross over to your side."

[1.207] On receiving this message, Cyrus summoned his leading counselors to advise him which of the alternatives he should choose. They were unanimous in proposing that Tomyris and her army should cross over to their side. But Croesus the Lydian, who was present at the council of war, took the opposite view, speaking as follows: "O king, I have said before that ever since Zeus gave me into your hands, I will do all I can to avert any danger threatening your house. My own misfortunes have taught me a bitter lesson. If you think that you and your army are immortal, it would be pointless to declare my opinion in this matter. But if you recognize that you are merely human, and your men too, then first learn this, that there is a cycle in human affairs that does not permit the same people to enjoy unbroken good fortune. In this matter I do not agree with your counselors. If we allow the enemy to cross over to our side of the river, in the event of defeat you will lose not only a battle but your entire empire. For it is obvious that the victorious Massagetae would not retreat but would continue to drive on right through your realm. If, on the other hand, victory falls to you, it would not be as decisive as it would be if you were to pursue a defeated enemy into their own land. Then again there is the further consideration that it would be intolerable for Cyrus, son of Cambyses, to retreat before a woman. My advice is to cross over the river and advance as far as the enemy withdraws and then employ this stratagem: I gather that the Massagetae have no experience of the good things that the Persians enjoy and are insensible to life's pleasures. Let us provide for them in our camp a most generous banquet, with huge numbers of sheep slaughtered and dressed for the table, bowls of strong wine on a liberal scale, and all kinds of other dishes. When this has been done, let the greater part of your army retire, leaving behind some inferior troops. Unless I am mistaken, on seeing this attractive banquet, the enemy will fall upon it, and this will afford you the opportunity to deliver a mighty stroke."

[1.208] These were the conflicting counsels presented to Cyrus, who elected to follow Croesus's advice and sent a message to Tomyris bidding her withdraw, as he was about to cross the river. She withdrew in accordance with her undertaking, and Cyrus, placing Croesus in the care of his son Cambyses, whom he named as his successor, with earnest instructions to treat him with honor and respect if he, Cyrus, should meet with disaster, sent them both back to Persia and crossed the river with his army.

[1.209] On the night after the crossing, as Cyrus was asleep in the land of the Massagetae, he had a dream. He dreamed that he saw the eldest son of Hystaspes with wings on his shoulders, one of which overshadowed Asia and the other Europe. Now the eldest son of Hystaspes, of the Achaemenid clan, was Darius, a young man of about twenty at the time, who had been left behind as not yet of military age. When Cyrus awoke, he reflected on the dream and, sending for Hystaspes, he spoke to him in private. "Hystaspes," he said, "I have discovered that your son is plotting against me and my throne, and I will disclose to you the reason for my certainty. The gods have me in their care and warn me of what is to come. Last night in a dream I saw your eldest son with wings on his shoulders, one overshadowing Asia and the other Europe. There can be no doubt of the significance to this—he is plotting against me. Do you therefore return to Persia with the utmost speed and see to it that you produce the young man for trial when I return victorious from this war."

[1.210] So spoke Cyrus, thinking that Darius was plotting against him. But the true meaning of the dream had escaped him. The god was forewarning Cyrus that he was about to meet his death, and Darius would thereby come to the throne.

Hystaspes replied, "O king, may there never be born a Persian who would plot against you, and if there be, may he straightaway die. You found the Persians slaves and made them free; you found them subject to others and made them rulers over all men. If a dream has told you that my son is stirring up revolution, I give him over to you to do as you will." With this answer, he crossed the Araxes to return to Persia and keep watch over his son Darius for Cyrus's sake.

[1.211] Cyrus now advanced a day's march from the Araxes and carried out Croesus's plan. Then he retired with the flower of his army, leaving behind some inferior troops. A detachment of the Massagetae, one-third of their army, fell upon these troops, overcame their feeble resistance, and slew them all. After this victory, seeing a banquet laid out before them, they betook themselves to feasting, and, sated with good food and wine, fell asleep. The Persians attacked, slew many of them, and took prisoner an even greater number, among whom was their general, Spargapises, Tomyris's son.

[1.212] The queen, learning of these events and of her son's capture, sent the following message: "Cyrus, you who cannot get your fill of blood, do not pride yourself on what you have accomplished. The fruit of the vine, wherewith you fill yourselves until you are so maddened that as the wine goes down shameful words float up on its fumes—*that* is the treacherous poison whereby you have got my son into your power, not by strength in battle. Now listen to me for your own good. Restore my son to me and get out of my land without hurt, gloating over your triumph over a third part of the Massagetae. If you refuse, I swear by the sun, our lord, that for all your gluttony I will give you more blood than you can drink."

[1.213] Cyrus paid no heed to this message. As for Tomyris's son, Spargapises, when he was sober again and realized the nature of his misfortune, he begged Cyrus to have his fetters removed, and as soon as he had the use of his hands, he did away with himself.

[1.214] When Cyrus had rejected her message, Tomyris gathered all her forces and met him in the field, and the battle that followed was, I consider, the most violent that has ever been between foreign nations. According to what I have learned, the manner of it was this. At first, the two sides stood at a distance and fired arrows at each other; then, when all their shafts were exhausted, they came into close combat with lances and swords. They fought this way for a long time, with neither side willing to retreat. Finally, the Massagetae got the upper hand. The greater part of the Persian army was destroyed on the spot, and Cyrus himself was killed. He had reigned twenty-nine years. Tomyris sought out his body among the dead, flung his severed head into a wineskin filled with human blood, and, enraged, spoke these words: "Though I have conquered you, and I live and you are dead, yet you have destroyed me by treacherously capturing my son. Now, as I promised you, I shall give you your fill of blood."

Of the many accounts of Cyrus's death, this is the one I believe true.

[1.215–16][40] The Massagetae dress as the Scythians do and have a similar way of life. In battle they fight both mounted and on foot, and some use the spear, bow and arrow, and the *sagaris* or battle-ax. The only metals they use are gold and bronze . . . for they have no iron or silver in their land, but gold and bronze in great quantity. The following are their customs: Each man takes a wife, but the wives are all held in common. The Greeks think it is the Scythians who do this, but in fact it's the Massagetae. Whenever a Massagetan man desires a woman, he simply hangs up his arrow case on the front of her wagon and enjoys her freely. As to life span, they set no other limit but this to old age: When one of them becomes very old, all his kin gather and sacrifice him, along with various animals, and then they roast all the meats and hold a huge feast. This they deem the happiest death, and they take pity on anyone who dies from disease, since this person must be buried in the ground and not eaten. They grow no crops but live off their flocks and also fishing, for fish are plentiful in the Araxes. They are great drinkers of milk. As to deities, they honor one alone, the sun; and to it they sacrifice horses, in the belief that the swiftest of creatures is owed to the swiftest of gods.

---

40. These two chapters were translated by James Romm.

FROM BOOK 3

Cambyses's Aithiopian Campaign

The conquest of Egypt by Cambyses, son of Cyrus, in the mid-520s BCE, provided Herodotus with the opportunity to devote the entire second book of the Histories *to a comprehensive account of the geography, culture, and history of Egypt that inaugurated the long series of Greek ethnographies of Egypt. After returning to the subject of the conquest of Egypt at the beginning of the third book and describing various examples of Cambyses's tyrannical actions in Egypt, Herodotus discusses his plans for further invasions of African territories bordering Egypt and their disastrous failure.*

[3.17–19][41] Cambyses planned three different campaigns: one against the Carthaginians, one against the Ammonians, and a third against the Long-lived Aithiopians,[42] who inhabit the part of Libya nearest the southern sea.[43] Against the Carthaginians he sent his navy, and against the Ammonians, a select part of his army; but to the Aithiopians he first sent spies, to see whether there really was such a thing as the so-called Table of the Sun[44] and to spy on the country generally. He gave these spies gifts to present to the Aithiopian king as a pretext for their visit. (The Table of the Sun, reportedly, is something like this: In front of the Aithiopian city there is a meadow, and it is filled with cooked meats from every type of animal; state officials go there every night to set out these meats, and in the daytime, anyone who wishes can come and partake of them. But the Aithiopians say that these meats spring forth from the earth itself.)[45] Having decided to use spies, then, Cambyses immediately sent for some of the Fish-eaters who live in Elephantine, since these men understand the Aithiopian language. . . .

---

41. Chapters 17–33 were translated by James Romm.
42. In order to avoid confusion with the modern country of "Ethiopia" and its people, the editor has replaced "Ethiopia" and "Ethiopians" in the translation with "Aithiopia" and "Aithiopians," the ancient Greek terms for the Nile Valley south of Egypt and its inhabitants.
43. The city of the "Long-lived Aithiopians" has often been identified with Meroe, the capital of the kingdom of Kush, but that is to ignore Herodotus's clear statement that they lived near the "southern sea," that is, "Ocean," where Homer located the pious Aithiopians. In other words, Herodotus assumed that Cambyses's campaign was directed at a people, who supposedly lived at the end of the earth and not a city located within the Nile Valley.
44. Scholars, who identify the city of the "Long-lived Aithiopians" with Meroe, also identify the Table of the Sun with the so-called Sun Temple at Meroe. The identification is not possible, however, since the Sun Temple dates to the first century BCE, not the sixth century BCE.
45. As he had done with the story of Cyrus being raised by a bitch, Herodotus rationalized the "fantastic" element of the story, namely, that the earth spontaneously provided food.

When they arrived, he sent them on their mission, giving orders what to say and loading them up with gifts: a purple cloak, a necklace and bracelets of gold, a container of myrrh, and a jar of Phoenician wine. [3.20] The Aithiopians to whom Cambyses sent these men are said to be the tallest and most beautiful of all peoples. Their customs are unlike those of other peoples, especially as concerns the king-ship: They select as king whomever they deem to be the tallest and to have strength commensurate with his size.

[3.21] So, the Fish-eaters arrived and presented the king with their gifts, saying: "Cambyses, king of the Persians, has sent us to negotiate with you and to give you these gifts, items that he himself most delights in, in the hopes of becoming your ally and visiting you in person." The Aithiopian king realized that they were spies, however, and spoke as follows: "It's not true that the Persian king has sent you here because he hopes to become my guest; nor do you fellows speak the truth (for it's obvious you're spying on my realm); nor is your king a righteous man; for if he were, he would not feel tempted to conquer land outside his own territory, nor would he enslave men who have done him no wrong. Here, give him this bow and say to him, 'The king of the Aithiopians advises the king of the Persians thus: If the Persians can draw bows as big as these with as much ease as we do, then let them come in full force against the Long-lived Aithiopians; if not, let them give thanks to the gods, who have never inspired in the children of the Aithiopians any desire to gain lands beyond their own.'" Then he picked up a bow, unstrung it, and handed it to them.

[3.22] Then, picking up the purple clothing, he asked what it was and how it had been made. The Fish-eaters gave him a true account of how purple cloth is dyed, to which he replied: "Disguised clothing for disguised men." Next he asked about the gold necklace and bracelets; when the Fish-eaters explained that they were jewelry, he laughed, think-ing they meant shackles. "We have shackles in our land far stronger than this," he said. Then he asked about the myrrh, and when they described its manufacture and its use as a perfume, he said the same thing he had said about the clothing. Finally he came to the wine; after learning how it was made and drinking some, he declared himself delighted. Then he asked what the Persian king ate and how long the oldest Persians lived. They described the making of bread out of grain and said that eighty years was the greatest complement of years allotted to their race. To this the Aithiopian replied that he was not surprised they lived such a short time while feeding on dung;[46] moreover, he said, they would not live even as long as eighty years if not for their drink (pointing to the wine); in this alone, he said, the Aithiopians were outdone by the Persians.

[3.23] Now the Fish-eaters asked in their turn about the Aithiopian way of life, and the king told them that many Aithiopians lived to 120 years, and some even longer than that, eating meat and drinking milk. When the spies expressed amazement at their longevity, the king led them to a spring, whose water made

---

46. According to Solon (F 27 Gerber), human life span consisted of ten seven-year periods, or seventy years.

their skin glisten just as if it were olive oil and gave off a smell of violets. The spies later reported that this water was so light that nothing would float on it; even wood, or things lighter than wood, would sink to the bottom. (If this water is really such as they described, then it must be through their constant use of it that they have become long-lived.) Next after the spring, he showed them the prison, where all the prisoners were bound with shackles of gold. (Bronze is the rarest and most precious substance among these Aithiopians.)[47] After their visit to the prison, he also showed them the so-called Table of the Sun.

[3.24] Finally the king showed them the Aithiopian tombs, which are said to be made of crystal and used in the following manner: After embalming the corpse (either in the Egyptian manner or some other way), they whiten it with gypsum and paint on it as close a likeness of the living person as they can. Next they surround the body with a pillar of crystal, hollowed out to form a chamber (this crystal is mined easily and in great quantities in their land). In the middle of the pillar stands the corpse, where it can be clearly seen from outside; no unpleasant smells or anything else unseemly can be sensed; the image of the corpse is not distorted in any way by the crystal. For the space of a year, the nearest and dearest of the dead person keep the pillar in their home, bringing it sacrifices and offering it the finest foods; after that they carry it outside and set it up in a circuit around the city.

[3.25] Having seen all this, then, the Fish-eaters departed and, returning to Egypt, made their report to Cambyses. Immediately Cambyses, enraged, marched against the Aithiopians, without first ordering provision of food or reckoning with the fact that he was setting out for the ends of the earth; when he heard what the Fish-eaters had to say, he became maddened and no longer in his right mind, and he marched. He ordered the Greeks who were with him to remain there in Egypt and took with him his entire infantry corps. When he came to Thebes in the course of his march, he split off five myriads[48] from the army and sent them to attack the Ammonians,[49] enslave them, and to set fire to the local oracle of Zeus, while he himself took the remaining forces and proceeded against the Aithiopians.

When Cambyses had not yet completed even a fifth of the march, his food supplies began to fail. Next the pack animals gave out—for they were devoured by the soldiers. If under these circumstances Cambyses had come to his senses and turned the army around, he would have been a wise man despite his original error; but in fact he paid no heed to his difficulties and pressed ahead. As long as the soldiers

---

47. Unlike gold, which has no practical use but is supposedly abundant in the remote lands at the ends of the earth and, therefore, inexpensive, bronze, which does not occur naturally but is useful, has to be imported and is valuable.

48. A myriad equals 10,000.

49. The Ammonians inhabited the oasis of Siwah west of Egypt, where was located the oracle of the Libyan god Ammon, whom the Greeks identified with the Egyptian god Amun and the Greek god Zeus.

could, they foraged grass and plants from the ground, but soon they came to the desert sand, and there some of them did a terrible thing: Drawing lots, they chose one man out of ten and the rest ate him. When Cambyses learned of this, shaken by the spectacle of his men devouring each other, he at last gave up his Aithiopian campaign and turned around, and got back to Thebes after having lost most of his army. From there he went north to Memphis and discharged the Greek fleet.

[3.26] Thus fared the campaign against the Aithiopians. As for those who were detached to attack the Ammonians: These troops set out from Thebes, with guides in the lead, and are known to have arrived at the city of Oasis, a seven days' journey across the desert (Oasis is settled by Samians, reportedly of the Aeschrionian tribe).[50] This place has a name that translates to "Islands of the Blessed." The army is said to have arrived at this place, but neither the Ammonians nor their neighbors nor any other sources know what happened thereafter. The men never reached the Ammonians and never returned home. This much, however, is told by the Ammonians: When the men were midway between Oasis and themselves on their journey through the desert, they stopped to prepare a meal and a violent south wind arose and buried them under heaps of sand; in this way they disappeared forever. So the Ammonians say regarding the expedition against them.

FROM BOOK 6

The Battle of Marathon

Persian rule in western Anatolia was challenged in the early 490s BCE (499 BCE–494 BCE) by a revolt of the Greek cities of Ionia that was supported by Athens. After the suppression of the revolt, which Herodotus called the "beginning of evils for the Greeks," in 494 BCE, an invasion of Greece was launched in 490 BCE in reprisal. After conquering Eretria, a small city in western Euboea and Athens's ally in the Ionian Revolt, and enslaving its population, the Persian force landed at Marathon in northeastern Attica, where they were met by the Athenian army. The unexpected defeat of the Persians was celebrated by Athenian artists and writers throughout the fifth and fourth centuries BCE.

[6.102] With the subjugation of Eretria,[51] after a few days' delay the Persians sailed for Attica,[52] confident that they could deal with the Athenians just as they

---

50. Herodotus has misinterpreted "Oasis" as the name of a city. Nothing is known about a Samian settlement in the interior of Libya.

51. The survivors of the sack of Eretria were enslaved and transported to Asia, where Darius I settled them near Susa in western Iran.

52. Attica is the region of Greece in which the city of Athens was located.

had dealt with the Eretrians. Marathon being a place in Attica suitable for cavalry and nearest to Eretria, it was to Marathon that they were guided by Hippias, son of Pisistratus.

[6.103] When the news reached the Athenians, they likewise marched out to Marathon under the command of ten generals,[53] of whom the tenth was Miltiades. Miltiades's father, Cimon, had been banished from Athens by the tyrant Pisistratus. While in exile it was his fortune to win the four-horse chariot race at Olympia, thereby acquiring the same honor as his half-brother Miltiades before him. At the next Olympiad he won the same prize with the same mares but surrendered his victory and caused Pisistratus to be proclaimed the victor, on the understanding that he would be allowed back to his own country. He won another Olympiad with the same mares, but was murdered by the sons of Pisistratus after their father had died. They set men to waylay him by night, and these slew him near the Council House. He was buried outside the city beyond what is called the Valley Road, and opposite the tomb were buried the mares that had won three prizes. At the time of Cimon's death, Stesagoras, the elder of his two sons, was living with Cimon's brother Miltiades in the Chersonese, while the younger, called Miltiades after his uncle, who had founded the Chersonese settlement, was with his father in Athens.

It was this Miltiades who was then elected one of ten generals of the Athenian troops. He had escaped from the Chersonese and twice come within an ace of losing his life—first when the Phoenicians, eager to seize him and carry him off to the Persian king, pursued him as far as Imbros, and then, after he had escaped that peril and reached his own country and thought himself safe, when his political enemies, having lain in wait for him, arraigned him before the court and prosecuted him for his rule of the Chersonese.[54] This attack he likewise escaped and was appointed general by popular vote.[55]

[6.105] But before leaving the city, the Athenians first sent off to Sparta a messenger, one Philippides,[56] an Athenian who was by profession and practice a courier. According to the account he later gave to the Athenians, this man, when he was in the neighborhood of Mount Parthenion above Tegea, encountered the god Pan,

---

53. Each year the Athenians elected ten *strategoi* or "generals," one from each of the ten tribes into which the Athenian citizen body was divided. The presence of all ten generals at Marathon implies that the entire Athenian military had been mobilized to meet the Persian invasion.

54. Miltiades II had been sent by the Athenian tyrant Hippias c. 516/15 BCE to succeed his uncle of the same name as ruler of the Chersonese, that is, the Gallipoli Peninsula, but returned to Athens in the 490s BCE.

55. The ostensible charge was that he had been a tyrant, but the real motive was probably to remove from Athenian politics the head of the one of the most influential families in Athens, the Philaids.

56. C. 150 miles. The story that he died after running the twenty-six miles from Marathon to Athens to report the Athenian victory is a later legend that was clearly unknown to Herodotus.

who called him by name and bade him ask the Athenians why they neglected him, though he was well disposed to them and had often been helpful to them in the past and would be so again. The Athenians, believing this to be a true account, when their affairs were once more in good order, set up a shrine to Pan beneath the acropolis, and from the time they received this message, they propitiate him with yearly sacrifices and a torch-race. [6.106] So Philippides, at this time—that is, when he was sent by the generals and when, as he said, the god Pan appeared to him—reached Sparta the day after leaving Athens and delivered this message to the Spartan authorities: "Men of Lacedaemon, the Athenians ask you to come to their assistance and not to permit a city that is the most ancient in Greece to be enslaved by the barbarians. Already Eretria has been reduced to slavery, and Greece is the weaker for the loss of a notable city." Thus spoke Philippides, as instructed, and the Spartans replied that, although they were willing to send help, they found it impossible to do so immediately because of the restrictions of their own laws. It was the ninth day of the month, and they said they could not take the field until the moon was at the full.[57] So they waited for the full moon.

[6.107] Meanwhile Hippias, son of Pisistratus, was guiding the Persians to Marathon. On the previous night he had dreamed a strange dream, that he was lying in his mother's arms. This dream he interpreted to mean that he would be restored to Athens, would recover his power, and would end his days peacefully in his own native country. Such were his first thoughts about the dream. Acting now as a guide to the Persians, he put the prisoners from Eretria ashore on Aegilia, an island belonging to the town of Styra, and then proceeded to lead the fleet to an anchorage off Marathon, where he landed the Persians and drew them up in formation.

As he was thus engaged, it so happened that he sneezed and coughed more vigorously than was his wont, and, since he was advanced in years and most of his teeth were loose, one of them fell out through the violence of his coughing. It fell somewhere in the sand, and in spite of all his efforts, he could not find it. He heaved a great sigh and, turning to some bystanders, he said: "This land is not ours and we shall never be able to hold it. Whatever of it was my portion, my tooth possesses." So Hippias believed that this was the manner in which his dream had come true.

****

[6.108] The Athenians were drawn up in an enclosure sacred to Heracles when they were joined by the Plataeans in full force.[58]

---

57. Sparta's failure to arrive at Marathon in time for the battle was clearly embarrassing. That Herodotus's religious explanation was not considered convincing is suggested by the philosopher Plato's reference (*Laws* 3.698) to the Spartans being delayed by a revolt in Messenia.
58. Plataea had been closely allied to Athens since 519 BCE when the city had sought Athenian assistance against her traditional enemy in Boeotia, Thebes. The Plataean dead were honored by being buried at Marathon.

[6.109] The Athenian generals were divided in their opinions, some arguing against risking a battle in view of their numerical inferiority, while others were in favor. Among the latter was Miltiades. Seeing that opinion was divided and that the less valiant view was likely to prevail, Miltiades resolved to approach the Polemarch, who held the eleventh and decisive vote. (At this period of time, the man on whom the lot fell to be Polemarch was entitled to an equal vote with the ten generals.) The Polemarch on this occasion was Callimachus of Aphidna, and it was he whom Miltiades approached, speaking as follows: "It is in your hands, Callimachus, either to enslave Athens, or to make her free, and to leave behind you for all time a memory surpassing even that of Harmodius and Aristogeiton.[59] Never in all their history have the Athenians faced a greater peril. If they bow their necks to the Medes, no one can doubt what they will suffer when given over to Hippias; but if our native city fights and wins, it can become the leading city of all Greece. How such things can be, and how it rests with you to determine the course of events, I shall now make clear. We generals, ten in number, are divided in our opinions, some in favor of risking a battle, some against. If we do not fight now, I expect to see bitter dissension break out in Athens, which will shake men's resolution and lead to submission to Persia. But if we join battle before the rot can spread throughout the citizen body, and if the gods do but grant us fair play, we can win in the engagement. So yours is now the decisive voice; all depends on you. If you cast your vote on my side, your country will be free and the foremost city of Greece. But if you support those who are against giving battle, then the opposite of those blessings I have mentioned will be your lot."

[6.110] These words of Miltiades convinced Callimachus, and with the Polemarch's vote added to the others, the decision to fight was made. Thereupon the generals who had been in favor of fighting, as each one got his turn to exercise supreme command for the day, all resigned authority in favor of Miltiades. He accepted their offer but nevertheless waited until his own turn of command came around before he would join battle.

[6.111] Then the Athenian army was drawn up for battle in the following order. The right wing was commanded by the Polemarch, for it was the custom of the Athenians at the time for the Polemarch to have the right wing. Then, in their regular order, the tribes were arrayed in an unbroken line, and finally on the left wing were stationed the Plataeans. And ever since this battle, whenever the Athenians offer sacrifice at their quadrennial festivals, the Athenian herald prays that the Plataeans, along with the Athenians, receive benefits. Now the way that the Athenian troops were arranged at Marathon had this result, that the extending of

---

59. The "tyrant-slayers" who had assassinated Hippias's brother Hipparchus in a failed attempted coup in 514 BCE. They were honored with the first public statue representing specific individuals set up in Athens, and their descendants received free meals for life in the *prytanaeum*, Athens's "city hall," the highest honor awarded by the city.

the Athenian front to equal that of the Medes left their center the weakest part of the line, being few ranks deep, whereas both wings were strengthened.

[6.112] These dispositions being made and the sacrifices being favorable, with the word being given, the Athenians charged the enemy at a run. The distance between the armies was about a mile.[60] The Persians, seeing them coming on at a run, prepared to receive them; they thought that the Athenians had lost their senses and were bent on self-destruction, for they were inferior in number and came on at a rush without cavalry or archers. Such were the thoughts of the barbarians, but the Athenians fell upon them in close order and fought in a way never to be forgotten. They were the first of the Greeks, as far as we know, to charge the enemy at a run and the first to look unafraid at Median dress and the men wearing it. Before this, the very name "Mede" had been a terror to the Greeks.

[6.113] The struggle at Marathon lasted a considerable time. In the center, which was held by the Persians themselves and the Sacae, the invaders had the upper hand. It was there that they broke the line and pursued the fugitives inland, whereas on the wings the Athenians and the Plataeans were victorious. Where they had prevailed they allowed the enemy to flee and, uniting both wings, they fell upon those who had broken the center and defeated them. They pursued the fleeing Persians and cut them down as they fled to the sea. Then, laying hold of the ships, they called for fire.

[6.114–15] It was in this phase of the battle that the Polemarch Callimachus, who had fought valiantly, lost his life, and one of the generals, Stesilaus, was slain, and Cynegirus,[61] as he was laying hold of the vessel's stern, had his hand cut off by an ax and so perished. So likewise did many other notable Athenians. Nevertheless, in this way the Athenians managed to secure seven of the ships. The rest succeeded in getting away, and the Persians, after taking on board the Eretrian prisoners from the island where they had left them, sailed around Sunium and headed for Athens, hoping to reach it before the Athenian army could return. In Athens the Alcmaeonids were accused of suggesting this tactic. They had, it was said, an agreement with the Persians and raised a shield to signal to them when they were embarked on their ships.[62]

[6.116] So the Persians were sailing around Sunium, but the Athenians made all possible speed in returning to the city and succeeded in arriving before the Persians. Just as at Marathon they had taken up a position in an enclosure sacred to Heracles,

---

60. Since hoplite armor could weigh as much as forty pounds, a mile-long charge at a run was clearly impossible. Presumably, what happened was that the Athenians closed with the Persians as quickly as possible, as soon as they came within range of the Persian archers.

61. The brother of the playwright Aeschylus.

62. That the Alcmaeonids and other prominent Athenians were suspected of aiding the Persians is suggested by ostraca, pieces of broken pottery used in ostracisms (see Aristotle, *The Constitution of Athens* 22, for *ostracism*) on which their names were accompanied by comments accusing them of betrayal and supporting the Medes.

so they now stationed themselves in another enclosure sacred to Heracles at Cynosarges. The Persian fleet lay off Phalerum, which was at that time the harbor for Athens, and after riding at anchor for a while sailed away for Asia.

[6.117] In the battle of Marathon some 6,400 were killed on the Persian side, and on the Athenian side 192. In this battle a strange event took place. The Athenian Epizelus, fighting gallantly in the thick of the fray, was struck blind, though untouched either by sword or arrow, and his blindness continued to the end of his life. I am told that in speaking of this event he used to say that there stood against him a man of great stature, heavily armed, whose beard cast a shadow over his entire shield, and that this phantom passed him by and slew the man beside him. Such is his story.

[6.120] When the moon reached its full, the Spartans set out for Athens, two thousand strong, so anxious to be in time that they were in Attica on the third day after leaving Sparta. Too late to take part in the battle, they were nevertheless eager to have sight of the Medes and went on to Marathon to view the bodies. Then, bestowing praise on the Athenians for their achievement, they returned home.

FROM BOOK 9

The Persian Retreat

Herodotus's first readers in the late fifth century BCE would have found ominous foreshadowings of things to come in the final chapters of the history. Many people would have remembered that barely a decade after the decisive Greek victory at Plataea in 479 BCE, which ended the Persian invasion of Greece, the Spartan regent Pausanias, who had scorned Persian luxury in the immediate aftermath of the war, was recalled to Sparta, charged with living in that luxurious style and conspiring to betray Greece to Persia. Likewise, the islanders, who Athens generously promised to defend against future Persian reprisals in the early 470s BCE, would become the increasingly restive subjects of the Athenian Empire led by Pericles, the son of the Xanthippus, whose brutal execution of the Persian Artayctes foreshadowed his son's equally brutal suppression of revolts by Athens's subjects. Finally, and most ominously, the Persians' decision to remain in their harsh land and avoid loss of their toughness would have reminded anyone who thought about politics during the Peloponnesian War that the Persian Empire was still a great and threatening power.

[9.77] The Mantineans arrived on the scene when all was over. Learning that they had come late for the fight, they were greatly distressed, declaring that they deserved to be punished. They were informed of the flight of the Medes with

Artabazus and were all for pursuing them, but the Lacedaemonians refused to allow this. Returning home, they sent the leaders of their army into exile. After the Mantineans came the Eleans, and they too returned home in distress, which they also showed by sentencing their leaders to exile.

[9.78] Serving with the Aeginetans at Plataea was a man named Lampon, son of Pytheas, and of the first rank among the Aeginetans. This man made haste to approach Pausanias with a most unholy suggestion. "Son of Cleombrotus," he said, "what you have accomplished is great and glorious, and God has indeed granted to you to save Greece and gain the greatest renown of all men that we know of. Now finish this work so as to acquire even greater renown, so that no foreigner will in future venture to commit outrage against the Greeks. When Leonidas was slain at Thermopylae, Mardonius and Xerxes had his head struck off and impaled on a pike. If you now reply in kind, you will gain the approval of all Spartans and indeed of all the Greeks. Impale Mardonius's body, and then Leonidas, your father's brother, will be avenged."

[9.79] Thus spoke Lampon, thinking to gratify Pausanias, but the other replied: "My Aeginetan friend, I thank you for your goodwill and your regard for me, but your suggestion is far from acceptable. First you raise me to the skies, praising my country and my achievement, then you cast me into the dirt, urging me to insult the dead and thereby gain repute among men. What you suggest would be more fitting for barbarians than for Greeks, and even in barbarians it would be detestable. I seek not to please the Aeginetans by such means, nor any others who would approve such things. It is enough for me to gain the approval of the Spartans by righteous deeds and righteous words. Leonidas, whom you bid me to avenge, is already abundantly avenged. The price has been paid, both for him and for the others who fell at Thermopylae, by these countless lives that were taken. Come not to me again with such a suggestion, nor counsel me in this way, and be thankful that you go from me unpunished." Thus did Lampon, with this answer, go on his way.

[9.80] Pausanias then made a proclamation that no one should lay hands on the booty, and he ordered the helots to gather it all together in one place. So the helots went over all the ground where the enemy had been encamped and found there tents furnished with abundant gold and silver, couches adorned with these same precious metals, bowls, goblets, and drinking vessels all of gold, and wagons laden with sacks containing basins of gold and silver. From the bodies of the dead, they stripped bracelets and chains and scimitars with golden hilts, not even bothering with the richly embroidered garments. What the helots could not conceal they declared to the authorities, but many things they stole and sold thereafter to the Aeginetans, who thus laid the foundation of their great wealth by purchasing gold from the helots who apparently thought it was bronze.

[9.81] Once the booty was collected, a tenth was set aside for the god at Delphi, from which was made the golden tripod that stands on the bronze serpent with three heads, close to the altar. Portions were also allotted to the god at Olympia, from which was made a bronze Zeus ten cubits high, and also to the god at the Isthmus, from which was made a bronze Poseidon seven cubits high. The rest of the spoil—the Persians' concubines, the gold, the silver, other valuables, and the pack animals—was distributed among the troops, each according to his deserts. As to special awards for those who had won distinction at Plataea, I find no record, but I imagine that such awards were made. As for Pausanias, the portion set aside and granted him consisted of ten of everything—women, horses, talents, camels, and everything else.

[9.82] A story is also told that Xerxes in his flight from Greece had left behind his personal tent for Mardonius, and when Pausanias saw it, with its adornments of gold and silver and embroidered hangings, he gave orders to the bakers and cooks to prepare a meal such as they did for Mardonius. They did as bidden, and when Pausanias saw the couches of gold and silver beautifully bestrewn and the tables of gold and silver and the magnificent array of a banquet, he was astonished at the good things laid before him, and for a joke he ordered his own servants to prepare a Spartan meal. Seeing such a vast difference between the two meals, Pausanias laughed and sent for the Greek commanding officers. When they had gathered, he said, pointing to the two tables, "Fellow Greeks, I have brought you together to demonstrate to you the folly of the Mede, who, while enjoying this lifestyle, came to our country to rob us of our poverty." That's what Pausanias is said to have told the Greek commanders.

[9.86] After the burial of the dead at Plataea, a council was held at which it was decided to proceed against Thebes and demand the surrender of those who had espoused the cause of the Medes, in particular Timagenides and Attaginus, the leaders of that faction. If the Thebans refused to surrender them, they would lay siege to the town until it fell. Accordingly, eleven days after the battle they besieged Thebes, demanding the surrender of the men. Meeting with a refusal, they laid waste the surrounding country and assaulted the walls.

[9.87] When the destruction had continued for twenty days, Timagenides addressed his countrymen thus: "Men of Thebes, since the Greeks are resolved to continue the siege until either they take the town or you surrender us to them, let not Boeotia suffer any longer for our sakes. If the demand for our surrender is merely a pretext and it is money that they really want, then let us give them money from the treasury, for it was the state, and not we alone, that espoused the cause of the Medes. But if the purpose of the siege is really the surrender of our persons, we will give ourselves up to answer their charges." This proposal seemed right and met with approval, and forthwith the Thebans sent a message to Pausanias indicating that they were willing to surrender the men.

[9.88] As soon as agreement was reached, Attaginus made his escape from the town. His children were surrendered in his place, but Pausanias released them, declaring that children could not be considered guilty of their father's treachery. The rest of the men delivered up by the Thebans expected to be put on trial and hoped to secure acquittal by bribery. But Pausanias suspected this, and as soon as he took them into custody he dismissed the entire allied army, took the men to Corinth, and executed them.

That was what happened at Plataea and at Thebes.

[9.89][63] Meanwhile Artabazus, who had fled the battlefield at Plataea, was making his way homeward. When he came to Thessaly, the inhabitants provided for his needs and asked him about the rest of the army; they knew nothing yet of the events at Plataea. Artabazus understood that if he told them the truth about the battle, the Thessalians might well attack him and he and his army would be destroyed. So weighing this risk, he had said nothing at all as he made his way through the Phocaeans, and now he spoke as follows to the Thessalians: "Men of Thessaly, you see how pressed and hurried I am on my march toward Thrace; I've been sent with these men to deal with matters there. You should expect Mardonius and his men to arrive here just after me. See to his needs and serve him well; he won't forget you later if you do." So saying, he marched his army straight through Thrace by way of Thessaly and Macedonia, "pressed and hurried" indeed; he kept to the inland route.[64] He arrived in Byzantium having lost many troops to Thracian raids and to hunger and exhaustion during the journey. From Byzantium he was ferried over to Asia.

Birth of the Delian League

> *Herodotus's interpretation of the foundation of the Delian League in view of its significance as the basis for the development of the Athenian Empire is particularly interesting for its positive view of Athens's actions. Instead of emphasizing the opposition of Sparta to Athens assuming a leading role in the ongoing war against Persia as does, for example, Aristotle (*The Constitution of Athens 23*), Herodotus portrays Athens as assuming the duty of protecting the islanders and Ionians only after the Spartans refused, thereby, in effect, laying the ultimate blame for Athenian imperialism on Spartan isolationism.*

[9.106][65] After the Greeks had finished off most of the enemy, both those who fought them and those who fled, they set fire to the Persian ships and to the barricade, having first removed the spoils and set them on the beach (including some chests of money they found there). Then they set sail, and when they got to Samos they held a council about the revolt of the Ionia. They thought it best to find a place to resettle the Ionians where the rest of the Greeks could protect them, and let

---

63. This chapter was translated by James Romm.
64. By so doing he avoided the danger of attack by the Greek fleet.
65. This chapter was translated by James Romm.

the barbarian have the Asian coast; for it seemed impossible that they could maintain a presence in Ionia and safeguard its freedom forever, whereas if they didn't do this, there was scant hope that the Persians would let the Ionians get off easy. The Peloponnesian commanders thought it best to seize the trading ports of those Greek cities that had fought on the Persian side, remove their populations, and then resettle the Ionians in these places. But the Athenians disliked the idea of removing the Ionians and also did not want the Peloponnesians making decisions about cities they had founded, and they pressed their case so urgently that the Peloponnesians gave in. And so they made a pact with the Samians, Chians, Lesbians, and other islanders who had fought with the fleet, exchanging oaths and swearing not to desert one another.

> One of Herodotus's main themes is the danger of crossing boundaries as the Persians had done when they invaded Europe. The Persian withdrawal from Europe in 479 BCE restored the proper boundaries with the Persians predominant in Asia and the Greeks in Europe. Herodotus, however, used the brutality of Xanthippus's execution of Artayctes and his family and the decision of the Persians to maintain their warlike character by remaining in their harsh homeland to foreshadow the later atrocities of Athenian imperial rule and the continuing reality of the Persian threat in the fifth century BCE.

Herodotus on Athens and Persia

[9.114–15][66] After leaving Mycale bound for the Hellespont, the Greeks . . . sailed to Abydus, where they found the Persian bridges already broken up.[67] They had expected to find them intact and, indeed, had come to the Hellespont on their account. So the Peloponnesians serving under Leotychides decided to sail home, whereas the Athenians, under the commander Xanthippus, stayed there to make sallies against places in the Chersonese. So while the Peloponnesians sailed off home, the Athenians crossed from Abydus to the Chersonese and put the town of Sestus under siege. Since this town had the strongest walls of any in the region, people had streamed into it from all the other towns nearby as soon as they heard that the Greek fleet had arrived from the Hellespont. From Cardia had come a Persian named Oeobazus, seeking safety after having first stored the cables used in building the bridges. Native Aeolians were in possession of Sestus but there were lots of Persians and their allies inside with them.

---

66. Chapters 115–22 were translated by James Romm.
67. A storm had already destroyed the bridges. The Athenians salvaged the cables used in their construction and brought them to Athens, where they were dedicated to the gods.

[9.116] The ruler of this region was a Persian named Artayctes, whom Xerxes had appointed governor. He was a fearsome and high-handed fellow. During Xerxes's march on Athens, he had stolen the wealth belonging to the hero Protesilaus[68] from out of his shrine at Elaeus. For in Elaeus, in the Chersonese, there is a tomb of Protesilaus and around it a sanctuary, containing lots of money, gold and silver drinking cups, bronze, clothing, and other offerings; all this Artayctes had plundered. Now he was under siege by the Athenians, without having made adequate provisions (for he did not expect the Greek attack; they had taken him by surprise).

[9.117] The siege went on until autumn, and the Athenians began to chafe at being away from home and at failing to break through the wall. They asked their commanders to give up and go back, but the response was that first either the city must be taken or the Athenian government must issue orders for their recall. So they made the best of their circumstances.

[9.118] Meanwhile, inside the walls, the holdouts had reached the final extremes of hardship, such that they were boiling and eating the leather straps from their bed frames. When even these were gone, the Persians, including Oeobazus and Artayctes, made an escape at night by lowering themselves down the wall at a point where the besiegers were fewest. When dawn arrived, the local population signaled to the Athenians what had happened and opened the gates. Many of the troops went off in pursuit of the runaways, while others took control of Sestus.

[9.119] Oeobazus made it to Thrace, where the Thracian tribe called Apsinoi caught him and sacrificed him to their god Pleistorus, as is their custom; those accompanying him were killed in some other way. Artayctes and his group had set out later from Sestus and were caught a little ways beyond Aegospotami. They fought off their pursuers for a long time and many were killed, but others were taken alive. The Greeks tied them up and brought them to Sestus, Artayctes and his son among them.

[9.120–21] And while one of the guards was frying dried fish, the following marvel occurred, according to the inhabitants of the Chersonese: The fish suddenly jumped and wriggled above the fire as though they had just been caught. And when Artayctes saw this, he said to the man frying the fish, "Don't fear this marvel, my Athenian friend; it is not meant for you, but to me it signifies that Protesilaus, the hero of Elaeus, though dead and dried out like these fish, still has power from the gods to punish wrongdoers. I wish now to make reparations for the money I took from the shrine. I will offer a hundred talents to the god in compensation, and I will give two hundred more to you Athenians for my own life and the life of my son." But Xanthippus, the Athenian commander, would not accept. The people of Elaeus wanted Artayctes killed in retribution for Protesilaus, and Xanthippus's own feelings tended the same way.

---

68. According to Greek legend, Protesilaus was the first Greek warrior to die in the Trojan War.

So, taking him to the headland where Xerxes had built his bridge (some say rather the hill above Madytus), they nailed him alive to a plank and set it upright; then they stoned his son to death before his eyes. After that, they sailed back to Greece, bringing with them many spoils and, in particular, the cables from the bridges, which they intended to dedicate as offerings in their temples. And in that year nothing more transpired.

[9.122] This Artayctes who was hung on the plank had an ancestor named Artembares, who once made a proposal to the Persians to which they gave serious consideration. They brought the matter before Cyrus, saying as follows: "Since Zeus has given empire to the Persians and to you, Cyrus, by way of your conquest of Astyages, let us leave this paltry and rocky land we live in and get other, better territory. Right here next door, and further beyond that, lie many lands, any one of which would make us far more splendid than we are. It's the fitting thing for an imperial race to do, and when shall we have a better opportunity than now, when we rule many peoples and have conquered all of Asia?"

Cyrus heard them out but did not admire their reasoning. He told them to go ahead and do what they proposed, but also to prepare themselves to be ruled rather than rule others; for, he said, soft lands produce soft men; no single land could produce both rich harvests and men skilled in war.[69]

The Persians agreed with his reasoning and went away, bested by the judgment of Cyrus. They chose to live in a harsh land and rule, rather than farm the level plains and be slaves to others.

---

69. Herodotus's use of the theory that a people's character was determined by their environment, which first appears in the Hippocratic work *On Airs, Waters, and Places*, illustrates his familiarity with fifth-century BCE trends in Greek intellectual development.

CHAPTER 2

Thucydides, *History of the Peloponnesian War*

FROM BOOK I

Preface

*Thucydides's history is the first example in European historiography of what
is today called "revisionist history." Specifically, he maintained that, contrary
to what his contemporaries believed, the Peloponnesian War was the greatest war in Greek history, lasting for twenty-seven years from 431 to 404 BCE
and involving all of Greece and its neighbors and causing more destruction
and suffering than any previous conflict, including the Trojan War and the
Persian War. To support this thesis, he analyzed in the first twenty chapters of book one of his history the evidence concerning the early history of
Greece provided by Greek legend to demonstrate that it was improbable
that any previous war could have been on the scale of the Peloponnesian
War. He then concluded his introduction in chapters twenty to twenty-three
by explaining the methodology he used in writing his history and introducing the distinction between pretexts and underlying causes to explain the
origin of the Peloponnesian War.*

[1] Thucydides, an Athenian, wrote up the war of the Peloponnesians and the
Athenians as they fought against each other. He began to write as soon as the war
was afoot, with the expectation that it would turn out to be a great one and that,
more than all earlier wars, this one would deserve to be recorded. He made this
prediction because both sides were at their peak in every sort of preparation for war,
and also because he saw the rest of the Greek world taking one side or the other,
some right away, others planning to do so.

This was certainly the greatest upheaval there had ever been among the Greeks.
It also reached many foreigners—indeed, one might say that it affected most people
everywhere. Because of the great passage of time it is impossible to discover clearly
what happened long ago or even just before these events; still, I have looked into the
evidence as far as can be done, and I am confident that nothing great happened in
or out of war before this.

Early History of Greece

[2] It is evident that what is now called "Hellas"[1] was not permanently settled in former times, but that there were many migrations, and people were ready to leave their land whenever they met the force of superior numbers. There was no trade, and they could not communicate with each other either by land or over the sea without danger. Each group used its ground merely to produce a bare living; they had no surplus of riches, and they planted nothing, because they could not know when someone would invade and carry everything away, especially since they had no walls. They counted themselves masters of just enough to sustain them each day, wherever they were, and so made little difficulty about moving on. Because of this they had no strength, either in the size of their cities or in any other resources. The best land was always the most subject to these changes of inhabitants: what is now called Thessaly, also Boeotia, most of the Peloponnesus except for Arcadia, and whatever was most fertile in the rest of Greece. For the excellence of the land increased the power of certain men, and this led to civil wars, by which they were ruined; and all this made them more vulnerable to the designs of outsiders. Accordingly, Attica has been free from civil war for most of its history, owing to the lightness of its soil; and that is why it has always been inhabited by the same people.[2]

Here is strong support for this account: because of the migrations, the rest of Greece did not develop at the same rate as Athens, since the most able refugees from wars and civil strife all over Greece retired to the safety of Athens. There they became citizens, and they added so much to the citizen population that Attica could no longer support them, and colonies were sent out to Ionia.

[3] I am further convinced of the weakness of Hellas in ancient times by this fact: before the Trojan War, Hellas evidently took no action in common. I do not believe, either, that the name "Hellas" was yet applied to the whole country. Before the time of Hellen, the son of Deucalion, there was no such name at all, but the various regions took the names of their own inhabitants, with "Pelasgian" naming the largest. When Hellen and his sons came to power in Phthiotis [a part of Thessaly], however, they were called in to the aid of other cities, which one by one came to be called Hellenes because of their association with them. That name cannot have prevailed over all of Greece until much later, however. The principal evidence for this is from Homer, who does not ever give them that name in general, though he was born long after the Trojan War. He does not use the name for anyone but those who came from Phthiotis with Achilles (who were the very first Hellenes);

---

1. "Hellas" and "Hellenes" are the ancient Greek names for Greece and Greeks.
2. By the late fifth century BCE, when Thucyides wrote, Athenians had come to believe that they were autochthonous in the sense that they had always lived in Attica, unlike other Greeks such as the Dorians who had immigrated to their contemporary territories.

but he calls the others "Danaans," "Argives," or "Achaeans" in his poems. He does not use the term "foreigner" (*barbaros*) either, because, it seems to me, the Hellenes were not yet marked off by one name in opposition to them. City by city, then, they came to be called Hellenes if they understood each others' language, and later they all had this name; but before the Trojan War they did not enter into any action with their forces joined, owing to their lack of strength and communication; and they joined in that expedition only because they had learned to make more use of the sea.

[4] Minos, by all reports, was the first to build a navy;[3] he made himself master of most of what is now the Hellenic Sea, ruled the islands called the Cyclades, and sent colonies to most of them, expelling the Carians and setting up his own sons there as governors. Also, as one would expect, he freed the seas from piracy as much as he could, so that his revenue could reach him more easily.

[5] In ancient times, you see, the Greeks had turned to piracy as soon as they began to travel more in ships from one place to another, and so had the foreigners who lived on the mainland shore or on the islands. Their most powerful leaders aimed at their own profit, but also hoped to support the weak; and so they fell upon cities that had no walls or were made up of settlements. They raided these places and made most of their living from that. Such actions were nothing to be ashamed of then, but carried with them a certain glory, as we may learn from some of the mainlanders for whom this is still an honor, even today, if done nobly. The same point is proved by the ancient poets, who show that anyone who sails by, anywhere, is asked the same question—"Are you a pirate?"—and that those who are asked are not insulted, while those who want to know are not reproachful.

They also robbed each other on the mainland, and even now much of Greece follows this old custom—the Ozolean Locrians, for example, and the Aetolians and Acarnanians and mainlanders near them. The fashion of carrying iron weapons survives among those mainlanders as well, from their old trade of thieving. [6] All of Greece used to carry arms, you see, because houses were unfenced and travel was unsafe; and so they became accustomed to living every day with weapons, as foreigners do. The fact that some parts of Greece still do so testifies that the practice was once universal.

The Athenians were the first Greeks to put their weapons away and change to a more relaxed and luxurious style of life. It was due to this refinement that the older men among the rich there only recently gave up the fashion of wearing long linen robes and tying up the hair on their heads in knots fastened with golden cicadas. (From them, because of their kinship with Athens, the same fashion spread to the older men of Ionia and lasted a long time.) The moderate sort of clothing that is now in style was first used by the Lacedaemonians, who had made the life-style of the

---

3. As pointed out in the Introduction, Greek historians did not doubt that legendary figures such as Minos had existed, only that reliable information concerning them could not be obtained.

rich equal to that of ordinary people, especially in regard to dress.[4] They were also the first to strip themselves naked for exercise and to oil themselves afterward. In the old days athletes used to wear loincloths around their private parts when they competed, even at the Olympic Games, and it has not been many years since this custom ended. Even now there are foreigners, especially in Asia, whose athletes wear loincloths in boxing matches. And in many other ways one could show that the life-style of the ancient Greeks was similar to that of foreigners today.

[7] As for the cities, those that were settled more recently—since the advance of navigation—had a surplus of money and so were built with walls right on the coasts. They took over the isthmuses both for commercial reasons and to strengthen themselves individually against their neighbors. The older cities, however, were built further from the sea, owing to the greater danger of piracy on the islands as well as on the mainland. They robbed each other and any non-seamen who lived by the coast, with the result that even today those people are still settled inland.

[8] Most of the pirates were islanders, the Carians or Phoenicians who had settled most of the islands. The evidence for this is as follows: when the Athenians purified Delos during this war,[5] they dug up the graves of those who had died on the island and found that more than half were Carian. They knew this by the style of the weapons that were buried with them and by the burial customs, which are still in use.[6]

Once Minos's navy was afloat, navigation became easier, since he expelled the evildoers from the islands and planted colonies of his own in many of them. And as those who lived along the coasts became more addicted to acquiring wealth, their settlements became more stable. Some, who had become richer than before, threw up walls around their towns. In their desire for gain, the weaker cities let themselves be subject to the stronger ones, while the more powerful cities used their surplus wealth to bring weaker ones under their rule. And that was the situation later, when they sent the expedition against Troy.

[9] In my view Agamemnon was able to get the fleet together because he had more power than anyone else at that time, and not so much because he was the leader of the suitors of Helen who were bound by oaths to Tyndareus.[7]

---

4. Although differences in wealth existed among Spartans, public display of wealth by, for example, wearing luxurious clothing, was discouraged to emphasize that all Spartan citizens were "similars" (*homoioi*).

5. That is, the war whose history Thucydides was writing, the Peloponnesian War.

6. This is an interesting use of archaeological evidence to reconstruct early history. In the fifth century BCE, the Carians lived in southwestern Anatolia. Scholars, however, are divided as to the validity of Thucydides's conclusion that Carians had once inhabited the Aegean islands.

7. This is a good example of Thucydides's use of the argument from probability as the key to using Greek legends, such as the story of the Trojan War, as evidence for reconstructing the early history of Greece.

Those who received the clearest account of the Peloponnesians from their predecessors say that Pelops used the great wealth he brought from Asia and was the first to win power among the Peloponnesian people (who were very poor at the time). Because of this he gave his own name to the land, though he was an outsider. Afterward, his descendants became still more powerful. After Eurystheus was killed in Attica by the Heraclids, Atreus made himself king of Mycenae and the other lands Eurystheus had ruled. (Eurystheus had entrusted the rule of Mycenae to him when he set off on campaign, because of their family relationship. Atreus was his mother's brother and happened to be living at the time with Eurystheus, in exile from his father for the death of Chrysippus.) When Eurystheus did not come back, the Mycenaeans wanted Atreus to be king, partly out of fear of the Heraclids and partly because they thought Atreus was an able man and, at the same time, because he had served the interests of the majority. That is how the descendants of Pelops became greater than those of Perseus.

Now Agamemnon was the son of Atreus and inherited this power; and besides this he had a stronger navy than anyone else. That is why I think he assembled his forces more on the basis of fear than goodwill. It is evident that most of the ships were his and that he had others to lend to the Arcadians, as Homer declares (whose evidence should be good enough for anyone). Besides, in the "Giving of the Scepter" Homer says that Agamemnon was lord "of many islands and all Argos."[8] Now since he lived on the mainland, he could not have controlled islands (except for the neighboring ones, of which there were only a few) unless he had a navy. And we should infer the character of earlier enterprises on the basis of that expedition.

[10] Of course Mycenae was small, and the cities of that time may not seem to be worth very much; but such weak evidence should not count against believing that the expedition was as great as the poets have said it was, and as tradition holds. For if the Lacedaemonians' city were wiped out, and if only their temples and building foundations remained, I think people in much later times would seriously doubt that their power had matched their fame; and yet they own two fifths of the Peloponnesus and are leaders of the rest, along with many allies outside. Still, it would seem to have been rather weak, since it was not settled as one city around the use of costly temples or other buildings, but was made up of villages in the old Greek style.[9] If the same thing were to happen to Athens, however, one would infer from what was plain to see that its power had been double what it is.

We have no good reason, then, to doubt those reports about the size of the army in the Trojan War, or to measure a city more by its appearance than its power. We should think of that army as indeed greater than those that went before it, but

---

8. *Iliad* 2.108.

9. Sparta received its first walls at the end of the third century BCE or the beginning of the second century BCE.

weaker than those we have now. This depends on our trusting Homer again on this point, where he would be expected as a poet to exaggerate; but on his account that army was still much weaker than modern ones: he makes the fleet consist of twelve hundred ships and reports that the Boeotian ships carried one hundred twenty men each, while those of Philoctetes carried fifty. I think he did this to show the maximum and minimum, but he makes no mention at all in his catalogue of the size of the other ships.[10] He does, however, show that all the rowers in Philoctetes's ships were also fighters, for he writes that all the oarsmen were archers. As for passengers on the ships, it is not likely that there were many, aside from the kings and other top people, especially since they had to cross the sea with military equipment on board, and in ships without the protection of upper decks, built in the old pirate fashion. So if we take the mean between the largest and smallest ships, we find that not many went to Troy, considered as a joint expedition from all of Greece.

[11] This is to be explained more by lack of wealth than by a shortage of men. Because of their lack of rations, they brought a smaller army—just the size they expected would be able to support itself while fighting. When they landed, they got the upper hand in fighting. (That is obvious; otherwise they could not have fortified their camp). After that, apparently, they did not use all their power, because they had to turn partly to farming in the Chersonese, and partly to piracy. Because they were dispersed in this way, the Trojans were better able to hold them off for those ten years and were an equal match for those Greeks who were left near Troy at any one time.

If they had gone out with plenty of rations, however, and concentrated their forces on continuous warfare without farming or piracy, they would easily have taken the city once they'd gotten the upper hand in fighting, since they were a match for the Trojans with the portion of the army that was present at any time. If they had settled down in a siege they would have taken Troy in less time with less trouble.

All enterprises were weak before the Trojan War for want of money, and this one was too, for all that it was the most famous expedition of ancient times. The facts show clearly that it was weaker than its fame would have it, and weaker than the verbal tradition that has come down to us from the poets.

[12] After the Trojan War the Greeks were still in motion, still resettling, and so could not make progress in one place. The Greeks came back from Troy after a long absence, and this brought about many changes: civil war broke out in most cities, and the people who were driven out founded new cities. The people now known as Boeotians were thrown out of Arnē by the Thessalians in the sixtieth year after Troy was taken; they settled in what is now Boeotia, but was then called Cadmeïs. (Only a portion of them were in that country before then, some of whom fought

---

10. For Homer's account of the Greek forces in the Trojan War, see the Catalogue of Ships in *Iliad* 2.484 ff.

against Troy.) And in the eightieth year the Dorians seized the Peloponnesus along with the Heraclids.[11]

With much ado, then, and after a long time, peace came with security to Greece; and now that they were no longer being uprooted they began to send colonies abroad. The Athenians settled Ionia and most of the islands, while the Peloponnesians planted colonies in most of southern Italy and Sicily, as well as in some other parts of Greece. And all these were founded after the Trojan War.

[13] Now that Greece was becoming more powerful, and the Greeks were more interested in making money than before, tyrannies were set up in most of the cities; with their incomes growing larger (the hereditary kings before them had had only fixed revenues) the Greeks built navies and became more attached to the sea. The Corinthians are said to have been the first to change the design of ships almost to their present form, and to have built the first triremes in Greece at Corinth.[12] The Corinthian shipbuilder Ameinocles evidently built four ships at Samos, and he went to Samos about three hundred years before the current war ended [i.e., in 704 BCE]. The earliest naval battle we know of was fought between Corinth and Corcyra, and that was only two hundred and sixty years before the same time [664 BCE]. Because it was settled on the Isthmus, Corinth had always been a center of commerce. (The old Greeks had traded by land more than by sea, so the Peloponnesians had no contact with outsiders except through Corinth.) So the Corinthians had the power of wealth, as the old poets show us when they named their land "the rich."[13] After the Greeks took more to the sea, the Corinthians scoured the sea of pirates with the ships they had; and their city had the power of a large income because they were a center for trade by sea and land alike.

Later, the Ionians got together a great navy in the time of Cyrus (the first Persian King) and his son Cambyses. The Ionians made war on Cyrus and for a time had control of the sea near them. Polycrates also had a strong navy; he was tyrant of Samos at the time of Cambyses, and used his navy to take over several islands, including Rheneia [near Delos] which he captured and dedicated to Apollo. The Phocaeans, too, when they were settling Massalia [probably Marseilles] defeated the Carthaginians in a sea battle [about 600 BCE].

[14] These were the greatest naval powers, yet even they evidently used only a few triremes, though this was many generations after the Trojan War. Instead, they

---

11. The reference is to the Dorian invasion, which historians used to believe had been an important factor in the collapse of the Mycenaean civilization but is now doubted to have taken place. According to the legend, the Heraclids or Sons of Heracles conquered the Peloponnese after a century of exile in Doris in central Greece and founded the Dorian dynasties of Argos, Sparta, and Messenia.

12. Triremes were warships rowed by three banks of oarsmen. In the fifth century BCE, the standard complement of a trireme was 170 rowers and 30 officers and marines.

13. Homer, Iliad 2.570.

were made up of fifty-oared boats and long ships like those used at Troy. It was only shortly before the Persian War and the death of Darius (who was king of Persia after Cambyses) that the tyrants of Sicily and the Corcyreans had triremes in any number. These were the only navies worth mentioning in all of Greece before the Persian invasion. The people of Aegina had only a few ships, most of them of fifty oars, while the Athenians, and any others that had navies were no stronger. So it was only recently that Themistocles—during the war with Aegina, and when the Persian invasion was expected—persuaded the Athenians to build the ships in which they fought sea battles.[14] But even these ships were not completely decked over.

[15] Such, then, were the navies of the Greeks, both the ancient and the more recent ones. Those who used them nevertheless gained great power for themselves in increasing their wealth and ruling other peoples, for they sailed to the islands and conquered them (especially if they did not have enough land). But there was no warfare on land that would lead to any power; such wars as they had were all between neighbors, and the Greeks had not yet sent an army abroad to conquer any nation far from home. They never agreed to be subject to the greatest cities, you see, and they never put a common army together on an equal basis, but they fought each other only as citizens of individual states. The most they did was in the old war between Chalcis and Eretria, when the rest of Greece was divided into alliances with one side or the other.[15]

[16] While the rest were being held back from progress by other factors, the Ionians were conquered by the Persians. The Persian Kingdom was flourishing; and after Cyrus had conquered Croesus,[16] he marched against all the lands between the Halys River and the sea, subduing all the Ionian cities on the mainland. Later, Darius used his Phoenician navy to take control of the islands as well.[17]

[17] As for the tyrants that used to rule in the Greek cities, they looked only to their own interests—about their own persons and the glory of their own families, with as much safety as was possible. They resided for the most part in the cities and did no action worth remembering except against their neighbors—not even the tyrants of Sicily, who had arrived at the greatest power. Thus Greece was held back for a long time, because its cities could not do anything remarkable together, and no city dared try anything by itself.

---

14. Such as the battles of Artemisium and Salamis in 480 BCE and during the expansion of the Athenian Empire in the mid-fifth century BCE.

15. The so-called Lelantine War that was supposedly fought c. 700 BCE between Chalcis and Eretria for control of the Lelantine Plain on the island of Euboea.

16. Croesus's defeat by Cyrus is described in the selections from the first book of Herodotus's *Histories*.

17. The Phoenician cities, particularly Tyre and Sidon, provided the bulk of Persian naval forces.

[18] But after that, the last of the tyrants were most of them put down by the Lacedaemonians, both in Athens and in the rest of Greece where there were tyrannies, except for those of Sicily. For although Lacedaemon was troubled with civil strife for longer than any other city we know after its foundation by the Dorians who live there now, it acquired good laws[18] even so at a very early time and has always been free from tyrants. For up to the end of this war it has been over four hundred years that the Lacedaemonians have followed one and the same constitution; and this has made them strong in themselves, and also given them the ability to arrange matters in the other cities.

After the dissolution of tyrannies in Greece, it was not long before the battle was fought by the Persians against the Athenians in the fields of Marathon. And in the tenth year again after that, Xerxes, king of Persia, came with his great fleet into Greece to subjugate it. Since a great danger now threatened Greece, the leadership of the Greeks that formed an alliance in that war was given to the Lacedaemonians, because they were foremost in power. When the Persians invaded Athens, the Athenians, who had planned in advance to leave their city and were already packed, went aboard ships and became seamen. Soon after they had jointly beaten back the foreigners, all the Greeks—both those who had rebelled from the Persian king and those who had jointly made war against him—divided themselves and one part followed the Athenians while the other followed the Lacedaemonians. For these two cities appeared to be the mightiest; one had power by land, and the other by sea. But the alliance [of all Greece against the Persians] lasted only a while, for afterward the Lacedaemonians and the Athenians began to disagree and made war on each other, along with their various allies. And any other Greek cities that quarreled went over to one side or the other. So Athens and Sparta spent the time between the war against the Persians and this present war partly in peace and partly in war (either one against the other or against allies in rebellion); and they both arrived at this war well furnished with military provisions and also very experienced in dealing with danger.

[19] The Lacedaemonians led their allies without requiring any payments from them, but took care that they were governed by oligarchy, which served their interests alone. Over time, however, the Athenians took into their hands the ships of all their allies except for Chios and Lesbos, and ordered each of them to make certain monetary payments. And so it came about that the military preparation of Athens alone was greater in the beginning of this war than that of the whole alliance between them and the rest of Greece had been when it was intact and flourishing at its greatest.

[20] Such, then, was the state of Greece in the past as I found it, though particular pieces of evidence may be hard to believe.

---

18. "It acquired good laws": "Eunomia" or "good laws" was the term used to characterize the laws of Sparta after the reforms of Lycurgus, that supposedly established the Spartan way of life.

Methodology

People take in reports about the past from each other all alike, without testing them—even reports about their own country. Most of the Athenians, for example, think that Hipparchus was tyrant when he was killed by Harmodius and Aristogeiton, and don't know that it was Hippias who was in power, since he was the eldest son of Pisistratus, and Hipparchus and Thessalus were his brothers. In fact, on the very day, and at the very moment of the deed, Harmodius and Aristogeiton suspected that some of their accomplices had told Hippias about the plot. So they avoided him as having been forewarned, but they still wanted to do something daring before they were captured. When they met Hipparchus by chance at the Leocorium, where he was organizing the Panathenaic Procession, they killed him.[19]

Other Greeks have wrong opinions about many subjects that are current and not forgotten in the passage of time, for example, that the Lacedaemonian kings have two votes each, instead of one, and that they have a military unit there called "Pitanate," which never existed.[20] That shows how much the search for truth strains the patience of most people, who would rather believe the first things that come to hand. [21] But if the evidence cited leads a reader to think that things were mostly as I have described them, he would not go wrong, as he would if he believed what the poets have sung about them, which they have much embellished, or what the prose-writers have strung together, which aims more to delight the ear than to be true. Their accounts cannot be tested, you see, and many are not credible, as they have achieved the status of myth over time. But the reader should believe that I have investigated these matters adequately, considering their antiquity, using the best evidence available. People always think the greatest war is the one they are fighting at the moment, and when that is over they are more impressed with wars of antiquity; but, even so, this war will prove, to all who look at the facts, that it was greater than the others.

[22] What particular people said in their speeches, either just before or during the war, was hard to recall exactly, whether they were speeches I heard myself or those that were reported to me at second hand. I have made each speaker say what I thought the situation demanded, keeping as near as possible to the general sense of what was actually said.

And as for the real action of the war, I did not think it right to set down either what I heard from people I happened to meet or what I merely believed to be true. Even for events at which I was present myself, I tracked down detailed information from other sources as far as I could. It was hard work to find out what happened,

---

19. For the assassination of Hipparchus, see Aristotle, *The Constitution of Athens* 18.
20. "Other Greeks have wrong opinions": This is probably a reference to Herodotus, who made these two errors about Sparta.

because those who were present at each event gave different reports, depending on which side they favored and how well they remembered.

This history may not be the most delightful to hear, since there is no mythology in it. But those who want to look into the truth of what was done in the past—which, given the human condition, will recur in the future, either in the same fashion or nearly so—those readers will find this *History* valuable enough, as this was composed to be a lasting possession and not to be heard for a prize at the moment of a contest.

[23] The greatest action before this was the one against the Persians, and even that was decided quickly by two battles at sea and two on land. But the Peloponnesian War went on for a very long time and brought more suffering to Greece than had ever been seen before: never had so many cities been captured and depopulated (some by foreigners, others by Greeks themselves at war with one another—some of which were resettled with new inhabitants); never had so many people been driven from their countries or killed, either in the war itself or as a result of civil strife.

Tales told about earlier times, but scantily confirmed in actuality, suddenly ceased to be incredible: tales of earthquakes, which occurred over most of the earth at this time, quite violent ones—eclipses of the sun, which were more frequent than is recorded in earlier times—great droughts in some places followed by famine—and, what caused enormous harm and loss of life, the plague.

All these hardships came upon them during this war, which began when the Athenians and Peloponnesians broke the Thirty Years' Peace that had been agreed between them after the conquest of Euboea. I will first write down an account of the disputes that explain their breaking the Peace, so that no one will ever wonder what ground so great a war could arise among the Greeks. I believe that the truest reason for the quarrel, though least evident in what was said at the time, was the growth of Athenian power, which put fear into the Lacedaemonians and so compelled them into war. . . .

FROM BOOK 2

Pericles's Funeral Oration

> In the winter of 430 BCE, the Athenian political leader Pericles delivered a speech at a public funeral honoring the Athenians who had died in the first year of the war. According to Thucydides, Pericles omitted the usual topics dealt with in such speeches—the glories of the Athenian past—but instead, he offered the Athenians a vivid account of Athens and its values for which their relatives had died. How closely Thucydides followed Pericles's original speech is unknown, but if he composed it according to the principles he set out in his first book, he probably retained the main themes of Pericles's oration.

[35] Most of those who have spoken before me on this occasion have praised the man who added this oration to our customs because it gives honor to those who have died in the wars; yet I would have thought it sufficient that those who have shown their mettle in action should also receive their honor in an action, as now you see they have, in this burial performed for them at public expense, so that the virtue of many does not depend on whether one person is believed to have spoken well or poorly.

It is a hard matter to speak in due measure when there is no firm consensus about the truth. A hearer who is favorable and knows what was done will perhaps think that a eulogy falls short of what he wants to hear and knows to be true; while an ignorant one will find some of the praise to be exaggerated, especially if he hears of anything beyond his own talent—because that would make him envious. Hearing another man praised is bearable only so long as the hearer thinks he could himself have done what he hears. But if a speaker goes beyond that, the hearer soon becomes envious and ceases to believe. Since our ancestors have thought it good, however, I too should follow the custom and endeavor to answer to the desires and opinions of every one of you, as far as I can.

[36] I will begin with our ancestors, since it is both just and fitting that they be given the honor of remembrance at such a time. Because they have always lived in this land, they have so far always handed it down in liberty through their valor to successive generations up to now. They deserve praise; but our fathers deserve even more, for with great toil they acquired our present empire in addition to what they had received, and they delivered it in turn to the present generation. We ourselves who are here now in the prime of life have expanded most parts of the empire; and we have furnished the city with everything it needs to be self-sufficient both in peace and in war. The acts of war by which all this was attained, the valiant deeds of arms that we and our fathers performed against foreign or Greek invaders—these I will pass over, to avoid making a long speech on a subject with which you are well acquainted. But the customs that brought us to this point, the form of government and the way of life that have made our city great—these I shall disclose before I turn to praise the dead. I think these subjects are quite suitable for the occasion, and the whole gathering of citizens and guests will profit by hearing them discussed.

[37] We have a form of government that does not try to imitate the laws of our neighboring states. We are more an example to others, than they to us. In name, it is called a democracy, because it is managed not for a few people, but for the majority. Still, although we have equality at law for everyone here in private disputes, we do not let our system of rotating public offices undermine our judgment of a candidate's virtue; and no one is held back by poverty or because his reputation is not well-known, as long as he can do good service to the city. We are free and generous not only in our public activities as citizens, but also in our daily lives: there is no suspicion in our dealings with one another, and we are not offended by our neighbor for following his own pleasure. We do not cast on anyone the censorious looks that—though they are no punishment—are nevertheless painful. We live together

without taking offense on private matters; and as for public affairs, we respect the law greatly and fear to violate it, since we are obedient to those in office at any time, and also to the laws—especially to those laws that were made to help people who have suffered an injustice, and to the unwritten laws[21] that bring shame on their transgressors by the agreement of all.

[38] Moreover, we have provided many ways to give our minds recreation from labor: we have instituted regular contests and sacrifices throughout the year, while the attractive furnishings of our private homes give us daily delight and expel sadness. The greatness of our city has caused all things from all parts of the earth to be imported here, so that we enjoy the products of other nations with no less familiarity than we do our own.

[39] Then, too, we differ from our enemies in preparing for war: we leave our city open to all; and we have never expelled strangers in order to prevent them from learning or seeing things that, if they were not hidden, might give an advantage to the enemy.[22] We do not rely on secret preparation and deceit so much as on our own courage in action. And as for education, our enemies train to be men from early youth by rigorous exercise, while we live a more relaxed life and still take on dangers as great as they do.

The evidence for this is that the Lacedaemonians do not invade our country by themselves, but with the aid of all their allies; when we invade our neighbors, however, we usually overcome them by ourselves without difficulty, even though we are fighting on hostile ground against people who are defending their own homes. Besides, no enemy has yet faced our whole force at once, because at the same time we are busy with our navy and sending men by land to many different places. But when our enemies run into part of our forces and get the better of them, they boast that they have beaten our whole force; and when they are defeated, they claim they were beaten by all of us. We are willing to go into danger with easy minds and natural courage rather than through rigorous training and laws, and that gives us an advantage: we'll never weaken ourselves in advance by preparing for future troubles, but we'll turn out to be no less daring in action than those who are always training hard. In this, as in other things, our city is worthy of admiration.

[40] We are lovers of nobility with restraint, and lovers of wisdom without any softening of character. We use wealth as an opportunity for action, rather than for boastful speeches. And as for poverty, we think there is no shame in confessing it; what is shameful is doing nothing to escape it. Moreover, the very men who take care of public affairs look after their own at the same time; and even those who are devoted to their own businesses know enough about the city's affairs. For we alone think that a man who does not take part in public affairs is good for nothing, while others

---

21. The reference is probably to religious laws, such as the obligation to give proper burial to relatives that is central to the plot of Sophocles's tragedy *Antigone*.
22. As was done by the Spartans.

only say he is "minding his own business."[23] We are the ones who develop policy, or at least decide what is to be done; for we believe that what spoils action is not speeches, but going into action without first being instructed through speeches. In this too we excel over others: ours is the bravery of people who think through what they will take in hand, and discuss it thoroughly; with other men, ignorance makes them brave and thinking makes them cowards. But the people who most deserve to be judged tough-minded are those who know exactly what terrors or pleasures lie ahead, and are not turned away from danger by that knowledge. Again we are opposite to most men in matters of virtue: we win our friends by doing them favors, rather than by accepting favors from them. A person who does a good turn is a more faithful friend: his goodwill toward the recipient preserves his feeling that he should do more; but the friendship of a person who has to return a good deed is dull and flat, because he knows he will be merely paying a debt—rather than doing a favor—when he shows his virtue in return. So that we alone do good to others not after calculating the profit, but fearlessly and in the confidence of our freedom.

[41] In sum, I say that our city as a whole is a lesson for Greece, and that each of us presents himself as a self-sufficient individual, disposed to the widest possible diversity of actions, with every grace and great versatility. This is not merely a boast in words for the occasion, but the truth in fact, as the power of this city, which we have obtained by having this character, makes evident.

For Athens is the only power now that is greater than her fame when it comes to the test. Only in the case of Athens can enemies never be upset over the quality of those who defeat them when they invade; only in our empire can subject states never complain that their rulers are unworthy. We are proving our power with strong evidence, and we are not without witnesses: we shall be the admiration of people now and in the future. We do not need Homer, or anyone else, to praise our power with words that bring delight for a moment, when the truth will refute his assumptions about what was done. For we have compelled all seas and all lands to be open to us by our daring; and we have set up eternal monuments on all sides, of our setbacks as well as of our accomplishments.

Such is the city for which these men fought valiantly and died, in the firm belief that it should never be destroyed, and for which every man of you who is left should be willing to endure distress.

[42] That is why I have spoken at such length concerning the city in general, to show you that the stakes are not the same, between us and the enemy—for their city is not like ours in any way—and, at the same time, to bring evidence to back up the eulogy of these men for whom I speak. The greatest part of their praise has already been delivered, for it was their virtues, and the virtues of men like

---

23. "Minding his own business" [being *apragmōn*]. Solon (Aristotle, *The Constitution of Athens* 8) is supposed to have included as one of his laws that a person would lose his rights as a citizen if he did not support one of the sides in a political crisis.

them, that made what I praised in the city so beautiful. Not many Greeks have done deeds that are obviously equal to their own reputations, but these men have. The present end these men have met is, I think, either the first indication, or the final confirmation, of a life of virtue. And even those who were inferior in other ways deserve to have their faults overshadowed by their courageous deaths in war for the sake of their country. Their good actions have wiped out the memory of any wrong they have done, and they have produced more public good than private harm. None of them became a coward because he set a higher value on enjoying the wealth that he had; none of them put off the terrible day of his death in hopes that he might overcome his poverty and attain riches. Their longing to punish their enemies was stronger than this; and because they believed this to be the most honorable sort of danger, they chose to punish their enemies at this risk, and to let everything else go. The uncertainty of success they entrusted to hope; but for that which was before their eyes they decided to rely on themselves in action. They believed that this choice entailed resistance and suffering, rather than surrender and safety; they ran away from the word of shame, and stood up in action at risk of their lives. And so, in the one brief moment allotted them, at the peak of their fame and not in fear, they departed.

[43] Such were these men, worthy of their country. And you who remain may pray for a safer fortune, but you must resolve to be no less daring in your intentions against the enemy. Do not weigh the good they have done on the basis of one speech. Any long-winded orator could tell you how much good lies in resisting our enemies; but you already know this. Look instead at the power our city shows in action every day, and so become lovers of Athens. When the power of the city seems great to you, consider then that this was purchased by valiant men who knew their duty and kept their honor in battle, by men who were resolved to contribute the most noble gift to their city: even if they should fail in their attempt, at least they would leave their fine character [aretē] to the city. For in giving their lives for the common good, each man won praise for himself that will never grow old; and the monument that awaits them is the most splendid—not where they are buried, but where their glory is laid up to be remembered forever, whenever the time comes for speech or action. For to famous men, all the earth is a monument, and their virtues are attested not only by inscriptions on stone at home; but an unwritten record of the mind lives on for each of them, even in foreign lands, better than any gravestone.

Try to be like these men, therefore: realize that happiness lies in liberty, and liberty in valor, and do not hold back from the dangers of war. Miserable men, who have no hope of prosperity, do not have a just reason to be generous with their lives; no, it is rather those who face the danger of a complete reversal of fortune for whom defeat would make the biggest difference: they are the ones who should risk their lives. Any man of intelligence will hold that death, when it comes unperceived to a man at full strength and with hope for his country, is not so bitter as miserable defeat for a man grown soft.

[44] That is why I offer you, who are here as parents of these men, consolation rather than a lament. You know your lives teem with all sorts of calamities, and that it is good fortune for anyone to draw a glorious end for his lot, as these men have done. While your lot was grief, theirs was a life that was happy as long as it lasted. I know it is a hard matter to dissuade you from sorrow, when you will often be reminded by the good fortune of others of the joys you once had; for sorrow is not for the want of a good never tasted, but for the loss of a good we have been used to having. Yet those of you who are of an age to have children may bear this loss in the hope of having more. On a personal level new children will help some of you forget those who are no more; while the city will gain doubly by this, in population and in security. It is not possible for people to give fair and just advice to the state, if they are not exposing their own children to the same danger when they advance a risky policy. As for you who are past having children, you are to think of the greater part of your life as pure profit, while the part that remains is short and its burden lightened by the glory of these men. For the love of honor is the one thing that never grows old, and useless old age takes delight not in gathering wealth (as some say), but in being honored.

[45] As for you who are the children or the brothers of these men, I see that you will have considerable competition. Everyone is used to praising the dead, so that even extreme virtue will scarcely win you a reputation equal to theirs, but it will fall a little short. That is because people envy the living as competing with them, but they honor those who are not in their way, and their goodwill toward the dead is free of rivalry.

And now, since I must say something about feminine virtue, I shall express it in this brief admonition to you who are now widows: your glory is great if you do not fall beneath the natural condition of your sex, and if you have as little fame among men as is possible, whether for virtue or by way of reproach.[24]

[46] Thus I have delivered, according to custom, what was appropriate in a speech, while those men who are buried here have already been honored by their own actions. It remains to maintain their children at the expense of the city until they grow up. This benefit is the city's victory garland for them and for those they leave behind after such contests as these, because the city that gives the greatest rewards for virtue has the finest citizens.

So now, when everyone has mourned for his own, you may go.

The Plague

Pericles had persuaded the Athenians to adopt a defensive strategy, concentrating the population in the city and maintaining domination of the sea while allowing the Spartans to raid Athenian territory at will. The resulting

---

24. It was considered shameful for a woman's name to be mentioned in public, as for example, in lawsuits.

crowding in the city, aggravated by lack of even rudimentary public sanitation, rendered the Athenians particularly vulnerable when plague broke out in 430 BCE and recurred during the next two years. The plague has not been identified, but evidence suggests that as much as a third of the Athenians died. Thucydides was one of the survivors and provided a firsthand account of its symptoms and the demoralization it caused that reveals his familiarity with fifth-century BCE rational medicine and served as a model for numerous later accounts of plagues and their effects.

[47] Such was the funeral they held that winter, and with the end of that season the first year of the war came to a close.

In the very beginning of summer the Peloponnesians and their allies, with two-thirds of their forces as before, invaded Attica under the command of Archidamus, king of Lacedaemon. After they had settled in, they started wasting the country around them.

They had not been in Attica for many days when the plague first began among the Athenians. Although it was said to have broken out in many other places, particularly in Lemnos, no one could remember a disease that was so great or so destructive of human life breaking out anywhere before. Doctors, not knowing what to do, were unable to cope with it at first, and no other human knowledge was any use either. The doctors themselves died fastest, as they came to the sick most often. Prayers in temples, questions to oracles—all practices of that kind turned out to be useless also, and in the end people gave them up, defeated by the evil of the disease.

[48] They say it first began in the part of Aithiopia that is above Egypt, and from there moved down to Egypt and Libya and into most of the Persian Empire. It hit Athens suddenly, first infecting people in Piraeus [the port of Athens], with the result that they said the Peloponnesians must have poisoned the water tanks (they had no wells there at the time). Afterward the plague moved inland to the city, where people died of it a good deal faster. Now anyone, doctor or layman, may say as much as he knows about where this probably came from, or what causes he thinks are powerful enough to bring about so great a change. For my part, I will only say what it was like: I will show what to look for, so that if the plague breaks out again, people may know in advance and not be ignorant.[25] I will do this because I had the plague myself, and I myself saw others who suffered from it.

---

25. None of the proposed identifications of the plague, including smallpox, typhoid fever, and typhus, have been convincing. Thucydides's motive for including the account of the plague was to allow it to be recognized should it recur, consistent with his belief that this would make his work useful to future readers (1.22). To that end, he provided a day-by-day account of its symptoms similar to those found in the medical diaries of Hippcratic doctors that are called the *Epidemics*, literally "visit records," so that it could be recognized in the future.

[49] This year of all years was the most free of other diseases, as everyone agrees. If anyone was sick before, his disease turned into this one. If not, they were taken suddenly, without any apparent cause, and while they were in perfect health. First they had a high fever in the head, along with redness and inflammation of the eyes; inside, the throat and tongue were bleeding from the start, and the breath was weird and unsavory. After this came sneezing and hoarseness, and soon after came a pain in the chest, along with violent coughing. And once it was settled in the stomach, it caused vomiting, and brought up, with great torment, all the kinds of bile that the doctors have named. Most of the sick then had dry heaves, which brought on violent spasms which were over quickly for some people, but not till long after for others. Outwardly their bodies were not very hot to the touch, and they were not pale but reddish, livid, and flowered with little pimples and ulcers; inwardly they were burning so much with fever that they could not bear to have the lightest clothes or linen garments on them—nothing but mere nakedness, and they would have loved to throw themselves into cold water. Many of them who were not looked after did throw themselves into water tanks, driven mad by a thirst that was insatiable, although it was all the same whether they drank much or little. Sleeplessness and total inability to rest persisted through everything.

As long as the disease was at its height, the body did not waste away, but resisted the torment beyond all expectation, so that they either died after six or eight days from the burning inside them, or else, if they escaped that, then the disease dropped down into the belly, bringing severe ulceration and uncontrollable diarrhea; and many died later from the weakness this caused, since the disease passed through the whole body, starting with the head and moving down. And if anyone survived the worst of it, then the disease seized his extremities instead and left its mark there: it attacked the private parts, fingers, and toes. Many people escaped with the loss of these, while some lost their eyes as well. Some were struck by total amnesia as soon as they recovered, and did not know themselves or their friends. [50] This was a kind of disease that defied explanation, and the cruelty with which it attacked everyone was too severe for human nature. What showed more clearly than anything else that it was different from the diseases that are bred among us was this: all the birds and beasts that feed on human flesh either avoided the many bodies that lay unburied, or tasted them and perished. Evidence for this was the obvious absence of such birds: they were not to be seen anywhere, and certainly not doing that. But this effect was more clearly observed in the case of dogs, because they are more familiar with human beings.

[51] Now this disease was generally as I have described it, if I may set aside the many variations that occurred as particular people had different experiences. During that time no one was troubled by any of the usual sicknesses, but whatever sickness came ended in this. People died, some unattended, and some who had every sort of care. There was no medical treatment that could be prescribed as beneficial, for what helped one patient did harm to another. Physical strength turned out to

be of no avail, for the plague carried the strong away with the weak, no matter what regimen they had followed.

But the greatest misery of all was the dejection of mind in those who found themselves beginning to be sick, for as soon as they made up their minds it was hopeless, they gave up and made much less resistance to the disease. Another misery was their dying like sheep, as they became infected by caring for one another; and this brought about the greatest mortality. For if people held back from visiting each other through fear, then they died in neglect, and many houses were emptied because there was no one to provide care. If they did visit each other, they died, and these were mainly the ones who made some pretense to virtue. For these people would have been ashamed to spare themselves, and so they went into their friends' houses, especially in the end, when even family members, worn out by the lamentations of the dying, were overwhelmed by the greatness of the calamity. But those who had recovered had still more compassion, both on those who were dying and on those who were sick, because they knew the disease firsthand and were now out of danger, for this disease never attacked anyone a second time with fatal effect. And these people were thought to be blessedly happy, and through an excess of present joy they conceived a kind of light hope never to die of any other disease afterward.

[52] The present affliction was aggravated by the crowding of country folk into the city, which was especially unpleasant for those who came in. They had no houses, and because they were living in shelters that were stifling in the summer, their mortality was out of control. Dead and dying lay tumbling on top of one another in the streets, and at every water fountain lay men half dead with thirst. The temples also, where they pitched their tents, were all full of the bodies of those who died in them, for people grew careless of holy and profane things alike, since they were oppressed by the violence of the calamity, and did not know what to do. And the laws they had followed before concerning funerals were all disrupted now, everyone burying their dead wherever they could. Many were forced, by a shortage of necessary materials after so many deaths, to take disgraceful measures for the funerals of their relatives: when one person had made a funeral pyre, another would get before him, throw on his dead, and give it fire; others would come to a pyre that was already burning, throw on the bodies they carried, and go their way again.

[53] The great lawlessness that grew everywhere in the city began with this disease, for, as the rich suddenly died and men previously worth nothing took over their estates, people saw before their eyes such quick reversals that they dared to do freely things they would have hidden before—things they never would have admitted they did for pleasure. And so, because they thought their lives and their property were equally ephemeral, they justified seeking quick satisfaction in easy pleasures. As for doing what had been considered noble, no one was eager to take any further pains for this, because they thought it uncertain whether they should die or not before they achieved it. But the pleasure of the moment, and whatever contributed to that, were set up as standards of nobility and usefulness. No one

was held back in awe, either by fear of the gods or by the laws of men: not by the gods, because men concluded it was all the same whether they worshipped or not, seeing that they all perished alike; and not by the laws, because no one expected to live till he was tried and punished for his crimes. But they thought that a far greater sentence hung over their heads now, and that before this fell they had a reason to get some pleasure in life.

[54] Such was the misery that weighed on the Athenians. It was very oppressive, with men dying inside the city and the land outside being wasted. At such a terrible time it was natural for them to recall this verse, which the older people said had been sung long ago:

> A Dorian war will come,
> and with it a plague.

People had disagreed about the wording of the verse: some said it was not *plague* (*loimos*) but *famine* (*limos*) that was foretold by the ancients; but on this occasion, naturally, the victory went to those who said "plague," for people made their memory suit their current experience. Surely, I think if there is another Dorian war after this one, and if a famine comes with it, it will be natural for them to recite the verse in that version. Those who knew of it also recalled an oracle that was given to the Lacedaemonians when they asked the god [Apollo] whether they should start this war or not. The oracle had said: *they would win if they fought with all their might, and that he himself would take their part* [1.118]. Then they thought that their present misery was a fulfillment of the prophecy; the plague did begin immediately when the Peloponnesians invaded, and it had no appreciable effect in the Peloponnesus, but preyed mostly on Athens and after that in densely populated areas. So much for the plague.[26]

Pericles's Last Speech

The combination of a second Spartan invasion of Attica in 430 BCE and the suffering caused by the plague provoked a backlash against Pericles and his policies. In this political crisis, Thucydides has Pericles deliver a speech urging the Athenians to continue to follow his defensive strategy despite their present misfortunes. Unlike Pericles's other speeches in Thucydides's history, his final speech failed to persuade the Athenians, who deposed him from his generalship and fined him, only to reelect him shortly thereafter, a prime example in Thucydides's view of the fickleness of the Athenian people.

---

26. No specific evidence concerning the number of Athenians who died as a result of the plague survives, but estimates range as high as one-third of the Athenian population.

Soon afterward, however, Pericles contracted the plague and died, allowing Thucydides the opportunity to provide an analysis of his leadership, emphasizing that had the Athenians continued to follow his defensive strategy, they would have won the war.

[59] After their second invasion by the Peloponnesians, now that their land had been wasted a second time, and the plague was lying over them along with the war, the Athenians changed their minds and blamed Pericles for persuading them to make war—as if the troubles that had come their way were due to him—and were in a hurry to come to terms with the Lacedaemonians. They sent ambassadors to them, without effect. They were altogether at their wit's end, and so they attacked Pericles.

When he saw that they were angry over their present circumstances, and were doing exactly what he had expected, he called an assembly—he was still general at the time—intending to put heart into them, to turn aside their anger, and so to make their minds calmer and more confident. He stood before them and spoke as follows:

[60] I expected you to get angry with me, and I can see why it has happened. I have called this assembly to remind you of certain points and to rebuke you for your misplaced anger at me and for your giving in too easily to misfortune.

I believe that if the city is sound as a whole, it does more good to its private citizens than if it benefits them as individuals while faltering as a collective unit. It does not matter whether a man prospers as an individual: if his country is destroyed, he is lost along with it; but if he meets with misfortune, he is far safer in a fortunate city than he would be otherwise. Since, therefore, a city is able to sustain its private citizens in whatever befalls them, while no one individual is strong enough to carry his city, are we not all obliged to defend it and not, as you are doing now, sacrifice our common safety? In your dismay at our misfortunes at home you are condemning yourselves along with me—me for advising you to go to war and yourselves for agreeing to it. And it is I at whom you are angry, a man who is second to none (in my opinion) for recognizing and explaining what must be done—I, a patriot, beyond corruption. A man who knows something but cannot make it clear might as well have had nothing in mind at all; while a man who can do both will not give such loyal advice if he has no love for his city; and a man who has all this and loyalty too, but can be overcome by money, will sell everything for this alone. It follows that if you were persuaded to go to war because you thought I had all those qualities, even in a moderately higher degree than other people, there is no reason for me to bear a charge of injustice now.

[61] Of course, for people who have the choice and are doing well in other ways, it is very foolish to go to war. But if (as is the case with us) they are compelled either to submit directly to the rule of their neighbors, or else to take on great dangers in order to survive, a man who runs away from danger is more to be blamed than one who stands up to it.

For my part, I am the man I was. I have not shifted ground. It is you who are changing: you were persuaded to fight when you were still unharmed, but now that times are bad, you are changing your minds; and to your weak judgment my position does not seem sound. That is because you already feel the pain that afflicts you as individuals, while the benefit to us all has not yet become obvious; and now that this great reversal has come upon you in so short a time you are too low in your minds to stand by your decisions, for it makes your thoughts slavish when something unexpected happens suddenly and defies your best-laid plans. That is what has happened to you on top of everything else, mainly because of the plague.

Still, you live in a great city and have been brought up with a way of life that matches its greatness; so you should be willing to stand up to the greatest disasters rather than eclipse your reputation. (People think it equally right, you see, to blame someone who is so weak that he loses the glorious reputation that was really his, as it is to despise someone who has the audacity to reach for a reputation he should not have.)

So set aside the grief you feel for your individual losses, and take up instead the cause of our common safety.

[62] As for your fear that we will have a great deal of trouble in this war, and still be no closer to success, I have already said something that should be enough for you: I proved many times that you were wrong to be suspicious of the outcome. I will tell you this, however, about your greatness in empire—something you never seem to think about, which I have not mentioned in my speeches. It is a rather boastful claim, and I would not bring it up now if I had not seen that you are more discouraged than you have reason to be. You think your empire extends only to your allies, but I am telling you that you are entirely the masters of one of the two usable parts of the world—the land and the sea. Of the sea, you rule as much as you use now, and more if you want. When you sail with your fleet as it is now equipped, there is no one who can stop you—not the king of Persia or any nation in existence. This power cannot be measured against the use of your land and homes, though you think it a great loss to be deprived of them. It makes no sense to take these so seriously; you should think of your land as a little kitchen garden, and your house as a rich man's trinket, of little value compared to this power. Keep in mind too that if we hold fast to our liberty and preserve it we will easily recover our land and houses; but people who submit to foreign domination will start to lose what they already had. Don't show yourselves to be doubly inferior to your ancestors, who took the empire—they did not inherit it from others—and, in addition, kept it safe and passed it on to you. No, what you should do is remember that it is more shameful to lose what you have than to fail in an attempt to get more. You should take on the enemy at close quarters, and go not only with pride, but with contempt. Even a coward can swell with pride, if he is lucky and ignorant; but you cannot have contempt for the enemy unless your confidence is based on a strategy to overcome them—which is your situation exactly. Even if you have only an even chance of

winning, if you are conscious of your superiority it is safer for you to be daring, for in that case you do not depend on hope (which is a bulwark only to those who have no resources at all), but on a strategy based on reality, which affords a more accurate prediction of the result.

[63] You have reason besides to support the dignity our city derives from her empire, in which you all take pride; you should not decline the trouble, unless you cease to pursue the honor, of empire. And do not think that the only thing we are fighting for is our freedom from being subjugated: you are in danger of losing the empire, and if you do, the anger of the people you have ruled will raise other dangers. You are in no position to walk away from your empire, though some people might propose to do so from fear of the current situation, and act the part of virtue because they do not want to be involved in public affairs. You see, your empire is really like a tyranny—though it may have been thought unjust to seize, it is now unsafe to surrender. People who would persuade the city to do such a thing would quickly destroy it, and if they set up their own government they would destroy that too. For those who stay out of public affairs survive only with the help of other people who take action; and they are no use to a city that rules an empire, though in a subject state they may serve safely enough.

[64] Don't be seduced by this sort of men. After all, it was you who decided in favor of this war along with me; so don't be angry at me. What the enemy did when they invaded was just what was to be expected when we refused to submit to them; and this plague has struck contrary to all expectations—it is the only thing, of all that has happened, that has defied our hopes. I know that I have become hated largely because of this; but that is an injustice, unless you will also give me credit whenever you do better than you'd planned to do. What heaven sends we must bear with a sense of necessity, what the enemy does to us we must bear with courage—for that is the custom in our city; that is how it used to be, and that custom should not end with you.

Keep this in mind: our city is famous everywhere for its greatness in not yielding to adversity and in accepting so many casualties and so much trouble in war; besides, she has possessed great power till now, which will be remembered forever by those who come after us, even if we do give way a little now (for everything naturally goes into decline): Greeks that we are, we have ruled most of the Greeks, and held out in great wars against them, all together or one city at a time, and our city has the most wealth of every sort, and is the greatest. And yet a man of inaction would complain about this! No matter, anyone who is active will want to be like us, and those who do not succeed will envy us. To be hated and to cause pain is, at present, the reality for anyone who takes on the rule of others, and anyone who makes himself hated for matters of great consequence has made the right decision; for hatred does not last long, but the momentary brilliance of great actions lives on as a glory that will be remembered forever after.

As for you, keep your minds on the fine future you know will be yours, and on the shame you must avoid at this moment. Be full of zeal on both counts. Send no more heralds to the Lacedaemonians, and do not let them know how heavy your troubles are at present. The most powerful cities and individuals are the ones that are the least sensitive in their minds to calamity and the firmest in their actions to resist it.

[65] With this speech Pericles tried to appease the anger of the Athenians and to divert their attention from their present afflictions. They were persuaded on the public matter, and no longer sent embassies to the Lacedaemonians, but applied themselves more to the war. As individuals, however, they were upset by what had happened to them—the people were upset because they had been deprived of the little they had, and the powerful because they had lost their fine possessions in the country, along with their houses and costly furnishings. Most of all, however, it was because they had war instead of peace. As a group, they did not give up their anger against him until they had punished him with a fine. Not long after, however, as is common with a mob, they made him general again and turned all public affairs over to him, for their pain over their private domestic losses was dulled now, and they thought he was the best man to serve the needs of the city as a whole.

As long as he was at the head of the city in time of peace, he governed it with moderation and guarded it securely; and it was greatest under him. After the war was afoot, it was obvious that he also foresaw what the city could do in this. He lived two years and six months after the war began. And after his death his foresight about the war was even better recognized, for he told them that if they would be quiet and take care of their navy, and not seek to expand the empire during this war or endanger the city itself, they should then have the upper hand. But they did the opposite on all points, and in other things that seemed not to concern the war they managed the state for their private ambition and private gain, to the detriment of themselves and their allies. Whatever succeeded brought honor and profit mostly to private individuals, while whatever went wrong damaged the city in the war.

The reason for Pericles's success was this: he was powerful because of his prestige and his intelligence, and also because he was known to be highly incorruptible. He therefore controlled the people without inhibition, and was not so much led by them, as he led them. He would not humor the people in his speeches so as to get power by improper means, but because of their esteem for him he could risk their anger by opposing them. Therefore, whenever he saw them insolently bold out of season, he would put them into fear with his speeches; and again, when they were afraid without reason, he would raise up their spirits and give them courage. Athens was in name a democracy, but in fact was a government by its first man. But because those who came after were more equal among themselves, with everyone aiming to be the chief, they gave up taking care of the commonwealth in order to please the people.[27]

---

27. The reference is to Pericles's successors, the so-called demagogues, literally "leaders of the people," such as Cleon who, unlike Pericles in Thucydides's opinion, maintained their influence in the assembly only by pandering to the desires of the Athenian citizens.

Since Athens was a great imperial city, these mistakes led to many others, such as the voyage against Sicily, which was due not so much to mistaking the power of those they attacked, as it was to bad decisions on the part of the senders, which were no use to the people they sent. They weakened the strength of the army through private quarrels about popular leadership, and they troubled the state at home with discord for the first time. After their debacle in Sicily, when they lost most of their navy along with the rest of the expedition, and the city was divided by civil strife, they still held out eight years against their original enemies, who were now allied with the Sicilians, against most of their own rebellious allies besides, and also eventually against Cyrus, the son of the king of Persia, who took part with, and sent money to, the Peloponnesians to maintain their fleet. And they never gave in until they had brought about their own downfall through private quarrels.

So Pericles had more than enough reasons to predict that the city might easily outlast the Peloponnesians in this war.

From Book 3

The Mytilenean Debate

As usually happens, the expectation that the war would be over quickly proved false. By the spring of 428 BCE, the Peloponnesian War had dragged on for three years when Mytilene, the main city on the island of Lesbos, and three other smaller cities revolted. After holding out for almost a year, Mytilene surrendered when promised Spartan aid did not materialize. Furious because Lesbos was one of only two allies still retaining their autonomy and fearful of further revolts, the Athenians determined to make an example of Mytilene, voting to execute the adult male population and sell the women and children into slavery. The next day, however, emotions had cooled, and the Athenians convened a second meeting of the assembly to reconsider their decision. How many persons spoke at the assembly we don't know, but Thucydides chose to provide versions of only two speeches that represented in his opinion the main point at issue: what was the best policy for an imperial power to follow to maintain its empire. According to Cleon, consistency was the best policy, however ruthless a particular action might seem to be, while Diodotus argued that a pragmatic approach that didn't leave rebels and potential rebels any option but fighting to the bitter end was more likely to succeed. In the end, Diodotus's recommendation carried, but even so the Athenians punished Mytilene severely, executing the 1,000 oligarchs and their supporters who were in their custody and confiscating much of Mytilene's territory.

SPEECH OF CLEON[28]

[37] For my part, I have often seen that a democracy is not capable of ruling an empire, and I see it most clearly now, in your change of heart concerning the Mytileneans. Because you are not afraid of conspiracies among yourselves in your daily life, you imagine you can be the same with your allies, and so it does not occur to you that when you let them persuade you to make a mistake, or you relent out of compassion, your softness puts you in danger and does not win you the affection of your allies; and you do not see that your empire is a tyranny,[29] and that you have unwilling subjects who are continually plotting against you. They obey you not because of any good turns you might do them to your own detriment, and not because of any goodwill they might have, but only because you exceed them in strength. But it will be the worst mischief of all if none of our decisions stand firm, and if we never realize that a city with inferior laws is better if they are never relaxed than a city with good laws that have no force, that people are more use if they are sensible without education than if they are clever without self-control, and that the more common sort of people generally govern a city better than those who are more intelligent. For those intellectuals love to appear wiser than the laws and to win a victory in every public debate—as if there were no more important ways for them to show their wisdom! And that sort of thing usually leads to disaster for their city. But the other sort of people, who mistrust their own wits, are content to admit they know less than the laws and that they cannot criticize a speech as powerfully as a fine orator can; and so, as impartial judges rather than contestants, they govern a city for the most part very well. We should do the same, therefore, and not be carried away by cleverness and contests of wit, or give to you, the people, advice that runs against our own judgment.

[38] As for me, I have the same opinion I had before, and I am amazed at these men who have brought this matter of the Mytileneans into question again, thus causing a delay that works more to the advantage of those who have committed injustice. After a delay, you see, the victim comes at the wrongdoer with his anger dulled; but the punishment he gives right after an injury is the biggest and most appropriate. I am also amazed that there is anyone to oppose me, anyone who will

---

28. Cleon was the most influential Athenian political figure of the 420s BCE. Ridiculed for his nonaristocratic social origins—his family's wealth came from owning a slave-run tannery—he supported a strong imperial policy and may have been responsible for Thucydides's exile. He achieved a notable success in capturing almost 300 Spartans and their allies on the island of Sphacteria near Pylos in the southwestern Peloponnesus in 425 BCE, but he was killed three years later in 422 BCE in an unsuccessful attempt to recapture Amphipolis in northern Greece for Athens.

29. The difference in rhetoric between Pericles (Thucydides, *Peloponnesian War* 2.63) telling the Athenians that their empire is "like a tyranny" and Cleon bluntly asserting that it "is a tyranny" is telling about Thucydides's view of the change in Athenian attitudes caused by several years of warfare.

try to prove that the injustice the Mytileneans have committed is good for us and that what goes wrong for us is really damaging to our allies. Clearly, he must have great trust in his eloquence if he is trying to make you believe that you did not decree what you decreed. Either that, or he has been bribed to try to lead you astray with a fine-sounding and elaborate speech.

Now the city gives prizes to others in contests of eloquence like this one, but the risks she must carry herself. You are to blame for staging these rhetorical contests so badly. The habits you've formed: why you merely look on at discussions, and real action is only a story to you! You consider proposals for the future on the basis of fine speeches, as if what they proposed were actually possible; and as for action in the past, you think that what has been done in front of your own eyes is less certain than what you have heard in the speeches of clever fault-finders. You are excellent men—at least for being deceived by novelties of rhetoric and for never wanting to follow advice that is tried and proved. You bow down like slaves to anything unusual, but look with suspicion on anything ordinary. Each of you wishes chiefly to be an effective speaker, but, if not, then you enter into competition with those who are. You don't want to be thought slow in following their meaning, so you applaud a sharp point before it is even made; and you are as eager to anticipate what will be said, as you are slow to foresee its consequences. You seek to hear about almost anything outside the experience of our daily lives, and yet you do not adequately understand what is right before your eyes. To speak plainly, you are so overcome with the delight of the ear that you are more like an audience for the sophists than an assembly deliberating for the good of the city.

[39] To put you out of these habits, I tell you that the Mytileneans have done us a far greater injustice than any other single city. For my part, I can forgive those cities that rebelled because they could not bear being ruled by us, or because they were compelled to do so by the enemy. But *these* people were islanders, their city was walled, and they had no fear of our enemies except by sea, where they were adequately protected by their fleet of triremes. Besides, they were governed by their own laws, and were held by us in the highest honor. That they should have done this! What is it but a conspiracy or a betrayal? It is not a rebellion, for a rebellion can only come from people who have been violently oppressed, whereas these people have joined our bitterest enemies to destroy us! This is far worse than if they had made war on us to increase their own power.

They'd learned nothing from the example of their neighbors' calamities—everyone who has rebelled against us so far has been put down—and their prosperity did not make them at all cautious before rushing into danger. They were bold in the face of the future and they had hopes above their power to achieve, though below what they desired. And so they started this war, resolved to put strength before justice, for as soon as they thought they could win, they attacked us, who had done them no injustice. It is usual for cities to turn insolent when they have suddenly come to great and unexpected prosperity. In general, good fortune is more secure in human hands when it comes in reasonable measure, than when it arrives unexpectedly; and, generally, it is easier to keep misfortune away than to preserve great happiness. Long ago we should have given the Mytileneans no more privileges than our other allies, and then they would not have come to this degree of insolence, for generally it is human nature to look with contempt on those who serve your interests, and to admire those who never give in to you.

They should be punished right now, therefore, as they deserve for their injustice. And do not put all the blame on the oligarchs and absolve the common people, for they all alike took up arms against you. The democrats could have come over to our side and would long since have recovered their city, but they thought it safer to join in the oligarchs' rebellion.

Now consider your allies. If you inflict the same punishment on those who rebel under compulsion by the enemy, as on those who rebel of their own accord, don't you think anyone would seize the slightest pretext to rebel, when if they succeed they will win their liberty, but if they fail they will suffer nothing that can't be mended? And then we would have to risk our lives and our money against one city after another. If we succeed we recover only a ruined city, and so lose its future revenue, on which our strength is based. But if we fail, we add these as new enemies to those we had before, and the time we need to spend fighting our old enemies we must use up fighting our own allies.

[40] We must not, therefore, give our allies any hope that pardon may be secured by bribery or by persuading us that "it is only human to err." For these people conspired against us in full knowledge and did us an injury of their own will, while only involuntary wrongs may be pardoned. Therefore I contend then and now that you ought not to alter your former decision, and you ought not to make the mistake of giving in to the three things that are most damaging to an empire: pity, delight in speeches, and a sense of fairness. It may be right to show pity to those who are likeminded, but not to those who will never have pity on us and who must necessarily be our enemies for ever after. As for the rhetoricians who delight you with their speeches—let them play for their prizes on matters of less weight, and not on a subject that will make the city pay a heavy price for a light pleasure, while the speakers themselves will be well rewarded for speaking well. And as for fairness, we should show that only toward people who will be our friends in the future, and not toward those who will still be as they are now if we let them live: our enemies.

In sum I say only this: if you follow my advice, you will do justice to the Mytileneans and promote your own interests at the same time. But if you see the matter differently, you will not win their favor; instead, you will be condemning yourselves: if they were right to rebel, you ought not to have been their rulers. But then suppose your empire is not justified: if you resolve to hold it anyway, then you must give these people an unreasonable punishment for the benefit of the empire, or else stop having an empire so that you can give charity without taking any risks.

If you keep in mind what it would have been reasonable for them to do to you if they had prevailed, then you—the intended victims—cannot turn out to be less responsive to perceived wrong than those who hatched the plot, and you *must* think they deserve the same punishment they'd have given you—especially since they were the first to commit an injustice. Those who wrong someone without any excuse are the ones who press him the hardest, even to the death, when they see how dangerous an enemy he will be if he survives; for (they will think) if one side is wronged without cause, and escapes, he will be more harsh than if the two sides had hated each other equally in the beginning.

Therefore, do not be traitors to yourselves. Recall as vividly as you can what they did to you, and how it was more important than anything else for you to defeat them then. Pay them back now, and do not be softened at the sight of their present condition, or forget how terrible a danger hung over us at that time. Give these people the punishment they deserve, and set up a clear example for our other allies, to show that the penalty for rebellion is death. Once they know this, you will less often have occasion to neglect your enemies and fight against your own allies.

[41] So spoke Cleon. After him, Diodotus, the son of Eucrates, who in the earlier assembly had strongly opposed putting the Mytileneans to death, came forward this time also, and spoke as follows:

SPEECH OF DIODOTUS[30]

[42] I find no fault with those who have brought the Mytilenean business forward for another debate, and I have no praise for those who object to our having frequent discussions on matters of great importance. In my opinion, nothing is more contrary to good judgment than these two—haste and anger. Of these, the one is usually thoughtless, while the other is ill-informed and narrow-minded. And anyone who contends that discussion is not instructive for action is either stupid or defending some private interest of his own. He is stupid if he thinks there is anything other than words that we can use to consider what lies hidden from sight in the future. And he has a private interest if he wants to persuade you to do something awful, but knows that a good speech will not carry a bad cause, and so tries to browbeat his opponents and audience with some good slander instead: the most difficult opponents are those who also accuse one of putting on a rhetorical show for a bribe. If the accusation were merely of ignorance, a speaker could lose his case and still go home with a reputation more for stupidity than injustice; but once corruption is

---

30. This is the only appearance of Diodotus in Thucydides's history, and he is mentioned in no other historical source. That should not be considered surprising, however, since the opening question in debates in the assembly—"who wishes to speak?"—implied that many people might speak in the assembly only once in their lifetime.

imputed to him, then he will be under suspicion even if he wins, and if he loses he will be thought both stupid and unjust. Such accusations do not do the city any good, since it loses good advisers from fear of them. The city would do best if this kind of citizen had the least ability as speakers, for they would then persuade the city to fewer errors. A good citizen should not go about terrifying those who speak against him, but should try to look better in a fair debate. A sensible city should neither add to, nor reduce, the honor in which it holds its best advisers, nor should it punish or even dishonor those whose advice it does not take. This would make it less attractive for a successful speaker to seek greater popularity by speaking against his better judgment, or for an unsuccessful one to strive in this way to gratify the people and gain a majority.

[43] But we do the opposite of that here; and besides, if anyone is suspected of corruption, but gives the best advice anyway, we are so resentful of the profit we think he is making (though this is uncertain), that we give up benefits the city would certainly have received. It has become the rule also to treat good advice honestly given as being no less under suspicion than bad, so that a man who has something rather good to say must tell lies in order to be believed, just as a man who gives terrible advice must win over the people by deception. Because of these suspicions, ours is the only city that no one can possibly benefit openly, without deception, since if anyone does good openly to the city, his reward will be the suspicion that he had something secretly to gain from this.

But on the most important matters, such as these, we orators must decide to show more foresight than is found in you short-sighted citizens, especially since we stand accountable for the advice we give, but you listeners are not accountable to anyone, because if you were subject to the same penalties as the advisers you follow, you would make more sensible decisions. As it is, whenever you fail, you give in to your momentary anger and punish the man who persuaded you for his one error of judgment, instead of yourselves for the many mistakes in which you had a part.

[44] For my part, I did not come forward to speak about Mytilene with any purpose to contradict or to accuse. Our dispute, if we are sensible, will concern not their injustice to us, but our judgment as to what is best for us. Even if I proved them guilty of terrible injustice, I still would not advise the death penalty for this, unless that was to our advantage. Even if they deserved to be pardoned, I would not have you pardon them if it did not turn out to be good for the city. In my opinion, what we are discussing concerns the future more than the present. And as for this point that Cleon insists on—that the death penalty will be to our advantage in the future, by keeping the others from rebelling—I maintain exactly the opposite view, and I too am looking at our future well-being. I urge you not to reject the usefulness of my advice in favor of the apparent attractions of his. In view of your present anger against the Mytileneans, you may agree that his argument is more in accord with justice. But we are not at law with them, and so have no need to speak of justice. We are in council instead, and must decide how the Mytileneans can be put to the best use for us.

[45] The death penalty has been ordained for many offenses in various cities, and these are minor offenses compared to this one; yet people still risk their lives when they are buoyed up by hope, and no one has ever gone into a dangerous conspiracy convinced that he would not succeed. What city would ever attempt a rebellion on the supposition that her resources, whether from home or from her alliance with other states, are too weak for this? They all have it by nature to do wrong, both men and cities, and there is no law that will prevent it. People have gone through all possible penalties, adding to them in the hope that fewer crimes will then be done to them by evildoers. It stands to reason that there were milder punishments in the old days, even for the most heinous crimes; but as the laws continued to be violated, in time most cities arrived at the death penalty. And still the laws are violated.

Either some greater terror than death must be found, therefore, or else punishment will not deter crime. Poverty compels the poor to be daring, while the powerful are led by pride and arrogance into taking more than their share. Each human condition is dominated by some great and incurable passion that impels people to danger. Hope and passionate desire, however, dominate every situation: with desire as the leader and hope as the companion, desire thinking out a plan, and hope promising a wealth of good fortune, these two cause the greatest mischief, and because they are invisible they are more dangerous than the evils we see. Besides these, fortune [*tuchē*] plays no less a part in leading men on, since she can present herself unexpectedly and excite you to take a risk, even with inadequate resources. This happens especially to cities, because of the serious issues at stake—their own freedom and their empire over others—and because an individual who is acting with everyone else has an unreasonably high estimate of his own ability. In a word, it is an impossible thing—you would have to be simple-minded to believe that people can be deterred, by force of law or by anything else that is frightening, from doing what human nature is earnestly bent on doing.

[46] We should not, therefore, make a bad decision, relying on capital punishment to protect us, or set such hopeless conditions that our rebels have no opportunity to repent and atone for their crime as quickly as possible. Consider this: if a city in rebellion knew it could not hold out, as things are it would come to terms while it could still pay our expenses and make its remaining contributions; but if we take Cleon's way, wouldn't any city prepare better for a rebellion than they do now, and hold out in a siege to the very last, since it would mean the same whether they gave in late or early? And what is this if not harmful to us—to have the expense of a siege because they will not come to terms, and then, when we have taken a city, to find it ruined and to lose its revenue for the future?[31] You see, our strength against our enemies depends on that revenue.

---

31. Maintaining sufficient revenue to sustain the war had become a serious issue by 427 BCE, leading to increased taxes on wealthy Athenians and higher levels of tribute in the empire.

We should not, then, be strict judges in punishing offenders, and so harm ourselves; instead, we should look for a way to impose moderate penalties to ensure that we will in the future be able to make use of cities that can make us substantial payments. We should not plan to keep them in check by the rigor of laws, but by watching their actions closely. We are doing the opposite now, if we think we should punish cruelly a city that used to be free, was held in our empire by force, rebelled from us for a good reason—to restore its autonomy—and now has been defeated. What we ought to do in the case of a city of free men is not to impose extreme penalties after they rebel, but to be extremely watchful before they rebel, and to take care that the idea of rebellion never crosses their minds. And once we have overcome them, we should lay the fault upon as few of them as we can.

[47] Consider also how great a mistake you will be making on this score if you follow Cleon's advice: as things are, the democrats in all the cities are your friends, and either they do not join the oligarchs in rebellion or, if they are forced to, they remain hostile to the rebels, so that when you go to war with them, you have their common people on your side; but if you destroy the democrats of Mytilene, who had no part in the rebellion, and who delivered the city into your hands of their own will as soon as they were armed, then you will, first, commit an injustice by killing those who have done you good service, and, second, accomplish exactly what oligarchs everywhere want the most: when they have made a city rebel, they will immediately have the democrats on their side, because you will have shown them in advance that those who are not guilty of injustice suffer the same penalty as those who are. And even if they were guilty, however, we should pretend that they were not, so that the only party still allied with us will not become our enemy. And in order to keep our empire intact, I think it much more advantageous for us to put up with an injustice willingly, than for us justly to destroy people we ought not to destroy. And as for Cleon's idea that justice and our own advantage come to the same in the case of punishment—these two cannot be found to coincide in the present case.

[48] Now I want you to accept my proposal because you see that it is the best course, and not because you are swayed more by pity or a sense of fairness. I would not have you influenced by those factors any more than Cleon would. But take my advice and judge the leaders of the rebellion at your leisure, while you let the rest enjoy their city. That will be good for the future, and it will strike fear into your enemies today. Those who plan well against their enemies, you see, are more formidable than those who attack with active force and foolishness combined.

[49] So spoke Diodotus. After these two quite opposite opinions were delivered, the Athenians were at odds with each other, and the show of hands was almost equal on both sides. But the opinion of Diodotus prevailed.

On this they immediately sent out another ship in haste, so they would not find the city already destroyed by coming in after the first ship (which had left a day and a night earlier). The Mytilenean ambassadors provided wine and barley cakes for the second ship and promised them great rewards if they overtook the first. And so they rowed in such haste that they ate their barley cakes steeped in wine and oil while they rowed, and took turns rowing while others slept. They were lucky in that there was no wind against them. And since the first ship was not sailing in any haste on its perverse mission, while the second one hurried on in the manner described, the first ship did arrive first, but only by the time it took Paches to read the decree. He was about to execute the sentence when the second ship came in and prevented the destruction of the city. That was how close Mytilene came to destruction.

[50] As for the other men Paches had sent away as being most to blame for the rebellion, the Athenians did kill them as Cleon had advised, just over a thousand of them. They also razed the walls of Mytilene and confiscated their ships. Afterward, they stopped collecting payments directly from Lesbos. Instead, they divided the land (all but that of Methymna[32]) into three thousand allotments, of which they consecrated three hundred to the gods, the rest going to Athenians who were chosen by lot and sent out as allotment holders.[33] The people of Lesbos were required to pay them two silver *minas*[34] annually for each lot, and worked the land themselves. The Athenians also took over the communities that Mytilene had controlled on the mainland and made them subject to Athens. So ended the business on Lesbos.

Civil War at Corcyra

Thucydides began his account of the run-up to the outbreak of the Peloponnesian War with the conclusion of the alliance between Athens and Corcyra—modern Corfu—in 433/32 BCE despite the vigorous objection of Corinth. Five years later in 427 BCE, civil war—the first of many as Thucydides noted—broke out in Corcya between pro-Athenian democrats and pro-Spartan oligarchs, a civil war that ended with the victory of the democrats as an Athenian fleet drove off the Peloponnesian fleet that had supported the oligarchs. The result was not peace and reconciliation, however, but a brutal massacre of the oligarchs and their supporters, 400 of whom had taken sanctuary as suppliants in the Temple of Hera together with others who had been persuaded to help man the thirty ships they had expected to use in the defense of Corcyra against the Peloponnesians.

---

32. Unlike Mytilene and the three other rebel cities on Lesbos, Methymna had a democratic government and had not joined the rebellion against Athens.

33. The Athenians established a cleruchy on Lesbos. Cleruchies were a uniquely Athenian form of colony commonly used in the fifth century BCE in which Athenian citizens were settled on land confiscated from another city to serve as a garrison for its future good behavior. Each settler in a cleruchy received a "kleros" or "allotment of land." Unlike other types of Greek colonies, cleruchies had no autonomy but were extensions of Athens in which each settler remained an active citizen of Athens.

34. A *mina* was equal to 100 drachmas or 100 days' wages for a skilled workman.

*Thucydides's account of the civil war at Corcyra contains some of the
most vivid writing in* The History of the Peloponnesian War, *but it is more
than just a dramatic narrative. In the first book, Thucydides observed
(1.22) that "those who want to look into the truth of what was done in the
past—which, given the human condition, will recur in the future, either in
the same fashion or nearly so—those readers will find this History valuable
enough." Just as his account of the plague was a case study of such an event
and its impact on a society, so that of the civil war at Corcyra was a case
study of a city in the grip of civil war and the transvaluation of values and
the transformation of behavior that accompanied such crises.*

[81.2] When the people of Corcyra heard that the Athenian ships were approaching, and that the Peloponnesians were leaving, they brought in the Messenian soldiers[35] who had been outside into the city, and ordered the ships they had manned
to come around into the Hyllaic port. While they were going around, the Corcyrean
democrats killed all the opposing faction they could lay hands on; and as for the ones
they had persuaded to man the ships, they killed them all as they disembarked. And
they came to the temple of Hera and persuaded fifty of the oligarchic sympathizers
who had taken sanctuary there to submit themselves to a trial; then they condemned
them all to death. When they saw what was being done, most of the suppliants—all
those who were not induced to stand trial by law—killed one another right there in
the temple; some hanged themselves on trees, and everyone made away with himself
by what means he could. For the seven days that the Athenian admiral Eurymedon
stayed there with his sixty ships, the Corcyreans went on killing as many of their
own people as they took to be their enemies. They accused them of subverting the
democracy, but some of the victims were killed on account of private hatred, and some
by their debtors for the money they had lent them. Every form of death was seen at
this time; and (as tends to happen in such cases) there was nothing people would not
do, and more: fathers killed their sons; men were dragged out of the temples and then
killed hard by; and some who were walled up in the temple of Dionysus died inside it.

[82] So cruel was the course of this civil war [*stasis*], and it seemed all the more
so because it was among the first of these. Afterward, virtually all Greece was in
upheaval, and quarrels arose everywhere between the democratic leaders, who
sought to bring in the Athenians, and the oligarchs, who wanted to bring in the
Lacedaemonians. Now in time of peace they could have had no pretext and would
not have been so eager to call them in, but because it was war, and allies were to be
had for either party to hurt their enemies and strengthen themselves at the same
time, invitations to intervene came readily from those who wanted a new government. Civil war brought many hardships to the cities, such as happen and will

---

35. The Messenians were former Helots who had been settled by the Athenians at Naupactus at
the western end of the Corinthian Gulf in 464 BCE after the end of their revolt against Sparta.

always happen as long as human nature is the same, although they may be more or less violent or take different forms, depending on the circumstances in each case. In peace and prosperity, cities and private individuals alike are better minded because they are not plunged into the necessity of doing anything against their will; but war is a violent teacher: it gives most people impulses that are as bad as their situation when it takes away the easy supply of what they need for daily life.

Civil war ran through the cities; those it struck later heard what the first cities had done and far exceeded them in inventing artful means for attack and bizarre forms of revenge. And they reversed the usual way of using words to evaluate activities.[36] Ill-considered boldness was counted as loyal manliness; prudent hesitation was held to be cowardice in disguise, and moderation merely the cloak of an unmanly nature. A mind that could grasp the good of the whole was considered wholly lazy. Sudden fury was accepted as part of manly valor, while plotting for one's own security was thought a reasonable excuse for delaying action. A man who started a quarrel was always to be trusted, while one who opposed him was under suspicion. A man who made a plot was intelligent if it happened to succeed, while one who could smell out a plot was deemed even more clever. Anyone who took precautions, however, so as not to need to do either one, had been frightened by the other side (they would say) into subverting his own political party. In brief, a man was praised if he could commit some evil action before anyone else did, or if he could cheer on another person who had never meant to do such a thing.

Family ties were not so close as those of the political parties, because their members would readily dare to do anything on the slightest pretext. These parties, you see, were not formed under existing laws for the good, but for avarice in violation of established law. And the oaths they swore to each other had their authority not so much by divine law, as by their being partners in breaking the law. And if their opponents gave a good speech, if they were the stronger party, they did not receive it in a generous spirit, but with an eye to prevent its taking effect.

To take revenge was of higher value than never to have received injury. And as for oaths of reconciliation (when there were any!), these were offered for the moment when both sides were at an impasse, and were in force only while neither side had help from abroad; but on the first opportunity, when one person saw the other unguarded and dared to act, he found his revenge sweeter because he had broken trust than if he had acted openly: he had taken the safer course, and he gave himself the prize for intelligence if he had triumphed by fraud. Evildoers are called skillful sooner than simpletons are called good, and people are ashamed to be called simpletons but take pride in being thought skillful.

The cause of all this was the desire to rule out of avarice and ambition, and the zeal for winning that proceeds from those two. Those who led their parties in the

---

36. Throughout this passage, Thucydides analyzes the corruption of language under the pressure of *stasis*, extreme partisan conflict.

cities promoted their policies under decent-sounding names: "equality for ordinary citizens" [*plēthous isonomia politikē*] on one side, and "moderate aristocracy" [*aristokratia sōphrōn*] on the other. And though they pretended to serve the public in their speeches, they actually treated it as the prize for their competition; and striving by whatever means to win, both sides ventured on most horrible outrages and exacted even greater revenge, without any regard for justice or the public good. Each party was limited only by its own appetite at the time, and stood ready to satisfy its ambition of the moment either by voting for an unjust verdict or seizing control by force.

So neither side thought much of piety. but they praised those who could pass a horrible measure under the cover of a fine speech. The citizens who remained in the middle were destroyed by both parties, partly because they would not side with them, and partly for envy that they might escape in this way.

[83] Thus was every kind of wickedness afoot throughout all Greece by the occasion of civil wars. Simplicity, which is the chief cause of a generous spirit, was laughed down and disappeared. Citizens were sharply divided into opposing camps, and, without trust, their thoughts were in battle array. No speech was so powerful, no oath so terrible, as to overcome this mutual hostility. The more they reckoned up their chances, the less hope they had for a firm peace, and so they were all looking to avoid harm from each other, and were unable to rely on trust. For the most part, those with the weakest minds had the greatest success, since a sense of their own inferiority and the subtlety of their opponents put them into great fear that they would be overcome in debate or by schemes due to their enemies' intelligence. They therefore went immediately to work against them in action, while their more intelligent opponents, scornful and confident that they could foresee any attack, thought they had no need to take by force what might be gotten by wit. They were therefore unprotected, and so more easily killed.

[85][37] Such was the anger that the Corcyreans expressed in their city— the first against fellow citizens.

Eurymedon and the Athenians sailed away with their ships. Later, refugees from Corcyra—about five hundred of them had escaped—seized forts on the mainland and took control of the Corcyrean territory opposite the island, which they used as a base for plundering Corcyra, causing considerable damage and a severe famine that broke out in the city. Meanwhile, they sent ambassadors to Lacedaemon and Corinth about going home.[38] After a time, when nothing came of that, they got boats and hired mercenary soldiers, then crossed over to the island, about six

---

37. Chapter 84 has been omitted because linguistic differences between it and the rest of Thucydides's work make it clear that it was written by a different author and inserted into his book sometime after he wrote.

38. The reference is to the Corcyrean oligarchs, who were seeking Corinthian and Spartan help in overthrowing the pro-Athenian democracy.

hundred in all. There they burned their boats so that their only hope would be to take control of the land. They went up to Mt. Istone[39] and built a fort there; then they preyed on those in the city and took control of the land.

FROM BOOK 4

The End of the Corcyrean Insurgents

> In 425, the Athenian general Eurymedon returned to Corcyra and attacked the fort on Mt. Istone. The oligarchs there surrendered on condition that they be tried by the people of Athens. The Athenians, for their part, required that the oligarchs accept temporary imprisonment on an island from which they must not try to escape.
> The Corcyrean democrats were afraid Athens would pardon the oligarchs, so they enticed some of them to try escaping. The escape was discovered, and the Athenians, considering the treaty broken, turned their captives over to the Corcyreans. This is what happened next:

[47.3] When the Corcyreans took over the prisoners they shut them up in a large building and later brought them out twenty at a time, bound them together, and made them go down a path lined with hoplites drawn up on both sides. They were beaten and stabbed by the troops in the lines, whenever any of them was spotted as someone's personal enemy. And to speed up the laggards, men with whips followed them down.

[48] They took about sixty men from the building, drove them down the path, and killed them, while those inside the building thought they were only being moved to another place. When someone told them, and they saw the truth, they cried out to the Athenians and asked them to kill them if they wanted, but said that they were no longer willing to leave the building, and that, as long as they had the power, they would not allow anyone to come in.

The Corcyreans, however, had no intention of forcing their way in at the door; they climbed up on the roof of the building, tore off the roofing, and began throwing roof tiles and shooting arrows inside. The inmates defended themselves as well as they could, but most of them killed themselves either by stabbing their throats with arrows that had been shot at them or by strangling themselves with cords from beds that happened to be there or ropes they made from their own clothes.

This went on most of the night (for it happened at night); and so they perished either at their own hands by strangulation or else struck down from above. At daybreak the Corcyreans threw them criss-cross on wagons and carted them out of the city. The women they had captured at the fort were made slaves.

---

39. Present-day Mount Pantocrator, the highest mountain on Corfu.

This is how the Corcyreans who had occupied the mountain fort were destroyed by the democrats; and at this point the civil war that had grown so large came to an end, at least as far as this war was concerned, since there was hardly anything left of one of the two sides.

FROM BOOK 5

The Second Preface

One of Thucydides's principal innovations was to treat the Peloponnesian War as a single twenty-seven-year war instead of two wars: the first war, which historians call the Archidamian War, lasted from 431 BCE to 421 BCE and ended in a stalemate, and a second war that began in 416 BCE and ended in 404 BCE with the surrender of Athens and the loss of her empire. In the following passage, which is known as the second preface, Thucydides sets out his thesis and explains why he was uniquely qualified to write its history.

[26] This history also has been written by Thucydides of Athens in order as each event came to pass, by summers and winters, up to the time when the Lacedaemonians and their allies put an end to the Athenian Empire and took the Long Walls and the Piraeus. At that point the war had lasted twenty-seven years in all.

As for the period of the treaty in the middle, anyone who thinks that this was not war is making a mistake. He should look at how the period was cut up by the actual events; then he'll find that it makes no sense to judge this a peace, when the two sides did not make the exchanges they had agreed on. Besides, there were violations on both sides in the Mantinean and Epidaurian wars, among other actions; and the allies in Thrace continued at war, while the Boeotians observed a mere ten-day truce. So, counting the first ten-year war, the doubtful cessation of hostilities that followed it, and the war that grew out of that, you will find just that many years, if you add up the times, with only a few days left over. And for those who think there is some certainty in oracles, here is one case in which an oracle happened to be reliable.[40] I have remembered all along, from the beginning of the war right up to its end, that many people predicted it would last three times nine years.

I lived through all this at a good age to observe the war,[41] and I applied my mind to gaining accurate knowledge of each event. It turned out that I was living in exile

---

40. For Thucydides's skepticism about oracles, see his comments about them in connection with the plague in 2.54.

41. Because the minimum age to be a general was thirty and Thucydides was a general in 424 BCE, this passage implies that he can't have been born any later than 455 BCE.

for twenty years after my command at Amphipolis, and because I spent time with both sides (more time, in fact with the Peloponnesians, owing to my exile) I was able to observe things more closely and without distraction. So I will now discuss the quarrel that followed the ten-years' war, the dissolution of the treaty, and what came afterward as they waged war.

The Melian Dialogue

Thucydides began his account of the "second phase" of the war with a minor but horrific event, the Athenian attack on the island of Melos. Melos was technically neutral but was believed to be a Spartan colony and had been sympathetic to Sparta during the Archidamian War. Thucydides treats Athens's attack on the island, which ended with the massacre of the adult-male Melians and the enslavement of the women and children, as an unprovoked act of aggression intended to intimidate Athens's subjects. His narrative of the actual invasion and its outcome is brief, while he devotes most of his account to the unsuccessful secret negotiations between representatives of Athens and Melos. That such negotiations took place and that the Athenians emphasized the folly of the Melians resisting their overwhelming power need not be doubted, but scholars are agreed that the so-called Melian Dialogue is essentially Thucydides's own composition and intended to make clear the realities of imperialism as they impact the strong and the weak when stripped of all moral considerations.

[84] (In 416) the Athenians made war against the island of Melos, with thirty ships of their own, six from Chios, and two from Lesbos. The Athenian contingent was twelve hundred hoplites, three hundred archers, and twenty mounted archers, while the allies, including islanders, contributed about fifteen hundred hoplites. The Melians are a colony of the Lacedaemonians,[42] and so did not want to be subject to Athens as the other islands were. At the beginning, they had stayed at peace with both sides. Later on, however, when the Athenians drove them to it by wasting their land,[43] they were openly at war.

Now the Athenian generals, Cleomedes and Tisias, set up camp in Melian territory with these forces. Before doing any harm to the Melian land, they first sent ambassadors to negotiate. The Melians refused to bring these ambassadors before

---

42. The only certain Spartan colony is Taras in South Italy. Evidence points to the settlement of Melos c. 900 BCE, but not to who founded it.
43. In 426 BCE. Melos would again have been neutral following the Peace of Nicias in 421 BCE, which ended the first phase of the Peloponnesian War.

the common people, but ordered them to deliver their message to a few officials and leading citizens.[44] The Athenians spoke as follows:

[85] *Athenians*: Since we may not speak before the common people, for fear that they would be led astray if they heard our persuasive and unanswerable arguments all at once in a continuous speech—we know that is what you had in mind in bringing us to the few leading citizens—you who are sitting here should make your situation still more secure: answer every particular point, not in a single speech, but interrupting us immediately whenever we say anything that seems wrong to you. And first, tell us whether you like this proposal.

[86] *To this the Melian Council replied*: We would not find fault with the fairness of a leisurely debate, but these acts of war—happening right now, not in the future—do not seem to be consistent with that. We see that you have come to be judges of this proceeding, so we expect the result to be this: if we make the better case for justice and do not surrender because of that, we will have war; but if you win the argument, we will have servitude.

[87] *Athenians*: Well, then, if you came to this meeting to reason on the basis of suspicions about the future, or for any other purpose than to work out how to save your city on the basis of what you see here today—we should stop now. But if that is your purpose, let's speak to it.

[88] *Melians*: People in our situation can be expected to turn their words and thoughts to many things, and should be pardoned for that. Since, however, this meeting is to consider only the point of our survival, let's have our discussion on the terms you have proposed, if that is your decision.

[89] *Athenians*: For our part, we will not make a long speech no one would believe, full of fine moral arguments—that our empire is justified because we defeated the Persians, or that we are coming against you for an injustice you have done to us. And we don't want you to think you can persuade us by saying that you did not fight on the side of the Lacedaemonians in the war, though you were their colony, or that you have done us no injustice. Instead, let's work out what we can do on the basis of what both sides truly accept: we both know that decisions about justice are made in human discussions only when both sides are under equal compulsion; but when one side is stronger, it gets as much as it can, and the weak must accept that.

[90] *Melians*: Well, then, since you put your interest in place of justice, our view must be that it is in your interest not to subvert this rule that is good for all: that a plea of justice and fairness should do some good for a man who has fallen into

---

44. The Melian Dialogue is the most controversial example of "direct speech" in the work for two reasons. First, it is not clear how Thucydides could have obtained a detailed account of what was said, if, indeed, it took place, and second, it is hard to believe that the negotiations could have been carried on in such an abstract manner. For these reasons, scholars assume that it is an example of Thucydides making them speak according to what he "thought the situation demanded."

danger, if he can win over his judges, even if he is not perfectly persuasive. And this rule concerns you no less than us: if you ever stumble, you might receive a terrible punishment and be an example to others.

[91] *Athenians*: We are not downhearted at the prospect of our empire's coming to an end, though it may happen. Those who rule over others (such as the Lacedaemonians, who are not our present concern) are not as cruel to those they conquer as are a subject people who attack their rulers and overcome them. But let us be the ones to worry about that danger. We will merely declare that we are here for the benefit of our empire, and we will speak for the survival of your city: we would like to rule over you without trouble, and preserve you for our mutual advantage.

[92] *Melians*: But how could it be as much to our advantage to serve, as it is yours to rule?

[93] *Athenians*: Because if you obey, you will save yourselves from a very cruel fate; and we will reap a profit from you if we don't destroy you.

[94] *Melians*: So you would not accept a peaceful solution? We could be friends rather than enemies, and fight with neither side.

[95] *Athenians*: No. Your enmity does not hurt us as much as your friendship would. That would be a sign of our weakness to those who are ruled by us; but your hatred would prove our power.

[96] *Melians*: Why? Do your subjects reason so unfairly that they put us, who never had anything to do with you, in the same category as themselves, when most of them were your colonies, or else rebels whom you defeated?

[97] *Athenians*: Why not? They think we have as good a justification for controlling you as we do for them; they say the independent cities survive because they are powerful, and that we do not attack them because we are afraid. So when you have been trampled down by us, you will add not only to our empire, but to our security, by not staying independent. And this is especially true because you are islanders who are weaker than the others, and we are masters of the sea.

[98] *Melians*: But don't you think there is safety in our proposal of neutrality? Here again, since you have driven us away from a plea for justice, and are telling us to surrender to whatever is in your interest, we must show you what would be good for us, and try to persuade you that your interests coincide with ours. Won't this turn the people who are now neutral into your enemies? Once they've seen this, they will expect you to attack them eventually also. And what would this accomplish, but to make the enemies you already have still greater, and to make others your enemies against their will, when they would not have been so?

[99] *Athenians*: We do not think the free mainlanders will be terrible enemies to us; it will be long before they so much as keep guard against us. But islanders worry us—those outside the empire like you, and those under the empire who resent the force that keeps them that way—these may indeed act recklessly and bring themselves and us into foreseeable danger.

[100] *Melians*: Yes, but if you would face such extreme danger to retain your empire, and if your subjects would do so to get free of you, then wouldn't it be great weakness and cowardice on our part, since we are still free, not to go to every extreme rather than be your subjects?

[101] *Athenians*: No, not if you think sensibly. Your contest with us is not an equal match of courage against courage; no honor is lost if you submit. This is a conference about your survival and about not resisting those who are far stronger than you.

[102] *Melians*: But we know that in war the odds sometimes are more even than the difference in numbers between the two sides, and that if we yield, all our hope is lost immediately; but if we hold out, we can still hope to stand tall.

[103] *Athenians*: Hope! It is a comfort in danger, and though it may be harmful to people who have many other advantages, it will not destroy them. But people who put everything they have at risk will learn what hope is when it fails them, for hope is prodigal by nature; and once they have learned this, it is too late to take precautions for the future. Do not let this happen to you, since you are weak and have only this one throw of the dice. And do not be like the ordinary people who could use human means to save themselves but turn to blind hopes when they are forced to give up their sensible ones—to divination, oracles, and other such things that destroy men by giving them hope.

[104] *Melians*: You can be sure we think it hard to contend against your power and good fortune, unless we might do so on equal terms. Nevertheless, we trust that our good fortune will be no less than yours. The gods are on our side, because we stand innocent against men who are unjust. And as for power, what we lack will be supplied by the alliance we will make with the Lacedaemonians, who must defend us as a matter of honor, if only because we are related to them. So our confidence is not as totally unreasonable as you might think.

[105] *Athenians*: Well, the favor of the gods should be as much on our side as yours. Neither our principles nor our actions are contrary to what men believe about the gods, or would want for themselves. Nature always compels gods (we believe) and men (we are certain) to rule over anyone they can control. We did not make this law, and we were not the first to follow it; but we will take it as we found it and leave it to posterity forever, because we know that you would do the same if you had our power, and so would anyone else. So as far as the favor of the gods is concerned, we have no reason to fear that we will do worse than you.

As for your opinion about the Lacedaemonians, your trust that they will help you in order to preserve their own honor—we admire your blessed innocence, but we don't envy you your foolishness. Granted, the Lacedaemonians do show a high degree of virtue toward each other according to their local customs; but one could say many things about their treatment of other people. We'll make this as brief and as clear as possible: of all the people we know, they are the ones who make it most obvious that they hold whatever pleases them to be honorable, and whatever profits them to be just. So your plan will not support your hope for survival, and it now seems reckless.

[106] *Melians*: But on that point we most firmly trust the Lacedaemonians to pursue their own advantage—*not* to betray their colonists, the Melians, for in doing so they would benefit their enemies by losing the confidence of their friends among the Greeks.

[107] *Athenians*: Don't you realize that advantage lies with safety, and that the pursuit of justice and honor brings danger? Which the Lacedaemonians are usually least willing to face?

[108] *Melians*: But we believe they will take a dangerous mission in hand for our sake. They will think it safer to do so for us than for anyone else, since we are close enough to the Peloponnesus for action, and we will be more faithful to them than others because our kinship gives us common views.

[109] *Athenians*: But the goodwill of those who call for help does not offer any security to those who might fight for them. They will be safe only if they have superior power in action. The Lacedaemonians are more aware of this than anyone else; at least they have no confidence in their own forces, and therefore take many allies along with them when they attack a neighbor. So while we are masters of the sea, you cannot reasonably expect them to cross over to an island.

[110] *Melians*: Yes, but they may have others to send. The Sea of Crete is wide; it is harder for its masters to seize ships there, than it is for people who want to escape to slip through. And if the Lacedaemonians failed in this, they would turn their arms against your own land or the lands of your allies that have still not been invaded by Brasidas.[45] And then you will be troubled about your own land, and that of your allies, and no longer about a country that does not concern you.

[111] *Athenians*: With your experience of what might happen, you are surely not unaware that Athens has never given up a single siege through fear of anyone else. We are struck by the fact that though you said you would confer about your survival, in all this discussion you have never mentioned a single thing that people could rely on and expect to survive. Your strongest points are mere hopes for the future, and your actual resources are too small for your survival in view of the forces arrayed against you. Your planning will be utterly irrational, unless (after letting us withdraw from the meeting) you decide on a more sensible policy. Do not be distracted by a sense of honor; this destroys people all too often, when dishonor and death stand before their eyes. Many have been so overcome by the power of this seductive word, "honor," that even when they foresee the dangers to which it carries them, they are drawn by a mere word into an action that is an irreparable disaster; and so, intentionally, they fall into a dishonor that is more shameful than mere misfortune, since it is due to their own foolishness.

---

45. Brasidas was the most successful Spartan commander during the 420s BCE. It was Thucydides's failure to prevent Brasidas's capture of Amphipolis in 424 BCE that brought about his exile.

You must guard against this if you are to deliberate wisely, and you must not think it unseemly for you to submit to a city of such great power, which offers such reasonable conditions—to be our allies, and to enjoy your own property under tribute to us. You are being given a choice between war and survival: do not make the wrong decision out of a passion for victory. Remember what is usually the best course: do not give way to equals, but have the right attitude toward your superiors and use moderation toward your inferiors. So think about this when we withdraw from the meeting, and keep this often in your mind: you are considering what to do for your country—your only country—and this one discussion will determine whether it meets success or failure.

[112] So the Athenians withdrew from the conference, and the Melians, left to themselves, decided on much the same position as they had taken in the debate. Then the Melians answered as follows:

Melians: Athenians, our resolution is no different from what it was before: we will not, in a short time, give up the liberty in which our city has remained for the seven hundred years since its foundation. We will trust in the fortune of the gods, which has preserved it up to now, and in the help of men—the Lacedaemonians—and we will do our best to maintain our liberty. We offer this, however: we will be your friends; we will be enemies to neither side; and you will depart from our land, after making whatever treaty we both think fit.

[113] That was the answer of the Melians. As they broke off the conference, the Athenians said:

Athenians: It seems to us, on the basis of this discussion, that you are the only men who think you know the future more clearly than what is before your eyes, and who, through wishful thinking, see doubtful events as if they had already come to pass. You have staked everything on your trust in hope, good fortune, and the Lacedaemonians; and you will be ruined in everything.

[114] Then the Athenian ambassadors went back to their camp. When the generals saw that the Melians would not submit, they turned immediately to war and surrounded the Melian city with a wall, after dividing up the work with their allies. After that, the Athenians left a contingent of Athenian and allied troops there to guard the city by land and sea, and went home with the greater part of their army. The rest stayed behind to besiege the place.

[115] (About the same time, the Argives invaded the country around Phlious, where they were ambushed by Phlians and exiles from Argos, losing about eighty men. Meanwhile, the Athenians at Pylos brought in a great deal of plunder from the Lacedaemonians. The Lacedaemonians did not go to war over this, because that would have broken the treaty. Instead they proclaimed that any of their people could plunder the Athenians in return. The Corinthians were at war with the Athenians, but this was over certain disputes of their own, and the rest of the Peloponnesus kept quiet.)

The Melians, in a night attack, captured part of the Athenian wall opposite the market place, killed the men there, and brought in grain and as many supplies as they could. Then they went back and kept quiet. After that the Athenians maintained a better watch.

And so the summer ended.

[116] (The following winter, the Lacedaemonians were about to march into the land of Argos, but they returned when they found that the sacrifices for the border crossing were not favorable. The Argives suspected some of their own people of being involved in the Lacedaemonian plan; they captured some of them, and the rest escaped.)

About the same time, the Melians took another part of the Athenian wall, because there were not many men to guard it. After that another army came from Athens under the command of Philocrates. Now that the city was besieged in force, there was some treachery, and the Melians on their own initiative surrendered to the Athenians, to be dealt with as the Athenians decided: they killed all the men of military age and made slaves of the women and children. Later, they settled the place themselves, sending five hundred colonists.

FROM BOOK 7

Battle in the Great Harbor

Shortly after the fall of Melos in 415 BCE, the Athenians voted to go to war in Sicily. Thucydides portrays the attempt to conquer Sicily as pure folly, the result of the Athenian people's ignorance of the scale of the undertaking, their unwillingness to follow Pericles's policy of restraint, and their susceptibility to the promises of unprincipled demagogues. After two years of bitter fighting focused on the siege of the city of Syracuse, which was supported by Sparta, everything came down to a sea battle on September 9, 413 BCE, in the Great Harbor of Syracuse in which the Athenian fleet suffered a total defeat. In the following passage, Thucydides vividly describes the battle and the terrible fate of the almost 40,000 survivors of the battle, most of whom either died in the retreat from Syracuse or were sold into slavery after months of confinement in stone quarries.

BATTLE IN THE GREAT HARBOR
September 9, 413

[69] The Syracusan generals and Gylippus gave this encouragement to their soldiers; then they manned their ships as soon as they saw the Athenians doing the same. Nicias was terrified by the present state of affairs, realizing how great

the danger was and how near, now that they were on the point of departing, and thought—as happens in a great crisis—that when all has been done there is still something missing, and that when everything has been said it is still not enough. In this state he once again called on each ship captain, one by one, addressing him by his father's name, his own, and that of his tribe, and entreated each one if he had a brilliant reputation not to betray it now, and not to tarnish the ancestral virtues that had distinguished their forefathers. He reminded them also of their country with its great liberty and the untrammeled freedom it gives everyone to live as he pleases; and he said whatever else people say at such a time when they are at the point of action and don't mind sounding old-fashioned, using words that fit nearly any occasion, bringing in wives and children and ancestral gods, crying out in the hope that such speeches will be helpful in the terror of the moment.

When he had exhorted them as long as he thought he could (which was less than he thought he should), Nicias withdrew and led his land forces along the shore, placing them as widely as he could so as to give the maximum benefit of their encouragement to those on board the ships. Meanwhile, Demosthenes, Menander, and Euthydemus—these men had embarked as commanders of the fleet—put out from their camp and sailed straight to the barrier at the mouth of the harbor, to the passage that had been left open, with the intention of forcing their way out.

[70] The Syracusans and their allies had already put out with about as many ships as before, some of them guarding the outlet and the rest forming a circle around the harbor so they could attack the Athenians from all sides at once. At the same time, their land forces came along to support them wherever their ships might put ashore. The Syracusan navy was under the command of Sicanus and Agatharchus, each of whom had charge of a wing, while the Corinthians under Pythen held the center. When the Athenians first reached the barrier, their initial charge overwhelmed the ships assigned to guard it, and they tried to break open the bars. But after that, when the Syracusans and their allies hit them from all sides, the battle spread from the barrier throughout the harbor and was more fiercely fought than any naval battle in history. The sailors were full of enthusiasm to row wherever they were ordered; the steersmen were full of ingenuity and there was great mutual rivalry among them. The soldiers on board did their utmost when one ship came alongside another to see that their fighting from the decks was not outdone by the sailors in other tasks. Each and every one of them, in fact, pushed himself eagerly to be the best at his assignment.

But with so many ships engaged in a small area (this was the largest sea battle in the narrowest quarters, for there were almost two hundred ships altogether) they could not ram each other very often, since there was no room to back up and charge; but they had frequent collisions, as one ship would run against another by chance while it was fleeing or attacking a third vessel. While a boat was approaching, the soldiers on the decks pelted it with javelins and arrows and stones in abundance; but once they were alongside they fell to hand-to-hand fighting as the marines tried to board each other's vessels. In many places, owing to the lack of room, it happened that one ship would be charging another while being charged itself, and that two ships, or sometimes more, would be forced against one, and the captains wound up having to defend on one side while preparing to attack on the other, not just one ship at a time but many from all directions. Meanwhile the great din of so many ships in combat was terrifying and drowned out orders coming from the officers. Officers were shouting out instructions and encouragement on both sides, of course, going beyond their normal duties in the excitement of battle: the Athenians were crying out to their men to force the passage and now if ever to show their spirit and secure a safe return to their country; the Syracusans and their allies were shouting about how fine it would be to prevent the Athenian escape and to bring honor to each country by their victory. The generals on both sides were shouting as well: if they saw anyone backing to stern unnecessarily they called on the ship-captain by name. The Athenians would ask if he was retreating because he thought he'd be more at home here, where the land was so terribly hostile, than on the open sea, which they had won at such cost. The Syracusans would ask why he was running away, since he knew perfectly well that the Athenians were desperate to escape any way they could.

[71] While the naval battle hung in the balance, the land forces on both sides were in an agony of suspense and conflict of mind, the local troops eager to win more glory than before, the invaders afraid that their situation might get even worse. Since everything depended on their ships, the Athenians were in the most extraordinary fear of what might happen, and since the battle was uneven in different parts of the harbor, the watchers on shore could only get uneven impressions of it. They were watching at close range and not all seeing the same thing at the same time. Those who saw their side winning took heart and fell to calling upon the gods not to take away their chance of escape; meanwhile, those who caught sight of defeat were wailing, even shrieking outright, and they were more overwhelmed in their minds by the sight of the battle than the actual combatants were. Others could see a part of the fighting that hung in the balance, and the protracted indecision of the struggle was agony for them as their bodies reflected their fears. These watchers had the hardest time of all, as they were always on the brink between escape and destruction. So it was that in one and the same army, while the sea battle was in doubt, you could hear all this at once: wailing, cheering, "we're winning," "we're losing," along with all the other confused shouting that has to come from a great army in serious trouble.

Much the same happened to the men on the ships, until at last, after a long-drawn out battle, the Syracusans and their allies clearly got the upper hand, forced the Athenians to retreat, and chased them back to land with a lot of shouting and cheering. Then the troops from the ships landed helter skelter—if they hadn't been taken at sea—and rushed to the camp. And now the soldiers on land were no longer of two minds: they all wailed and groaned from the same impulse, all unable to bear what had happened. Some of them ran to help the ships, others rushed to guard what was left of the wall; most of them, however, were only looking for a way to save their own skins. The panic at this point was greater than it had ever been. Their disaster was comparable to the one they had inflicted on the Lacedaemonians at Pylos: when the Lacedaemonians lost their ships there they also lost the men they had put on the island; and now the Athenians had no hope of escaping over land unless by a miracle.

[72] After this cruel battle, which consumed many ships and men on both sides, the victorious Syracusans and their allies picked up their dead and the wreckage of their ships, sailed back to the city, and put up a trophy. The Athenians, however, were so cast down by the enormity of the present disaster that they never thought to ask permission to pick up their dead or their wreckage; all they wanted was to get away that very night. Demosthenes went to Nicias and proposed that they man the remaining ships and, if possible, break out at dawn, since, as he said, they still had more serviceable ships than the enemy. The Athenians had sixty ships remaining, while the enemy had fewer than fifty. Nicias accepted this proposal, but when they asked the sailors to man the ships they refused to go aboard. They were in such a panic from their defeat that they thought they could never win a victory ever again.

[73] And so they all resolved to break out by land. Hermocrates of Syracuse suspected they had such a plan, however, and thought it would be terrible if an army of that size withdrew by land, found a base somewhere in Sicily, and planned a new campaign against them. So he went and told the authorities what he was thinking, and urged them not to let the Athenians slip away by night, but to send out all the Syracusan and allied forces to occupy the roads, seize the narrow passes, and keep watch. The authorities agreed with him and felt as strongly as he did that this should be done, but they were afraid that they could not easily get the soldiers to obey, since they were now happily resting after the great battle and enjoying a festival besides (by coincidence this was the day for worshipping Heracles). Most of the men had been celebrating their victory by drinking heavily at the festival, and now the very last thing they would agree to do would be to take up their arms again and sally out to fight. Hermocrates saw that the authorities were convinced his proposal was impossible, and, because he could not persuade them, he came up with this stratagem on his own: he was afraid the Athenians might easily get a head start during the night and cross over the most difficult terrain, so as soon as it grew dark he sent some of his friends on horses to the Athenian camp. They rode up within earshot and called to a few Athenians, pretending to be friendly to their cause (Nicias did have some informants inside the city); then they instructed them to tell Nicias not to take the army out at night, since the Syracusans were guarding the roads, but to prepare for an easy departure the next day. The horsemen said this and rode off, while those who heard them took the message to the Athenian generals.

[74] It never occurred to the generals that this message was a fraud, so they decided to stay the night. Then, since they had not set off immediately after their defeat, they decided to wait another day to give the soldiers time to pack as well as they could, taking what they needed the most and leaving all the rest behind. Their aim was to take only what was necessary for physical survival.

Meanwhile the Syracusans and Gylippus took their land forces out ahead of them and blocked the roads in the area the Athenians were likely to cross; they also guarded the river and stream crossings and posted troops to receive and hold the Athenian army where they thought best. They also sailed up and dragged the Athenian ships off the beach. They burned some of these (as the Athenians would have done) and easily tied up the others wherever they lay and towed them into the city, since there was no one to stop them.

The Athenian Retreat

Retreat and destruction of the Athenian force

[75] Later, two days after the sea battle, Nicias and Demosthenes decided they were ready enough, and the army began its withdrawal. It was a lamentable departure, and not just because of the single fact that by losing all their ships they had dashed all their great hopes and put themselves and their city in danger: as they left the camp each one of them was struck by the sight or the thought of some great grief. The dead were lying about unburied, and when anyone saw the body of a friend on the ground he was seized with fear and horror, while the living who were left behind sick or wounded were a more horrible sight than the dead and were far worse off than those who had passed away. Their continual pleading and wailing brought home the utter helplessness of the army; they begged to be taken along, and if any of them saw a friend or relative he'd call on him by name, and they would hang on the necks of their departing tent-mates, or follow them as far as they could, till strength or life failed them and they were left behind with no shortage of prayers and lamentations.

As a result the entire army was full of tears, and in this state of helplessness it was not easy for them to start their retreat, though they were leaving a hostile place and had already suffered more than tears could express; still, they were afraid of the suffering their unknown future might bring them. They hung down their heads and many thought themselves worthless. They seemed like a whole city of refugees trying to escape from a siege, and not a small city either, as there were no fewer than 40,000 people in the entire crowd that was on the march. Each of them carried whatever provisions he could; even hoplites and horsemen did this, although it went against custom for them to carry their own rations while under arms; some did so because they'd lost their servants, others because they did not trust them, since they had been deserting for a long time and now most of them had just run away. Even so, they did not carry enough, since the army was running out of food. And the other indignities they bore were too great for them to take lightly at this point, even though sharing troubles equally with many other people usually lightens the load. The worst part was that they had come down from such a height of splendor and glory to this miserable end—the greatest reversal that had ever happened to a Greek army: these men who had come to enslave other people now had to leave in fear of being enslaved themselves; in place of the prayers and battle-hymns with which they had sailed out they now left with the omens against them; besides, this force that had traveled by sea was now reduced to foot soldiers, depending on hoplites more than on sailors. Still, in view of the great danger hanging over them, they felt they had to bear all this. [76] When Nicias saw that the army had lost its spirit and was so greatly changed, he passed through the ranks and gave them whatever encouragement and comfort he could in the circumstances, his voice rising higher and higher as he went along because he was so serious and so eager that his exhortation should benefit as many men as possible.

Nicias's Speech

[77] "Even now, allies and Athenians, we should keep hope alive. People have been saved ere now from greater dangers than these. You should not think too badly of yourselves, either for your past losses or present suffering, which is undeserved. I may have less strength than any of you—you see how sick I am—but I have as good a reputation as anyone for success in both private and public life, and I am now in the same danger as the worst men here. Still, I have passed my life in the great piety that is ordained toward the gods, while toward men I have shown great justice and given no offense. In view of this my hope for the future is still confident, and these losses cause me no anxiety so far as our merit is concerned; indeed, we may well have some relief from them. Our enemies have now had their share of good luck, and if we have offended any of the gods in this campaign we have already had enough punishment. Others have invaded their neighbors before we did, and what they suffered for doing what human beings do has been bearable. And now we have a reason to hope for milder treatment from the gods, since we have come to deserve their pity more than their anger. And just look at yourselves: with so many fine hoplites, marching in good order, you shouldn't give way to panic. Wherever you settle down you will immediately be a city, and no other force in Sicily will be able to withstand your attack or force you out once you're established.

As for the journey, you must take care that it be safe and orderly. And each of you keep this thought above all: that whatever place you are forced to fight in will be your country, with your walls. We will hurry along our way equally by night and day, since our supplies are short. If we can reach a friendly town of Sicels, then you should consider yourselves secure. A message has been sent to them telling them to meet us and bring food. To conclude, soldiers, you must see that your only choice is to be brave; there is no place of safety near enough for cowards to reach. But if you now escape our enemies, you will all see what you desire, and those of you who are Athenians will restore the fallen power of Athens to its former greatness. It is the men, you see, and not the walls or empty ships, that are the city.

[78] As Nicias made this exhortation he went along the troops, collecting any stragglers he saw out of position and putting them in their places. Demosthenes did no less for his troops and said much the same things. Then they marched out in hollow rectangle formation, Nicias commanding the front and Demosthenes the rear, hoplites on the outside and baggage carriers and general rabble inside. When they came to the crossing of the Anapus River they found a unit of Syracusans and their allies drawn up on the bank. These they put to flight, took control of the ford, and marched forward, harassed by the pressure of the Syracusan cavalry and the javelins of their light-armed troops. On that day they advanced about four miles and a half and spent the night by a certain hill. The next day they left at dawn and went about two miles further, reaching a flat place where they set up camp, planning to get food from the houses (for the place was inhabited) and to take water from there along with them, since it was scarce for many miles ahead of them on their intended route. But the Syracusans got ahead of them and walled off the passage in front of them where there is a steep hill with precipitous ravines on either side, called the Acraean cliff. The next day the Athenians went on, while great numbers of Syracusan cavalry and javelin-throwers pressed them from both sides by charging them or throwing javelins. The Athenians fought for a long time and then returned to their camp. They had less food than before, now that the Syracusan cavalry would no longer let them leave their position.

[79] Early in the morning they set off on their way up to the hill that had been fortified by the enemy. In front of them, below the wall, they found the enemy foot soldiers lined up many shields deep, as the place was narrow. The Athenians charged and attacked the wall under heavy fire from the soldiers on the steep hill above them, who could easily reach their targets since they were throwing their javelins from above. When the Athenians could not force through, they backed down and rested. Just then a small thunderstorm blew up and drenched them, as often happens when autumn is near. At this the Athenians lost heart still more and thought that all these events were meant to destroy them.[46] While they were resting, Gylippus and the Syracusans sent a detachment to dig in behind them where they had entered the gorge; but the Athenians sent some of their own men in response and stopped them. After that the Athenians took their whole army down to more level ground and camped.

---

46. Earlier Nicias had delayed the army's retreat for a month because of his superstitious concerns over an eclipse.

The next day they went on while the Syracusans pelted them with javelins from all sides in a circle and wounded many of them. And when the Athenians went after them, they withdrew, but when the Athenians backed off they attacked. They were especially fierce in attacking the Athenians at the rear, in hopes that routing a small number of them would throw the whole army into a panic. The Athenians held out against this for a long time, and after advancing a little over half a mile they rested on the plain while the Syracusans retired to their own camp.

[80] That night Nicias and Demosthenes made a decision. The army was in terrible shape: they had run out of all their supplies and many of them had been wounded in all those encounters with the enemy. So they decided to light as many fires as they could and take the army out of there, not the way they had originally planned, but toward the sea—the opposite direction from the route guarded by the Syracusans. (All along, they had been marching not toward Catana but toward the other part of Sicily, around Camarina and Gela and the Greek or foreign cities in that area.) And so, when they had lighted a good many fires, they moved off in the night. And then—well, in any army, especially a large one, fear and terror are likely to strike, and more so at night, in enemy territory, and when the enemy is not far off—*then* they fell into a total panic. Nicias's unit, which led the way, stayed together and made good progress, while Demosthenes's troops, much more than half the army, got separated and went on without much order. Still, they reached the sea at dawn and set off on the Helorus Road toward the Cacyparis River, which they planned to cross so they could head for the interior. There they hoped to meet the Sicels whom they had sent for. When they got to the river they found another unit of the Syracusan guard digging in and putting stakes across the ford. They forced their way across and went on to the next river, the Erineus, on the advice of their guides.

[81] Meanwhile, when the Syracusans and their allies realized at daybreak that the Athenians had gone, many of them accused Gylippus of letting them go intentionally, and went after them in hot pursuit. Their route was easy to follow, and they caught up around lunchtime. First they found Demosthenes's troops, who were in the rear and had moved more slowly and in greater disorder because of that panic during the night. Immediately, the Syracusans attacked and surrounded them with cavalry—which was easy since they were divided—and herded them into one place. Nicias's troops, however, were almost six miles further on; he was moving faster because he thought that their safety lay in not willingly staying to fight at this point and that they should retreat as quickly as possible and fight only where compelled to do so. But Demosthenes was having a much worse time of it, under constant pressure from the enemy because he was in the rear where they attacked first. When he saw that the Syracusans were in pursuit, he stopped his advance and went into battle formation. During this lengthy process, however, he got surrounded by enemy cavalry, and then he and his Athenians were in serious trouble. They were huddled up in a place with a wall around it, roads on this side and that, and a good many olive

trees; and they were being hit by javelins from all sides. The Syracusans had a good reason for attacking them in this way rather than at close quarters: it would only have helped the Athenians for them to expose themselves to danger at the hands of such desperate men. Besides, now that victory was assured, everyone felt a certain reluctance to throw away his life, and they hoped that their tactics would enable them to subdue the Athenians and take them alive.

[82] After hitting them all day from all sides, Gylippus saw that the Athenians were worn out with wounds and other troubles, so he and the Syracusans and their allies made a proclamation: any of the islanders with the Athenians could freely come over to their side if they wished (and troops from a few cities did cross over). Afterward they made an agreement with all the rest of Demosthenes's troops: if they laid down their arms, no one would be killed by violence or imprisonment or starvation. So they surrendered, six thousand of them in all;[47] and they threw all the money they had into the hollow of some shields, filling up four shields. They were then taken immediately to the city.

Meanwhile, Nicias and his army reached the Erineus River that day, crossed, and set up camp on high ground. [83] Next day the Syracusans caught up with him and told him that Demosthenes's troops had surrendered. They ordered him to do the same. Nicias did not trust them, so he sent a horseman under truce to find out. When the horseman brought back word of the surrender, Nicias sent a herald to Gylippus and the Syracusans to say that he was ready to agree on behalf of the Athenians to repay Syracuse for the cost of the war if they would let his army go away. He also promised to give them Athenian hostages till the money was paid—one man for each talent. But the Syracusans and Gylippus did not accept the terms. They attacked and surrounded the Athenians, hitting them with missiles from all sides, as they had the others, till evening. Then, although they were pinched by their lack of food and supplies, they kept watch that night intending to leave as soon as it was quiet. But when they took up their weapons the Syracusans heard them and raised the battle-hymn. The Athenians realized they had been found out and returned to camp, all but about three hundred of them who forced their way through the Syracusan guards and went as far as they could that night.

[84] When day came, Nicias led his army forward, while the Syracusans and their allies laid into them as before, hitting them from all sides with javelins and other missiles. The Athenians hurried on to the Assinarus River, partly because

---

47. The total number of men lost is unknown, but a fleet of 200 ships implies a force of at least 40,000 men, a number far larger than Athens could raise by itself. A large percentage of these men, therefore, must have been allied troops, but nevertheless, losses on this scale must have been devastating and not only for Athens's military forces. The resulting social disruption is indicated by references in late fifth-century BCE and early fourth-century BCE literature to women who could not find husbands and had to find ways to support themselves and their children.

they were under pressure on all sides from attack by the cavalry and the rest of the mob (which they hoped would ease off once they had crossed the river), and partly because they were exhausted and desperate for water. As soon as they were there, they rushed in without any order, each man wanting to be the first to cross, while the enemy laid into them and made the crossing even harder. They were forced to go into the river in heaps, and so they fell upon one another and got trampled under foot. Some died immediately on each other's spears, others got tangled in the baggage and were washed away. On the other side of the river were Syracusans who stood on the steep bank and threw javelins down at the Athenians while most of them were drinking greedily or getting in each other's way in the river hollow. The Peloponnesians also came down and killed them in the river. This immediately fouled the water, but they went on drinking it nonetheless; and though it was full of mud and blood, many of them even fought over it.

[85] In the end, when many dead lay heaped in the river, and the army was utterly defeated, partly at the river, and partly by horsemen who chased down those who ran away, Nicias personally surrendered to Gylippus because he trusted him more than he did the Syracusans. He told Gylippus and the Lacedaemonians to do whatever they liked with him, but to stop slaughtering the other soldiers. After that, Gylippus ordered his troops to take live captives. The remaining soldiers were brought to the city alive (except for the many who were hidden away)[48] while the three hundred who had broken through the guard during the night were chased down and captured also. The number of Athenian captives collected as public property was not large, but a great many were secretly stolen away and all Sicily was filled with them. (That was because there had been no agreement in their case, as there had for those captured with Demosthenes.) A large part of the army was dead, for the slaughter at the river had been dreadful, exceeding that of any other action in this war, while a good many had been killed earlier during those frequent attacks along the way. Still, many escaped. Some got away then and there, while others were made slaves and ran away later. All these fugitives made their way toward Catana.

[86] The Syracusans and their allies formed up and returned to the city with their booty and as many prisoners as they could take. The remaining Athenian and allied captives were sent down into the stone quarries, which they considered the easiest place to guard safely; but Nicias and Demosthenes were executed, though Gylippus was opposed to this, since he thought it would be a fine prize for him if he could deliver the enemy generals to the Lacedaemonians on top of everything else. One of the two happened to be their worst enemy—Demosthenes, for what he did on the island and at Pylos; while the other had been extremely helpful to them over the same affair. Nicias had worked hard on behalf of the Lacedaemonians on the island; it was he who had persuaded the Athenians to make the treaty that released

---

48. To be sold as slaves by their captors.

them.[49] For this the Lacedaemonians were friendly toward him, and that was the main reason he had trusted Gylippus enough to surrender to him. Some of the Syracusans, however, had conspired with him earlier (so it is said) and were afraid that he would speak out under torture and so get them into trouble just when all was going well. Others, mainly Corinthians, were afraid that with his great wealth he would bribe certain people, make his escape, and be the cause of some fresh mischief to them. So they persuaded the allies to kill him. This or something like it was the cause of his death, though of all the Greeks in my time he was the one who least deserved such a misfortune, since he had regulated his whole life in the cultivation of virtue (*aretē*).

[87] The Syracusans treated the men in the quarries badly at first. They were crowded together in a small sunken area without a roof where they were tormented by the sun's heat and stifling air, followed by cold nights, as autumn was coming on—a change that gave them new diseases. They had to do everything in the same narrow space, and besides that [i.e., the excrement] the carcasses of the dead, who had died of their wounds or the change in temperature or some such cause, were heaped up together and the stench was unbearable. All the while they were afflicted with hunger and thirst, for during an eight-month period they fed each man a cup of water and two cups of grain each day.[50] In short, they were not spared a single one of the miseries you'd expect when men are thrown into a place like that.

For seventy days they lived like this all together. After that they kept the Athenians, along with the Sicels and Italians who had joined them, but sold all the rest. It is hard to say how many men were captured altogether, but there were at least seven thousand.

This was the greatest action of the war—in my opinion, the greatest in all Greek history—the most glorious victory for the winners, and the worst calamity for the losers. They were utterly vanquished on all points, and none of their losses was small. It was "total destruction" as the saying is, for the army and navy alike. There was nothing that was not lost, and few out of many returned home.[51] That is what happened on Sicily.

[viii.1] When the news was told in Athens, even though the messengers were actual soldiers who had fled from the scene itself, and gave a clear report, people refused for a long time to believe that the loss had been so utterly complete. When

---

49. These are the 120 Spartans who had been captured by the Athenians on the island of Sphacteria near Pylos in 425 BCE and whose release was a major reason for Sparta signing the Peace of Nicias in 421 BCE.

50. Four cups of wheat per day was the normal Athenian ration for a man, so the Syracusans fed the Athenian prisoners half rations without any of the protein or oils necessary for a healthy diet.

51. According to a story famous in antiquity, the Syracusans so admired the poetry of the tragedian Euripides that they released any Athenian who could recite his verses.

they did realize the truth, they were furious with the orators who had joined in promoting the expedition (as if they had not voted for it themselves!). They were also angry with the prophets and soothsayers and all those who had claimed to give them assurances from the gods that they would take Sicily. Everything from every side was a grief to them, and on top of this overwhelming loss they were stricken with fear and panic, the worst ever. It was bad enough that every private family, and the city as a whole, was burdened with the loss of so many hoplites and cavalry and men of military age for whom replacements were nowhere to be seen. But when they did not see enough ships in the boathouses, or money in the treasury, or officers to staff the ships, then they lost hope of surviving this crisis altogether. They thought their enemies from Sicily would immediately sail a navy into the Piraeus,[52] especially after such a great victory, while their enemies in Greece would double all their preparations and lay into them fiercely by land and by sea with the support of their former allies, who would now rebel.

Nevertheless, they decided they ought not to give in while they still had resources. They voted to build a fleet using wood and money from wherever they could find it, and also to make sure of their allies' loyalty, especially those on Euboea. Then they decided to slash public expenses and to select a committee of senior men to advise them on the crisis as the situation demanded. Now that they were face to face with real danger, the people were ready—as often in democracy—to turn over all their affairs to good management. Then they carried out the decisions they had made. And so the summer ended.

---

52. The harbor of Athens.

CHAPTER 3

Xenophon, *The Hellenica*

FROM BOOK 2

The End of the Peloponnesian War

The end of the Peloponnesian War and the Tyranny of the Thirty were both traumatic for Athens. Xenophon's account of them is the earliest and fullest that we possess, full of vivid details about the overthrow of the Athenian democracy and the brutal events in Athens during the rule of the Thirty afterward that suggest that he was an eyewitness. While his account of the final defeat of the Athenian democracy is relatively evenhanded, not concealing either the harshness of Lysander's actions or the Athenian atrocities that people thought justified them, that is not the case with his treatment of the Tyranny of the Thirty.

One would have expected his account to be sympathetic. After all, he was a known sympathizer of the Spartans and, as a follower of Socrates, he also would have known Critias and probably other members of the Thirty and may even have been a member of the Three Thousand. Nevertheless, his account is distinctly hostile, as is illustrated by his observation that the Thirty killed more Athenians in eight months than the Spartans did in ten years. Perspective is what accounts for Xenophon's unexpected view of the Thirty. He wrote his account of the Thirty several decades after finishing his narrative of the end of the Peloponnesian War, including it as the beginning of the general history of Greece that is contained in the final five books of the Hellenica. By then, he had seen that Lysander's policy of governing the Spartan Empire by establishing oligarchies like the Thirty had led to the collapse not only of the Spartan Empire but also of Sparta itself as a major power. The failure of the Thirty was the first step in that process, and it was that recognition that shaped his interpretation of its rule.

2.1. In the following year—[Archytas being now ephor, and Alexias archon at Athens][1]—Lysander[2] arrived at Ephesus and sent for Eteonicus to come thither from Chios with the ships, while he also gathered together all the other ships that were anywhere to be found; then he occupied himself with refitting these vessels and building more at Antandrus. Meantime he went to Cyrus[3] and asked for money; and Cyrus told him that the funds provided by the King had been spent, in fact much more besides, showing him how much each of the admirals had received; nevertheless he did give him money. And upon receiving it Lysander appointed to each trireme its captain and paid his sailors the wages that were due them. Meanwhile the Athenian generals also were getting their fleet in readiness, at Samos.

At this point Cyrus sent for Lysander, for a messenger had come to him from his father with word that he was ill and summoned him, being at Thammeria, in Media, near the country of the Cadusians, against whom he had made an expedition, for they were in revolt. And when Lysander arrived, Cyrus warned him not to give battle to the Athenians unless he should far outnumber them in ships; for, Cyrus said, both the King and he had money in abundance, and hence, so far as that point was concerned, it would be possible to man many ships. He then assigned to Lysander all the tribute which came in from his cities and belonged to him personally, and gave him also the balance he had on hand; and, after reminding Lysander how good a friend he was both to the Lacedaemonian state and to him personally, he set out on the journey to his father.

Now Lysander, when Cyrus had thus given over to him all his money and set out, in response to the summons, to visit his sick father, distributed pay to his men and set sail to the Ceramic Gulf, in Caria. There he attacked a city named Cedreiae which was an ally of the Athenians, and on the second day's assault captured it by storm and reduced the inhabitants to slavery; they were a mixture of Greek and barbarian blood. Thence he sailed away to Rhodes. As for the Athenians, they harried the territory of the King, using Samos as a base, and sailed against Chios and Ephesus; they were also making their preparations for battle, and had chosen three generals in addition to the former number—Mendander, Tydeus, and Cephisodotus. Meanwhile Lysander sailed from Rhodes along the coast of Ionia to the Hellespont,

---

1. 405/4 BCE. Some scholars believe that several passages containing dates, lists of officials, and references to events in Sicily were not written by Xenophon but were added to the *Hellenica* by later writers. Although this issue is still not settled, I have placed the passages in question in brackets.

2. Lysander was the most influential Spartan military and political figure in the final years of the Peloponnesian War, being responsible for the final defeat of Athens and the establishment of Spartan imperial rule in the Aegean.

3. Cyrus was the younger son of the Persian king Darius II (424 BCE–404 BCE) and overall governor of Persian territories in western Anatolia during the final years of the Peloponnesian War. He was killed during a revolt against his brother, Artaxerxes II (405/4 BCE–359/58 BCE), in 401 BCE.

in order to prevent the passing out of the grain-ships[4] and to take action against the cities which had revolted from the Lacedaemonians. The Athenians likewise set out thither from Chios, keeping to the open sea; for Asia was hostile to them. But Lysander coasted along from Abydus to Lampsacus, which was an ally of the Athenians; and the people of Abydus and the other cities were at hand on the shore to support him, being commanded by Thorax, a Lacedaemonian. Then they attacked the city and captured it by storm, whereupon the soldiers plundered it. It was a wealthy city, full of wine and grain and all other kinds of supplies. But Lysander let go all the free persons who were captured. Now the Athenians had been sailing in the wake of Lysander's fleet, and they anchored at Elaeus, in the Chersonese,[5] with some hundred and eighty ships. While they were breakfasting there, the news about Lampsacus was reported to them, and they set out immediately to Sestus. From there, as soon as they had provisioned, they sailed to Aegospotami, which is opposite Lampsacus, the Hellespont at this point being about fifteen stadia wide. There they took dinner. And during the ensuing night, when early dawn came, Lysander gave the signal for his men to take breakfast and embark upon their ships, and after making everything ready for battle and stretching the side screens, he gave orders that no one should stir from his position or put out. At sunrise the Athenians formed their ships in line for battle at the mouth of the harbor. Since, however, Lysander did not put out against them, they sailed back again, when it grew late in the day, to Aegospotami.[6] Thereupon Lysander ordered the swiftest of his ships to follow the Athenians and when they had disembarked, to observe what they did, and then to sail back and to report to him; and he did not disembark the men from their vessels until these scout ships had returned. This he did for four days; and the Athenians continued to sail out and offer battle. Meanwhile Alcibiades, who could discern from his castle that the Athenians were moored on an open shore, with no city nearby, and were fetching their provisions from Sestus, a distance of fifteen stadia[7] from their ships, while the enemy, being in a harbor and near a city, had everything needful, told the Athenians that they were not moored in a good place, and advised them to shift their anchorage to Sestus and thus gain a harbor and a city; "for if you are there," he said, "you will be able to fight when you please." The generals, however, and especially Tydeus and Menander, bade him be gone; for they said that they were in command now, not he. So he went away. And now Lysander, on the fifth day the Athenians sailed out against him, told his men, who followed them back, that as soon as they saw that the enemy had disembarked and scattered

---

4. At the end of the fifth century BCE Athens relied for much of its supply of grain on imports from the Black Sea.
5. The Chersonese is the present-day Gallipoli Peninsula on the European side of the Hellespont.
6. The "Goat River." The battle of Aegospotami took place in August 405 BCE.
7. Approximately 1.7 miles. There are approximately eight stades to a mile.

up and down the Chersonese,—and the Athenians did this far more freely every day, not only because they bought their provisions at a distance, but also because they presumed to think lightly of Lysander for not putting out to meet them,—they were to sail back to him and to hoist a shield when midway in their course. And they did just as he had ordered. Straightway Lysander gave a signal to his fleet to sail with all speed, and Thorax with his troops went with the fleet. Now when Conon saw the oncoming attack, he signaled the Athenians to hasten with all their might to their ships. But since his men were scattered here and there, some of the ships had but two banks of oars manned, some but one, and some were entirely empty;[8] Conon's own ship, indeed, and seven others accompanying him, which were fully manned, put to sea in close order, and the Paralus[9] with them, but all the rest Lysander captured on the beach. He also gathered up on the shore most of the men of their crews; some, however, gained the shelter of the neighboring strongholds.

But when Conon, fleeing with his nine ships, realized that the Athenian cause was lost, he put in at Abarnis, the promontory of Lampsacus, and there seized the cruising sails that belonged to Lysander's ships;[10] then he sailed away with eight ships to seek refuge with Evagoras in Cyprus, while the Paralus went to Athens with tidings of what had happened. As for Lysander, he took his prizes and prisoners and everything else back to Lampsacus, the prisoners including Philocles, Adeimantus, and some of the other generals. Furthermore, on the day when he achieved this victory he sent Theopompus, the Milesian pirate, to Lacedaemon to report what had happened, and Theopompus arrived and delivered his message on the third day. After this Lysander gathered together the allies and bade them deliberate regarding the disposition to be made of the prisoners. Thereupon many charges began to be urged against the Athenians, not only touching the outrages they had already committed and what they had voted to do if they were victorious in the battle,—namely, to cut off the right hand of every man taken alive,[11]—but also the fact that after capturing two triremes, one a Corinthian and the other an Andrian, they had thrown the crews overboard to a man. And it was Philocles, one of the Athenian generals, who had thus made away with these men. Many other stories were told, and it was finally resolved to put to death all of the prisoners who were Athenian, with the exception of Adeimantus, because he was the one man who in the Athenian Assembly had opposed the decree in regard to cutting off the hands of captives; he was charged, however, by the people with having betrayed the fleet.

---

8. Being triremes, the Athenian ships needed all three banks of oars to be manned to be fully operational.

9. The Paralus was one of a number—twenty to thirty—of sacred triremes that the Athenians used for public business.

10. Greek warships left their sails on shore to save weight during battle. By seizing the sails of the Spartan ships, Conon prevented the Spartans from mounting an effective pursuit of his ships.

11. According to other sources, the Athenians voted to cut off the right thumb of prisoners so that they could not use an oar or throw a spear.

As to Philocles [who threw overboard the Andrians and Corinthians], Lysander first asked him what he deserved to suffer for having begun outrageous practices toward Greeks, and then had his throat cut.

2.2. After setting in order the affairs of Lampsacus, Lysander sailed against Byzantium and Calchedon. And the people of those cities admitted him, allowing the Athenian garrisons, by the terms of the surrender, to withdraw. And those who had betrayed Byzantium to Alcibiades fled at this time to the Pontus,[12] but afterward they went to Athens and became Athenian citizens. Now the Athenian garrisons, and in fact every other Athenian whom he saw anywhere, Lysander sent home to Athens, giving them safe conduct if they sailed to that one place and not if they went to any other; for he knew that the more people were collected in the city and Piraeus, the more quickly there would be a scarcity of provisions. Then, after leaving Sthenelaus, a Laconian, as governor of Byzantium and Calchedon, he sailed back to Lampsacus and occupied himself with refitting his ships.

It was at night that the Paralus arrived at Athens with tidings of the disaster, and a sound of wailing ran from Piraeus through the long walls to the city, one man passing on the news to another; and during that night no one slept, all mourning, not for the lost alone, but far more for own selves, thinking that they would suffer such treatment as they had visited upon the Melians, colonists of the Lacedaemonians, after reducing them by siege,[13] and upon the Histiaeans and Scionaeans and Toronaeans and Aeginetans and many other Greek peoples. On the following day they convened an Assembly, at which it was resolved to block up all the harbors except one, to repair the walls, to station guards, and in all other respects to get the city ready for a siege. They busied themselves, accordingly, with these matters.

Meanwhile Lysander, sailing out of the Hellespont with two hundred ships, arrived at Lesbos and arranged the affairs of Mytilene and the other cities of the island; and he sent Eteonicus with ten triremes to the places on the Thracian coast, and Eteonicus brought over everything in that region to the side of the Lacedaemonians. Indeed, the rest of the Greek world also had fallen away from the Athenians immediately after the battle, with the exception of Samos; there the people slaughtered the aristocrats and held possession of their city. After this Lysander sent word to Agis,[14] at Decelea, and to Lacedaemon that he was coming with two hundred ships. Thereupon the Lacedaemonians took the field with their whole force and likewise the rest of the Peloponnesians excepting the Argives, at the command of Pausanias, the other king of the Lacedaemonians.[15] And when all had been

---

12. The Black Sea.

13. See Thucydides 5.84, "The Melian Dialogue."

14. Agis II, king of Sparta from 427 BCE to 398 BCE.

15. There were two royal houses at Sparta, each providing one king. Normally, only one king was away from Sparta at any one time. Pausanias (445 BCE–426 BCE and 408 BCE–395 BCE) represented the Agiad royal house and sought to undermine Lysander's influence in Sparta.

gathered together, Pausanias led them to Athens and encamped in the Academy. Meanwhile Lysander, upon reaching Aegina, restored the state to the Aeginetans, gathering together as many of them as he could, and he did the same thing for the Melians also and for all the others who had been deprived of their native states. Then, after laying waste Salamis, he anchored at Piraeus with one hundred and fifty ships and closed the entrance to the harbor against all merchantmen.

Now the Athenians, being thus besieged by land and by sea, knew not what to do, since they had neither ships nor allies nor provisions; and they thought that there was no way out, save only to suffer the pains which they had themselves inflicted, not in retaliation, but in wantonness and unjustly upon the people of small states, for no other single reason than because they were in alliance with the Lacedaemonians. On this account they restored to the disfranchised their political rights and held out steadfastly, refusing to make overtures for peace even though many were dying in the city from starvation. When, however, their provisions had entirely given out, they sent ambassadors to Agis declaring their wish to become allies of the Lacedaemonians while still keeping their walls and Piraeus, and on these terms to conclude a treaty. But Agis bade them go to Lacedaemon, saying that he himself had no authority. And when the ambassadors reported to the Athenians this reply, they sent them to Lacedaemon. But when they were at Sellasia, near Laconia, and the ephors[16] learned from them what proposals they were bringing,—the same, namely, as those which they had presented to Agis,—they directed them to go back again without coming a step farther and, if they really had any desire for peace, to take better counsel before they returned. And when the ambassadors reached home and reported this to the people, despondency descended upon all; for they imagined that they would be reduced to slavery, and that while they were sending another set of ambassadors, many would die of the famine. Nevertheless, no one wanted to make any proposal involving the destruction of the walls; and when Archestratus said in the Council[17] that it was best to make peace with the Lacedaemonians on the terms they offered—and the terms were that they should tear down a portion ten stadia long of each of the two long walls[18]—he was thrown into prison, and a decree was passed forbidding the making of a proposal of this sort.

This being the condition of affairs in Athens, Theramenes[19] said in the Assembly that if they were willing to send him to Lysander, he would find out before he came

---

16. The five highest-elected officials at Sparta. Ephors were elected for one-year terms, and all Spartan citizens were eligible to hold the office.

17. Probably the Council of Five Hundred, whose primary functions were to preside over the Athenian assembly and prepare its agenda, supervise the administration of the various institutions of Athens's government, and review the performance of its officials.

18. About 1.5 miles.

19. Theramenes was an important oligarchic politician at Athens during the Peloponnesian War, being instrumental in the establishment of both the Oligarchy of the Four Hundred in 411 BCE and the Tyranny of the Thirty in 404 BCE.

back whether the Lacedaemonians were insistent in the matter of the walls because they wished to reduce the city to slavery, or in order to obtain a guarantee of good faith. Upon being sent, however, he stayed with Lysander three months and more, waiting for the time when, on account of the failure of provisions, the Athenians would agree to anything and everything which might be proposed. And when he returned in the fourth month, he reported in the Assembly that Lysander had detained him all this time and had then directed him to go to Lacedaemon, saying that he had no authority in the matters concerning which Theramenes asked for information but only the ephors. After this Theramenes was chosen ambassador to Lacedaemon with full power, being at the head of an embassy of ten. Lysander meanwhile sent Aristoteles, an Athenian exile, in company with some Lacedaemonians, to report to the ephors that the answer he had made to Theramenes was that they only had authority in the matter of peace and war. Now when Theramenes and the other ambassadors were at Sellasia and, on being asked with what proposals they had come, replied that they had full power to treat for peace, the ephors thereupon gave orders to summon them to Lace-daemon. When they arrived, the ephors called an Assembly, at which the Corinthians and Thebans in particular, though many other Greeks agreed with them, opposed making a treaty with the Athenians and favored destroying their city. The Lacedae-monians, however, said that they would not enslave a Greek city which had done great service amid the greatest perils that had befallen Greece,[20] and they offered to make peace on these conditions: that the Athenians should destroy the long walls and the walls of Piraeus, surrender all their ships except twelve, allow their exiles to return, count the same people friends and enemies as the Lacedaemonians did, and follow the Lacedaemonians both by land and sea wherever they should lead the way.

So Theramenes and his fellow ambassadors brought back this word to Athens. And as they were entering the city, a great crowd gathered around them, fear-ful that they had returned unsuccessful; for it was no longer possible to delay, on account of the number who were dying of the famine. On the day the ambassadors reported to the Assembly the terms on which the Lacedaemonians offered to make peace; Theramenes acted as spokesman for the embassy, and urged that it was best to obey the Lacedaemonians and tear down the walls. And while some spoke in opposition to him, a far greater number supported him, and it was voted to accept the peace. After this Lysander sailed into Piraeus, the exiles returned, and the Peloponnesians with great enthusiasm began to tear down the walls to the music of flute-girls, thinking that that day was the beginning of freedom for the Greeks.

[So the year ended, in the middle of which Dionysius of Syracuse, the son of Her-mocrates, became tyrant,[21] after the Carthaginians had been defeated in battle by the Syracusans, but had captured Acragas by famine, the Siceliots abandoning the city.]

---

20. The reference is to Athens's role in the war against Persia in 480/79 BCE.
21. Dionysius I was tyrant of Syracuse from 406 BCE to 367 BCE. Acragas was captured by the Carthaginians in 406 BCE.

The Tyranny of the Thirty

2.3. In the following year—[in which was celebrated an Olympiad, wherein Crocinas the Thessalian was victorious in the stadium,[22] Endius being now ephor at Sparta and Pythodorus archon at Athens. Since, however, Pythodorus was chosen during the time of the oligarchy, the Athenians do not use his name to mark the year, but call it "the archonless year."[23] And this oligarchy came into being in the way hereafter described—it was voted by the people to choose thirty men to frame the ancient laws into a constitution under which to conduct the government. And the following men were chosen: Polychares, Critias, Melobius, Hippolochus, Eucleides, Hieron, Mnesilochus, Chremon, Theramenes, Aresias, Diocles, Phaedrias, Chaereleos, Anaetius, Peison, Sophocles, Eratosthenes, Charicles, Onomacles, Theognis, Aeschines, Theogenes, Cleomedes, Erasistratus, Pheidon, Dracontides, Eomathes, Aristoteles, Hippomachus, Mnesitheides.] When this had been done, Lysander sailed off to Samos, while Agis withdrew the land force from Decelea and dismissed the several contingents to their cities.

It was near this date, and at about the time of an eclipse of the sun,[24] that Lycophron of Pherae,[25] who wanted to make himself ruler of all Thessaly, defeated in battle those of the Thessalians who opposed him, namely the Larisaeans and others, and slew many of them.

It was at the same time also that Dionysius, the tyrant of Syracuse, was defeated in battle by the Carthaginians and lost Gela and Camarina.[26] Shortly afterward also the Leontines, who had been dwelling at Syracuse, revolted from Dionysius and the Syracusans and returned to their own city. And immediately thereafter the Syracusan horsemen were dispatched by Dionysius to Catana.

Meanwhile the Samians were being besieged by Lysander on every side, and when, seeing that at first they refused to come to terms, he was on the point of making an attack upon them, they came to an agreement with him that every free person should depart from the city with but one cloak and that all else should be surrendered; and on these terms they withdrew. And Lysander gave over the city and everything therein to the former citizens, and appointed ten rulers to guard it; then he dismissed the naval contingents of the allies to their several cities and sailed home with the Laconian ships to Lacedaemon, taking with him the prows of the captured ships, the triremes from Piraeus except twelve, the crowns which he had received from the cities as gifts to himself individually,

---

22. The stadium was the original and most prestigious Olympic event, a sprint approximately 200 meters or 656 feet in length.

23. 404/3 BCE. Since the Athenian year began in mid-summer, usually July, the Tyranny of the Thirty was established in late summer 404 BCE.

24. The solar eclipse took place on September 3, 404 BCE.

25. Lycophron's career lasted from c. 406 BCE to 390 BCE.

26. Summer 405 BCE.

four hundred and seventy talents[27] in money, being the balance that remained of the tribute money which Cyrus had assigned to him for the prosecution of the war, and whatever else he had obtained during the course of the war. All these things he delivered over to the Lacedaemonians at the close of the summer[28]—[with which ended the twenty-eight years and six months of the war, during which years the eponymous ephors were the following: Aenesias first, in whose term the war began,[29] in the fifteenth year of the thirty years' truce which followed the conquest of Euboea,[30] and after him the following: Brasidas, Isanor, Sostratidas, Exarchus, Agesistratus, Angenidas, Onomacles, Zeuxippus, Pityas, Pleistolas, Cleionomachus, Ilarchus, Leon, Chaerilas, Patesiades, Cleosthenes, Lycarius, Eperatus, Onomantius, Alexippidas, Misgolaïdas, Isias, Aracus, Euarchippus, Pantacles, Pityas, Archytas, and Endius; it was in Endius's term that Lysander sailed home after performing the deeds above described.]

Now at Athens the Thirty had been chosen as soon as the long walls and the walls round Piraeus were demolished; although chosen, however, for the purpose of framing a constitution under which to conduct the government, they continually delayed framing and publishing this constitution, but they appointed a Council[31] and the other magistrates as they saw fit. Then, as a first step, they arrested and brought to trial for their lives persons who, by common knowledge, had made a living in the time of the democracy by acting as informers and had been offensive to the aristocrats;[32] and the Council was glad to pronounce these people guilty, and the rest of the citizens—at least all who were conscious that they were not of the same sort themselves—were not at all displeased. When, however, the Thirty began to consider how they might become free to do just as they pleased with the state, their first act was to send Aeschines and Aristoteles to Lacedaemon and persuade Lysander to help them to secure the sending of a Lacedaemonian garrison, to remain until, as they said, they could put "the scoundrels" out of the way and establish their government; and they promised to maintain this garrison at their own charges. Lysander consented, and helped them to secure the dispatch of the

---

27. A talent was not a coin but a weight equal in value to 6,000 drachmas. Since a drachma was equivalent to the wages of a skilled worker for a day's labor, one talent equaled the pay of a skilled worker for 6,000 days' labor.

28. At this point, Xenophon's continuation of Thucydides's *History of the Peloponnesian War* ended.

29. 431 BCE.

30. The Thirty Years Peace was signed in 446/45 BCE.

31. The "Council" was the Council of Five Hundred, but it reorganized to consist of sympathizers of the new regime.

32. "Informers" or "sycophants" were individuals who were accused of exploiting a law of Solon that allowed any Athenian to bring a suit against another Athenian by maliciously suing rich Athenians on unjustified grounds. They supposedly profited from such suits either by receiving a portion of the fine if they won their case or by accepting a bribe to drop the suit before it went to court.

troops and of Callibius as governor. But when they had got the garrison, they paid court to Callibius in every way, in order that he might approve of everything they did, and as he detailed guardsmen to go with them, they arrested the people whom they wished to reach,—not now "the scoundrels" and persons of little account, but from this time forth the men who, they thought, were least likely to submit to being ignored, and who, if they undertook to offer any opposition, would obtain supporters in the greatest numbers.

Now in the beginning Critias[33] and Theramenes were agreed in their policy and friendly; but when Critias showed himself eager to put many to death, because, for one thing, he had been banished by the democracy, Theramenes opposed him, saying that it was not reasonable to put a man to death because he was honored by the commons, provided he was doing no harm to the aristocrats. "For," said he, "you and I also have said and done many things for the sake of winning the favor of the city." Then Critias (for he still treated Theramenes as a friend) replied that it was impossible for people who wanted to gain power not to put out of the way those who were best able to thwart them. "But if," he said, "merely because we are thirty and not one, you imagine that it is any the less necessary for us to keep a close watch over this government, just as one would if it were an absolute monarchy, you are foolish." But when, on account of the great numbers continually—and unjustly— put to death, it was evident that many were banding together and wondering what the state was coming to, Theramenes spoke again, saying that unless they admitted an adequate number of citizens into partnership with them in the management of affairs, it would be impossible for the oligarchy to endure. Accordingly, Critias and the rest of the Thirty, who were by this time alarmed and feared above all that the citizens would flock to the support of Theramenes, enrolled a body of three thousand, who were to share, as they said, in the government. Theramenes, however, objected to this move also, saying that, in the first place, it seemed to him absurd that, when they wanted to make the best of the citizens their associates, they should limit themselves to three thousand, as though this number must somehow be good men and true and there could neither be excellent men outside this body nor rascals within it. "Besides," he said, "we are undertaking, in my opinion, two absolutely inconsistent things,—to rig up our government on the basis of force and at the same time to make it weaker than its subjects."

This was what Theramenes said. As for the Thirty, they held a review, the Three Thousand assembling in the market place and those who were not on "the roll"[34] in various places here and there; then they gave the order to pile arms and while the men were off duty and away, they sent their Lacedaemonian guardsmen and such

---

33. Critias (c. 460 BCE–403 BCE) was a relative of the philosopher Plato and a close associate of Socrates. He was an important intellectual noted for writing tragedies and holding a favorable view of Sparta.

34. The reference is to Athenians who were not on the list of the Three Thousand.

citizens as were in sympathy with them, seized the arms of all except the Three Thousand, carried them up to the Acropolis, and deposited them in the temple.[35] And now, when this had been accomplished, thinking that they were at length free to do whatever they pleased, they put many people to death out of personal enmity, and many also for the sake of securing their property. The measure that they resolved upon, in order to get money to pay their guardsmen, was that each of their number should seize one of the aliens residing in the city, and that they should put these men to death and confiscate their property. So they bade Theramenes also to seize anyone he pleased; and he replied: "But it is not honorable, as it seems to me," he said, "for people who style themselves the best citizens to commit acts of greater injustice than the informers used to do. For they allowed those from whom they got money to live; but shall we, in order to get money, put to death men who are guilty of no wrong-doing? Are not such acts altogether more unjust than theirs were?" Then the Thirty, thinking that Theramenes was an obstacle to their doing whatever they pleased, plotted against him, and kept accusing him to individual councilors, one to one man and another to another, of injuring the government. And after passing the word to those young men, who seemed most audacious, to be in attendance with daggers hidden under their arms, they convened the Council. Then when Theramenes arrived, Critias arose and spoke as follows:

"Gentlemen of the Council, if anyone among you thinks that more people than is fitting are being put to death, let them reflect that where governments are changed these things always take place; and it is inevitable that those who are changing the government here to an oligarchy should have most numerous enemies, both because the state is the most populous of the Greek states and because the commons have been bred up in a condition of freedom for the longest time. Now we, believing that for men like ourselves and you democracy is a grievous form of government, and convinced that the commons would never become friendly to the Lacedaemonians, our preservers, while the aristocrats would continue ever faithful to them, for these reasons are establishing, with the approval of the Lacedaemonians, the present form of government. And if we find anyone opposed to the oligarchy, so far as we have the power we put him out of the way; but in particular we consider it to be right that, if any one of our own number is harming this order of things, he should be punished.

"Now in fact we find this man Theramenes trying by what means he can, to destroy both ourselves and you. As proof that this is true you will discover, if you consider the matter, that no one finds more fault with the present proceedings than Theramenes here, or offers more opposition when we wish to put some demagogue out of the way. Now if he had held these views from the beginning, he was, to be sure, an enemy, but nevertheless he would not justly be deemed a scoundrel. In fact, however, he was the very man who took the initiative in the policy of establishing a cordial understanding with the Lacedaemonians; he was the very man who began

---

35. The Parthenon.

the overthrow of the democracy, and who urged you most to inflict punishment upon those who were first brought before you for trial; but now, when you and we have manifestly become hateful to the democrats, he no longer approves of what is going on,—just that *he* may get on the safe side again, and that *we* may be punished, not merely as an enemy, but also as a traitor both to you and to ourselves. And treason is a far more dreadful thing than war, inasmuch as it is harder to take precaution against the hidden than against the open danger, and a far more hateful thing, inasmuch as men make peace with enemies and become their trustful friends again, but if they catch a man playing the traitor, they never in any case make peace with that man or trust him thereafter.

"Now to let you know that the man's present doings are nothing new, but that he is, rather, a traitor by nature, I will recall to you his past deeds. This man in the beginning, although he had received honors at the hands of the democracy, was extremely eager, like his father Hagnon,[36] to change democracy into the oligarchy of the Four Hundred,[37] and he was a leader in that government. When, however, he perceived that some opposition to the oligarchy was gathering, he took the lead again—as champion of the democrats against the oligarchs! That is the reason, you know, why he is nicknamed 'Kothornos,' for as the *kothornos*[38] seems to fit both feet, so he faces both ways. But Theramenes, the man who deserves to live ought not to be clever at leading his comrades into dangerous undertakings and then, if any hindrance offers itself, to turn around on the instant, but he ought, as one on shipboard, to hold to his task until they come into a fair breeze. Otherwise, how in the world would sailors reach the port for which they are bound, if they should sail in the opposite direction the moment any hindrance offered itself? It is true, of course, that all sorts of changes in government are attended by loss of life, but you, thanks to your changing sides so easily, share the responsibility, not merely for the slaughter of a large number of oligarchs by the commons, but also for the slaughter of a large number of democrats by the aristocracy. And this Theramenes, you remember, was the man who, although detailed by the generals to pick up the Athenians whose ships were disabled in the battle off Lesbos, failed to do so, and nevertheless was the very one who accused the generals and brought about their death in order that he might save his own life!"[39]

---

36. Hagnon was an important Athenian politician and associate of Pericles, who was responsible for the founding of the Athenian colony of Amphipolis in Thrace in 437/36 BCE.

37. A pro-Spartan oligarchy that seized power in Athens after the failure of the invasion of Sicily and briefly governed the city from September 411 BCE to June 410 BCE.

38. A *kothornos* was a high boot worn by men or women and able to be worn on either foot.

39. The reference is to the battle of Arginousai in 406 BCE in which the Athenians defeated a Spartan fleet but could not rescue the survivors or recover the bodies of the dead because of a storm. Theramenes had been one of the accusers of the generals commanding the fleet who were condemned and executed in an irregular trial authorized by the assembly over the objections of Socrates, who was the presiding officer at the assembly on that day.

"Now when a man clearly shows that he is always looking out for his own advantage and taking no thought for honor or his friends, how in the world can it be right to spare him? Ought we not surely, knowing of his previous changes, to take care that he shall not be able to do the same thing to us also? We therefore arraign him on the charge of plotting against and betraying both ourselves and you. And in proof that what we are thus doing is proper, consider this fact also. The constitution of the Lacedaemonians is, we know, deemed the best of all constitutions. Now in Lacedaemon if one of the ephors should undertake to find fault with the government and to oppose what was being done instead of yielding to the majority, do you not suppose that he would be regarded, not only by the ephors themselves but also by all the rest of the state, as having merited the severest punishment? Even so you, if you are wise, will not spare this Theramenes, but rather yourselves; for to leave him alive would cause many of those who hold opposite views to yours to cherish high thoughts, while to destroy him would cut off the hopes of them all, both within and without the city."

When Critias had so spoken, he sat down; and Theramenes rose and said: "I will mention first, gentlemen, the last thing Critias said against me. He says that I brought about the death of the generals by my accusation. But it was not I, as you know, who began the matter by accusing them; on the contrary, it was they who accused me by stating that although that duty was assigned me by them, I failed to pick up the unfortunates in the battle off Lesbos. I said in my defense that on account of the storm it was not possible even to sail, much less to pick up the men, and it was decided by the state that my plea was a reasonable one, while the generals were clearly accusing themselves. For though they said it was possible to save the men, they nevertheless sailed away and left them to perish. I do not wonder, however, that Critias has misunderstood the matter; for when these events took place, it chanced that he was not here; he was establishing a democracy in Thessaly along with Prometheus and arming the *Penestai*[40] against their masters. God forbid that any of things which he was doing there should come to pass here.

"I quite agree with him, however, on this point, that if anyone is desirous of deposing you from your office and is making strong those who are plotting against you, it is just for him to incur the severest punishment. But I think you can best judge who it is that is doing this, if you will consider the course which each of us two has taken and is now taking. Well then, up to the time when you became members of the Council and magistrates were appointed and the notorious informers were brought to trial, all of us held the same views; but when these Thirty began to arrest men of worth and standing, then I, on my side, began to hold views opposed to theirs. For when Leon the Salaminian[41] was put to death,—a man of capacity, both

---

40. The *Penestai* were an enslaved subject population similar to the Helots in Sparta who worked the estates of the Thessalian aristocracy.
41. According to Plato, Socrates was ordered by the Thirty to arrest Leon, but he refused to do so, apparently to no avail since this passage indicates that Leon was, in fact, executed.

actually and by repute,—although he was not guilty of a single act of wrong-doing, I knew that those who were like him would be fearful, and, being fearful, would be enemies of this government. I also knew, when Niceratus, the son of Nicias, was arrested,—a man of wealth who, like his father, had never done anything to curry popular favor,—that those who were like him would become hostile to us. And further, when Antiphon, who during the war supplied from his own means two fast sailing triremes, was put to death by us, I knew that all those who had been zealous in the state's cause would look upon us with suspicion. I objected, also, when they said that each of us must seize one of the *metics*;[42] for it was entirely clear that if these men were put to death, the whole body of such aliens would become enemies of the government. I objected likewise when they took away from the people their arms, because I thought that we ought not to make the state weak; for I saw that, in preserving us, the purpose of the Lacedaemonians had not been that we might become few in number and unable to do them any service; for if this had been what they desired, it was within their power, by keeping up the pressure of famine a little while longer, to leave not a single man alive. Again, the hiring of guardsmen did not please me, for we might have enlisted in our service an equal number of our own citizens, until we, the rulers, should easily have made ourselves masters of our subjects. And further, when I saw that many in the city were becoming hostile to the government and that many were becoming exiles, it did not seem to me best to banish either Thrasybulus or Anytus or Alcibiades; for I knew that by such measures the opposition would be made strong, if once the commons should acquire capable leaders and if those who wished to be leaders should find a multitude of supporters.

"Now would the man who offers openly this sort of admonition be fairly regarded as a well-wisher, or as a traitor? It is not, Critias, the men who prevent one's making enemies in abundance nor the men who teach one how to gain allies in the greatest numbers,—it is not these, I say, who make one's enemies strong; but it is much rather those who unjustly rob others of property and put to death people who are guilty of no wrong, who, I say, make their opponents numerous and betray not only their friends but also themselves, and all to satisfy their covetousness. And if it is not evident in any other way that what I say is true, look at the matter in this way: do you suppose that Thrasybulus and Anytus[43] and the other exiles would prefer to have us follow here the policy which I am urging by word, or the policy which these men are carrying out in deed? For my part, I fancy that now they believe every spot is full of allies, while if the best element in the state were friendly to us, they would count it difficult even to set foot anywhere in the land! Again, as to his statement that I have a propensity to be always changing sides, consider these facts also: it was

---

42. *Metics* were non-Athenians who lived at Athens either temporarily or permanently and were required to pay a special tax and do military service but were protected by Athenian law and were prominent in Athenian economic life.
43. Possibly the principal accuser of Socrates.

the people itself, as everybody knows, which voted for the government of the Four Hundred, being advised that the Lacedaemonians would trust any form of government sooner than a democracy. But when the Lacedaemonians did not in the least relax their efforts in prosecuting the war, and Aristoteles, Melanthus, Aristarchus, and their fellow generals were found to be building a fort on the peninsula, into which they proposed to admit the enemy and so bring the state under the control of themselves and their oligarchical associates,—if I perceived the plan and thwarted it, is that being a traitor to one's friends?

"He dubs me 'Kothornos,' because, as he says, I try to fit both parties. But for the man who pleases neither party,—what in the name of the gods should we call him? For you in the days of the democracy were regarded as the bitterest of all haters of the commons, and under the aristocracy you have shown yourself the bitterest of all haters of the better classes. But I, Critias, am forever at war with the men who do not think there could be a good democracy until the slaves and those who would sell the state for lack of a drachma should share in the government, and on the other hand I am forever an enemy to those who do not think that a good oligarchy could be established until they should bring the state to the point of being ruled absolutely by a few. But to direct the government in company with those who have the means to be of service, whether with horses or with shields,—this plan I regarded as best in former days and I do not change my opinion now. And if you can mention any instance, Critias, where I joined hands with demagogues or despots and undertook to deprive men of standing of their citizenship, then speak. For if I am guilty either of doing this thing now or ever having done it in the past, I admit that I should justly suffer the very uttermost of all penalties and be put to death."

When with these words he ceased speaking and the Council had shown its good will by applause, Critias, realizing that if he should allow the Council to pass judgment on the case, Theramenes would escape, and thinking that this would be unendurable, went and held a brief consultation with the Thirty, and then went out and ordered the men with the daggers to take their stand at the railing in plain sight of the Council. Then he came in again and said: "Councilors, I deem it the duty of a leader who is what he ought to be, in case he sees that his friends are being deceived, not to permit it. I, therefore, shall follow that course. Besides, these men who have taken their stand here say that if we propose to let a man go who is manifestly injuring the oligarchy, they will not suffer us to do so. Now it is provided in the new laws that while no one of those who are on the roll of the Three Thousand may be put to death without your vote, the Thirty shall have power of life or death over those outside the role. I, therefore," he said, "strike off this man Theramenes from the roll, with the approval of all the Thirty. That being done," he added, "we now condemn him to death."

When Theramenes heard this, he sprang to the altar and said: "And I, sirs," said he, "beg only bare justice,—that it be not within the power of Critias to strike off either me or whomsoever of you he may wish, but rather that both in your case and in mine the judgment may be rendered strictly in accordance with that law which these men have made regarding those on the roll. To be sure," said he, "I know, I swear by the gods, only too well, that this altar will avail me nothing, but I wish to show that these Thirty are not only most unjust toward men, but also most impious toward the gods. But I am surprised at you," he said, "gentlemen of the aristocracy, that you are not going to defend your own rights, especially when you know that my name is not a whit easier to strike off than the name of each of you." At this moment the herald of the Thirty ordered the Eleven to seize Theramenes; and when they came in, attended by their servants and with Satyrus, the most audacious and shameless of them, at the head, Critias said: "We hand over to you," said he, "this man Theramenes, condemned according to the law. Do you, the Eleven, take him and lead him to the proper place and do that which follows."

When Critias had spoken these words, Satyrus dragged Theramenes away from the altar, and his servants lent their aid. And Theramenes, as was natural, called upon gods and men to witness what was going on. But the councilors kept quiet, seeing that the men at the rail were of the same sort as Satyrus and that the space in front of the council-house was filled with the guardsmen, and being well aware that the former had come armed with daggers. So they led the man away through the market-place, while he proclaimed in a very loud voice the wrongs he was suffering. One saying of his that is reported was this: when Satyrus told him that if he did not keep quiet, he would suffer for it, he asked: "Then if I do keep quiet, shall I not suffer?" And when, being compelled to die, he had drunk the hemlock, they said that he threw out the last drops, like a man playing *kottabos*,[44] and exclaimed: "Here's to the health of my beloved Critias." Now I am not unaware of this, that these are not sayings worthy of record; still, I deem it admirable in the man that when death was close at hand, neither self-possession nor the spirit of playfulness departed from his soul.

2.4. So, then, Theramenes died; but the Thirty, thinking that now they could play the tyrant without fear, issued a proclamation forbidding those who were outside the roll to enter the city and evicted them from their estates, in order that they themselves and their friends might have these people's lands. And when they fled to Piraeus, they drove many of them away from there also, and filled both Megara and Thebes with the refugees.

Presently Thrasybulus set out from Thebes with about seventy companions and seized Phyle,[45] a strong fortress. And the Thirty marched out from the city with the Three Thousand and the cavalry, the weather being very fine indeed. When they reached Phyle, some of the young men were so bold as to attack the fortress at once, but they accomplished nothing and suffered some wounds themselves before they

---

44. *Kottabos* was a game in which guests seated on couches at a party threw wine dregs from their cups at a target in the center of the dining room.
45. Phyle was a fortress in northern Attica guarding the main road from Athens to Thebes in Boeotia. Thrasybulus and the exiles seized Phyle in winter, 404/3 BCE.

retired. And while the Thirty were planning to invest the place, so as to force them to surrender by shutting off their avenues for receiving provisions, a very heavy snow storm came on during the night and continued on the following day. So they came back to the city in the snow, after losing a goodly number of their camp followers by the attacks of the men in Phyle. Then the Thirty, knowing that the enemy would also gather plunder from the farms if there were no force to protect them, sent out all but a few of the Laconian guardsmen and two divisions of the cavalry to the outlying districts about fifteen stadia[46] from Phyle. These troops made their camp in a bushy spot and proceeded to keep guard. Now by this time about seven hundred men were gathered at Phyle, and during the night Thrasybulus marched down with them; and about three or four stadia[47] from the guardsmen he had his troops ground their arms and keep quiet. Then when it was drawing toward day and the enemy were already getting up and going away from their camp withersoever each had to go, and the grooms were keeping up a hubbub as they curried their horses, at this moment Thrasybulus and men picked up their arms and charged on the run. They struck down some of the enemy and turned them all to flight, pursuing them for six or seven stadia;[48] and they killed more than one hundred and twenty of the hoplites, and among the cavalry Nicostratus, nicknamed "the beautiful," and two more besides, catching them while still in their beds. Then after returning from the pursuit and erecting a trophy and packing up all the arms and baggage they had captured, they went back to Phyle. And when the cavalry from the city came to rescue, there were none of the enemy left to be seen; so after waiting until after their relatives had taken up the bodies of the dead, they returned to the city.

After this, the Thirty, deeming their government no longer secure, formed a plan to appropriate Eleusis,[49] so as to have a place of refuge if it should prove necessary. Accordingly Critias and the rest of the Thirty, having issued orders to the cavalry to accompany them, went to Eleusis. There they held a review of the townspeople under guard of the cavalry, pretending that they wanted to know how numerous they were and how large an additional garrison they would require, and then ordered them all to register; and each man when he had registered had to pass out by the gate in the town wall in the direction of the sea. Meanwhile they had stationed the cavalry on the shore on either side of the gate, and as each man passed out their servants bound him fast. And when all had thus been seized, they ordered Lysimachus, the cavalry commander, to take them to Athens and turn them over to the Eleven. On the following day they summoned to the Odeum[50] the hoplites who

---

46. Almost two miles.
47. Almost half a mile.
48. Almost a mile.
49. Eleusis was the westernmost town in Attica, near the border with Megara.
50. The Odeum was a roofed concert hall modeled after the royal tent of the Persian Great king that was built by Pericles below the south side of the Acropolis.

were on the roll and the cavalry also. Then Critias rose and said: "We, gentlemen," said he, "are establishing this government no less for you than for ourselves. Therefore you must vote condemnation of the Eleusinians who have been seized, that you may have the same hopes and fears as we." Then he showed them a place and bade them cast their ballots therein, in plain sight of everybody. Now the Laconian guardsmen were in one half of the Odeum, fully armed; and these proceedings were pleasing also to such of the citizens as cared only for their own advantage.

Soon after this Thrasybulus took the men of Phyle, who had now gathered to the number of about one thousand and came by night to Piraeus.[51] When the Thirty learned of this, they at once set out against him, with the Laconian guardsmen and their own cavalry and hoplites; then they advanced along the carriage road which leads up to Piraeus. And for a time the men from Phyle tried to prevent their coming up, but when they saw that the line of the town wall, extensive as it was, need a large force for its defense, whereas they were not yet numerous, they gathered in a compact body on the hill of Munichia.[52] And the men from the city, when they came to the market place of Hippodamus,[53] first formed themselves in line of battle, so that they filled the road which leads to the temple of Artemis of Munichia and the sanctuary of Bendis;[54] and they made a line not less than fifty shields in depth; then, in this formation, they advanced up the hill. As for the men from Phyle, they too filled the road, but they made a line not more than ten hoplites in depth. Behind the hoplites, however, were stationed peltasts and light javelin-men and behind them the stone-throwers. And of these there were many, for they came from the neighborhood.

And now, while the enemy were advancing, Thrasybulus ordered his men to ground their shields and did the same himself, though still keeping the rest of his arms, and then took his stand in the midst of them and spoke as follows: "Fellow citizens, I wish to inform some of you and to remind others that those who form the right wing of the approaching force are the very men whom you turned to flight and pursued four days ago, but the men upon the extreme left—they, yes they, are the Thirty, who robbed us of our city when we were guilty of no wrong, and drove us from our homes, and proscribed those who were dearest to us. But now, behold, they have found themselves in a situation in which they never expected to be, but we always prayed that they might be. For with arms in our hands we stand face to face with them; and the gods, because once we were seized while dining or sleeping or

---

51. The battle of Piraeus and the overthrow of the Thirty took place in spring 403 BCE.
52. Munichia was a hill overlooking the harbor of Piraeus, which was strategically located to control Piraeus.
53. Hippodamus of Miletus was a fifth-century BCE town-planner who was famous for the invention of the grid street plan and was responsible for planning the Piraeus.
54. A Thracian goddess, possibly a huntress like Artemis, who was introduced to Athens in the second half of the fifth century BCE.

trading, because some of us also were banished when we were not only guilty of no offence, but were not even in the city, are manifestly fighting on our side. For in fair weather they send a storm, when it is to our advantage, and when we attack, they grant us, though we are few in number and our enemies are many, to set up trophies of victory; and now in like manner they have brought us to a place where the men before you, because they are marching up hill, cannot throw spears and javelins over the heads of those in front of them, while we, throwing both spears and javelins and stones downhill, shall reach them and strike down many. And though one would have supposed that we should have to fight with their front ranks at least on even terms, yet in fact, if you let fly your missiles with a will, as you should, no one will miss his man when the road is full of them, and they in their efforts to protect themselves will be continually skulking under their shields. You will therefore be able just as if they were blind men, to strike them wherever you please and then leap upon them and overthrow them. And now, comrades, we must so act that each man shall feel in his breast that he is chiefly responsible for the victory. For victory, God willing, will now give back to us country and homes, freedom and honors, children, to such as have them, and wives. Happy, indeed, are those of us who shall win the victory and live to behold the gladdest day of all! And happy he who is slain; for no one, however rich he may be, will gain a monument so glorious. Now, when the right moment comes, I will strike up the Paean;[55] and when we call Enyalius[56] to our aid, then let us all, moved by one spirit, take vengeance upon these men for the outrages we have suffered."

After saying these words and turning about to face the enemy, he kept quiet; for the seer bade them not to attack until one of their own number was either killed or wounded. "But as soon as that happens," he said, "we shall lead on, and to you who follow will come victory, but death methinks to me." And his saying did not prove false, for when they had taken up their shields, he, as though led on by a kind of fate, leaped forth first of all, fell upon the enemy, and was slain, and he lies buried at the ford of the Cephisus; but the others were victorious, and pursued the enemy as far as the level ground. In this battle fell two of the Thirty, Critias and Hippomachus, one of the Ten who ruled in Piraeus, Charmides, the son of Glaucon,[57] and about seventy of the others. And the victors took possession of their arms, but they did not strip off the tunic of any citizen. When this had been done and while they were giving back the bodies of the dead, many on either side mingled and talked with one another. And Cleocritus, the herald of the initiated, a man with a very fine voice, obtained silence and said: "Fellow citizens, why do you drive us out of the city? Why do you wish to kill us? For we never did you any harm, but we have shared with you in the most solemn rites and sacrifices and the most splendid festivals, we have been

---

55. A choral song addressed to Apollo, sung often at the beginning of a battle.
56. The war god Ares.
57. Charmides was an uncle of the philosopher Plato.

companions in the dance and schoolmates and comrades in arms, and we have braved many dangers both by land and by sea in defense of the common safety and freedom of us both. In the name of the gods of our fathers and mothers, in the name of our ties of kinship and marriage and comradeship,—for all these many of us share with one another,—cease, out of shame before gods and men, to sin against your fatherland, and do not obey those most accursed Thirty, who for the sake of their private gain have killed in eight months more Athenians almost, than all the Peloponnesians in ten years of war. And when we might live in peace as fellow citizens, these men bring upon us war with one another, a war most utterly shameful and intolerable, utterly unholy and hated by both gods and men. Yet for all that, be well assured that for some of those now slain by our hands not only you, but we also have wept bitterly."

Thus he spoke; but the surviving officials of the oligarchy, partly because their followers were hearing such things, led them back to the city. On the following day the Thirty, utterly dejected and with but few adherents left, held their session in the council-chamber; and as for the Three Thousand, wherever their several detachments were stationed, everywhere they began to quarrel with one another. For all those who had done any act of especial violence and were therefore fearful, urged strenuously that they ought not to yield to the men in Piraeus; while those who were confident that they had done no wrong, argued in their own minds and set forth to the others that there was no need of their suffering these evils, and they said that they ought not to obey the Thirty or allow them to ruin the state. In the end they voted to depose the Thirty and choose others. And they chose ten, one from each tribe.

The Thirty thereupon retired to Eleusis; and the Ten, with the aid of the cavalry commanders, took care of the men in the city, who were in a state of great disquiet and distrust of one another. In fact, even the cavalry did guard duty by night, being quartered in the Odeum and keeping with them both their horses and their shields; and such was the suspicion that prevailed, that they patrolled along the walls from evening onward with their shields, and toward dawn with their horses, fearing continually that they might be attacked by parties of men from Piraeus. The latter, who were now numerous and included all sorts of people, were engaged in making shields, some of wood, others of wicker-work, and in painting them. And having given pledges that whoever fought with them should be accorded equality in taxation with citizens even if they were foreigners, they marched forth before ten days had passed, a large body of hoplites with numerous light troops; they also got together about seventy horsemen; and they made forays and collected wood and produce, and then came back to spend the night in Piraeus. As for the men in the city, none of them went forth from the walls under arms except the cavalry, who sometimes captured foraging parties made up of the men from Piraeus and inflicted losses upon their main body. They also fell in with some people of Aexone who were going to their own farms after provisions; and Lysimachus, the cavalry commander, put these men to the sword, although they pleaded earnestly and many of the cavalrymen were much opposed to the proceeding. In retaliation, the men in Piraeus killed one of the cavalrymen, Callistratus, of the tribe of Leontis, having captured him in the country. For by this time they were very confident, so that they even made attacks upon the wall of the city. And perhaps it is proper to mention also the following device of the engineer in the city; when he learned that the enemy were intending to bring up their siege-engines by the race course which leads from the Lyceum, he ordered all his teams to haul stones each large enough to load a wagon and drop them at whatever spot in the course each driver pleased. When this had been done, each single one of the stones caused the enemy a great deal of trouble.

And now, when the Thirty in Eleusis sent ambassadors to Lacedaemon, and likewise those in the city who were on the roll, asked for aid on the plea that the commons had revolted from the Lacedaemonians, Lysander, calculating that it was possible to blockade the men in Piraeus both by land and by sea and to force them to a quick surrender if they were cut off from provisions, lent his assistance to the ambassadors, with the result that a hundred talents was loaned to the Athenian oligarchs and that Lysander himself was sent out as governor on land and his brother Libys as admiral of the fleet. Accordingly, Lysander proceeded to Eleusis and busied himself with gathering a large force of Peloponnesian hoplites; meanwhile the admiral kept guard on the sea, to prevent any supplies from coming in by water to the besieged; so that the men in Piraeus were soon in difficulties again, while the men in the city again had their turn of being confident, in reliance upon Lysander. While matters were proceeding in this way, Pausanias the king, seized with envy of Lysander, because, by accomplishing this project, he would not only win fame but also make Athens his own, persuaded three of the ephors and led forth a Lacedaemonian army. And all the allies likewise followed with him, excepting the Boeotians and the Corinthians; and the plea of these was that they did not think they would be true to their oaths if they took the field against the Athenians when the latter were doing nothing in violation of the treaty; in fact, however, they acted as they did because they supposed that the Lacedaemonians wanted to make the territory of the Athenians their own sure possession.

So Pausanias encamped on the plain which is called Hailpedium, near Piraeus, himself commanding the right wing, while Lysander and his mercenaries formed the left. Then, sending ambassadors to the men in Piraeus, Pausanias bade them disperse to their homes; and when they refused to obey, he attacked them, at least so far as to raise the war-cry, in order that it might not be evident that he felt kindly toward them. And when they had retired without accomplishing anything by his attack, on the next day he took two regiments of the Lacedaemonians and three tribes of the Athenian cavalry and proceeded along the shore to the Still Harbor, looking to see where Piraeus could best be shut off by a wall. As he was returning, some of the enemy attacked him and caused him trouble, whereupon, becoming angry, he ordered the cavalry to charge upon them at full speed, and the infantrymen within ten years of military age to follow the cavalry; while he himself with the rest of his troops came along in the rear. And they killed nearly thirty of the enemy's light troops and pursued the rest to the theater in Piraeus. There, as it chanced, the whole body of the light troops and likewise the hoplites of the men in Piraeus were arming themselves. And the light troops rushing forth at once, set to throwing javelins, hurling stone, shooting arrows, and discharging slings; then the Lacedaemonians, since many of them were being wounded and they were hard pressed, gave ground, though still facing the enemy; and at this the latter attacked much more vigorously. In this attack Chaeron and Thibracus, both of them polemarchs, were slain, and Lacrates, the Olympic victor, and other Lacedaemonians who lie buried before the gates of Athens in the Cerameicus.[58] Now Thrasybulus and the rest of his troops—that is, the hoplites—when they saw the situation, came running to lend aid, and quickly formed in line, eight deep, in front of their comrades. And Pausanias, being hard pressed and retreating about four or five stadia to a hill, sent orders to the Lacedaemonians and to the allies to join him. There he formed an extremely deep phalanx and led the charge against the Athenians. The Athenians did indeed accept battle at close quarters; but the in the end some of them were pushed into the mire at the marsh of Halae and others gave way; and about one hundred and fifty of them were slain.

Thereupon Pausanias set up a trophy and returned to his camp; and despite what had happened he was not angry with them, but sent secretly and instructed the men in Piraeus to send ambassadors to him and the ephors who were with him, telling them also what proposals these ambassadors should offer; and they obeyed him. He also set about dividing the men in the city, and gave directions that as many of them as possible should gather together and come to him and the ephors and say that they had no desire to wage war with the men in Piraeus, but rather to be reconciled with them and in common with them to be friends of the Lacedaemonians. Now Naucleidas also, who was an ephor, was pleased to hear this. For, as it is customary for two of the ephors to be with a king on a campaign, so in this instance Naucleidas and one other were present, and both of them held to the policy of Pausanias rather than to that of Lysander. For this reason they eagerly sent to Lacedaemon both the envoys from Piraeus, having the proposals for peace with the Lacedaemonians, and the envoys from the city party as private individuals, namely Cephisophon and Meletus.[59] When, however, these men had departed for Lacedaemon, the authorities in the city also proceeded to send ambassadors, with message that they surrendered both the walls which they possessed and themselves to the Lacedaemonians, to do with them as they wished; and they said they counted it only fair that the men in Piraeus, if they claimed to be friends of the Lacedaemonians, should in like manner surrender Piraeus and Munichia. When the ephors and the members of the Lacedaemonian Assembly had heard all the ambassadors, they dispatched fifteen men to Athens and commissioned them, in conjunction with Pausanias, to effect a reconciliation in the best way they could. And they effected a reconciliation on these terms, that the two parties should be at peace with one another and that

---

58. The "Potters' District," a section in the northwest of Athens that contained a major cemetery including official public burials.

59. Meletus may be identical with the accuser of Socrates of the same name.

every man should depart to his home except the members of the Thirty and of the Eleven, and of the Ten who had ruled in Piraeus. They also decided that if any of the men in the city were afraid, they should settle in Eleusis.

When these things had been accomplished, Pausanias disbanded his army and the men from Piraeus went up to the Acropolis under arms and offered sacrifice to Athena. When they had come down, the generals convened an Assembly. There Thrasybulus spoke as follows: "I advise you," he said, "men of the city, to 'know yourselves.' And you would best learn to know yourselves were you to consider what grounds you have for arrogance, that you should undertake to rule over us. Are you more just? That the commons, though poorer than you, never did you any wrong for the sake of money; while you, though richer than any of them, have done many disgraceful things for the sake of gain. But since you can lay no claim to justice, consider then whether it is courage that you have a right to pride yourselves upon. And what better test could there be of this than the way we made war upon one another? Well then, would you say that you are superior in intelligence, you who having a wall, arms, money, and the Peloponnesians as allies, have been worsted by men who had none of these? Is it the Lacedaemonians, then, think you, that you may pride yourselves upon? How so? Why, they have delivered you up to this outraged populace, just as men fasten a clog upon the necks of snapping dogs and deliver them up to keepers, and now have gone away and left you. Nevertheless, my comrades, I am not the man to ask you to violate any one of the pledges to which you have sworn, but I ask you rather to show this virtue also, in addition to your other virtues,—that you are true to your oaths and are god-fearing men." When he had said this and more to the same effect, and had told them that there was no need of their being disturbed, but that they had only to live under the laws that had previously been in force, he dismissed the Assembly.

So at that time they appointed their magistrates and proceeded to carry on their government; but at a later period, on learning that the men at Eleusis were hiring mercenary troops, they took the field with their whole force against them, put to death their generals when they came for a conference, and then, by sending to the others their friends and kinsmen, persuaded them to become reconciled. And, pledged as they were under oath, that in very truth they would not remember past grievances, the two parties even to this day live together as fellow citizens and the commons abide by their oaths.[60]

---

60. The amnesty of 403 BCE was unique in Greek history. One result of it was that because suits against persons believed complicit with the Thirty were forbidden, such persons were charged with other offenses. Socrates, for example, was charged with "impiety and corrupting the youth of Athens," although it was well known that his real offense was his friendship with members of the Thirty, such as Critias and Charmides.

CHAPTER 4

Aristotle, *The Constitution of Athens*

The historical section of The Constitution of Athens *is not just a chronicle of Athenian history. Besides providing basic information on Athenian history, its author, probably Aristotle, also intended to trace the stages through which Athenian government passed before reaching the form of democracy that existed in his own time, namely, the second half of the fourth century BCE. The author identified eleven such stages or changes. The translated sections treat the five critical stages from the emergence of the earliest form of democracy due to the reforms of Solon at the beginning of the sixth century BCE to the appearance of the so-called radical democracy of the fifth century BCE following the reforms of Ephialtes in the late 460s BCE.*

THE REFORMS OF SOLON

5. While this system[1] prevailed in the state and the common people were serving as slaves to the rich, the people rose up against the upper class. The struggle was intense, and the two sides had fought each other for a long time when by mutual agreement they chose Solon as their mediator and leader and turned the state over to his control.[2] He had already composed an elegy that began "I look on, and my heart is filled with grief when I see the oldest land of the Ionian world being laid waste." In this poem he fights both for and against each faction, evaluating the good and weak points of either side. He then urges both parties to end their dispute.

Solon was by birth and reputation one of the most distinguished men in the state, but in wealth and occupation he belonged to the middle class. This can be deduced from many facts and also from Solon's own testimony in the following words of a poem in which he urges the wealthy not to demand too much for themselves: "You who have gained an ocean of wealth, hold back the powerful greed in your breasts, fix your proud ambition on moderation, set your spirit on control, for we will not give way, nor will all go easily for you."

---

1. The reference is to the organization of Athens after the reforms of the city's first lawgiver, Draco, which was in force from c. 621 BCE until the archonship of Solon in 594 BCE.
2. Solon was appointed sole archon in 594 BCE.

And as a whole, he attaches the blame for the civil warfare on the wealthy and, as he states at the beginning of his poem, he always feared love of money and arrogance of mind, making it clear that these had been the causes of the war between factions of citizens.

6. Once in control of the state, Solon freed the people by forbidding loans on the person of the debtor for both the present and the future. He proclaimed laws and enacted the cancellation of debts, both private and public, a measure that they call the *seisachtheia* (shaking off of burdens), since their burden had been lifted.[3] With regard to these matters, some people seek to slander Solon. For there came a time when, as he was about to proclaim the *seisachtheia*, he informed some of his friends in advance of his plans, and when he did so, according to the version of the popular party, his friends were enriched, but, according to those wishing to slander him, he himself shared in the gain. For these people borrowed money and bought a great deal of land, and soon after, when the cancellation of debts was announced, they suddenly became very rich. This is said to be the origin of those who were viewed as being "of ancient wealth."

Nevertheless, the version of the friends of the people appears the more credible, since it is not likely that in other respects Solon should have been so moderate and public spirited that, when he could have subdued all others and set himself up as a tyrant, he preferred the criticism of both parties and valued his honor and the common good of the state higher than his personal enrichment.

7. Next, Solon drew up a constitution for Athens and enacted new laws; the ordinances of Draco ceased to be used, with the exception of those relating to murder.[4] The laws were inscribed on wooden stands and set up in the King's Porch, and all swore to obey them. The nine Archons[5] took an oath, declaring that they would dedicate a golden statue if they should transgress any of them. This is the

---

3. The "burdens" are those connected to people called *hectemors* ("sixth-parters") because, according to Aristotle (chapter 2), "for this rent [sc. 1/6 of their crops] they worked the fields of the rich." How people became hectemors is not certain, but it is clear that if they failed to pay their rent, they and their families could be enslaved and even sold.

4. The principal innovations of Draco's homicide law were two: requiring a trial in cases of homicide if families could not agree on compensation for the victim instead of allowing personal retribution, which might set off a feud, and introducing the distinction between intentional and unintentional killing in homicide cases. The death penalty was allowed only in the case of intentional killing, while exile was the severest penalty permitted in the case of the latter.

5. The Archons (rulers) served for one-year terms and were the highest magistrates in Athens. The nine Archons were the Archon after whom years were named, the Basileus or king Archon who was Athens's chief religious official, the Polemarch or war Archon who led the army until the early fifth century BCE, and six Thesmothetai, law determiners, whose functions were primarily judicial.

origin of the oath to that effect, which they take to the present day. Solon designed his laws to endure for a hundred years, and the following was the fashion in which he organized the constitution.

He divided the population according to property into four classes, just as it had been divided before—that is, *Pentacosiomedimni* (500 bushel men),[6] *Hippeis* (Knights), Zeugitae, and Thetes (*sing.* Thes).[7] The various magistracies, namely, the nine Archons, the Treasurers, the *Poletae* (Commissioners for Public Contracts), the Eleven,[8] and Clerks he assigned to the *Pentacosiomedimni*, the Knights, and the Zeugitae, giving offices to each class in proportion to the value of their ratable property. To those who ranked among the Thetes he gave nothing but a place in the Assembly and on the juries. A man ranked as a *Pentacosiomedimnus* if from his own land he made five hundred measures, whether liquid or solid. A man ranked as a Knight if he made three hundred measures—or, as some say, could maintain a horse. To support this latter definition they cite the name of the class *Hippeis* (Knight) and also some votive offerings of early times, for on the Acropolis there is a votive offering, a statue of Diphilus, bearing this inscription:

> The son of Diphilus, known as Athenion, rose from the ranks of the Thetes
> to become a Knight. As a thank offering for this promotion, he brought to the
> gods this sculpture of a horse.

This horse stands in evidence beside the man, implying that this was what was meant by belonging to the rank of Knight. At the same time it seems reasonable to suppose that this class, like the *Pentacosiomedimni*, was defined by the possession of an income of a certain number of measures. Those who ranked as Zeugitae made two hundred measures, liquid or solid; the rest ranked as Thetes, and were not eligible for any office. Hence it is that even at the present day, when a candidate for any office is asked to what class he belongs, no one would think of saying that he belonged to the Thetes.

8. The elections to the various offices Solon enacted should be by lot, from candidates selected by each of the tribes. For the nine archonships, each tribe selected ten candidates, among whom the lot was cast. Hence it is still the custom for each tribe to choose ten candidates by lot, and then the lot is again cast among these. A proof that Solon regulated the elections to office according to the property classes may be found in the law still in force with regard to the Treasurers, which enacts that they shall be chosen from the *Pentacosiomedimni*.

---

6. A *medimnos* was a dry measure equal to about 110 pints or 52.2 liters.

7. Thetes were free individuals who were either landless or whose farms were too small to support a family and had to supplement their income by wage labor.

8. The Eleven were in charge of public prisons and the city's executioners.

Such was Solon's legislation with respect to the nine Archons, whereas in early times the Council of the Areopagus[9] summoned suitable persons according to its own judgment and appointed them for the year to the several offices. There were four tribes, as before, and four tribe-kings. Each tribe was divided into three Trittyes (thirds), with twelve Naucraries in each. The Naucraries had officers of their own called Naucrari,[10] whose duty it was to superintend the current receipts and expenditures. Thus it is that among the laws of Solon that are now obsolete, it is repeatedly written that the Naucrari are to receive and to spend out of the Naucraric fund. Solon also appointed a Council of four hundred, a hundred from each tribe; but he assigned to the Council of the Areopagus the duty of superintending the laws, acting as before as the guardian of the constitution in general. It kept watch over the affairs of the state in most of the more important matters and corrected offenders, with full powers to inflict either fines or personal punishment. The money received in fines it brought up into the Acropolis, without assigning the reason for the penalty.

It also tried those who conspired to overthrow the state, Solon having enacted a process of impeachment to deal with such offenders. Further, since he saw the state often engaged in internal disputes, while many of the citizens from sheer indifference accepted whatever might turn up, he made a law with express reference to such people, enacting that anyone who in a time of civil unrest did not take up arms with any party, ceased to play any part in the state.

9. Such, then, was his legislation concerning the magistracies. There are three points in the constitution of Solon that are agreed to be its most democratic features: first and foremost, the prohibition of loans on the security of the debtor's person; second, the right of every person who so willed to claim redress on behalf of anyone to whom wrong was being done; and third, the institution of the appeal to the jury courts.

It is to this last, they say, that the masses have owed their strength most of all, because when the democracy is master of the voting power, it is master of the constitution. Moreover, since the laws were not drawn up in simple and explicit terms (but like the one concerning inheritances and wards of state), disputes inevitably occurred, and the courts had to decide in every matter, whether public or private. Some people in fact believe that Solon deliberately made the laws unclear, in order that the final decision might be in the hands of the people. This, however, is not probable, and the reason no doubt was that it is impossible to attain the ideal of perfection when framing a law in general terms. We must judge his intentions, not

---

9. The "Council of the Areopagus," which consisted of ex-Archons, met on the Mount of Ares, an outcrop of rock near the Acropolis sacred to the war god Ares from whom it and the council took their names.
10. Probably "shipmasters," which suggests that they were originally officials in charge of districts required to provide ships during wars.

from the actual results in the present day, but from the general tenor of the rest of his legislation.

10. These are agreed to be the democratic features of his laws; but in addition, before the period of his legislation, he first carried through his abolition of debts and then his increase in the standards of weights and measures and of the currency. During his administration the measures were made larger than those of Pheidon, and the mina, which previously had a standard of seventy drachmas, was raised to the full hundred.[11] The standard coin in earlier times was the two-drachma piece. He also made weights corresponding to the coinage, with sixty-three minas going to the talent, the odd three minas being distributed among the staters and other values.

11. When he had completed his organization of the constitution in the manner described, he found himself beset by people coming to him and harassing him about his laws, criticizing here and questioning there until, as he wished neither to alter what he had decided nor yet to be an object of ill will to everyone by remaining in Athens, he set off on a journey to Egypt with the combined objects of trade and travel, letting it be known that he would not return for ten years. He considered that it was not right for him to expound the laws in person, but that everyone should obey them just as they were written.

Many members of the upper class had been estranged from him on account of his abolition of debts, and both classes were alienated through their disappointment at the condition of things that he had created. The mass of the people had expected him to make a complete redistribution of all property, whereas the upper class hoped he would restore everything to its former position, or at any rate make only a small change. Solon, however, had resisted both classes. He might have made himself a tyrant by attaching himself to whichever party he chose, but he preferred, though at the cost of incurring the enmity of both, to be the savior of his country and the ideal lawgiver.

12. The truth of this view of Solon's policy is established both by common consent and by the mention he has himself made of the matter in his poems. Thus:

> I gave to the mass of the people such rank as befitted their need,
> I took not away their honor, and I granted naught to their greed;
> While those who were rich in power, who in wealth were glorious and great,

---

11. Aristotle mistakenly believed that Solon inflated the value of Athenian coins by reducing the amount of silver in the standard two drachma coin so that one mina in the system supposedly established by the seventh-century BCE king of Argos, Pheidon, which was used in the Peloponnesus and was equal to 70 drachmas (= 35 two drachma coins) would be equal to 100 drachmas (= 50 lighter two drachma coins). Actually, Athens did not mint coins at the time of Solon's reforms, so that what he may have done was standardize the weights and measures used at Athens.

I bethought me that naught should befall them unworthy of their splendor and state;
So I stood with my shield outstretched, and both were safe in its sight,
And I would not that either should triumph, when the triumph was not with right.

Again he declares how the mass of the people ought to be treated:

But thus will the people best the voice of their leaders obey,
When neither too slack is the rein, nor violence holds sway;
For indulgence breeds a child—the presumption that spurns control,
When riches too great are poured upon men of unbalanced soul.

And again elsewhere he speaks about the people who wished to redistribute the land:

So they came in search of plunder, and their cravings knew no bound,
Every one among them deeming endless wealth would here be found.
And that I with flattering smoothness hid a cruel mind within.
Fondly then and vainly dreamt they; now they raise an angry din,
And they glare askance in anger, and the light within their eyes
Burns with hostile flames upon me. Yet therein no justice lies.
All I promised, fully wrought I with the gods at hand to cheer,
Naught beyond in folly ventured. Never to my soul was dear
With a tyrant's force to govern, nor to see the good and base
Side by side in equal portion share the rich home of our race.

Once more he speaks of the abolition of debts and of those who before were in servitude, but were released owing to the *seisachtheia*:

Of all the aims for which I summoned forth
The people, was there one I compassed not?
You, when slow time brings justice in its train,
O mighty mother of the Olympian gods,
Dark Earth, you best can witness from whose breast
I swept the pillars broadcast-planted there,[12]
And made you free, who had been slave of yore.
And many a man whom fraud or law had sold
Far from his god-built land, an outcast slave,
I brought again to Athens; yes, and some,

---

12. The pillars or *horoi* were stone markers which named the person to whom the hectemor, who worked the land, had to pay his rent. By removing the pillars, Solon canceled the obligation to pay the rent and returned full title to the land to the hectemor.

Exiles from home through debt's oppressive load,
Speaking no more the dear Athenian tongue,
But wandering far and wide, I brought again;
And those that here in vilest slavery
Crouched beneath a master's frown, I set them free.
Thus might and right were yoked in harmony,
Since by the force of law I won my ends
And kept my promise. Equal laws I gave
To evil and to good, with even hand
Drawing straight justice for the lot of each.
But had another held the goad as
One in whose heart was guile and greediness,
He had not kept the people back from strife.
For had I granted, now what pleased the one,
Then what their foes devised in counterpoise,
Of many a man this state had been bereft.
Therefore I showed my might on every side,
Turning at bay like a wolf among the hounds.

And again he reviles both parties for their grumblings in the times that followed:

Nay, if one must lay blame where blame is due,
Were it not for me, the people never had set
Their eyes upon these blessings even in dreams;
While greater men, the men of wealthier life,
Should praise me and should court me as their friend.

For had any other man, he says, received this exalted post:

He had not kept the people back, nor ceased
Till he had robbed the richness of the milk.
But I stood forth a landmark in the midst,
And barred the foes from battle.

THE TYRANNY OF PEISISTRATUS AND HIS SONS

13. Such then, were Solon's reasons for leaving the country. Even after his departure, the city was still torn by divisions. For four years, they did indeed live in peace; but in the fifth year (590/89 BCE) after Solon's government they were unable

to elect an Archon[13] on account of their dissensions, and again four years later (586/85 BCE) they elected no Archon for the same reason. Subsequently, after a similar period had elapsed, Damasias was elected Archon; he governed for two years and two months (582/81 BCE to 580/79 BCE) until he was forcibly expelled from office.

After this it was agreed, as a compromise, to elect ten Archons—five from the Eupatridae,[14] three from the Agroeci (farmers), and two from the Demiurgi (artisans)—and they ruled for the year following Damasias.[15] It is clear from this that the Archon was at the time the magistrate who possessed the greatest power, since it is always in connection with this office that conflicts are seen to arise. But altogether they were in a continual state of internal disorder. Some found the cause and justification of their discontent in the abolition of debts because they had been reduced to poverty; others were dissatisfied with the political constitution because it had undergone a revolutionary change; while with others the motive lay in personal rivalries among themselves.

The parties at this time were three in number. First, there was the party of the shore led by Megacles the son of Alcmeon, which was considered to aim at a moderate form of government; second, there were the men of the plain, who desired an oligarchy and were led by Lycurgus; and third, there were the men of the highlands, at the head of whom was Peisistratus, who was looked on as an extreme democrat. This latter party was reinforced by those who had been deprived of the debts due to them, from motives of poverty, and by those who were not of pure descent, from motives of fear. Proof of this is seen in the fact that after the tyranny was overthrown a revision was made of the citizen roll, on the grounds that many people were partaking of the franchise without having a right to it. The names given to the respective parties were derived from the districts in which they farmed their lands.

14. Peisistratus had the reputation of being an extreme democrat, and he also had distinguished himself greatly in the war with Megara.[16] Taking advantage of this, he wounded himself, and by representing that his injuries had been inflicted by his political rivals, he persuaded the people, through a motion proposed by Aristion, to grant him a bodyguard. After he had got these "club bearers" as they were called, he used them to launch an attack on the people and seized the Acropolis. This happened in the archonship of Comeas (561/60 BCE), thirty-one years after the legislation of Solon.[17] It is said that, when Peisistratus asked for his bodyguard, Solon opposed the request, and declared that in so doing he proved himself wiser

---

13. There was, therefore, an "anarchy," that is, a year without an Archon.

14. "Eupatrids" were the people with "Good Fathers"; that is, they were members of Athenian noble families who claimed descent from gods or heroes.

15. They ruled, that is, for the remainder of Damasias's third year.

16. The exact date of this war is unknown, but its principal result was the acquisition by Athens of the island of Salamis off the southwest coast of Attica.

17. Actually thirty-three years.

than half the people and braver than the rest—wiser than those who did not see that Peisistratus designed to make himself tyrant, and braver than those who saw it and kept silence. But when all his words had no effect, he took out his armor and set it up in front of his house, saying that he had helped his country so far as lay in his power (he was already a very old man), and that he called on all others to do the same.

Solon's exhortations, however, proved fruitless, and Peisistratus assumed the sovereignty. His administration was more like a constitutional government than the rule of a tyrant, but before his power was firmly established, the adherents of Megacles and Lycurgus formed a coalition and drove him out. This took place in the archonship of Hegesias (556/55 BCE), five years after the first establishment of his rule. Eleven years later Megacles, embroiled in a party struggle, again opened negotiations with Peisistratus, proposing that the latter should marry his daughter.

On these terms he brought him back to Athens, using a very primitive and simple-minded device. He first spread abroad a rumor that Athena was bringing back Peisistratus, and then, having found a woman of great stature and beauty named Phye (according to Herodotus, of the deme of Paeania, but to others a Thracian flower seller of the deme of Collytus), he dressed her to resemble the goddess and brought her into the city with Peisistratus. The latter drove in on a chariot with this woman beside him, and the inhabitants of the city, struck with awe, received him with adoration.

15. In this manner his first return took place. He did not, however, hold his power long: about six years after his return he was again expelled. He refused to treat the daughter of Megacles as his wife, and being afraid, in consequence, of a combination of the two opposing parties, he retired from the country. First he led a colony to a place called Rhaicelus, in the region of the Thermaic gulf, and from there he passed to the country in the neighborhood of Mt. Pangaeus. Here he acquired wealth and hired mercenaries, and not until ten years had elapsed did he return to Eretria and make an attempt to recover the government by force. In this he had the assistance of many allies, notably the Thebans and Lygdamis of Naxos, and also the Knights who held the supreme power in the constitution of Eretria.

After his victory in the battle at Pallene[18] he captured Athens, and when he had disarmed the people, he at last had his tyranny securely established, and was able to take Naxos and set up Lygdamis as ruler there. He effected the disarmament of the people in the following manner. He ordered a parade in full armor in the Theseum, and began to make a speech to the people. He spoke for a short time, until the people called out that they could not hear him, whereupon he bade them come up to the entrance of the Acropolis, in order that his voice might be better heard. Then, while he continued to speak to them at great length, men whom he had appointed for the purpose collected the arms and locked them up in the chambers of the

---

18. The battle of Pallene is conventionally dated c. 546/45 BCE.

Theseum nearby, and gave a signal to him that it was done. Peisistratus accordingly, when he had finished the rest of what he had to say, told the people also what had happened to their arms; adding that they were not to be surprised or alarmed, but to go home and attend to their private affairs, while he would himself for the future manage all the business of the state.

16. Such was the origin and such the vicissitudes of the tyranny of Peisistratus. His administration was moderate, as has been said before, and more like constitutional government than a tyranny. Not only was he in every respect humane and mild and ready to forgive those who offended, but, in addition, he advanced money to the poorer people to help them in their labors so that they might make their living by agriculture. In this he had two objectives: first, that they might not spend their time in the city but might be scattered over all the face of the country, and second, that being moderately well off and occupied with their own business, they might have neither the wish nor the time to attend to public affairs. At the same time his revenues were increased by the thorough cultivation of the country, since he imposed a tax of one-tenth on all the produce.

For the same reasons he instituted local justices, and often made expeditions in person into the country to inspect it and to settle disputes between individuals, that they might not come into the city and neglect their farms. It was in one of these tours that, as the story goes, Peisistratus had his encounter with the man of Hymettus, who was cultivating the spot afterward known as "Tax-free Farm." He saw a man digging and working at a very stony piece of ground and, being surprised, he sent his attendant to ask the man what he got out of this plot of land. "Aches and pains," said the man, "and that's what Peisistratus ought to have his tenth of." The man spoke without knowing the identity of his questioner, but Peisistratus was so pleased with his frank speech and his industry that he granted him exemption from all taxes.

And so in matters in general he burdened the people as little as possible with his government, but always cultivated peace and kept them quiet. Thus the tyranny of Peisistratus was often spoken of proverbially as "the age of gold," for when his sons succeeded him the government became much harsher. But most important of all was his popular and kindly disposition. He was accustomed to observe the laws in all things without giving himself any exceptional privileges. Once he was summoned on a charge of homicide before the Areopagus; he appeared in person to make his defense, but the prosecutor was afraid to present himself and abandoned the case.

For these reasons he held power for a long time, and whenever he was expelled he regained his position easily. The majority both of the upper class and of the people were in his favor; the former he won through social intercourse, the latter by the assistance he gave to their private purses: his nature fitted him to win the hearts of both. Moreover, the laws in reference to tyrants at that time in force at Athens were very mild, especially the one that applied more particularly to the establishment of a tyranny. The law ran as follows: "These are the ancestral statutes of the Athenians; if any persons shall make an attempt to establish a tyranny, or if any person shall join in setting up a tyranny, he shall lose his civic rights, both he and his whole house."

17. Thus did Peisistratus grow old while in power, and he died of illness in the archonship of Philoneos (528/27 BCE), thirty-three years from the time when he first established himself as tyrant, during nineteen[19] of which he was in power; the rest he spent in exile. It is thus evident that the story is mere gossip, which states that Peisistratus was the youthful favorite of Solon and commanded in the war against Megara for the recovery of Salamis. This does not harmonize with their respective ages, as anyone may see who reckons up the years of the life of each of them, and the dates when they died. After the death of Peisistratus his sons seized the government and conducted it on the same system. He had two sons, Hippias and Hipparchus, by his first and legitimate wife, and two sons, Iophon and Hegesistratus (surnamed Thessalus), by his Argive consort. For Peisistratus took a wife from Argos, Timonassa, the daughter of Gorgilus, a man of Argos; she had previously been the wife of Archinus of Ambracia, one of the descendants of Cypselus. This relationship was the origin of his friendship with the Argives, owing to which a thousand Argives were brought by Hegesistratus to fight on Peisistratus's side in the battle at Pallene. Some authorities say that this marriage took place after Peisistratus's first expulsion from Athens, others while he was still in power.

18. Hippias and Hipparchus assumed control of affairs on the basis of both standing and age, but Hippias, as being also naturally of a statesmanlike and shrewd disposition, was really head of the government. Hipparchus was youthful in disposition, amorous, and fond of literature (it was he who invited Anacreon, Simonides, and other poets to Athens), while Thessalus was much younger and was both violent and headstrong. His character was the source of all the evils that befell the house. He became enamored of Harmodius, and, when he failed to win his affection, lost all restraint on his passion; in addition to other exhibitions of rage he finally prevented the sister of Harmodius from taking the part of a basket-bearer in the Panathenaic procession,[20] alleging that Harmodius was a person of loose

---

19. Other sources suggest that he ruled for seventeen years. The apparent precision of the dates of Peisistratus's three periods of tyranny in chapters 14 and 15 is misleading since they imply that he was in exile for thirty-two years, leaving only one year of rule between the battle of Pallene and his death instead of the extended period of rule indicated here. No fully satisfactory explanation of the nature of Aristotle's error has been proposed.

20. The reference to the "procession" indicates that Hipparchus was assassinated during the Great Panathenaea of 514/13 BCE, which took place every four years in the first month of the Athenian year—approximately August—during which a cross section of the Athenian population marched from the agora (marketplace) to the Acropolis and presented the cult statue of Athena with a new robe.

morals. Thereupon, in a frenzy of rage, Harmodius and Aristogeiton did their celebrated deed, in conjunction with a number of confederates. But while they were lying in wait for Hippias in the Acropolis at the time of the Panathenaea (Hippias was at this moment awaiting the arrival of the procession, while Hipparchus was organizing it), they saw one of the men who was privy to the plot talking familiarly with Hipparchus. Thinking that this man was betraying them, and wishing to do something before they were arrested, they rushed down and struck without waiting for the rest of their confederates. They succeeded in killing Hipparchus near the Leocoreum while he was engaged in arranging the procession, but ruined the plan as a whole: of the two leaders, Harmodius was killed on the spot by the guards, while Aristogeiton was arrested and perished later after suffering lengthy torture. While under torture he accused many men who belonged by birth to the most distinguished families and were also personal friends of the tyrants. At first the government could find no clue to the conspiracy; for the current story—that Hippias made all who were taking part in the procession leave their arms, and then detected those who were carrying secret daggers—cannot be true, since at that time they did not bear arms in processions, this being a custom instituted at a later period by the democracy.

According to the story of the popular party, Aristogeiton accused the friends of the tyrants with the deliberate intention that the latter might commit an impious act, and at the same time weaken themselves, by putting to death innocent men who were their own friends; others say that he told no falsehood, but was betraying the actual accomplices. At last, when for all his efforts he could not obtain release by death, he promised to give further information against a number of other people; and, having induced Hippias to give him his hand to confirm his word, as soon as he had hold of it he reviled him for giving his hand to the murderer of his brother, till Hippias, in a frenzy of rage, lost control of himself, snatched out his dagger, and dispatched him.

19. After this event the tyranny became much harsher. In consequence of his vengeance for his brother, and of the execution and banishment of a large number of men, Hippias became a distrusted and embittered man. About three years after the death of Hipparchus, finding his position in the city insecure, he set about fortifying Munichia, with the intention of establishing himself there. While he was still engaged on this work, however, he was expelled by Cleomenes,[21] king of Lacedaemon, in consequence of the Spartans being continually incited by oracles to overthrow the tyranny.

These oracles were obtained in the following way. The Athenian exiles, headed by the Alcmeonidae, could not by their own power effect their return, failing continually in their attempts. Among their other failures they fortified a post in Attica—Lipsydrium, above Mt. Parnes—and were there joined by some partisans

---

21. Cleomenes I, king of Sparta from c. 520 BCE to c. 490 BCE.

from the city; but they were besieged by the tyrants and forced to surrender. After this disaster the following became a popular drinking song:

> Ah! Lipsydrium, faithless friend!
> Lo, what heroes to death did send,
> Nobly born and great in deed!
> Well did they prove themselves at need
> Of noble sires a noble seed.

Having failed, then, in every other method, they took the contract for rebuilding the temple at Delphi, thereby obtaining ample funds, which they used to secure the help of the Lacedaemonians. All this time the Pythia kept pressing the Lacedaemonians who came to consult the oracle that they must free Athens. She finally succeeded in impelling the Spartans to that step, although the house of Peisistratus was connected with them by ties of hospitality.

The resolution of the Lacedaemonians was, however, at least equally due to the friendship that had been formed between the house of Peisistratus and Argos. Accordingly they first sent Anchimolus by sea at the head of an army; but he was defeated and killed, following the arrival of Cineas of Thessaly to support the sons of Peisistratus with a force of a thousand horsemen. Then, being roused to anger by this disaster, they sent their king, Cleomenes, by land at the head of a larger force; and he, after defeating the Thessalian cavalry when they attempted to intercept his march into Attica, shut up Hippias within what was known as the Pelargic wall and blockaded him there with the assistance of the Athenians.

While he was besieging the place, it so happened that the sons of the Peisistratidae were captured while attempting to slip out; at this point the tyrants capitulated on condition of the safety of their children, and surrendered the Acropolis to the Athenians, five days being first allowed them to remove their effects. This took place in the archonship of Harpactides (511/10 BCE), after they had held the tyranny for about seventeen years since their father's death, that is to say, including the period of their father's rule, for forty-nine years.[22]

THE REFORMS OF CLEISTHENES

20. After the overthrow of the tyranny, the rival leaders in the state were Isagoras, son of Tisander, a partisan of the tyrants, and Cleisthenes, who belonged to the

---

22. Hippias ruled from 528/27 BCE to 511/10 BCE. The family held power continuously for thirty-six years from 546/45 BCE to 511/10 BCE. Aristotle's forty-nine years—actually fifty years—omit the periods of Peisistratus's exile, reckoning the family's tyranny as beginning with his first seizure of power in 561/60 BCE.

family of the Alcmeonidae. Cleisthenes, being defeated in the political clubs, called the people to him by ceding the *politeia* (the constitution) to the masses. Thereupon Isagoras, finding his power reduced, invited Cleomenes, who was united to him by ties of hospitality, to return to Athens and persuaded him to "drive out the pollution," a plea derived from the fact that the Alcmeonidae were supposed to be under the curse of pollution.[23] On this Cleisthenes retired from the country, and Cleomenes, entering Attica with a small force, expelled, as polluted, seven hundred Athenian families.

Having effected this, he next attempted to dissolve the Council and to set up Isagoras and three hundred of his partisans as the supreme power in the state. The Council, however, resisted, the populace flocked together, and Cleomenes and Isagoras, with their adherents, took refuge on the Acropolis. Here the people besieged them for two days; on the third day they agreed to let Cleomenes and all his followers depart, while they summoned Cleisthenes and the other exiles back to Athens. When the people had thus obtained the command of affairs, Cleisthenes was their chief and popular leader. And this was natural as the Alcmeonidae were perhaps the chief cause of the expulsion of the tyrants, and for the greater part of their rule were at perpetual war with them.[24] But even earlier than the attempts of the Alcmeonidae, one Cedon made an attack on the tyrants, from which arose another popular drinking song addressed to him:

> Pour a health yet again, boy, to Cedon; forget not this duty to do,
> If a health is an honor befitting the name of a good man and true.

21. The people, therefore, had good reason to place confidence in Cleisthenes. Accordingly, now that he was the popular leader, three years after the expulsion of the tyrants in the archonship of Isagoras (508/7 BCE), his first step was to distribute the whole population into ten tribes in place of the existing four, with the object of intermixing the members of the different tribes and so ensuring that more men might have a share in the franchise. From this arose the saying "Do not judge a man by his tribe," addressed to those who wished to scrutinize the lists of the old families.

---

23. The clan of the Alcmeonidae supposedly murdered the supporters of Cylon, who had attempted to establish a tyranny in Athens in the late seventh century BCE and had taken refuge at the altar of Athena, and became polluted as a result of the sacrilege. The demand to "expel the polluted" continued to be used against Alcmeonid politicians, most notably Pericles, throughout the fifth century BCE.

24. Cleisthenes's hostility to the tyrants is exaggerated since the discovery of a fragment of a list of Athenian Archons revealed that he was Archon in 525/24 BCE, one year after Hippias was Archon, which indicates that he was a prominent political figure in Athens during at least the early part of Hippias's reign.

Next he reorganized the Council to consist of five hundred rather than four hundred members; each tribe now contributed fifty, whereas formerly each had sent one hundred. The reason he did not organize the people into twelve tribes was to discontinue the existing division into *trittyes* (thirds). The four tribes had formed twelve trittyes, and creating twelve tribes would not have achieved his object of redistributing the population into fresh combinations.

He further divided the country into thirty groups of demes,[25] ten from the districts around the city, ten from the coastal area, and ten from the interior. These groups he now called trittyes; he assigned three of them by lot to each tribe, in such a way that each group should have one portion in each of the three localities. All who lived in any given deme he declared fellow-demesmen, to the end that the new citizens might not be identified by the habitual use of family names, but that men might be officially described by the names of their demes; accordingly, it is by the names of their demes that the Athenians speak of one another.[26]

He also instituted Demarchs (deme Archons), who had the same duties as the previously existing Naucrari, the demes having replaced the Naucraries. He gave names to the demes, some according to the localities to which they belonged and some from the people who founded them, since some of the areas no longer corresponded to localities possessing names. On the other hand he allowed everyone to retain his family and clan and religious rites according to ancestral custom. The names given to the tribes were the ten that the Pythia appointed out of the hundred selected national heroes.

CLEISTHENIC DEMOCRACY

22. By these reforms the constitution became much more democratic than that of Solon. The laws of Solon had been obliterated by disuse during the period of the tyranny, while Cleisthenes substituted new ones with the object of securing the good will of the masses. Among these was the law concerning ostracism.[27] Four

---

25. A deme was a village or, in the case of the city of Athens, a residential district. Since the assembly met in the city of Athens, the long-term effect of this reform was to increase the influence of the residents of the city of Athens in the assembly as opposed to those living in rural areas.

26. Henceforth, Athenians would identify themselves as So and so, son of So and so, from deme X, instead of So and so, son of So and so, of the family Y, which allowed individuals to be identified as belonging to Eupatrid, that is, noble, families or not.

27. Ostracism took its name from "ostracon," a piece of broken pottery on which Athenians wrote the name of the person they wished to be "ostracized." If the people voted in a particular year to hold an ostracism, citizens came to Athens on a specific day and turned in their ostraca in places assigned to their tribe. If the total of ostraca turned in was at least 6,000,

years after the establishment of this system, in the archonship of Hermocreon (501/0 BCE), they first imposed upon the Council of Five Hundred the oath that they take to the present day.

Next they began to elect the generals by tribes, one from each tribe, while the Polemarch was the commander of the whole army. Then, eleven years later, in the archonship of Phaenippus (490/89 BCE), they won the battle of Marathon; and two years after this victory (488/87 BCE), when the people had now gained self-confidence, they for the first time made use of the law of ostracism. This had originally been passed as a precaution against men in high office, because Peisistratus took advantage of his position as a popular leader and general to make himself tyrant. The first person ostracized was one of his relatives, Hipparchus son of Charmus of the deme of Collytus, the very person on whose account especially Cleisthenes had enacted the law, as he wished to get rid of him. Hitherto, however, Hipparchus had escaped; the Athenians, with the usual leniency of the democracy, allowed all the partisans of the tyrants who had not joined in their evil deeds in the time of the troubles, to remain in the city: the chief and leader of these was Hipparchus.

Then in the very next year, in the archonship of Telesinus (487/86 BCE), for the first time since the tyranny they elected by lot, tribe by tribe, the nine Archons out of the five hundred candidates selected by the demes, all the earlier ones having been elected by vote; in the same year Megacles, son of Hippocrates of the deme of Alopece, was ostracized. Thus for three years they continued to ostracize the friends of the tyrants, on whose account the law had been passed; but in the following year they began to remove others as well, including anyone who seemed to be more powerful than was expedient.

The first person unconnected with the tyrants who was ostracized was Xanthippus son of Ariphron. Two years later, in the archonship of Nicodemus (483/82 BCE), the mines of Maroneia were discovered, and the state made a profit of a hundred talents from working them. Some men advised the people to distribute the money among themselves, but this was prevented by Themistocles. He refused to say on what he proposed to spend the money, but he bade them lend it to the hundred richest men in Athens, one talent to each. Then, if the manner in which the money was employed pleased the people, the expenditure should be charged to the state, but otherwise the state should receive the sum back from those to whom it was lent. On these terms he received the money and with it had a hundred triremes built, each of the hundred individuals building one, and it was with these ships that they fought the battle of Salamis against the barbarians.

About this time Aristides the son of Lysimachus was ostracized. Three years later, however, in the archonship of Hypsichides (481/80 BCE), all the ostracized

---

the ostracism was valid and the person whose name appeared on a plurality of ostraca was exiled from Athens for ten years. The person ostracized retained his property and his family suffered no other penalty.

men were recalled as the army of Xerxes was advancing; and it was laid down for the future that people under sentence of ostracism must live between Geraestus and Scyllaeum, on pain of losing their civic rights irrevocably.

The Supremacy of the Areopagus

23. So far, then, had the city progressed by this time, growing gradually with the growth of the democracy. However, after the Persian wars the Council of the Areopagus once more developed strength and assumed control of the state. It did not acquire this supremacy by virtue of any formal decree, but as a result of its leadership leading up to the battle of Salamis. When the generals were utterly at a loss as to how to meet the crisis and made a proclamation that everyone should see to his own safety (every man for himself), the Areopagus distributed eight drachmas to each member of the ships' crews, and thus prevailed on them to go on board.

On these grounds people bowed to the prestige of the Council, and during this period Athens was well administered. At this time they devoted themselves to the prosecution of the war and were in high repute among the Greeks so that the command by sea was conferred upon them, in spite of the opposition of the Lacedaemonians. The leaders of the people[28] during this period were Aristides, son of Lysimachus, and Themistocles, son of Neocles; the latter appeared to devote himself to the conduct of war, while the former had the reputation of being a clever statesman and the most upright man of his time. Accordingly the one was usually employed as general, the other as political adviser. The rebuilding of the fortifications they conducted in combination, although they were political opponents.

However it was Aristides who, seizing the opportunity afforded by the discredit brought upon the Lacedaemonians by Pausanias, guided public policy in the matter of the defection of the Ionian states from the alliance with Sparta. It follows that it was he who made the first assessment of tribute from the various allied states, two years after the battle of Salamis, in the archonship of Timosthenes; and it was he who took the oath of offensive and defensive alliance with the Ionians, on which occasion they cast the masses of iron into the sea.[29]

24. After this, seeing the state growing in confidence and much wealth accumulated, Aristides advised the people to seize the leadership of the league, to quit the country districts, and to settle in the city. He pointed out to them that all would

---

28. Apparently, Aristotle means only that Aristides and Themistocles were the two most prominent political figures in Athens at this time without treating them as representing ideologically opposed points of view, Aristides being aristocratic and Themistocles democratic, as later writers did.

29. The allies and Athens supposedly swore an oath to remain faithful to the alliance until the iron floated.

be able to gain a living there—some by service in the army, others in the garrisons, others by taking part in public affairs—and in this way they would secure the leadership. Persuaded that this was the right policy, the people assumed the supreme control and proceeded to treat their allies in a more imperious fashion, with the exception of the people of Chios, Lesbos, and Samos. These they maintained to protect their empire, leaving their constitutions untouched, and allowing them to retain whatever dominion they then possessed.

The people of Athens also secured an ample maintenance for the mass of the population in the way that Aristides had pointed out to them. Out of the proceeds of the tributes and taxes and the contributions of the allies more than twenty thousand people were maintained. There were 6,000 jurymen, 1,600 bowmen, 1,200 Knights, 500 members of the Council, 500 guards of the dockyards, in addition to 50 guards in the Acropolis. There were some 700 magistrates at home, and some 700 abroad. Further, when they subsequently went to war, there were in addition 2,500 heavily armed troops, 20 guard-ships, and other ships that collected the tributes, with crews amounting to 2,000 men, selected by lot. Besides these there were the people maintained at the Prytaneum, orphans, and jailers, since all these were supported by the state.

THE REFORMS OF EPHIALTES

25. Such was the way in which the people earned their livelihood. The supremacy of the Areopagus lasted for about seventeen years after the Persian wars, although it gradually declined. But as the strength of the masses increased, Ephialtes, son of Sophonides, a man with a reputation for incorruptibility and public virtue who had become the leader of the people, attacked the Council. First of all he removed many of its members by bringing actions against them with reference to their administration. Then, in the archonship of Conon (462/61 BCE), he stripped the Council of all the acquired prerogatives from which it derived its guardianship of the constitution,[30] and assigned some of their duties to the Council of Five Hundred, and others to the Assembly and the law courts.

In this revolution he was assisted by Themistocles,[31] who was himself a member of the Areopagus, but was expecting to be tried before it on a charge of treasonable dealings with Persia. This made him anxious that the Council of the Areopagus should be overthrown, and accordingly he warned Ephialtes that the Council intended to arrest him, while at the same time he informed the Areopagites that he would reveal to them certain people who were conspiring to subvert the constitution.

---

30. These "acquired prerogatives" are nowhere specified. After Ephialtes's reforms, the Areopagus's most important function was to serve as the court in cases of homicide.

31. Themistocles cannot have been Ephialtes's sally since he was ostracized c. 472 BCE and spent the rest of his life in Anatolia in Persian service.

He then conducted the representatives delegated by the Council to the residence of Ephialtes, promising to show them the conspirators who assembled there, and proceeded to converse with them in an earnest manner. Ephialtes, seeing this, was seized with alarm and, wearing the single garment of a supplicant, took refuge at the altar. Everyone was astounded, and presently, when the Council of Five Hundred met, Ephialtes and Themistocles together proceeded to denounce the Areopagus to them. This they repeated in similar fashion in the Assembly, until they succeeded in depriving the Areopagus of its power. Not long afterward, however, Ephialtes was assassinated by Aristodicus of Tanagra.

26. In this way the Council of Areopagus was deprived of its guardianship of the state. After this revolution the administration of the state became more and more lax, in consequence of the eager rivalry of candidates for popular favor. During this period the moderate party, as it happened, had no real chief, their leader being Cimon son of Miltiades, who was a comparatively young man and had only recently entered public life; at the same time the general populace suffered great losses in war. Soldiers for active service were selected at that time from the roll of citizens, and as the generals were men of no military experience, who owed their position solely to their family standing, it continually happened that some two or three thousand of the troops perished on an expedition; thus it was that the best men of the lower and the upper classes were exhausted. Consequently in most matters of administration less heed was paid to the laws than had formerly been the case.

No alteration, however, was made in the method of election of the nine Archons, except that five years after the death of Ephialtes[32] it was decided that the candidates to be submitted to the lot for that office might be selected from the Zeugitae as well as from the higher classes. The first Archon from that class was Mnesitheides. Up to this time all the Archons had been taken from the *Pentacosiomedimni* and Knights, while the Zeugitae were confined to the ordinary magistracies, save where an evasion of the law was overlooked. Four years later, in the archonship of Lysicrates (453/52 BCE), the thirty "local justices," as they were called, were reestablished; and two years later, in the archonship of Antidotus, as a consequence of the great increase in the number of citizens, it was resolved, on the motion of Pericles, that no one should be admitted to the franchise who was not of citizen birth by both parents.

27. After this Pericles came forward as popular leader, having first distinguished himself while still a young man by prosecuting Cimon on the audit of his official accounts as general. Under his auspices the constitution became still more democratic. He took away some of the privileges of the Areopagus, and, above all, he turned the policy of the state in the direction of sea power, which caused the masses to become more self-confident and consequently to take the conduct of affairs more and more into their own hands. Moreover, forty-eight years after the battle of

---

32. 457/56 BCE.

Salamis, in the archonship of Pythodorus (432/31 BCE), the Peloponnesian war broke out, during which the populace was shut up in the city and became accustomed to gain its livelihood by military service, and so, partly voluntarily and partly involuntarily, determined to assume the administration of the state itself.

Pericles was also the first to institute pay for service in the law courts, as a bid for popular favor to counterbalance the wealth of Cimon. The latter, having private possessions on a regal scale, not only performed the regular public services magnif- icently, but also maintained a large number of his fellow-demesmen. Any member of the deme of Laciadae could go every day to Cimon's house and there receive a reasonable provision; meanwhile there were no fences to guard his estate, so that anyone who liked might help himself to the fruit from it.

Pericles's private property was quite unequal to this magnificence and accordingly he took the advice of Damonides of Oia (who was commonly supposed to be the person who prompted Pericles in most of his measures, and was therefore subsequently ostracized), which was that, as he was beaten in the matter of private possessions, he should make gifts to the people from their own property; and thus it was he instituted pay for the members of the juries. Some critics accuse him of thereby causing deterioration in the character of the juries, since it was always the common people who put themselves forward for selection as jurors, rather than men of higher standing. Moreover, after this bribery came into existence, the first person to introduce it being Anytus, after his command at Pylos. He was prosecuted by certain individuals on account of his loss of Pylos, but by bribing the jury he escaped.

CHAPTER 5

The Parian Marble[1]

The Parian Marble *is a unique document. Unlike the other works in this book, it was a public document, a huge marble stele almost seven feet high and three feet wide that was displayed somewhere on the island of Paros. Unfortunately, only two badly damaged fragments of this remarkable monument survive today. The first and larger fragment—Fragment A—which treats legendary and archaic Greek history, was brought to England from Turkey in 1627 and, although part of it was lost in the English Civil War, the remainder is now preserved in Oxford. The second and smaller fragment—Fragment B—which treats the late fourth and early third centuries BCE, was found on Paros in 1897.*

Despite its damaged condition, the Parian Marble's *unknown author clearly intended to provide the citizens of Paros with a comprehensive and precisely dated list of the most important events in Greek history, compiled, he claimed, from all kinds of records and general histories. Although it is unknown whether the monument was commissioned by the government of Paros or was a gift to the city, its purpose was clearly educational, and like all textbooks, its content was not chosen at random. Instead, its particular emphases—the antiquity of Greek history, the achievements of archaic and classical Greek writers, and the emergence of monarchy in Greece—had particular relevance in the third century BCE, when Paros was ruled by one of the successors of Alexander the Great, Ptolemy II of Egypt, who was actively supporting scholars organizing a canon of great Greek writers. As such it provides unique insight into the view of Greek history held by an educated Greek living in one of the Hellenistic kingdoms.*

Precise dates, of course, made the story set out in the Parian Marble *easier to follow and more persuasive. Since Greek cities did not have a common dating system, however, the author invented an ingenious system of his own that would provide its readers with a unified account of Greek history. To achieve that end, he recorded for each event listed in his chronicle the number of years that had elapsed between the event and the year in which he composed his chronicle, namely, the year in which the archon in Athens was Diognetus—264/63 BCE in our calendar—and a now unknown person was*

---

1. Translated by the editor.

archon at Paros, thereby connecting the history of Paros to that of Athens, which had become the principal cultural center of Greece as a whole.[2]

FRAGMENT A

Preface

I have recounted ancient times from records of all sorts and general histories, beginning from Cecrops, the first king of Athens, until the archonship of [. . .]anax[3] in Paros and Diognetus in Athens.

The Legendary Period

Since Cecrops became king of Athens and the country was called Cecropia, having previously been named Actice, from Actaios,[4] who was autochthonous.[5] Years 1318 (= 1581/80 BCE).[6]

Since Deucalion ruled near Mount Parnassus in Lycorea, and Cecrops ruled the Athenians. Years 1310 (= 1573/72 BCE).

------

2. Unfortunately, his system had a serious flaw that made it difficult to use. Since dates in the *Parian Marble* were keyed to the year of the archonship of Diognetus in which the chronicle was composed, as time passed, an increasing gap inevitably developed between that date and that of readers who consulted it.

3. Because of damage to the surface of the stone, many letters and words are missing or so damaged as to be unreadable. Ellipses marks inside brackets indicate that letters or words have been lost at that point. Words inside brackets no longer exist on the stone but have been restored by scholars based on other evidence.

4. Greek historians explained the names of peoples and states as being derived from the name of their first ancestor or ruler.

5. Athenians claimed that they were autochthonous. Most writers, like Thucydides (*Peloponnesian War* 1.2), understood this claim as meaning that the Athenians were the original inhabitants of Attica, unlike other Greeks who migrated to the regions where they lived in historical times. A minority of authors, however, claimed that the original Athenians literally sprang from the earth of Attica.

6. The precise dates assigned to figures and events in Greek legend in the Parian Marble are illusory as they were not based on documentary evidence but were calculated by converting into years the number of generations supposedly separating, for example, a legendary ruler such as Cecrops from a key event such as the Trojan War, by assigning an average length— thirty or forty years—to a generation.

Since the judgment by the Athenians between Ares and Poseidon about Halirrhothius, the son of Poseidon, and the place was called Areopagus, years 1268 (= 1531/30 BCE), when Cranaos ruled the Athenians.

Since the flood took place in the time of Deucalion, and Deucalion took refuge from the storms in Lycorea in Athens with Cranaos, and he built the temple of Zeus Olympios and performed the salvation sacrifice. Years 1265 (= 1531/30 BCE), when Cranaos ruled the Athenians.

Since Amphictyon, the son of Deucalion, ruled at Thermopylae, and gathered together the peoples dwelling around the temple and named them Amphictyons, and first offered sacrifice where the Amphictyons also now still sacrifice, years 1258 (= 1521/20 BCE), when Amphyction ruled the Athenians.

Since Hellen, the son of Deucalion, ruled Phthiotis, and the people previously called Greeks were named Hellenes,[7] and the Panathenaic contest [. . . years] 1257 (= 1520/19 BCE), when Amphyction ruled the Athenians.

Since Cadmus, the son of Agenor, came to Thebes [. . . and] founded the Cadmea, years 1255 (= 1518/17 BCE), when Amphyction ruled the Athenians.

Since [. . .]nike ruled, years 1252, when Amphyction ruled the Athenians.

Since the first ship,[8] which was equipped with fifty oars by Danaus, sailed from Egypt to Greece and was called a pentecontor, and Danaus's daughters . . . and Helice and Archedice were chosen by the rest, and they founded the temple of Athena Lindia and they offered sacrifice on the promontory at . . . Lindos on Rhodes, years 1247 (1510/9 BCE), when Erechthonius ruled the Athenians.

Since Erechthonius harnessed a chariot at the first Panathenaia and made the contest known and named the Athenians. The statue of the mother of the gods appeared in Cybela, and Hyagnis the Phrygian first discovered flutes in . . . the Phrygians, and he first played on the flute the mode called Phrygian and other modes of the Mother, Dionysos, Pan, and the . . . , years 1242 (1505/4 BCE), when Erechthonius ruled the Athenians and harnessed the chariot.

Since the first Minos[9] ruled Crete and settled Apollonia, and iron was discovered at Mt. Ida by the Idaian Dactyls, Celmis and Damnameneus, years 1100(?), when Pandion ruled the Athenians.

---

7. In antiquity, Hellenes was the accepted name for Greeks, apparently derived from a region named Hellas in central Greece near Thermopylae. The origin of the name "Greeks (*Graikoi*)" is unknown as is why the Romans adopted it as the general name for Greeks instead of Hellenes.

8. Greek and Roman historians wrote the history of technology by compiling lists of "first inventors," that is, the persons who were believed to have first constructed or discovered a technology such as, in this case, shipbuilding.

9. A common way in which ancient historians solved the problem of multiple dates in their sources for a figure such as Minos in this passage was to assume that the different dates referred to more than one person with the same name.

Since Demeter came to Athens and discovered grain, and the first Proerosia was held, Triptolemus, the son of Celeus, and Neaera having established it, years 1146 (= 1409/8 BCE), when Erechtheus ruled the Athenians.

Since Triptolemus domesticated grain, which he planted in a place called Rharia at Eleusis, years 1145 (= 1408/7 BCE), when Erechtheus ruled the Athenians.

Since Orpheus . . . published his own poetry, the seizure of Core and the search of Demeter and the harvest created by her and the number of those who received the harvest, years 1135 (= 1398/97 BCE), when Erechtheus ruled the Athenians.

Since Eumolpus . . . revealed the mysteries in Eleusis and published the poems of his father Mousaeus, years 1100 (?), when Erechtheus, the son of Pandion, ruled the Athenians.

Since purification first took place . . . , years 1062 (= 1325/24 BCE), when Pandion, the son of Cecrops, ruled the Athenians.

Since the gymnastic competition in Eleusis . . . the Lycaea in Arcadia took place, . . . of Lycaon were given . . . to the Greeks, years (?), when Pandion, the son of Cecrops, ruled the Athenians.

Since . . . Heracles . . . when Aigeus ruled the Athenians.

Since there was a famine in Athens and Apollo responded to the Athenians consulting his oracle that they should pay whatever penalty Minos demanded, years 1031 (= 1294/93 BCE), when Aigeus ruled the Athenians.

Since Theseus ruled the Athenians and united the twelve poleis and gave the constitution and democracy to . . . [demos] of the Athenians, and established the Isthmian games after killing Sinis, years 995 (= 1259/58 BCE).

Since the invasion of the Amazons into Attica, years 992 (= 1256/55 BCE), when Theseus ruled the Athenians.

Since the Argives together with Adrastus marched against Thebes and established the games at Nemea at Archemorous, years 987 (= 1251/50 BCE), when Theseus ruled the Athenians.

Since the Greeks marched against Troy, years 954 (1218/17 BCE), in the thirteenth year of Menestheus's reign over the Athenians.[10]

---

10. Unlike nineteenth-century historians of Greece, ancient Greek historians viewed the Trojan War as the dividing line between the legendary and historical periods in the history of Greece. Because it was a Panhellenic war involving heroes from the whole of Greece, events before and after it could be dated by counting the number of generations in the genealogies of the various heroes and assigning an average number of years to a generation, as explained in note 6. It is noteworthy that the author ignores the first celebration of the Olympic Games in 776 BCE, which later modern historians treated as the first securely datable event in Greek history.

Since Troy was captured, years 945 (1209/8 BCE),[11] in the twenty-second year of the reign of Menestheus over the Athenians, on the seventh day from the end of the month of Thargelion.

Beginning of History

Since the trial of Orestes, the son of Agamemnon, and Erigone, the daughter of Aegisthus on behalf of Aegisthos and Clytemnestra took place on the Areopagus, in which Orestes was acquitted because the votes were equal, years 944 (= 1208/7 BCE), when Demophon ruled the Athenians.

Since Teucer founded Salamis on Cyprus, years 938 (= 1202/1 BCE), when Demophon ruled the Athenians.

Since Neleus founded Miletus and the all the rest of Ionia: Ephesus, Erythrae, Clazomenae, Priene, Lebedus, Teos, Colophon, Myus, Phocaea, Samos, Chios, and the Panionia took place, years 813 (= 1077/76 BCE), in the thirteenth year of the reign of Menestheus over the Athenians.

Archaic Period

Since the poet Hesiod lived, years 670 (= 937/36 BCE), when [. . . ?] ruled the Athenians.

Since the poet Homer lived, years 643 (= 917/16 BCE), when Diognetus ruled the Athenians.

Since Pheidon, the Argive, who was eleventh from Heracles, established weights and measures, and struck silver coins in Aigina, years 631 (= 895/94 BCE), when Pherecles ruled the Athenians.

Since Archias, the son of Euagetus, who was tenth from Temenus, led the colony from Corinth and founded Syracuse, years [——] in the twenty-first year of the reign of Aeschylus over the Athenians.

Since the archon held office annually, years 420 (= 683/82 BCE).

Since [. . .], years 418 (= 681/80 BCE), when Lysiades was archon at Athens.

Since Terpander, the son of Derden[es], the Lesbian, introduced the (?) for the cythera and transformed previous music, years 381 (= 645/44 BCE), when Dropides was archon at Athens.

---

11. Various dates were assigned to the end of the Trojan War, depending on the reference point from which it was calculated. Herodotus (2.145) dated it to c. 800 years before his time, that is, about 1230 BCE, while other historians placed it a thousand years before the reign of Alexander the Great, about 1330 BCE. The most widely accepted date, 1184 BCE, was proposed by the third-century BCE chronicler and geographer Eratosthenes of Cyrene.

Since Alyattes ruled the Lydians, years 341 (= 605/4 BCE), when Aristocles was archon at Athens.

Since Sappho sailed from Mytilene to Sicily, having fled . . . , when the elder Critias was archon at Athens, and the *Gamori* (= Landholders) seized rule at Syracuse.

Since the Amphictyons sacrificed after having defeated Cyrrha, and the gymnastic contest was established with prizes provided from the plunder, years 327 (= 591/90 BC), when Simon was archon at Athens.

Since the contest with a crown as prize was established for the second time, years 318 (= 582/81 BCE), when Damasius was archon at Athens for the second time.

Since the comic chorus was established at Athens, the Icarians competing for the first time, Susarion having invented it, and the prize was established for the first time as a basket of dried figs and an amphora of wine, years 200+, when [. . . ?] was archon at Athens.

Since Pisistratus became tyrant of the Athenians, years 297 (= 561/60 BCE), when Comeas was archon at Athens.

Since Croesus sent sacred envoys from Asia to Delphi, years 292 (= 556/55 BCE), when Euthydemus was archon at Athens.

Since Cyrus (II), the king of the Persians, seized Sardis and Croesus . . . , years 277 (= 541/40 BCE), when [. . . ?] was archon at Athens and at the same time Hipponax the iambic poet lived.

Since Thespis, the poet, who created drama in Athens, played a part for the first time, and a goat was set as the prize, years 270 (= 536/35 BCE), when [. . . ?] was archon at Athens. for the second time.

Since Darius (I) became king of the Persians after the death of the Magus, years 256 (520/19 BCE), when [. . . ?] was archon in Athens.

Since Harmodius and Aristogeiton killed Hipparchus, the successor of Pisistratus and the Athenians drove the Pisistratids from the Pelasgic wall, years 248 (= 511/10 BCE), when Harpactides was archon at Athens.[12]

Since male choruses first competed, and the one that was trained by Hypodicus, the Chalcidian, was victorious, years 246 (= 510/19), when Lysagoras was archon at Athens.

Since Melanippides, the Melian, was victorious at Athens, years 231 (= 494/93 BCE), when Pythocritus was archon at Athens.

Classical Period

Since the battle of the Athenians against the Persians and Artaphernes, the nephew of Darius, and the general Datis took place, in which the Athenians were victorious,

---

12. The author of the *Parian Marble* mistakenly assumed that Hipparchus was tyrant of Athens instead of Hippias and that his assassination, therefore, ended the Athenian tyranny, an error already exposed by Thucydides 1.20.

years 227 (= 490/89 BCE), when Phaenippides the second was archon at Athens; and Aeschylus the poet fought in the battle, being 33 years old.[13]

Since Simonides, the grandfather of Simonides the poet, who was also a poet himself, was victorious at Athens, and Darius died, and Xerxes, his son, became king, years 226 (= 489/88 BCE), when Aristides was archon at Athens.

Since Aeschylus, the poet, was first victorious in tragedy, and Euripides, the poet, was born, and Stesichorus, the poet, came to Greece, years 226 (= 485/84 BCE), when Philocrates was archon at Athens.

Since Xerxes built the bridge of boats at the Hellespont and dug through Athos, and the battle at Thermopylae took place and the naval battle of the Greeks against the Persians near Salamis, in which the Greeks were victorious took place, years 217 (= 480/79 BCE), when Calliades was archon at the Athens.

Since the battle took place of the Athenians against Mardonius, the general of Xerxes, in which the Athenians were victorious, and Mardonius died, years 216 (= 479/78 BCE), when Xanthippus was archon at Athens.[14]

Since Gelon, the son of Deinomenes, began to be tyrant of the Syracusans, years 215 (= 478/78 BCE), when Timosthenes was archon at Athens.

Since Simonides, the son of Leoprepes, the Cean, who invented the mnemonic technique and trained, was victorious at Athens, and the statues of Harmodius and Aristogeiton were set up,[15] years 213 (= 477/76 BCE), when Adeimantus was archon at Athens.

Since Hieron became tyrant of the Syracusans, years 208 (= 472/71 BCE), when Chares was archon at Athens; and Epicharmus, the poet, lived at the same time.

Since Sophocles, the son of Sophilus, from Colonus, was victorious in tragedy, being 28 years old, years 206 (= 469/68 BCE), when Apsephion was archon at Athens.

Since a meteor fell at Aegospotami, and Simonides, the poet, died, having lived 90 years, years 205 (468/67 BCE), when Theagenides was archon at Athens.

Since Alexander (I) died, and his son Perdiccas (II) became king of the Macedonians, years 199 (= 461/60 BCE), when Euthippus was archon at Athens.

Since Aeschylus, the poet died in Gela in Sicily, having lived 69 years, years 193 (= 455/54 BCE), when the elder Callias was archon at Athens.

---

13. The reference is to the battle of Marathon.

14. This passage is a good example of the pro-Athenian bias of the compiler of the *Parian Marble*. The reference is to the battle of Plataea in 479 BCE in which the army of the Hellenic League under the command of the Spartans and not just the Athenians defeated the Persian forces led by Mardonius.

15. The statues mentioned in this passage were set up at Athens to replace two bronze statues of Harmodius and Aristogeiton that were looted by the Persians in 480/79 BC and taken to Susa. Alexander the Great found them there and returned them to Athens, where they remained for the rest of antiquity.

Since Euripides at the age of 43 was victorious in tragedy for the first time, years 179 (= 442/41 BCE), when Diphilus was archon at Athens; and Socrates and Anaxagoras lived at the same time as Euripides.

Since Archelaus became king of the Macedonians, at the death of Perdiccas, years 157 (= 420/19 BCE), when Astiphilus was archon at Athens.

Since Dionysius became tyrant of the Syracusans, years 147 (= 408/7 BCE), when Euctemon was archon at Athens.

Since Euripides died at the age of 75 + (?), years 145 (= 407/6 BC), when Antigenes was archon at Athens.

Since Sophocles died at the age of 92, and Cyrus (i.e., the Younger) marched upcountry [years 143 (= 406/5 BCE)], when the elder Callias[16] was archon at Athens.

Since Telestes, the Selinuntian, was victorious at Athens, years 139 (= 402/1 BCE), when Micion was archon at Athens.

Since the Greeks, who had marched upcountry with Cyrus,[17] returned, and Socrates, the philosopher, died at the age of 70, years 137 (= 400/399 BCE), when Laches was archon at Athens.

Since Ariston . . . was victorious at Athens, years 135 (= 399/98 BCE), when Aristocrates was archon at Athens.

Since Polyeides, the Selymbrian, was victorious in the dithyramb at Athens, years 110+, when (. . . ?) was archon at Athens.

Since Philoxenus, the dithyrambic poet, died at the age of 55, years 116 (= 380/79 BCE), when Pytheas was archon at Athens.

Since Anaxandrides, the comic poet, was victorious at Athens, years 113 (= 377/76 BCE), when Calleas was archon at Athens.

Since Astydamus was archon at Athens, years 109 (= 373/72 BCE), when Asteius was archon at Athens. The temple at Delphi also burned at that time.

Since the battle at Leuctra between the Thebans and the Lacedaemonians in which the Thebans were victorious took place, years 107 (= 371/70 BCE), when Phrasicleides was archon at Athens. Amyntas also died and his son Alexander became king of the Macedonians.

Since Stesichorus the younger from Himera was victorious at Athens, and Megalopolis was founded [in Arcadia, years 105* (370/69 BCE, when [. . . ?] was archon in Athens].

Since Dionysius, the Sicilian, died, and Dionysius, his son, became tyrant, and Alexander (II) died and Ptolemy, the Alorite, became king of the Macedonians, years 104 (= 368/67 BCE), when Nausigenes was archon at Athens.

---

16. There is an error in the text at this point, since "the elder Callias" was already recorded as archon under the year 455/54 BCE. No satisfactory correction has been proposed.

17. The exploits of the Greek mercenaries, who supported Cyrus the Younger's rebellion against his brother, Artaxerxes II, were narrated by Xenophon in the *Anabasis*.

Since the Phocians seized the oracle . . . , years 102 (= 366/65 BCE), when Cephisodorus was archon at Athens.

Since Timotheus died at the age of 90, years [*], when (. . . ?) was archon at Athens.

From the time when Philip (II), the son of Amyntas, became king of the Macedonians, and Artaxerxes died, and Ochos, his son, became king, years [*], when (. . . ?) was archon at Athens.

Since [. . .] was victorious at Athens, years 93 (= 357/56 BCE), when Agathocles was archon at Athens.

Since [. . .] happened, years [91 (= 355/54 BCE)], when Callistratus was archon at Athens.

FRAGMENT B

Alexander the Great and His Successors

[Since . . .] Philip died and Alexander (III) became king, years 72 (= 336/35 BCE), when Pythodelus was archon at Athens.

Since Alexander campaigned against the Triballi and the Illyrians, and the Thebans revolted and besieged the garrison, and he returned, captured the city by force and razed it, years 71 (= 335/34 BCE), when Euainetus was archon at Athens.

Since the crossing of Alexander into Asia and the battle near the Granicus and after it the battle at Issus of Alexander against Darius, years 70 (= 334/33 BCE), when Ctesicles was archon at Athens.

Since Alexander became master of Phoenicia and Cyprus and Egypt, years 69 (= 332/31 BCE), when Nicocrates was archon at Athens.

Since the battle of Alexander against Darius near Arbela in which Alexander was victorious; and he captured Babylon, and released the allies, and Alexandria was founded, years 68 (= 332/31 BCE), when Nicetes was archon at Athens.

Since Callippus explained astronomy,[18] and Alexander seized Darius, and he hung Besos,[19] years 66 (= 330/29), when Aristophon was archon at Athens.

---

18. Callippus of Cyzicus was an astronomer and colleague of Aristotle. Although he wrote several important astronomical works, the reference is probably to the book in which he published what is known as the Callippic Cycle, a system for synchronizing lunar calendars, such as those used by the Greeks with a solar year of 365 ¼ days, and predicting lunar eclipses. According to the Callippic Cycle, a lunar year and a solar year would begin on the same day once every seventy-nine years, beginning in 330 BCE.

19. Besos (usually spelled Bessos), the satrap of Bactria, was the leader of the assassins of Darius III, king of Persia, and ruled briefly as Artaxerxes V.

Since Philemon, the comic poet, was victorious, years 64 (= 328/27 BCE), when Euthycritus was archon at Athens. A Greek city was founded near the Tanais.

Since Alexander died and Ptolemy took control of Egypt, years 60 (= 324/23 BCE), when Hegesias was archon at Athens.

Since the war of the Athenians against Antipater that took place near Lamia and the sea battle of the Macedonians against the Athenians near Amorgus, in which the Macedonians were victorious, years 59 (= 323/22 BCE), when Cephisodorus was archon at the Athens.

Since Antipater captured Athens and Ophelas, who had been dispatched by Ptolemy, captured Cyrene, years 58 (= 322/21 BCE), when Philocles was archon at Athens.

Since Antigonus crossed into Asia, and Alexander was brought to Memphis, and Perdiccas invaded Egypt and died, and Craterus and Aristotle, the sophist, died at the age of 50, years 57 (= 321/20 BCE), when Archippus was archon at Athens. Ptolemy also traveled to Cyrene.

Since the death of Antipater and the withdrawal of Cassander from Macedonia, and from the siege of Cyzicus, which was besieged by Aridaeus, and from the time when Ptolemy captured Syria and Phoenicia, years 55 (= 319/18 BCE), when Apollodorus was archon at Athens. Also in this same year Agathocles was chosen general with full power for the defense of Sicily.

Since the sea battle of Cleitus and Nicanor near the temple of the Calchedonians, and when Demetrius[20] issued laws for the Athenians, years 53 (= 317/16 BCE), when Demogenes was archon at Athens.

Since Cassander returned to Macedon, and Thebes was built, and Olympias died, and Cassandreia was founded, and Agathocles became tyrant of the Syracusans, years 52 (= 316/15 BCE), when Democleides was archon at Athens. Also at that time, Menander, the comic poet, was victorious for the first time at Athens.

Since Sosiphanes, the poet died, years 49 (= 313/12 BCE), when Theophrastus was archon at Athens at the age of 45.

Since the sun was eclipsed, and Ptolemy defeated Demetrius at Gaza and sent Seleucus to Babylon, years 48 (= 312/11 BCE), when Polemon was archon at Athens.

Since Nicocreon died and Ptolemy gains control of the island, years 47 (= 311/10 BCE), when Simonides was archon at Athens.

Since Alexander (IV), the son of Alexander, dies, and another son, Heracles, the son of the daughter of Artabazus, also died, and Agathocles crossed over to Carthage [. . . years] 46 (= 310/19 BCE), when Hieromnemon was archon at Athens.

Since the city of Lysimacheia was founded, and Ophelas [to Carthage . . .], and Ptolemy, the son, was born on Cos, and Cleopatra died at Sardis [. . . years] 35 (= 309/8 BCE), when Demetrius was archon at Athens.

---

20. Demetrius of Phaleron, a colleague of Aristotle, who ruled Athens from 317 to 307 BCE.

Since Demetrius[21] besieged and captured the Peiraeus, and Demetrius of Phaleron was banished from Athens, years 44 (= 308/7 BCE), when Caerimus was archon at Athens.

Since Demetrius razed Munichia, and captured Cyprus, and Phill[ip. . . years] 43 (= 307/6 BCE), when Anaxicrates was archon at Athens.

Since Sosiphanes, the poet, was born [. . . years 42 (= 306/5 BCE), when the archon at Athens] was Coroebus.

Since the siege at Rhodes, and from the time when Ptolemy (I) assumed the kingship, [years 41 (= 305/4 BCE), when Euxenippus was archon at Athens].

Since the earthquakes that happened in Ionia, and when Demetrius occupied Chalcis by agreement and [. . .] of Demetrius, years 40 (= 304/3 BCE), when Phere-cles was archon at Athens.

Since a comet appeared, and Lysimachus crossed into Asia, years 39 (= 303/2 BCE), when Leostratus was archon at Athens.

Since the truce between Cassander and Demetrius took place [. . .] Cassander [. . . died], years 38 (= 302/1 BCE), when Nicocles was archon at Athens.

Since the ascent of Demetrius to Chalcis, and the Athenians Cas[sander . . .] Ptolemy, years 35 (= 299/98 BCE), when [Euctemon was archon at Athens].

---

21. Demetrius, the son of Antigonus the One-Eyed.

CHAPTER 6

Polybius, *The Histories*

FROM BOOK I

Preface

The emergence of world history as an important field of study was a major development of the late twentieth century. Left unanswered, however, was the question of the best way to write a world history: whether to trace the history of humanity from the prehistoric origins of humanoids in Africa to the present or to focus on some topic that unified a particular historical period, such as, for example, globalization. The same problem faced ancient historians who attempted to write "universal histories," that is, histories that embraced the world known to the Greeks. The most common solution was to organize such histories around the theme of the succession of world empires: Assyrian, Median, Persian, Macedonian, and Roman. Polybius chose the alternative solution, claiming that during his lifetime, the known world was unified for the first time by a common process: Roman imperialism. In his preface, he explained his rationale for the innovative way in which he organized his history.

1. Had previous chroniclers neglected to speak in praise of History in general, it might perhaps have been necessary for me to recommend everyone to choose for study and welcome such treatises as the present, since men have no more ready corrective of conduct than knowledge of the past. But all historians, one may say without exception, and in no half-hearted manner, but making this the beginning and end of their labor, have impressed on us that the soundest education and training for a life of active politics is the study of History, and that the surest and indeed the only method of learning how to bear bravely the vicissitudes of fortune, is to recall the calamities of others. Evidently therefore no one, and least of all myself, would think it his duty at this day to repeat what has been so well and so often said. For the very element of unexpectedness in the events I have chosen as my theme will be sufficient to challenge and incite everyone, young and old alike, to peruse my systematic history. For who is so worthless or indolent as not to wish to know by what means and under what system of government the Romans in less than fifty-three years[1] have succeeded in subjecting nearly the whole inhabited world to

---

1. 220 BCE to 167 BCE.

their sole government—a thing unique in history? Or who is there so passionately devoted to other spectacles or studies as to regard anything as of greater moment that the acquisition of this knowledge?

2. How striking and grand is the spectacle presented by the period with which I propose to deal, will be most clearly apparent if we set beside and compare with the Roman dominion the most famous empires of the past, those which have formed the chief theme of historians. Those worthy of being set beside it and compared are these. The Persians for a certain period possessed a great rule and dominion, but so often as they ventured to overstep the boundaries of Asia they imperiled not only the security of their empire, but their own existence. The Lacedaemonians, after having for many years disputed the hegemony of Greece, at length attained it but to hold it uncontested for scarce twelve years. The Macedonian rule in Europe extended but from the Adriatic region to the Danube, which would appear a quite insignificant portion of the continent. Subsequently, by overthrowing the Persian empire they became supreme in Asia also. But though their empire was now regarded as the greatest geographically and politically that had ever existed, they left the larger part of the inhabited world as yet outside it. For they never even made a single attempt to dispute possession of Sicily, Sardinia, or Libya, and the most warlike nations of Western Europe were, to speak the simple truth, unknown to them. But the Romans have subjected to their rule not portions, but nearly the whole of the world [and possess an empire which is not only immeasurably greater than any which preceded it, but need not fear rivalry in the future]. In the course of this work it will become more clearly intelligible [by what steps this power was acquired], and it will also be seen how many and how great advantages accrue to the student from the systematic treatment of history.

3. The date from which I propose to begin my history is the 140th Olympiad,[2] and the events are the following: (1) in Greece the so-called Social War, the first waged against the Aetolians by the Achaeans in league with and under the leadership of Philip of Macedon, the son of Demetrius and father of Perseus, (2) in Asia the war for Coele-Syria between Antiochus and Ptolemy Philopator, (3) in Italy, Libya, and the adjacent regions, the war between Rome and Carthage, usually known as the Hannibalic War. These events immediately succeed those related at the end of the work of Aratus of Sicyon. Previously the doings of the world had been, so to say, dispersed, as they were held together by no unity of initiative, results, or locality; but ever since this date history has been an organic whole, and the affairs of Italy and Libya have been interlinked with those of Greece and Asia, all leading up to one end. For it was owing to their defeat of the Carthaginians in

---

2. 220 BCE to 216 BCE. Olympiad dating was introduced by the late fourth/early third-century BCE Sicilian historian Timaeus. Because all Greeks recognized the Olympic Games, Olympiads—the four-year intervals between games—provided a convenient common dating system for Greeks for events occurring after the first Olympiad, 776 BCE to 772 BCE.

the Hannibalic War that the Romans, feeling that the chief and most essential step in their scheme of universal aggression had now been taken, were first emboldened to reach out their hands to grasp the rest and cross with an army to Greece and the continent of Asia.

Now were the Greeks well acquainted with the two states which disputed the empire of the world, it would not perhaps have been necessary for me to deal at all with their previous history, or to narrate what purpose guided them, and on what sources of strength they relied, in entering on such a vast undertaking. But as neither the former power nor the earlier history of Rome and Carthage is familiar to most of the Greeks, I thought it necessary to prefix this Book and the next to the actual history, in order that no one after becoming engrossed in the narrative proper may find himself at a loss, and ask by what counsel and trusting to what power and resources the Romans embarked on that enterprise which has made them lords over land and sea in our part of the world; but that from those Books and the preliminary sketch in them, it may be clear to readers that they had quite adequate grounds for conceiving the ambition of a world empire and adequate means for achieving their purpose.

4. For what gives my work its peculiar quality, and what is most remarkable in the present age, is this. Fortune[3] has guided almost all the affairs of the world in one direction and has forced them toward one and the same end; a historian should likewise bring before his readers under one synoptical view the operations by which she has accomplished her general purpose. Indeed it was this chiefly that invited and encouraged me to undertake my task; and secondarily the fact that none of my contemporaries have undertaken to write a general history, in which case I should have been much less eager to take this in hand. As it is, I observe that while several modern writers deal with particular wars and certain matters connected with them, no one, as far as I am aware, has even attempted to inquire critically when and whence the general and comprehensive scheme of events originated and how it led up to the end. I therefore thought it quite necessary not to leave unnoticed or allow to pass into oblivion this the finest and most beneficent of the performances of Fortune. For though she is ever producing something new and ever playing a part in the lives of men, she has not in a single instance ever accomplished such a work, ever achieved such a triumph as in our times. We can no more hope to perceive this from histories dealing with particular events than to get at once a notion of the form of the whole world, its disposition and order, by visiting, each in turn, the most famous cities, or indeed by looking at separate plans of each: a result by no means likely. He indeed who believes that by studying isolated histories he can acquire a fairly just view of history as a whole, is, as it seems to me, much in the case of one, who, after having looked at the dissevered limbs of an animal once alive and beautiful, fancies

3. Polybius adduces Fortune (*Tyche*) to explain events for which people find it difficult or impossible to find natural causes.

he has been as good as an eyewitness of the creature itself in all its action and grace. For could anyone put the creature together on the spot, restoring its form and the comeliness of life, and then show it to the same man, I think he would quickly avow that he was formerly very far away from the truth and more like one in a dream. For we can get some idea of a whole from a part, but never knowledge or exact opinion. Special histories therefore contribute very little to the knowledge of the whole and conviction of the truth. It is only indeed by study of the interconnection of all the particulars, their resemblances and differences, that we are enabled at least to make a general survey, and thus derive both benefit and pleasure from history.

From Book 2

The Achaean League

> Greeks in the Hellenistic period found themselves in a world dominated by powerful kingdoms. As a result, individual city states tended to be eclipsed in the third and second centuries BCE by federal states such as the Achaean and Aetolian Leagues that were better able to compete politically and militarily with the kingdoms, particularly Macedon, which aimed to maintain the dominant role in Greek affairs it had gained during the reign of Philip II in the mid-fourth century BCE. It is not surprising, therefore, that the Achaean League, of which Polybius was an important political figure, is prominent in his history or that later political thinkers, including American Federalists, found his account of the league and its institutions of great interest.

37.7. As regards the Achaean nation and the royal house of Macedon, it will be proper to refer briefly to earlier events, since our times have seen, in the case of the latter its complete destruction, and in the case of the Achaeans, as I have said above, a growth of power and political union in the highest degree remarkable.[4] For while many have attempted in the past to induce the Peloponnesians to adopt a common policy, no one ever succeeding, as each was working not in the cause of general liberty, but for his own aggrandizement, this object has been so much advanced, and so nearly attained in my own time that not only have they formed an allied and friendly community, but they have the same laws, weights, measures, and coinage, as well as the same magistrates, senate, and courts of justice, and the whole Peloponnesus only falls short of being a single city in the fact of its inhabitants not

---

4. The reference is to the end of the Third Macedonian War in 168 BCE, when Rome abolished the Macedonian monarchy and the Achaean League expanded to include the whole Peloponnesus. Ignored is the exile of 1,000 Achaean politicians, including Polybius, to Rome because of their suspected anti-Roman tendencies.

being enclosed by one wall, all other things being, both as regards the whole and as regards each separate town, very nearly identical.

38. In the first place it is of some service to learn how and by what means all the Peloponnesians came to be called Achaeans. For the people whose original and ancestral name this was are distinguished neither by the extent of their territory, nor by the number of their cities, nor by exceptional wealth or the exceptional valor of their citizens. Both the Arcadian and Laconian nations far exceed them, indeed, in population and the size of their countries, and certainly neither of the two could ever bring themselves to yield to any Greek people the palm for military valor. How is it, then, that both these two peoples and the rest of the Peloponnesians have consented to change not only their political institutions for those of the Achaeans, but even their name? It is evident that we should not say it is the result of chance, for that is a poor explanation. We must rather seek for a cause, for every event whether probable or improbable must have some cause. The cause here, I believe to be more or less the following. One could not find a political system and principle so favorable to equality and freedom of speech, in a word so sincerely democratic, as that of the Achaean league. Owing to this, while some of the Peloponnesians chose to join it of their own free will, it won many over by persuasion and argument, and those whom it forced to adhere to it when the occasion presented itself suddenly underwent a change and became quite reconciled to their position. For by reserving no special privileges for original members, and putting all new adherents exactly on the same footing, it soon attained the aim it had set itself, being aided by two very powerful coadjutors, equality and humanity. We must therefore look upon this as the initiator and cause of that union that has established the present prosperity of the Peloponnese.

These characteristic principles and constitution had existed in Achaea from an early date. There is abundant testimony of this, but for the present it will suffice to cite one or two instances in confirmation of this assertion. 39. When, in the district of Italy, then known as Greater Hellas,[5] the clubhouses of the Pythagoreans were burnt down, there ensued, as was natural, a general revolutionary movement, the leading citizens of each city having thus unexpectedly perished, and in all the Greek towns of the district murder, sedition, and every kind of disturbance were rife. Embassies arrived from most parts of Greece offering their services as peacemakers, but it was the Achaeans on whom these cities placed most reliance and to whom they committed the task of putting an end to their present troubles. And it was not only at this period that they showed their approval of Achaean political principles; but a short time afterward, they resolved to model their own constitution exactly on that of the League. The Crotonians, Sybarites, and Caulonians, having

---

5. "Greater Hellas" refers to the area of Greek settlement in South Italy. The Pythagoreans fled to Croton from Samos in the late sixth century BCE and governed it and neighboring cities until the mid-fifth century BCE when their regimes were overthrown.

called a conference and formed a league, first of all established a common temple and holy place of Zeus Amarius in which to hold their meetings and debates, and next, adopting the customs and laws of the Achaeans, decided to conduct their government according to them. It was only indeed the tyranny of Dionysius of Syracuse[6] and their subjection to the barbarian tribes around them which defeated this purpose and forced them to abandon these institutions, much against their will. Again, subsequently, when the Lacedaemonians were unexpectedly defeated at Leuctra,[7] and the Thebans, as unexpectedly, claimed the hegemony of Greece, great uncertainty prevailed in the whole country and especially among these two peoples, the Lacedaemonians not acknowledging their defeat, and the Thebans not wholly believing in their victory. They, however, referred the points in dispute to the Achaeans alone among all the Greeks, not taking their power into considerations, for they were then almost the weakest state in Greece, but in view of their trustworthiness and high character in every respect. For indeed this opinion of them was at that time, as is generally acknowledged, held by all.

Up to now, these principles of government had merely existed among them, but had resulted in no practical steps worthy of mention for the increase of the Achaean power, since the country seemed unable to produce a statesman worthy of their principles, anyone who showed a tendency to act so being thrown into the dark and hampered either by the Lacedaemonian power or still more by that of Macedon. 40. When, however, in due time, they found statesmen capable of enforcing them, their power at once became manifest, and the League achieved the splendid result of uniting all the Peloponnesian states. Aratus of Sicyon[8] should be regarded as the initiator and conceiver of the project; it was Philopoemen[9] of Megalopolis who promoted and finally realized it, while Lycortas[10] and his party were those who assured the permanency, for a time at least, of this union. I will attempt to indicate how and at what date each of the three contributed to the result, without transgressing the limits I have set to this part of my work. Aratus's government, however, will be dealt with here and in future quite summarily, as he published a truthful and clearly written account of his own career; but the achievements of the two others will be narrated in greater detail and at more length. I think it will be easiest for myself to set forth the narrative and for my readers to follow it if I begin from the period when, after the dissolution of the Achaean League by the kings of

---

6. Dionysius I was tyrant of Syracuse from 405 BCE to 367 BCE.

7. 371 BCE.

8. Aratus lived from 271 to 213 BCE and was the dominant figure in Achaean politics from 245 BCE to the end of his life.

9. Philopoemen lived from c. 253 to 182 BCE and was the Achaean League's most prominent politician in the early second century BCE. Polybius wrote a biography of Philopoemen that does not survive but which was the main source of knowledge of his career.

10. Polybius's father.

Macedonia, the cities began again to approach each other with a view to its renewal. Henceforward the League continued to grow until it reached in my own time the state of completion I have just been describing.

41. It was in the 124th Olympiad[11] that Patrae and Dyme took the initiative, by entering into a league just about the date of the deaths of Ptolemy son of Lagus, Lysimachus, Selecucus, and Ptolemy Ceraunus, which all occurred in this Olympiad. The condition of the Achaean nation before this date had been more or less as follows. The first king was Tisamenus the son of Orestes, who, when expelled from Sparta on the return of the Heraclidae, occupied Achaea, and they continued to be ruled by kings of his house down to Ogygus. Being dissatisfied with the rule of Ogygus's sons, which was despotical and not constitutional, they changed the government to a democracy. After this, down to the reigns of Alexander and Philip, their fortunes varied according to circumstances, but they always endeavored, as I said, to keep their League a democracy. This consisted of twelve cities, which still all exist with the exception of Olenus and of Helice[12] which was engulfed by the sea a little before the battle of Leuctra. These cities are Patrae, Dyme, Pharae, Tritaea, Leontium, Aegium, Aegira, Pellene, Pharae, and Caryneia. After the time of Alexander and previous to the above Olympiad they fell, chiefly thanks to the kings of Macedon, into such a state of discord and ill-feeling that all the cities separated from the League and began to act against each others' interests. The consequence was that some of them were garrisoned by Demetrius and Cassander and afterward by Antigonus Gonatas, and some even had tyrants imposed on them by the latter, who planted more monarchs in Greece than any other king. But, as I said above, about the 124th Olympiad they began to repent and form fresh leagues. (This was just about the date of Pyrrhus's crossing to Italy.)[13] The first cities to do so were Dyme, Patrae, Tritaea, and Pharae, and for this reason we do not even find any formal inscribed record of their adherence to the League. About five years afterward the people of Aegium expelled their garrison and joined the League, and the Burians were the next to do so, after putting their tyrant to death. Caryneia joined almost at the same time, for Iseas, its tyrant, when he saw the garrison expelled from Aegium, and the monarch of Bura killed by Margus and the Achaeans, and war just about to be made on himself by all the towns around, abdicated and, on receiving an assurance from the Achaeans that his life would be spared, added his city to the League.

42. Why, the reader will ask, do I go back to these times? It is, firstly, to show which of the original Achaean cities took the first steps to re-form the League and at what dates and, secondly, that my assertion regarding their political principle may be confirmed by the actual evidence of facts. What I asserted was that the

---

11. 284–280 BCE.

12. Helice was destroyed by an earthquake and tsunami in 373 BCE.

13. Pyrrhus, king of Epirus, came to Italy to support several cities of South Italy against Rome in 280 BCE and returned to Epirus in 275 BCE.

Achaeans always followed one single policy, ever attracting others by the offer of their own equality and liberty and ever making war on and crushing those who either themselves or through the kings attempted to enslave their native cities, and that, in this manner and pursuing this purpose, they accomplished their task in part unaided and in part with the help of allies. For the Achaean political principle must be credited also with the results furthering their end, to which their allies in subsequent years contributed. Though they took so much part in the enterprises of others, and especially in many of those of the Romans which resulted brilliantly, they never showed the least desire to gain any private profit from their success, but demanded, in exchange for the zealous aid they rendered their allies, nothing beyond the liberty of all states and the union of the Peloponnesians. This will be more clearly evident when we come to see the League in active operation.

43. For twenty-five years,[14] then, the league of cities continued, electing for a certain period a Secretary of state and two Strategi [generals]. After this they decided to elect one Strategus and entrust him with the general direction of their affairs, the first to be nominated to this honorable office being Margus of Caryneia. Four years later[15] during Margus's term of office, Aratus of Sicyon, though only twenty years of age, freed his city from its tyrant by his enterprise and courage, and, having always been a passionate admirer of the Achaean polity, made his own city a member of the League. Eight years after this[16] during his second term of office as Strategus, he laid a plot to rule the citadel of Corinth[17] which was held by Antigonus,[18] thus delivering the Peloponnesians from a great source of fear, and induced the city he had liberated to join the League. In the same term of office he obtained the adhesion of Megara to the Achaeans by the same means. These events took place in the year before that defeat of the Carthaginians which forced them to evacuate Sicily and submit for the first time to pay tribute to Rome.[19] Having in so short a space of time thus materially advanced his projects, he continued to govern the Achaean nation, all his schemes and action being directed to one object, the expulsion of the Macedonians from the Peloponnese, the suppression of the tyrants, and the establishment on a sure basis of the ancient freedom of every state. During the life of Antigonus Gonatas he continued to offer a most effectual opposition to the meddlesomeness of this king and the lust for power of the Aetolians, although the two were so unscrupulous and venturesome that they entered into an arrangement for the purpose of dissolving

---

14. 280/79 to 256/55 BCE.

15. 251/50 BCE.

16. 243 BCE.

17. Acrocorinthus ("the top of Corinth") was the acropolis of Corinth, which together with Demetrias in Thessaly and Chalcis on Euboea were the "Fetters of Greece," the three fortresses which were the anchors of Macedonian influence in Greece.

18. Antigonus Gonatas, king of Macedon from 283 BCE to 239 BCE.

19. That is, 242 BCE, the year before the end of the First Punic War in 241 BCE.

the Achaean League. 44. But, on the death of Antigonus, the Achaeans even made an alliance with the Aetolians and supported them ungrudgingly in the war against Demetrius, so that, for the time at least, their estrangement and hostility ceased, and a more or less friendly and sociable feeling sprang up between them. Demetrius only reigned for ten years,[20] his death taking place at the time the Romans first crossed to Illyria, and after this the tide of events seemed to flow for in favor of the Achaean's constant purpose; for the Peloponnesian tyrants were much cast down by the death of Demetrius, who had been, so to speak, their furnisher and paymaster, and equally so by the threatening attitude of Aratus, who demanded they should depose themselves, offering abundance of gifts and honors to those who consented to do so, and menacing those who turned a deaf ear to him with still more abundant chastisement on the part of the Achaeans. They therefore hurried to accede to his demand, laying down their tyrannies, setting their respective cities free, and joining the Achaean League. Lydiades of Megalopolis had even foreseen what was likely to happen, and with great wisdom and good sense had forestalled the death of Demetrius and of his own free will laid down the tyranny and adhered to the national government. Afterward Aristomachus, tyrant of Argos, Xenon, tyrant of Hermione, and Cleonymus, tyrant of Phlius, also resigned and joined the democratic Achaean League.

The Cleomenic War (229 BCE to 222 BCE)

Cleomenes III (236 BCE to 222 BCE) of Sparta was that rare thing in Greek history: a genuine revolutionary. By the mid-third century BCE, the number of Spartans with the rights of full citizens had fallen to about 700, and Sparta was negligible as a military power. Building on reforms proposed by his predecessor Agis IV (c. 262 BCE to 241 BCE), Cleomenes reconstituted the Spartan state, canceling debts, redistributing land, restoring the Spartan educational system, and raising the number of citizens to almost 5,000. Faced with a resurgent Sparta allied with its principal rival for influence in Greece, the Aetolian League, the Achaean League turned to Macedon for help. Polybius's account of the Cleomenic War is an illuminating account based on the lost memoirs of Aratus of Sicyon, the dominant figure of the Achaean League, of how Aratus sacrificed his political ideals to the needs of realpolitik.

45. The League being thus materially increased in extent and power, the Aetolians, owing to that unprincipled passion for aggrandizement which is natural to them, either out of envy or rather in the hope of partitioning the cities, as they

---

20. Demetrius II ruled Macedon from 239 BCE to 229 BCE.

had partitioned those of Acarnania with Alexander and had previously proposed to do regarding Achaea with Antigonus Gonatas, went so far as to join hands with Antigonus Doson,[21] then regent of Macedonia and guardian to Philip, who was still a child, and Cleomenes, king of Sparta.[22] They saw that Antigonus was undisputed master of Macedonia and at the same time the open and avowed enemy of the Achaeans owing to their seizure by treachery of the Acrocorinthus, and they supposed that if they could get the Lacedaemonians also to join them in their project, exciting first their animosity against the League, they could easily crush the Achaeans by attacking them at the proper time all at once and from all quarters. This indeed they would in all probability soon have done, but for the most important factor which they had overlooked in their plans. They never took into consideration that in this undertaking they would have Aratus as their opponent, a man capable of meeting any emergency. Consequently the result of their intrigues and unjust aggression was that not only did they fail in their designs, but on the contrary consolidated the power of the League, and of Aratus who was then Strategus, as he most adroitly diverted and spoilt all their plans. How he managed all this the following narrative will show.

46. Aratus saw that the Aetolians were ashamed of openly declaring war on them, as it was so very recently that the Achaeans had helped them in their war against Demetrius, but that they were so much of one mind with the Lacedaemonians and so jealous of the Achaeans that when Cleomenes broke faith with them and possessed himself of Tegea, Mantinea, and Orchomenos,[23] cities which were not only allies of the Aetolians, but at the same time members of their league, they not only showed no resentment, but actually set their seal to his occupation. He saw too that they, who on previous occasions, owing to their lust of aggrandizement, found any pretext adequate for making war on those who had done them no wrong, now allowed themselves to be treacherously attacked and to suffer the loss of some of their largest cities simply in order to see Cleomenes become a really formidable antagonist of the Achaeans. Aratus, therefore, and all the leading men of the Achaean League decided not to take the initiative in going to war with anyone, but to resist Spartan aggression. This at least was their first resolve; but when shortly afterward Cleomenes boldly began to fortify against them the so-called Athenaeum in the territory of Megalopolis, and to show himself their avowed bitter

---

21. Antigonus Doson ("he who will give") ruled Macedon and served as regent for Philip V (221 BCE to 179 BCE) from 229 BCE to 221 BCE.

22. Cleomenes III belonged to the Agiad dynasty and was king of Sparta from 236 BCE to 222 BCE. He carried through a series of reforms intended to restore Sparta's "ancestral constitution" and rebuild Spartan military power by redistributing land and thereby increasing Sparta's citizen body.

23. The three most important cities in Arcadia, the mountainous region in the central Peloponnesus.

enemy, they called the Council of the League together and decided on open war with Sparta.

This was the date at which the war known as the Cleomenic War began;[24] and such was its origin. 47. The Achaeans at first decided to face the Lacedaemonians single-handed, considering it in the first place most honorable not to owe their safety to others but to protect their cities and country unaided, and also desiring to maintain their friendship with Ptolemy[25] owing to the obligations they were under to him, and not to appear to him to be seeking aid elsewhere. But when the war had lasted for some time and Cleomenes, having overthrown the ancient system of government at Sparta and changed the constitutional kingship into a tyranny,[26] showed great energy and daring in the conduct of the campaign, Aratus, foreseeing what was likely to happen and dreading the reckless audacity of the Aetolians, determined to be beforehand with them and spoil their plans. He perceived that Antigonus was a man of energy and sound sense, and that he claimed to be a man of honor, but he knew that kings do not regard anyone as their natural foe or friend, but measure friendship and enmity by the sole standard of expediency. He therefore decided to approach that monarch and put himself on confidential terms with him, pointing out to him to what the present course of affairs would probably lead. Now for several reasons he did not think it expedient to do this overtly. In the first place he would thus expose himself to being outbidden in his project by Cleomenes and the Aetolians and next he would damage the spirit of the Achaean troops by thus appealing to an enemy and appearing to have entirely abandoned the hopes he had placed in them—this being the very last thing he wished them to think. Therefore, having formed this plan, he decided to carry it out by covert means. He was consequently compelled in public both to do and to say many things quite contrary to his real intention, so as to keep his design concealed by creating the exactly opposite impression. For this reason there are some such matters that he does not even refer to in his *Memoirs*.

48. He knew that the people of Megalopolis were suffering severely from the war, as, owing to their being on the Lacedaemonian border, they had to bear the full brunt of it, and could not receive proper assistance from the Achaeans, as the latter were themselves in difficulties and distress. As he also knew for a surety that they were well disposed to the royal house of Macedon ever since the favors received in the time of Philip, son of Amyntas,[27] he felt sure that, hard pressed as they were

---

24. The Cleomenic War between Sparta and its allies and the Achaean League, Macedon, and their allies began in 229 BCE and ended in 222 BCE.

25. Ptolemy III Euergetes ("Benefactor") was king of Egypt from 246 BCE to 222 BCE.

26. As part of his revolution, Cleomenes III abolished the office of ephor and assassinated the Eurypontid king Archidamus V and appointed his own brother king in Archidamus's place.

27. Philip II, the father of Alexander the Great.

by Cleomenes, they would be very ready to take refuge in Antigonus and hopes of safety from Macedonia. He therefore communicated his project confidentially to Nicophanes and Cercidas of Megalopolis who were family friends of his own and well suited for the business, and he had no difficulty through them in inciting the Megalopolitans to send an embassy to the Achaeans begging them to appeal to Antigonus for help. Nicophanes and Cercidas themselves were appointed envoys by the Megalopolitans, in the first place to the Achaeans and next, if the League consented, with orders to proceed at once to Antigonus. The Achaeans agreed to allow the Megalopolitans to send an embassy; and with the other ambassadors hastened to meet the king. They said no more than was strictly necessary on the subject of their own city, treating this matter briefly and summarily, but dwelt at length on the general situation, in the sense that Aratus had directed and prompted. 49. He had charged them to point out the importance and the probable consequences of the common action of the Aetolians and Cleomenes, representing that in the first place the Achaeans were imperiled by it and next and in a larger measure Antigonus himself. For it was perfectly evident to all that the Achaeans could not hold out against both adversaries, and it was still more easy for any person of intelligence to see that, if the Aetolians and Cleomenes were successful, they would surely not rest content and be satisfied with their advantage. The Aetolian schemes of territorial aggrandizement would never stop short of the boundaries of the Peloponnese or even those of Greece itself, while Cleomenes's personal ambition, and far-reaching projects, though for the present he aimed only at supremacy in the Peloponnese, would, on his attaining this, at once develop into a claim to be overlord of all Hellas, a thing impossible without his first putting an end to the dominion of Macedon. They implored him then to look to the future and consider which was most in his interest, to fight in the Peloponnese against Cleomenes for the supremacy of Greece with the support of the Achaeans and Boeotians, or to abandon the greatest of the Greek nations to its fate and then do battle in Thessaly for the throne of Macedon with the Aetolians, Boeotians, Achaeans, and Spartans all at once. Should the Aetolians, still pretending to have scruples owing to the benefits received from the Achaeans in their war with Demetrius, continue their present inaction, the Achaeans alone, they said, would fight against Cleomenes, and, if Fortune favored them, would require no help; but should they meet with ill-success and be attacked by the Aetolians also, they entreated him to take good heed and not let the opportunity slip, but come to the aid of the Peloponnesians while it was still possible to save them. As for conditions of alliance and the return they could offer him for his support, they said he need not concern himself, for once the service they demanded was being actually rendered, they promised him that Aratus would find terms satisfactory to both parties. Aratus himself, they said, would also indicate the date at which they required his aid.

50. Antigonus, having listened to them, felt convinced that Aratus took a true and practical view of the situation, and carefully considered the next steps to be

taken, promising the Megalopolitans by letter to come to their assistance if such was the wish of the Achaeans too. Upon Nicophanes and Cercidas returning home and delivering the king's letter, assuring at the same time their people of his goodwill toward them and readiness to be of service, the Meagalopolitans were much elated and most ready to go to the Council of the League and beg them to invite the aid of Antigonus and at once put the direction of affairs in his hands. Aratus had private information from Nicophanes of the king's favorable inclination toward the League and himself, and was much gratified to find that his project had not been futile, and that he had not, as the Aetolians had hoped, found Antigonus entirely alienated from him. He considered it a great advantage that the Megalopolitans had readily consented to approach Antigonus through the Achaeans; for, as I said above, what he chiefly desired was not to be in need of asking for help also, but if it became necessary to resort to this, he wished the appeal to come not only from himself personally, but from the League as a whole. For he was afraid that if the king appeared on the scene and, after conquering Cleomenes and the Lacedaemonians, took any measures the reverse of welcome regarding the League, he himself would be universally blamed for what happened, as the king would seem to have justice on his side owing to Aratus's offence against the house of Macedon in the case of the Acrocorinthus. Therefore, when the Megalopolitans appeared before the General Council of the League, and showing the king's letter, assured them of his general friendly sentiments, at the same time begging the Achaeans to ask for his intervention at once, and when Aratus saw that this was the inclination of the Achaeans also, he rose, and after expressing his gratification at the king's readiness to assist them and his approval of the attitude of the meeting, he addressed them at some length, begging them if possible to attempt to save their cities and country by their own efforts, that being the most honorable and advantageous course, but, should adverse fortune prevent this, then, but only when they had no hope left in in their own resources, he advised them to resort to an appeal to their friends for aid. 51. The people applauded his speech, and a decree was passed to leave things as they were for the present and conduct the war unaided. But a series of disasters overtook them. In the first place Ptolemy threw over the League and began to give financial support to Cleomenes with a view of setting him on to attack Antigonus, as he hoped to be able to keep in check more effectually the projects of the Macedonian kings with the support of the Lacedaemonians than with that of the Achaeans. Next the Achaeans were worsted by Cleomenes while on the march near the Lycaeum and again in a pitched battle at a place in the territory of the Megalopolitans called Ladoceia, Lydiades falling here, and finally their whole force met with utter defeat at the Hecatombaeum in the territory of Dyme. Circumstances now no longer permitting delay, they were compelled by their position to appeal with one voice to Antigonus. Aratus on this occasion sent his son as envoy to the king and ratified the terms of the alliance. They were, however, in considerable doubt and difficulty about the Acrocorinthus, as they did not think Antigonus would come to their assistance unless it were restored to him, so that he could use Corinth as a base for the present war, nor could they go to the length of handing over the Corinthians against their will to Macedon. This even caused at first an adjournment of the Council for a consideration of the guarantees they offered.

52. Cleomenes, having inspired terror by the victories I mentioned, henceforth made an unimpeded progress through the cities, gaining some by persuasion and others by threats. He annexed in this manner Caphyae, Pellene, Pheneus, Argos, Phlius, Cleonae, Epidaurus, Hermione, Troezen, and finally Corinth. He now sat down in front of Sicyon, but he had solved the chief difficulty of the Achaeans; for the Corinthians by ordering Aratus, who was then Strategus, and the Achaeans to quit Corinth, and by sending to invite Cleomenes, furnished the Achaeans with good and reasonable ground for offering to Antigonus the Acrocorinthus then held by them. Availing himself of this, Aratus not only atoned for his former offence to the royal house, but gave sufficient guarantee of future loyalty, further providing Antigonus with a base for the war against the Lacedaemonians.

Cleomenes, when he became aware of the understanding between the Achaeans and Antigonus, left Sicyon and encamped on the Isthmus, uniting by a palisade and trench the Acrocorinthus and the mountain called the Ass's Back, regarding confidently the whole Peloponnese as being henceforth his own domain. Antigonus had been for long making his preparations, awaiting the turn of events, as Aratus had recommended, but now, judging from the progress of events that Cleomenes was on the point of appearing in Thessaly with his army, he communicated with Aratus and the Achaeans reminding them of the terms of their treaty, and passing through Euboea with his forces, reached the Isthmus, the Aetolians having, in addition to other measures they took to prevent his assisting the Achaeans, forbidden him to advance with an army beyond Thermopylae, threatening, if he attempted it, to oppose his passage.

Antigonus and Cleomenes now faced each other, the former bent on penetrating into the Peloponnese and the latter on preventing him. 53. The Achaeans, although they had suffered such very serious reverses, yet did not abandon their purpose or their self-reliance, but on Aristoteles of Argos revolting against the partisans of Cleomenes, they sent a force to his assistance and entering the city by surprise under the command of their Strategus, Timoxenus, established themselves there. We should look on this achievement as the principal cause of the improvement in their fortunes which ensued. For events clearly showed that it was this which checked Cleomenes's ardor and subdued in advance his troops. Though his position was stronger than that of Antigonus and he was much better off for supplies, as well as animated by greater courage and ambition, no sooner did the news reach him that Argos had been seized by the Achaeans than he instantly took himself off, abandoning all these advantages, and made a precipitate retreat, fearing to be surrounded on all sides by the enemy. Gaining entrance to Argos he possessed himself of part of the city, but, on the Achaeans making a gallant resistance, in which the Argives joined with all the zeal of renegades, this plan broke down too, and, marching by way of Mantinea he returned to Sparta.

54. Antigonus now safely entered the Peloponnese and took possession of the Acrocorinthus and, without wasting any time there, pushed on and reached Argos. Having thanked the Argives and put matters in the city on a proper footing, he moved on again at once, making for Arcadia. After having ejected the garrisons from the forts that Cleomenes had built there to command the country in the territory of Aegys and Belbina, and handed over these forts to the Megalopolitans, he returned to Aegium where the Council of the Achaean League was in session. He gave them an account of the measures he had taken and arranged with them for the future conduct of the war. They hereupon appointed him commander-in-chief of all the allied forces, and after this he retired for a short time to his winter quarters near Sicyon and Corinth. Early in Spring he advanced with his army and reached Tegea in three days. Here the Achaeans joined him and the siege of the city was opened. The Macedonians conducted the siege energetically, especially by mining, and the Tegeans soon gave up all hope of holding out and surrendered. Antigonus, after securing the city, continued to pursue his plan of campaign and advanced rapidly on Laconia. He encountered Cleomenes posted on the frontier to defend Laconia and began to harass him, a few skirmishes taking place; but on learning from his scouts that the troops from Orchomenus had left to come to the aid of Cleomenes, he at once hastily broke up his camp and hurried thither. He surprised Orchomenus, and captured it by assault, and after this he laid siege to Mantinea which likewise the Macedonians soon frightened into submission and then he advanced on Heraea and Telphusa which the inhabitants surrendered to him of their own accord. The winter was now approaching. Antigonus came to Aegium to be present at the meeting of the Achaean Synod, and dismissing all his Macedonians to their homes for the winter, occupied himself in discussing the present situation with the Achaeans and making joint plans for the future.

55. Cleomenes at this juncture had observed that Antigonus had dismissed his other troops and, keeping only his mercenaries with him, was spending the time at Aegium at a distance of three days march from Megalopolis. He knew that this latter city was very difficult to defend, owing to its extent and partial desolation, that it was at present very carelessly guarded owing to the presence of Antigonus in the Peloponnese, and above all it had lost the greater part of its citizens of military age in the battles at the Lycaeum and at Ladoceia. He therefore procured the co-operation of certain Messenian exiles then living in Megalopolis and by their means got inside the walls secretly by night. On day breaking, he came very near not only being driven out, but meeting with complete disaster owing to the bravery of the Megalopolitans, who had indeed expelled and defeated him three months previously when he entered the city surprise in the quarter called Colaeum. But on this occasion, owing to the strength of his forces, and owing to his having had time to seize on the most advantageous positions, his project succeeded, and finally he

drove out the Megalopolitans and occupied their city. On possessing himself of it, he destroyed it with such systematic cruelty and animosity, that nobody would have thought it possible that it could ever be re-inhabited. I believe him to have acted so, because the Megalopolitans and Stymphalians were the only peoples from among whom in the varied circumstances of his career he could never procure himself a single partisan to share in his projects or a single traitor. For in the case of the Clitorians their noble love of freedom was sullied by the malpractice of one man Thearces whom, as one would expect, they naturally deny to have been a native-born citizen, affirming that he was the son of a foreign soldier and foisted in from Orchomenus.

How Not To Write History

More than any other Greek historian, Polybius discussed issues concerning historiography, even devoting his twelfth book—unfortunately lost except for fragments—to the subject. His discussions take the form of what we would call "critical book reviews" of the works of his predecessors. A particularly good example is the following extended analysis of the history of the third-century BCE Athenian historian Phylarchus, which contains some of Polybius's most important comments on how he believed that history should and should not be written.

56. Since, among those authors who were contemporaries of Aratus, Phylarchus,[28] who on many points is at variance and in contradiction with him, is by some received as trustworthy, it will be useful or rather necessary for me, as I have chosen to rely on Aratus's narrative for the history of the Cleomenic War and not leave the question of their relative credibility undiscussed, so that truth and falsehood in their writings may no longer be of equal authority. In general Phylarchus through his whole work makes many random and careless statements; but while perhaps it is not necessary for me at present to criticize in detail the rest of these, I must minutely examine such as relate to events occurring in the period with which I am now dealing, that of the Cleomenic War. This partial examination will however be quite sufficient to convey an idea of the general purpose and character of his work. Wishing, for instance, to insist on the cruelty of Antigonus and the Macedonians and also on that of Aratus and the Achaeans, he tells us that the Mantineans, when they surrendered, were exposed to terrible sufferings and that such were misfortunes that overtook this, the most ancient and greatest city in Arcadia, as to

---

28. Phylarchus was an Athenian historian who wrote in the late third century BCE a history of Greece from the death of Pyrrhus in 272 BCE to the death of Cleomenes III in 220 BCE. Phylarchus was one the principal exponents of what has been called "tragic history" in which vivid writing was used to arouse emotional responses in readers to the experiences of people caught in terrible events, similar to the responses produced by drama.

impress deeply and move to tears all the Greeks. In his eagerness to arouse the pity and attention of his readers he treats us to a picture of clinging women with their hair disheveled and their breasts bare, or again of crowds of both sexes together with their children and aged parents weeping and lamenting as they are led away to slavery. This sort of thing he keeps up throughout his history, always trying to bring horrors vividly before our eyes. Leaving aside the ignoble and womanish character of such a treatment of his subject, let us consider how far it is proper or serviceable to history. A historical author should not try to thrill his readers by such exaggerated pictures, nor should he, like a tragic poet, try to imagine the probable utterances of his characters or reckon up all the consequences probably incidental to the occurrences with which he deals, but simply record what really happened and what really was said, however commonplace. For the object of tragedy is not the same as that of history, but quite the opposite. The tragic poet should thrill and charm his audience for the moment by the verisimilitude of the words he puts into his characters' mouths, but it is the task of the historian to instruct and convince for all time serious students by the truth of the facts and the speeches he narrates, since in the one case it is the probable that takes precedence, even if it be untrue, the purpose being to confer benefit on learners. Apart from this, Phylarchus simply narrates most of such catastrophes and does not even suggest their causes or the nature of these causes, without which it is impossible in any case to feel either legitimate pity or proper anger. Who, for instance, does not think it an outrage for a free man to be beaten? But if this happens to one who was the first to resort to violence, we consider that he got only his desert, while where it is done for the purpose of correction or discipline, those who strike free men are not only excused but deemed worthy of thanks and praise. Again, to kill a citizen is considered the greatest of crimes and that deserving the highest penalty, but obviously he who kills a thief or adulterer is left untouched, and the slayer of a traitor or tyrant everywhere meets with honor and distinction. So in every such case the final criterion of good and evil lies not in what is done, but in the different reasons and different purposes of the doer.

57. Now the Mantineans had, in the first instance, deserted the Achaean League, and of their own free will put themselves and their city into the hands first of the Aetolians and then of Cleomenes. They had deliberately ranged themselves on his side and been admitted to Spartan citizenship, when, four years before the invasion of Antigonus, their city was betrayed to Aratus and forcibly occupied by the Achaeans. On this occasion, so far from their being cruelly treated owing to their recent delinquency, the circumstances became celebrated because of the sudden revulsion of sentiments on both sides. For immediately Aratus had the city in his hands, he at once issued orders to his troops to keep their hands off the property of others and next, calling an assembly of the Mantineans, bade them be of good courage and retain possession of all they had; for if they joined the Achaean League he would assure their perfect security. The prospect of safety thus suddenly revealed to them took the Mantineans completely by surprise, and there was an instantaneous and

universal reversal of feeling. The very men at whose hands they had seen, in the fight that had just closed, many of their kinsmen slain and many grievously wounded, were now taken into their houses, and received into their families with whom they lived on the kindest possible terms. This was quite natural, for I never heard of any men meeting with kinder enemies or being less injured by what is considered the greatest of calamities than the Mantineans, all owing to their humane treatment by Aratus and the Achaeans. 58. Subsequently, as they foresaw discord among themselves and plots by the Aetolians and Lacedaemonians, they sent an embassy to the Achaeans asking for a garrison. The Achaeans consented and chose by lot three hundred of their own citizens, who set forth, abandoning their own houses and possessions, and remained in Mantinea to watch over the liberty and safety of its townsmen. At the same time they sent two hundred hired soldiers, who aided this Achaean force in safe-guarding the established government. Very soon however the Mantineans fell out with the Achaeans, and, inviting the Lacedaemonians, put the city into their hands and massacred the garrison the Achaeans had sent them. It is not easy to name any greater or more atrocious act of treachery than this. For in resolving to forswear their friendship and gratitude, they should at least have spared the lives of these men and allowed them to depart under terms. Such treatment is, by the common law of nations, accorded even to enemies; but the Mantineans simply in order to give Cleomenes and the Lacedaemonians a satisfactory guarantee of their good faith in this undertaking violated the law recognized by all mankind and deliberately committed the most heinous of crimes. Vengeful murderers of the very men who previously on capturing their city had left them unharmed, and who now were guarding their liberties and lives—against such men, one asks oneself, can any indignation be too strong? What should we consider to be an adequate punishment for them? Someone might say that now when they were crushed by armed force they should have been sold into slavery with their wives and children. But to this fate the usage of war exposes those who have been guilty of no such impious crime. These men therefore were worthy of some far heavier and more extreme penalty; so that had they suffered what Phylarchus alleges, it was not to be expected that they should have met with pity from the Greeks, but rather that approval and assent should have been accorded to those who executed judgment on them for their wickedness. Yet, while nothing more serious befell the Mantineans in this their hour of calamity, than the pillage of their property and the enslavement of their male citizens, Phylarchus, all for the sake of making his narrative sensational, composed a tissue not only of falsehoods, but of improbable falsehoods, and, owing to his gross ignorance, was not even able to compare an analogous case and explain how the same people at the same time, on taking Tegea by force, did not commit any such excesses. For if the cause lay in the barbarity of the perpetrators, the Tegeans should have met with the same treatment as those who were conquered at the same time. If only the Mantineans were thus exceptionally treated, we must evidently infer that there was some exceptional cause for anger against them.

FROM BOOK 5

The Death of Cleomenes

After being defeated by Antigonus and his allies at the battle of Sellasia in July 222 BCE, Cleomenes fled from Sparta and went into exile in Egypt, where he became a member of the court first of Ptolemy III and then of Ptolemy IV. Polybius portrays Cleomenes as a "fish out of water" in the corrupt environment of Ptolemaic Alexandria, unable to cope with the plots of the devious courtiers of Ptolemy IV who entrapped him until he felt his only option was to die bravely like a true Spartan in a doomed attempt to incite rebellion by the king's subjects.

35. Cleomenes, during the lifetime of Ptolemy Euergetes, to whom he had linked his fortunes and pledged his word, had kept quiet, in the constant belief that he would receive sufficient assistance from him to recover the throne of his ancestors. But after the death of this king, as time went on, and circumstances in Greece almost called aloud for Cleomenes, Antigonus being dead, the Achaeans being engaged in war, and the Spartans now, as Cleomenes had from the first planned and purposed, sharing the hatred of the Aetolians for the Achaeans and Macedonians, he was positively compelled to bestir himself and do his best to get away from Alexandria. Consequently, he at first approached Ptolemy[29] more than once with the request that he would furnish him with adequate supplies and troops for an expedition; but as the king would not listen to this, he earnestly besought him to allow him to leave with his household, for the state of affairs, he said, held out a sufficiently fair prospect of his recovering his ancestral throne. The king, however, who for the reasons I stated above neither concerned him at all with such questions, nor took any thought for the future, continued in his thoughtlessness and folly to turn a deaf ear to Cleomenes. Meanwhile Sosibius, who, if anyone was now at the head of affairs, took counsel with his friends and came to the following decision with regard to him. On the one hand they judged it inadvisable to send him off on an armed expedition, as owing to the death of Antigonus they regarded foreign affairs as of no importance and thought that money they expended on them would be thrown away. Besides which, now that Antigonus was no more and there was no general left who was a match for Cleomenes, they were afraid that he would have little trouble in making himself the master of Greece and thus become a serious and formidable rival to themselves, especially as he had seen behind the scenes in Egypt and had formed a poor opinion of the king, and as he was aware that many parts of the kingdom were loosely attached or dissevered by distance, thus offering

---

29. Ptolemy IV, king of Egypt from 222 BCE to 205 BCE.

plenty of opportunity for intrigue—for they had a good many ships at Samos and a considerable military force at Ephesus. These, then, were the reasons which made them dismiss the project of sending Cleomenes off with supplies for an expedition; but at the same time they thought it would by no means serve their interests to send away such an eminent man after inflicting a slight on him, as this was sure to make him their enemy and antagonist. The only course left then was to keep him back against his will, and this they all indeed rejected at once and without discussion, thinking it by no means safe for a lion to lie in the same fold as the sheep, but it was especially Sosibius who was apprehensive of the effects of such a measure for the following reason. 36. At the time when they were plotting the murder of Magas and Berenice,[30] being in great fear of their project failing owing to the high courage of Berenice, they were compelled to conciliate the whole court, holding out hopes of favor to everyone if things fell out as they wished. Sosibius on this occasion, observing that Cleomenes was in need of assistance from the king, and that he was a man of judgment with a good grasp of facts, confided the whole plot to him, picturing the high favor he might expect. Cleomenes, seeing that he was in a state of great alarm and in fear chiefly of the foreign soldiers and mercenaries, bade him be of good heart, promising him that the mercenaries would do him no harm, but would rather be helpful to him. When Sosibius showed considerable surprise at this promise, "Don't you see," he said, "that nearly three thousand of them are from the Peloponnese and about a thousand are Cretans, and I need but make a sign to these men and they will all put themselves joyfully at your service. Once they are united whom do you have to fear? The soldiers from Syria and Caria, I suppose!" At the time Sosibius was delighted to hear this and pursued the plot against Berenice with doubled confidence, but afterward, when he witnessed the king's slackness, the words were always coming back to his mind, and the thought of Cleomenes's daring and popularity with the mercenaries kept on haunting him. It was he therefore who on this occasion was foremost in instigating the king and his friends to take Cleomenes into custody before it was too late. To reinforce this advice he availed himself of the following circumstance.

37. There was a certain Messenian called Nicagoras who had been a family friend of Archidamus the king of Sparta. In former times their intercourse had been of the slightest, but when Archidamus took flight from Sparta for fear of Cleomenes, and came to Messenia, Nicagoras not only gladly received him in his house and provided for his wants but ever afterward they stood on terms of the closest intimacy and affection. When therefore Cleomenes held out hopes to Archidamus of return and reconciliation, Nicagoras devoted himself to negotiating and concluding the treaty. When this had been ratified, Archidamus was on his way home to Sparta, relying on the terms of the agreement brought about by Nicagoras, but Cleomenes coming to meet him put Archidamus to death, sparing Nicagoras and the rest of his

---

30. Berenice II, the widow of Ptolemy III, and the mother of Magas and Ptolemy IV.

companions. To the outside world, Nicagoras pretended to be grateful to Cleomenes for having spared his life, but in his heart he bitterly resented what had occurred, for it looked as if he had been the cause of the king's death. This Nicagoras had arrived not long ago at Alexandria with a cargo of horses and on disembarking he found Cleomenes, with Panteus and Hippitas, walking on the wharf. When Cleomenes saw him he came up to him and greeted him affectionately and asked on what business he had come. When he told him he had brought horses to sell, Cleomenes said, "I very much wish you had brought catamites and sambuka girls[31] instead of the horses, for those are the wares this king is after." Nicagoras at the time smiled and held his tongue, but a few days afterward, when he had become quite familiar with Sosibius owing to the business of the horses, he told against Cleomenes the story of what he had recently said, and noticing that Sosibius listened to him with pleasure, he gave him a full account of his old grievance against that prince. 38. When Sosibius saw that he was ill-disposed to Cleomenes, he persuaded him by a bribe in cash and a promise of a further sum to write a letter against Cleomenes and leave it sealed, so that a few days after Nicagoras had left his servant might bring him the letter as having been sent by Nicagoras. Nicagoras entered into the plot, and when the letter was brought to Sosibius by the servant after Nicagoras had sailed, he at once took the servant and the letter to the king. The servant said that Nicagoras had left the letter with orders for him to deliver it to Sosibius, and as the letter stated that Cleomenes, unless he were furnished with a properly equipped expeditionary force, intended to revolt against the king, Sosibius at once availed himself of this pretext for urging the king not to delay, but to take the precaution of placing him in custody. This was done, a huge house being put at his disposal in which he resided under watch and ward, differing from ordinary prisoners only in that he had a bigger jail to live in. Seeing his position and having but poor hopes of the future, Cleomenes decided to make a dash for freedom at any cost, not that he really believed he would attain his object—for he had nothing on his side likely to conduce to success—but rather desiring to die a glorious death without submitting to anything unworthy of the high courage he had ever exhibited, and I suppose that there dwelt in his mind and inspired him those words of the hero which are wont to commend themselves to men of dauntless spirit:[32]

"Well, this is fate,
But I will not perish without doing some great deed
That future generations will remember."

---

31. Male prostitutes and girls, who played a four-stringed musical instrument called a sambuka.
32. Homer, *Iliad* 22, lines 331–33 (translation by Stanley Lombardo) = Homer, *Iliad*, lines 303–5 (Greek text).

39. Waiting then for a day on which Ptolemy made an excursion to Canobus he spread a report among his guards that he was going to be set at liberty by the king, and upon this pretense he entertained his own attendants, and sent presents of meat, garlands, and wine to the guards. When the soldiers, suspecting nothing, had indulged freely in these good things and were quite drunk, he took the friends who were with him and his own servants and at about midday they rushed out of the house unnoticed by the guards, and armed with daggers. As they advanced they met in the square with Ptolemy who had been left in charge of the city,[33] and overawing his attendants by the audacity of their attack, they dragged him from his chariot and shut him up, and now began to call on the people to assert their freedom. But when no one paid any attention or consented to join the rising, as the whole plan had taken everyone completely by surprise, they retraced their steps and made for the citadel with the intention of forcing the gates and getting the prisoners to join them. But when this design also failed, as the guards of the prison got word of their intention and made the gates fast, they died by their own hands like brave men and Spartans.

Thus perished Cleomenes, a man tactful in his bearing and address, with a great capacity for the conduct of affairs and in a word designed by nature to be a captain and a prince.

FROM BOOK 6

From the Preface to Book 6

What chiefly attracts and chiefly benefits students of history is just this—the study of causes and the consequent power of choosing what is best in each case. Now the chief cause of success or the reverse in all matters is the form of a state's constitution; for springing from this, as from a fountain-head, all designs and plans of action not only originate, but reach their consummation.

The Cycle of Constitutions

Polybius viewed Roman resilience after the devastating Carthaginian victory at Cannae in 216 BCE as the decisive factor in explaining Rome's ultimate defeat of Carthage in the Second Punic War. In book six, he argued that the true explanation of Rome's superiority to Carthage lay in its mixed constitution, which delayed its inevitable decline, while Carthage had already begun to decline and, as a result, despite initial victories, could not mount an

---

33. The governor of Alexandria, not the king.

effective military response to Roman power. Unfortunately, only fragments remain of book six, but the main stages of Polybius's argument are clear. After explaining the cycle of constitutions experienced by all states and the respective places of Rome and Carthage in the cycle, he described in a now lost passage the development of the Roman mixed constitution. An extensive description of Rome's political and military institutions, that is omitted here, followed; and the argument concluded with a comparative analysis demonstrating the superiority of Rome's mixed constitutions to other less successful examples of such governments like that of Sparta.

3. In the case of those Greek states which have often risen to greatness and have often experienced a complete change of fortune, it is an easy matter both to describe their past and to pronounce on their future. For there is no difficulty in reporting the known facts, and it is not hard to foretell the future by inference from the past. But about the Roman state it is neither at all easy to explain the present situation owing to the complicated character of the constitution, nor to foretell the future owing to our ignorance of the peculiar features of public and private life at Rome in the past. Particular attention and study are therefore required If one wishes to attain a general view of the distinctive qualities of their constitution.

Most of those whose object it has been to instruct us methodically concerning such matters,[34] distinguish three kinds of constitutions, which they call kingship, aristocracy, and democracy. Now we should, I think, be quite justified in asking them to enlighten us as to whether they represent these three to be the sole varieties or rather to be the best; for in either case my opinion is that they are wrong. For it is evident that we must regard as the best constitution a combination of all these three varieties, since we have had proof of this not only theoretically but by actual experience, Lycurgus having been the first to draw up a constitution—that of Sparta—on this principle.[35] Nor on the other hand can we admit that these are the only three varieties; for we have witnessed monarchical and tyrannical governments, which while they differ very widely from kingship, yet bear a certain resemblance to it, this being the reason why monarchs in general falsely assume and use, as far as they can, the regal title. There have also been several oligarchical constitutions which seem to bear some likeness to aristocratic ones, though the divergence is, generally, as wide as possible. The same holds good about democracies. 4. The truth of what I say is evident from the following considerations. It is by no means every monarchy which

---

34. Polybius does not identify "most of those," probably because the theory of three basic forms of constitutions was a commonplace by his time.

35. As will become obvious, Polybius actually recognized seven forms of constitutions, the three basic forms and their corruptions and mixed constitutions. The idea that Lycurgus, the legendary lawgiver of Sparta, created a mixed constitution is found already in fourth-century BCE thinkers like Plato and Aristotle.

we can call straight off a kingship, but only that which is voluntarily accepted by the subjects and where they are governed rather by an appeal to their reason than by fear and force. Nor again can we style every oligarchy an aristocracy, but only that where the government is in the hands of a selected body of the justest and wisest men. Similarly that is no true democracy in which the whole crowd of citizens is free to do whatever they wish or purpose, but when, in a community where it is traditional and customary to reverence the gods, to honor our parents, to respect our elders, and to obey the laws, the will of the greater number prevails, this is to be called a democracy. We should therefore assert that there are six kinds of governments, the three above mentioned which are in everyone's mouth and three which are naturally allied to them, I mean monarchy, oligarchy, and mob-rule. Now the first of these to come into being is monarchy, its growth being natural and unaided; and next arises kingship derived from monarchy by the aid of art and by the correction of defects. Monarchy first changes into its vicious allied form, tyranny; and next, the abolishment of both gives birth to aristocracy. Aristocracy by its very nature degenerates into oligarchy; and when the commons, inflamed by anger take vengeance on this government for its unjust rule, democracy comes into being; and in due course the license and lawlessness of this form of government produces mob-rule to complete the series. The truth of what I have just said will be quite clear to anyone who pays due attention to such beginnings, origins, and changes as are in each case natural. For he alone who has seen how each form naturally arises and develops, will be able to see when, how, and where the growth, perfection, change, and end of each are likely to occur again. And it is to the Roman constitution above all that this method, I think, may be successfully applied, since from the outset its formation and growth have been due to natural causes.

5. Perhaps this theory of the natural transformation into each other of the different forms of government is more elaborately set forth by Plato and certain other philosophers; but as the arguments are subtle and are stated at great length, they are beyond the reach of all but a few. I therefore will attempt to give a short summary of the theory, as far as I consider it to apply to the actual history of facts and to appeal to the common intelligence of mankind.[36] For if there appear to be omissions in my general exposition of it, the detailed discussion which follows will afford the reader ample compensation for any difficulties now left unsolved.

What then are the beginnings I speak of and what is the first origin of political societies? When owing to floods, famines, failure of crops, or other such causes there occurs such a destruction of the human race as tradition tells us more than

---

36. Two points should be noted. First, Polybius did not claim to have invented the theory of the cycle of constitutions but only to provide a summary of a theory held by numerous philosophers including Plato; and second, he understood it to be a natural process which all states must undergo. Consequently, identifying what point in the cycle a state has reached indicates how effective its government will be.

once happened, and as we must believe will often happen again, all arts and crafts perishing at the same time, then in the course of time, when springing from the survivors as from seeds men have again increased in numbers and just like other animals form herds—it being a matter of course that they too should herd together with those of their kind owing to their natural weakness—it is a necessary consequence that the man who excels in bodily strength and in courage will lead and rule over the rest. We observe and should regard as a most genuine work of nature this very phenomenon in the case of other animals which act purely by instinct and among whom the strongest are always indisputably the masters—I speak of bulls, boars, cocks, and the like. It is probable then that at the beginning men lived thus, herding together like animals and following the lead of the strongest and bravest, the ruler's strength being here the sole limit to his power and the name we should give his rule being monarchy.

But when in time feelings of sociability and companionship begin to grow in such gatherings of men, then kingship has struck root; and the notions of goodness, justice, and their opposites begin to arise in men.

6. The manner in which these notions come into being is as follows. Men being all naturally inclined to sexual intercourse, and the consequence of this being the birth of children, whenever one of those who have been reared does not on growing up show gratitude to those who reared him or defend them, but on the contrary takes to speaking ill of them or ill-treating them, it is evident that he will displease and offend those who have been familiar with his parents and have witnessed the care and pains they spent on attending to and feeding their children. For seeing that men are distinguished from the other animals by possessing the faculty of reason, it is obviously improbable that such a difference of conduct should escape them, as it escapes the other animals; they will notice the thing and be displeased at what is going on, looking to the future and reflecting that they may all meet with the same treatment. Again when a man who has been helped or succored when in danger by another does not show gratitude to his preserver, but even goes to the length of attempting to do him injury, it is clear that those who become aware of it will naturally be displeased and offended by such conduct, sharing the resentment of their injured neighbor and imagining themselves in the same situation. From all this there arises in everyone a notion of the meaning and theory of duty, which is the beginning and end of justice. Similarly, again, when any man is foremost in defending his fellows from danger, and braves and awaits the onslaught of the most powerful beasts, it is natural that he should receive marks of favor and honor from the people, while the man who acts in the opposite manner will meet with reprobation and dislike. From this again some idea of what is base and what is noble and of what constitutes the difference is likely to arise among the people; and noble conduct will be admired and imitated because it is advantageous, while base conduct will be avoided. Now when the leading and most powerful man among the people always throws the weight of his authority on the side of the notions on such matters which

generally prevail, and when in the opinion of his subjects he apportions rewards and penalties accordingly to desert, they yield obedience to him no longer because they fear his force, but rather because their judgment approves him; and they join in maintaining his rule even if he is quite enfeebled by age, defending him with one consent and battling against those who conspire to overthrow his rule. Thus by insensible degrees the monarch becomes a king, ferocity and force having yielded the supremacy to reason.

7. Thus is formed naturally among men the first notion of goodness and justice, and their opposites; this is the beginning and birth of true kingship. For the people maintain the supreme power not only in the hands of these men themselves, but in those of their descendants, from the conviction that those born from and reared by such men will also have principles like to theirs. And if they ever are displeased with the descendants, they now choose their kings and rulers no longer for their bodily strength and brute courage, but for the excellence of their judgment and reasoning powers, as they have gained experience from actual facts of the difference between the one class of qualities and the other. In old times, then, those who had once been chosen to the royal office continued to hold it until they grew old, fortifying and enclosing fine strongholds with walls and acquiring lands, in the one case for the sake of the security of their subjects and in the other to provide them with abundance of the necessities of life. And while pursuing these aims, they were exempt from all vituperation or jealousy, as neither in their dress nor in their food did they make any great distinction, but lived very much like everyone else, not keeping apart from the people. But when they received the office by hereditary succession and found their safety now provided for, and more than sufficient provision of food, they gave way to their appetites owing to this superabundance, and came to think that the rulers must be distinguished from their subjects by a peculiar dress, that there should be a peculiar luxury and variety in the dressing and serving of their food, and that they should meet with no denial in the pursuit of their loves, however lawless. These habits having given rise in the one case to envy and offense and in the other to an outburst of hatred and passionate resentment, the kingship changed into a tyranny; the first steps toward its overthrow were taken by the subjects, and conspiracies began to be formed. These conspiracies were not the work of the worst men, but of the noblest, most high-spirited, and most courageous, because such men are least able to brook the intolerance of princes. 8. The people now having got leaders, would combine with them against the ruling powers for the reasons I stated above; kingship and monarchy would be utterly abolished, and in their place aristocracy would begin to grow. For the commons, as if bound to pay at once their debt of gratitude to the abolishers of monarchy, would make them their leaders and entrust their destinies to them. At first these chiefs gladly assumed this charge and regarded nothing as of greater importance than the common interest, administering the private and public affairs of the people with paternal solicitude. But here again when children inherited this position of authority from their authority from

their fathers, having no experience of misfortune and none at all of civil equality and liberty of speech, and having been brought up from the cradle amid the evidences of the power and high position of their fathers, they abandoned themselves some to greed of gain and unscrupulous money-making, others to indulgences in wine and the convivial excess which accompanies it, and others again to the violation of women and the rape of boys; and thus converting the aristocracy into an oligarchy aroused in the people feelings similar to those of which I just spoke, and in consequence met with the same disastrous end as the tyrant. 9. For whenever anyone who has noticed the jealousy and hatred with which they are regarded by the citizens, has the courage to speak or act against the chiefs of the state he has the whole mass of the people ready to back him. Next, when they have either killed or banished the oligarchs, they no longer venture to set a king over them, as they still remember with terror the injustice they suffered from the former ones, nor can they entrust the government with confidence to a select few, with the evidence before them of their recent error in doing so. Thus the only hope still surviving unimpaired is in themselves, and to this they resort, making the state a democracy instead of an oligarchy and assuming the responsibility for the conduct of affairs. Then as long as some of those survive who experienced the evils of oligarchical dominion, they are well pleased with the present form of government, and set a high value on equality and freedom of speech. But when a new generation arises and the democracy falls into the hands of the grandchildren of its founders, they have become so accustomed to freedom and equality that they no longer value them, and begin to aim at pre-eminence; and it is chiefly those of ample fortune who fall into this error. So when they begin to lust for power and cannot attain it through themselves or their own good qualities, they ruin their estates, tempting and corrupting the people in every possible way. And hence when by their foolish thirst for reputation they have created among the masses an appetite for gifts and the habit of receiving them, democracy in its turn is abolished and changes into a rule of force and violence. For the people, having grown accustomed to feed at the expense of others and to depend for their livelihood on the property of others, as soon as they find a leader who is enterprising but is excluded from the honors of office by his poverty, institute the rule of violence; and now uniting their forces massacre, banish, and plunder, until they degenerate again into perfect savages and find once more a master and monarch.

Such is the cycle of political revolution, the course appointed by nature in which constitutions change, disappear, and finally return to the point from which they started. Anyone who clearly perceives this may indeed in speaking of the future of any state be wrong in his estimate of the time the process will take, but if his judgment is not tainted by animosity or jealousy, he will very seldom be mistaken as to the stage of growth or decline it has reached, and as to the form into which it will change. And especially in the case of the Roman state will this method enable us to arrive at a knowledge of its formation, growth, and greatest perfection, and likewise of the change for the worse which is sure to follow some day. For, as I said, this state, more than any other, has been formed and has grown naturally, and will undergo a natural decline and change to its contrary.[37] The reader will be able to judge of the truth of this from the subsequent parts of this work.

10. At present I will give a brief account of the legislation of Lycurgus, a matter not alien to my present purpose. Lycurgus had perfectly well understood that all the above changes take place necessarily and naturally, and had taken into consideration that every variety of constitution which is simple and formed on one principle is precarious, as it is soon perverted into the corrupt form which is proper to it and naturally follows on it. For just as rust in the case of iron and wood-worms and ship-worms in the case of timber are inbred pests, and these substances, even though they escape all external injury, fall a prey to the evils engendered in them, so each constitution has a vice engendered in it and inseparable from it. In kingship it is despotism, in aristocracy oligarchy, and in democracy the savage rule of mob violence; and it is impossible, as I said above, that each of these should not in course of time change into this vicious form. Lycurgus, then, foreseeing this, did not make his constitution simple and uniform, but united in it all the good and distinctive features of the best governments, so that none of the principles should grow unduly and be perverted into its allied evil, but that, the force of each being neutralized by that of the others, neither of them should prevail and outbalance another but that the constitution should remain for long in a state of equilibrium like a well-trimmed boat, kingship being guarded from arrogance by the fear of the commons, who were given a sufficient share in the government, and the commons on the other hand not venturing to treat the kings with contempt from fear of the elders, who being selected from the best citizens would be sure all of them to be always on the side of justice; so that that part of the state which was weakest owing to its subservience to traditional custom, acquired power and weight by the support and influence of the elders. The consequence was that by drawing up his constitution thus he preserved liberty at Sparta for a longer period than is recorded elsewhere.

Lycurgus then, foreseeing, by a process of reasoning, whence and how events naturally happen, constructed his constitution untaught by adversity, but the Romans while they have arrived at the same final result as regards their form of government, have not reached it by any process of reasoning, but by the discipline of many struggles and troubles, and always choosing the best by the light of the experience gained in disaster have thus reached the same result as Lycurgus, that is to say, the best of all existing constitutions.

---

37. It is important to recognize that while the development of a mixed constitution as Polybius believed had happened first at Sparta and later at Rome could slow the cycle of constitutions, it was not abolished. Rome, therefore, just as Sparta before it would eventually decline as its mixed constitution decayed.

Comparison of Constitutions

After a detailed description of Roman political and military institutions as Polybius believed they functioned during the Second Punic War, he concludes his discussion of constitutions with a comparative analysis of what he considers the best constitutions known to him. It is noteworthy that his criterion of constitutional excellence is the success of the states governed under them as imperial powers.

43. One may say that nearly all authors have handed down to us the reputation for excellence enjoyed by the constitutions of Sparta, Crete, Mantinea, and Carthage. Some make mention also of those of Athens and Thebes. I leave these aside; for I am myself convinced that the constitutions of Athens and Thebes need not be dealt with at length, considering that these states neither grew by a normal process, nor did they remain for long in their most flourishing state, nor were the changes they underwent immaterial; but after a sudden effulgence so to speak, the work of chance and circumstance, while still apparently prosperous and with every prospect of a bright future, they experienced a complete reverse of fortune. For the Thebans, striking at the Lacedaemonians through their mistaken policy and the hatred their allies bore them, owing to the admirable qualities of one or at most two men, who had detected these weaknesses, gained in Greece a reputation for superiority. Indeed, that the successes of the Thebans at that time were due not to the form of their constitution, but to the high qualities of their leading men, was made manifest to all by Fortune immediately afterward. For the success of Thebes grew, attained its height, and ceased with the lives of Epaminondas and Pelopidas; and therefore we must regard the temporary splendor of that state as due not to its constitution, but to its men. 44. We must hold very much the same opinion about the Athenian constitution. For Athens also, though she perhaps enjoyed more frequent periods of success, after her most glorious one of all which was coeval with the excellent administration of Themistocles,[38] rapidly experienced a complete reverse of fortune owing to the inconstancy of her nature. For the Athenian populace always more or less resembles a ship without a commander. In such a ship when fear of the billows or the danger of a storm induces the mariners to be sensible and to attend to the orders of the skipper, they do their duty admirably. But when they grow overconfident and begin to entertain contempt for their superiors and to quarrel with each other, as they are no longer all of the same way of thinking, then with some

---

38. Polybius's identification of Athens's greatest period of power and prosperity with the preeminence of Themistocles, essentially the time of the Persian Wars and their immediate aftermath in the early fifth century BCE, was unusual in antiquity, when most historians would have placed it later, specifically in the several decades after the mid-century during the time of Pericles as also do most modern historians.

of them determined to continue the voyage, and others putting pressure on the skipper to anchor, with some letting out the sheets and others preventing them and ordering the sails to be taken in, not only does the spectacle strike anyone who watches it as disgraceful owing to their disagreement and contention, but the position of affairs is a source of actual danger to the rest of those on board; so that often after escaping from the perils of the widest seas and fiercest storms they are shipwrecked in harbor and when close to the shore. This is what has more than once befallen the Athenian state. After having averted the greatest and most terrible dangers owing to the high qualities of the people and their leaders, it has come to grief at times by sheer heedlessness and unreasonableness in seasons of unclouded tranquility. Therefore I need say no more about this constitution or that of Thebes, states in which everything is managed by the uncurbed impulse of a mob in the one case exceptionally headstrong and ill-tempered and in the other brought up in an atmosphere of violence and passion.

45. To pass to the constitution of Crete, two points here demand out attention. How was it, the most learned of the ancient writers—Ephorus, Xenophon, Callisthenes, and Plato—state in the first place that it is one and the same with that of Lacedaemon and in the second place pronounce it worthy of commendation? In my opinion, neither of these assertions is true. Whether or not I am right the following observations will show. And first as to its dissimilarity with the constitution of Sparta. The peculiar features of the Spartan state are said to be first the land laws by which no citizen may own more than another, but all must possess an equal share of the public land; secondly their view of money-making; for, money being esteemed of no value at all among them, the jealous contention due to the possession of more or less is utterly done away with; and thirdly the fact that of the magistrates by whom or by whose co-operation the whole administration is conducted, the kings hold a hereditary office and members of the Gerousia[39] are elected for life. 46. In all these respects the Cretan practice is exactly the opposite. Their laws go as far as possible in letting them acquire land to the extent of their power, as the saying is, and money is held in such high honor among them that its acquisition is not only regarded as necessary, but as most honorable. So much in fact do sordid love of gain and lust for wealth prevail among them, that the Cretans are the only people in the world in whose eyes no gain is disgraceful. Again their magistracies are annual and elected on a democratic system. So that it often causes surprise how these authors proclaim to us, that two political systems the nature of which is so opposed are allied and akin to each other. Besides overlooking such differences, these writers go out of their way to give us their general views, saying that Lycurgus was the only man who ever

---

39. The Gerousia or Council of Elders consisted of the two kings and twenty-eight Spartans elected from those sixty years of age or older and prepared business for the Spartan assembly. It served as the city council and highest court of Sparta and could cancel decisions of the assembly with which it disagreed.

saw the point of vital importance for good government. For, there being two things to which a state owes it preservation, bravery against the enemy and concord among the citizens, Lycurgus by doing away with the lust for wealth did away also with all civil discord and broils. In consequence of which the Lacedaemonians, being free from these evils, excel all the Greeks in the conduct of their internal affairs and in their spirit of union. After asserting this, although they witness that the Cretans, on the other hand, owing to their ingrained lust of wealth are involved in constant broils both public and private, and in murders and civil wars, they regard this as immaterial, and have the audacity to say that the two political systems are similar. Ephorus actually, apart from the names, uses the same phrases in explaining the nature of the two states; so that if one did not attend to the proper names it would be impossible to tell of which he is speaking.

Such are the points in which I consider these two political systems to differ, and I will now give my reasons for not regarding that of Crete as worthy of praise or imitation. 47. In my opinion there are two fundamental things in every state, by virtue of which its principles and constitution is either desirable or the reverse. I mean customs and laws. What is desirable in these makes men's private lives righteous and well ordered and the general character of the state gentle and just, while what is to be avoided has the opposite effect. So just as when we observe the laws and customs of a people to be good, we have no hesitation in pronouncing that the citizens and the state will consequently be good also, thus when we notice that men are covetous in their private lives and that their public actions are unjust, we are plainly justified in saying that their laws, their particular customs, and the state as a whole are bad. Now it would be impossible to find except in some rare instances personal conduct more treacherous or a public policy more unjust than in Crete. Holding then the Cretan constitution to be neither similar to that of Sparta nor in any way deserving of praise and imitation, I dismiss it from the comparison which I have proposed to make.

Nor again is it fair to introduce Plato's republic which also is much belauded by some philosophers. For just as we do not admit to athletic contests artists or athletes who are not duly entered and have been in training, so we have no right to admit this constitution to the competition for the prize of merit, unless it first gives an exhibition of its actual working. Up to the present it would be just the same thing to discuss it with a view to comparison with the constitutions of Sparta, Rome, and Carthage, as to take some statue and compare it with living and breathing men. For even if the workmanship of the statue were altogether praiseworthy, the comparison of a lifeless thing with a living being would strike spectators as entirely imperfect and incongruous.

48. Dismissing, therefore, these constitutions, we will return to that of Sparta. To me it seems that as far as regards the maintenance of concord among the citizens, the security of the Laconian territory and the preservation of the freedom of Sparta, the legislation of Lycurgus and the foresight he exhibited were so admirable

that one is forced to regard his institutions as of divine rather than human origin. For the equal division of landed property and the simple and common diet were calculated to produce temperance in the private lives of the citizens and to secure the commonwealth as a whole from civil strife, as was the training in the endurance of hardships and dangers to form brave and valorous men. Now when both these virtues, fortitude and temperance, are combined in one soul or one city, evil will not readily originate within such men or such peoples, nor will they be easily overmastered by their neighbors. By constructing, therefore, his constitution in this manner and out of these elements, Lycurgus secured the absolute safety of the whole territory of Laconia, and left to the Spartans themselves a lasting heritage of freedom. But as regards the annexation of neighboring territories, supremacy in Greece, and generally speaking, an ambitious policy, he seems to me to have made absolutely no provision for such contingencies, either in particular enactments or in the general constitution of the state. What he left undone, therefore, was to bring to bear on the citizens some force or principle, by which, just as he had made them simple and contented in their private lives, he might make the city as a whole likewise contented and moderate. But now, while he made them most unambitious and sensible people as regards their private lives and the institutions of their city, he left them most ambitious, domineering, and aggressive toward the rest of the Greeks.

49. For who is not aware that they were almost the first of the Greeks to cast longing eyes on the territory of their neighbors, making war on the Messenians out of covetousness and for the purpose of enslaving them?[40] And is it not narrated by all historians how out of sheer obstinacy they bound themselves by an oath not to desist from the siege before they had taken Messene? It is no less universally known that owing to their desire of domination in Greece they were obliged to execute the behests of the very people they had conquered in battle. For they conquered the Persians when they invaded Greece, fighting for her freedom; but when the invaders had withdrawn and fled they betrayed the Greek cities to them by the peace of Antalcidas, in order to procure money for establishing their sovereignty over the Greeks; and here a conspicuous defect in their constitution revealed itself.[41] For as long as they aspired to rule over their neighbors or over the Peloponnesians alone, they found the supplies and resources furnished by Laconia itself adequate, as they

---

40. The reference is to the First Messenian War, traditionally believed to have lasted for twenty years in the late eighth century BCE. Polybius's interpretation of it as caused by Spartan aggression is counter to the more common pro-Spartan view that the war was a response to Messenians killing a Spartan king who was trying to protect young Spartan women threatened with rape.

41. Actually, almost a century intervened between the defeat of the Persians in 479 BCE and the conclusion of the so-called King's Peace or Peace of Antalcidas in 386 BCE, in which Sparta recognized Persian sovereignty over the Greeks of Asia and the Persian king's right to intervene in affairs in Greece proper.

had all they required ready to hand, and quickly returned home whether by land or by sea. But once they began to undertake naval expeditions and to make military campaigns outside the Peloponnese, it was evident that neither their crops nor the exchange of their crops for commodities which they lacked, as permitted by the legislation of Lycurgus, would suffice for their needs, since these enterprises demanded a currency in universal circulation[42] and supplies drawn from abroad; and so they were compelled to be beggars from the Persians, to impose tribute on the islanders, and to exact contributions from all the Greeks, as they recognized that under the legislation of Lycurgus it was impossible to aspire, I will not say to supremacy in Greece, but to any position of influence.

50. But what is the purpose of this digression? It is to show from the actual evidence of facts, that for the purpose of remaining in secure possession of their own territory and maintaining their freedom the legislation of Lycurgus is amply sufficient, and to those who maintain this to be the object of political constitutions we must admit that there is not and never was any system or constitution superior to that of Lycurgus. But if anyone is ambitious of greater things, and esteem it finer and more glorious than that to be the leader of many men and to rule and lord it over many and have the eyes of all the world turned to him, it must be admitted that from this point of view the Laconian constitution is defective, while that of Rome is superior and better framed for the attainment of power, as is indeed evident from the actual course of events. For when the Lacedaemonians endeavored to obtain supremacy in Greece, they very soon ran the risk of losing their own liberty; whereas the Romans, who had aimed merely at the subjection of Italy, in a short time brought the whole world under their sway, the abundance of supplies they had at their command conducing in no small measure to this result.

51. The constitution of Carthage seems to me to have been originally well contrived as regards its most distinctive points. For there were kings,[43] and the house of Elders was an aristocratical force, and the people were supreme in matters proper to them, the entire frame of the state much resembling that of Rome and Sparta. But at the time when they entered on the Hannibalic War,[44] the Carthaginian constitution had degenerated, and that of Rome was better. For as every body or state or action has its natural periods of decay, and as everything in them is at its best when they are in their prime, it was for this reason that the difference between the two states manifested itself at this time. For by as much as the power and prosperity of Carthage had been earlier than that of Rome, by so much had Carthage already begun to decline; while Rome was exactly at her prime, as far at least as her system of government was concerned. Consequently the multitude at Carthage had already

---

42. The Spartans were famous for using an iron currency which had no value outside Sparta.

43. What Polybius calls "kings" were the two annually elected *sufetes* ("judges") who were the chief magistrates at Carthage.

44. More commonly known as the Second Punic War (218–202 BCE).

acquired the chief voice in deliberations; while at Rome the senate still retained this; and hence, as in one case the masses deliberated and in the other the most eminent men, the Roman decisions in public affairs were superior, so that although they met with complete disaster, they were finally by the wisdom of their counsels victorious over the Carthaginians in the war.

52. But to pass to differences of detail, such as, to begin with, the conduct of war, the Carthaginians naturally are superior at sea both in efficiency and equipment, because seamanship has long been their national craft, and they busy themselves with the sea more than any other people; but as regards military service on land the Romans are much more efficient. They indeed devote their whole energies to this matter, whereas the Carthaginians entirely neglect their infantry, though they do pay some slight attention to their cavalry. The reason of this is that the troops they employ are foreign and mercenary whereas those of the Romans are natives of the soil and citizens. So that in this respect also we must pronounce the political system of Rome to be superior to that of Carthage, the Carthaginians continuing to depend for the maintenance of their freedom on the courage of a mercenary force but the Romans on their own valor and on the aid of their allies. Consequently even if they happen to be worsted at the outset, the Romans redeem defeat by final success, while it is the contrary with the Carthaginians. For the Romans, fighting as they are for their country and their children, never can abate their fury but continue to throw their whole hearts into the struggle until they get the better of their enemies. It follows that though the Romans are, as I said, much less skilled in naval matters, they are on the whole successful at sea owing to the gallantry of their men; for although skill in seamanship is of no small importance in naval battles, it is chiefly the courage of the marines that turns the scale in favor of victory.[45] Now not only do Italians in general naturally excel Phoenicians and Africans in bodily strength and personal courage, but by their institutions also they do much to foster a spirit of bravery in the young men. A single instance will suffice to indicate the pains taken by the state to turn out men who will be ready to endure everything in order to gain a reputation in their country for valor.

53. Whenever any illustrious man dies, he is carried at his funeral into the forum to the so-called rostra,[46] sometimes conspicuous in an upright posture and more rarely reclined. Here with all the people standing round, a grown-up son, if he has left one who happens to be present, or if not some other relative mounts the rostra and discourses on the virtues and successful achievements of the dead. As a consequence the multitude and not only those who had a part in these achievements, but those also who had none, when the facts are recalled to their minds and

---

45. The Romans were famous for winning naval victories in the First Punic War (264–241 BCE) by using boarding tactics.

46. The speaker's platform at Rome during the Republic. It was located in the *comitium*, the place where Roman assemblies met just north of the Forum.

brought before their eyes, are moved to such sympathy that the loss seems to be not confined to the mourners, but a public one affecting the whole people. Next after the interment and the performance of the usual ceremonies, they place the image of the departed in the most conspicuous position in the house, enclosed in a wooden shrine. This image is a mask reproducing with remarkable fidelity both the features and complexion of the deceased. On the occasion of public sacrifices they display these images, and decorate them with much care, and when any distinguished member of the family dies they take them to the funeral, putting them on men who seem to them to bear the closest resemblance to the original in stature and carriage. These representatives wear togas, with a purple border if the deceased was a consul or praetor, whole purple if he a censor, and embroidered with gold if he had celebrated a triumph or achieved anything similar. They all ride in chariots preceded by the fasces, axes, and other insignia by which the different magistrates are wont to be accompanied according to the respective dignity of the offices of state held by each during his life; and when they arrive at the rostra they all seat themselves in a row on ivory chairs. There could not easily be a more ennobling spectacle for a young man who aspires to fame and virtue. For who would not be inspired by the sight of the images of men renowned for their excellence, all together and as if alive and breathing? What spectacle could be more glorious than this? 54. Besides, he who makes the oration over the man about to be buried, when he has finished speaking of him recounts the successes and exploits of the rest whose images are present, beginning from the most ancient. By this means, by this constant renewal of the good report of brave men, the celebrity of those who performed noble deeds is rendered immortal, while at the same time the fame of those who did good service to their country becomes known to the public and a heritage for future generations. But the most important result is that young men are thus inspired to endure every suffering for the public welfare in the hope of winning the glory that attends on brave men. What I say is confirmed by the facts. For many Romans have voluntarily engaged in single combat in order to decide a battle, not a few faced certain death, some in war to save the lives of the rest, and others in peace to save the republic. Some even when in office have put their own sons to death contrary to every law or custom, setting a higher value on the interest of their country than on the ties of nature that bound them to their nearest and dearest.

Many such stories about many men are related in Roman history, but one told of a certain person will suffice for the present as an example and as a confirmation of what I say. 55. It is narrated that Horatius Cocles[47] was engaged in combat with two of the enemy at the far end of the bridge over the Tiber that lies in front of the town, he saw large reinforcements coming up to help the enemy, and fearing lest

---

47. This is the earliest version of the story of the legendary bravery of Horatius Cocles (the One-Eyed) whose deed is supposed to have occurred during an Etruscan invasion in 508 BCE. In later versions, Horatius survives by swimming to the Roman side of the Tiber.

they should force the passage and get into the town, he turned round and called to those behind him to retire and cut the bridge with all speed. His order was obeyed, and while they were cutting the bridge, he stood to his ground receiving many wounds, and arrested the attack of the enemy who were less astonished at his physical strength than at his endurance and courage. The bridge once cut, the enemy were prevented from attacking; and Cocles, plunging into the river in full armor as he was, deliberately sacrificed his life, regarding the safety of his country and the glory which in future would attach to his name as of more importance than his present existence and the years of life which remained to him. Such, if I am not wrong, is the eager emulation of achieving noble deeds engendered in the Roman youth by their institutions.

56. Again, the laws and customs relating to the acquisition of wealth are better in Rome than at Carthage. At Carthage nothing which results in profit is regarded as disgraceful; at Rome nothing is considered more so than to accept bribes and seek gain from improper channels. For no less strong than their approval of money making by respectable means is their condemnation of unscrupulous gain from forbidden sources. A proof of this is that at Carthage candidates for office practice open bribery, whereas at Rome death is the penalty for it. Therefore as the rewards offered for merit are the opposite in the two cases, it is natural that the steps taken to gain them should also be dissimilar.

But the quality in which the Roman commonwealth is most distinctly superior is in my opinion the nature of their religious convictions. I believe that it is the very thing which among other peoples is an object of reproach, I mean superstition, which maintains the cohesion of the Roman State. These matters are clothed in such pomp and introduced to such an extent into their public and private life that nothing could exceed it, a fact which will surprise many. My own opinion at least is that they have adopted this course for the sake of the common people. It is a course which perhaps would not have been necessary had it been possible to form a state composed of wise men, but as every multitude is fickle, full of lawless desires, unreasoned passion, and violent anger, the multitude must be held in by invisible terrors and suchlike pageantry. For this reason I think, not that the ancients acted rashly and at haphazard in introducing among the people notions concerning the gods and beliefs in the terrors of hell, but that the moderns are most rash and foolish in banishing such beliefs. The consequence is that among the Greeks, apart from other things, members of the government, if they are entrusted with no more than a talent, though they have ten copyists and as many seals and twice as many witnesses, cannot keep their faith; whereas among the Romans those who as magistrates and legates are dealing with large sums of money maintain correct conduct just because they have pledged their faith by oath. Whereas elsewhere it is a rare thing to find a man who keeps his hands off public money, and whose record is clean in this respect, among the Romans one rarely comes across a man who has been detected in such conduct.

POLYBIUS ON THE FUTURE OF THE ROMAN
REPUBLICAN CONSTITUTION

57. That all existing things are subject to decay and change is a truth that scarcely needs proof; for the course of nature is sufficient to force this conviction on us. There being two agencies by which every kind of state is liable to decay, the one external and the other a growth of the state itself, we can lay down no fixed rule about the former, but the latter is a regular process. I have already stated what kind of state is the first to come into being, and what is the next, and how the one is transformed into the other; so that those who are capable of connecting the opening propositions of this inquiry with its conclusion will now be able to foretell the future unaided. And what will happen is, I think, evident. When a state has weathered many great perils and subsequently attains to supremacy and uncontested sovereignty, it is evident that under the influence of long-established prosperity, life will become more extravagant and the citizens more fierce in their rivalry regarding office and other objects than they ought to be. As these defects go on increasing, the beginning of the change for the worse will be due to love of office and the disgrace entailed by obscurity, as well as to extravagance and purse-proud display; and for this change the populace will be responsible when on the one hand they think they have a grievance against certain people who have shown themselves grasping, and when, on the other hand, they are puffed up by the flattery of others who aspire to office. For now, stirred to fury and swayed by passion in all their counsels, they will no longer consent to obey or even to be the equals of the ruling caste, but will demand the lion's share for themselves. When this happens, the state will change its name to the finest sounding of all, freedom and democracy, but will change its nature to the worst thing of all, mob-rule.

CHAPTER 7

Memnon,[1] *History of Heracleia*

Heracleia Pontica was a Greek city founded by the cities of Megara and Thebes on the southwest coast of the Black Sea in the mid-sixth century BCE. Books nine through sixteen of Memnon's history treated the history of Heracleia from the establishment of the Heracleote tyranny in 364 BCE to the refoundation of the city by Julius Caesar in the 40s BCE after its capture and destruction by the Romans in the Third Mithridatic War in 70 BCE. Three themes dominated books nine through twelve: the reigns of the Heracleote tyrants and their characters,[2] the fate of the Heracleote exiles, and relations between Heracleia and the great powers, namely, Persia and then Alexander the Great and his successors.

THE EVIL TYRANTS: CLEARCHUS (364 BCE TO 352 BCE) AND SATYRUS (352 BCE TO 346 BCE)

[1] [Memnon] says that Clearchus was the first to attempt to make himself tyrant of the city. Clearchus had received an education in philosophy; he was one of the pupils of Plato, and for four years he had been a pupil of the rhetorician Isocrates. But he turned out to be truly savage and bloodthirsty toward his subjects, and reached the peak of arrogance, so that he called himself the son of Zeus, and tinged his face with unnatural dyes, adorning it in all kinds of different ways to make it appear glistening or ruddy to those who saw him; and varied his clothing to appear fearsome or elegant.[3] This was not his only vice; he showed no gratitude to his benefactors, was extremely violent, and ventured to carry out the most appalling

---

1. This translation of Memnon is used courtesy of Dr. Andrew Smith.
2. In his summary of Memnon's history, Photius focused on Memnon's account of the tyrants: "We read the historical work of Memnon from the ninth book to the sixteenth book. This history sets out to describe the noteworthy things which happened in Heracleia Pontica. It lists the tyrants of Heracleia, their character and deeds, the lives of the other [distinguished citizens], the manner of their death, and the sayings which were associated with them."
3. Claiming to be son of a god, as Clearchus did, did not mean that he claimed to be divine, but at most a hero like Heracles and other figures of Greek legend.

deeds.[4] He ruthlessly destroyed those he attacked, not only among his own people but whenever he perceived a threat elsewhere. However, he was the first of those who were called tyrants to establish a library.

Because of his murderous, cruel, and arrogant character many plots were formed against him, but he escaped them all until eventually Chion the son of Matris, a high-minded man who was a blood relation of Clearchus, formed a conspiracy with Leon, Euxenon, and many others. They gave Clearchus a fatal blow, and he died miserably from his wound.[5] When the tyrant was making a public sacrifice, Chion and his associates thought that this would be an opportunity for action, and Chion plunged a sword into the side of their common enemy. Clearchus was racked by a great and piercing pain, and he was tormented by horrible visions (these visions were the ghosts of those he had cruelly murdered). Two days later he expired, after living for 58 years, of which he was tyrant for 12 years. At that time Artaxerxes was king of Persia,[6] and after him his son Ochus.[7]

Clearchus sent many embassies to them during his lifetime. However almost all the tyrant's assassins were killed. Some were cut down by the bodyguard at the time of the attack, fighting bravely. Others were captured later and subjected to terrible tortures.

[2] Satyrus the brother of Clearchus took over the government, acting as guardian of the tyrant's sons, Timotheus and Dionysius. Satyrus exceeded not only Clearchus but all the other tyrants in his cruelty. Not only did he take vengeance on those who had plotted against his brother, but he inflicted equally intolerable harm on their children, who had taken no part in what their parents had done, and he punished many innocent people as if they were criminals. He was completely uninterested in learning, philosophy, and all the other liberal arts. His only passion was for murder, and he did not want to learn about or practice anything which was humane or civilized. He was evil in every way, even if time lessened his [desire to] sate himself with murders and the blood of his countrymen; but he did show a conspicuous affection toward his brother. He kept [the succession to] the leadership of the state safe for the children of his brother, and valued the welfare of the boys so highly that, although he had a wife and loved her dearly, he was determined not to have a child, and used every possible device to render himself childless, in order that he should not leave behind anyone who could be a rival to his nephews.

---

4. While in exile and serving with a Persian official named Mithridates, Clearchus was recalled to Heracleia by members of an oligarchic faction in the expectation that he would suppress their democratic opponents. Instead, he betrayed them, drove them into exile, and made himself tyrant.

5. Chion was also a student of Plato. Plato was accused of training tyrants like Clearchus so that tyrannicides such as Chion were celebrated as proof that the charge was false.

6. Artaxerxes II, 404 BCE to 359 BCE.

7. Artaxerxes III Ochus, 359 BCE to 338 BCE.

While he was still alive, but weighed down by old age, Satyrus passed on control of the state to Timotheus, the elder son of his brother, and shortly afterward he was afflicted by a severe and untreatable illness. A cancerous growth spread underneath between his groin and his scrotum, and irrupted painfully toward his inwards. An opening formed in his flesh and discharges ran out with a foul and unbearable smell, so that his retinue and his doctors could no longer conceal the all-pervading stench of the putrefaction.

Continual sharp pains racked his whole body, consigning him to sleeplessness and convulsions, until eventually the disease spread to his internal organs, and deprived him of his life. Like Clearchus, Satyrus gave to those who saw him when he was dying the impression that he was paying the penalty for his savage and lawless abuse of the citizens. They say that often during his illness he would vainly pray for death, and after he had been consumed by this harsh and grievous affliction for many days, he finally paid his due. He had lived for 65 years, and was tyrant for seven years, while Archidamus was king of Sparta.

THE GOOD TYRANTS: TIMOTHEUS (346 BCE TO 337 BCE) AND DIONYSIUS (337 BCE TO 305 BCE)

[3] Timotheus took over the government and reformed it to a milder and more democratic regime, so that his subjects no longer called him a tyrant, but a benefactor and savior. He paid off their debts to the moneylenders from his own resources, and gave interest-free loans to the needy for their trade and for the rest of their living expenses. He released innocent men, and even the guilty, from the prisons. He was a strict but humane judge, and in other respects he had a good and trustworthy nature. So, he cared for his brother Dionysius like a father in every way, making him joint ruler at the start, and then appointing him to be his successor. He also showed a brave spirit in matters of war. He was magnanimous and noble in body and in mind, and he was fair and gracious in the settlement of wars. He was skillful at grasping an opportunity, and vigorous in achieving what he contemplated; he was merciful and just in character, and relentless in his boldness; he was moderate, kind and compassionate. Therefore, in his lifetime he was an object of great fear to his enemies, who all dreaded and hated him; but to his subjects he was agreeable and gentle, so that when he died he was much missed, and his death aroused grief mixed with longing. His brother Dionysius cremated his body magnificently, pouring out tears from his eyes and groans from his heart. He held horse races in his honor; and not only horse races, but theatrical and choral and gymnastic contests. He held some of the contests immediately and others, yet more splendid, later on.

That, in brief, is what is related in books nine and ten of Memnon's history.

[4] Dionysius became the next ruler [of Heracleia] and increased its power; Alexander's victory over the Persians at the river Granicus had opened the way for those who wanted to increase their power, by cutting down the strength of the Persians, which had previously been an obstacle to them all. But later he experienced many dangers, especially when the exiles from Heracleia sent an embassy to Alexander, who had by then completely conquered Asia, asking him to grant their return and to restore the city to its traditional democracy.[8] Because of this Dionysius was almost removed from power, and he would have been removed if he had not been very clever and quick-witted, earning the goodwill of his subjects and courting the favor of Cleopatra. And so, he resisted the enemies who threatened him; sometimes he yielded to their demands, mollifying their anger and putting them off with delays, and at other times he took measures against them.

When Alexander died at Babylon from [? poison][9] or disease, Dionysius set up a statue of Joy [*Euthymia*] after hearing the news. In his great delight when the message first arrived, he suffered the same effect which extreme grief might produce: he almost collapsed with the shock, and seemed to have become senseless. The exiles from Heracleia urged Perdiccas,[10] who had taken over the government, to follow the same policy but Dionysius, though on a knife's edge, by similar methods escaped all the dangers which were facing him. Perdiccas was a poor leader and was killed by his men; the hopes of the exiles were extinguished, and Dionysius enjoyed prosperity in all his undertakings.

The greatest good fortune came to him from his second marriage. He married Amastris, the daughter of Oxathres; this Oxathres was the brother of Darius (III), whose daughter Stateira Alexander took as his wife after killing her father.[11] So, the two women were cousins, and also they had been brought up together, which gave them a special affection for each other. When he married Stateira, Alexander gave this Amastris to Craterus, one of his closest friends. After Alexander departed from this world, Craterus turned to Phila the daughter of Antipater, and with the agreement of her former husband Amastris went to live with Dionysius.

From this time onward, his realm flourished greatly, because of the wealth which the marriage brought to him and his own love of display. He decided to

---

8. In 324 BCE, Alexander issued a decree ordering Greek cities to allow exiles to return. Dionysius warded off this threat by consolidating his support within Heracleia and enlisting the assistance of Alexander's sister, Cleopatra.

9. The text is corrupt at this point, reading, "Alexander died by death or disease." The translator's suggestion that Memnon wrote "poison" implies that he alluded to the popular theory that Alexander was poisoned at a banquet by one of the sons of Antipater, his general in Macedon, who feared that he was about to be replaced.

10. The regent for Alexander's brother Philip III and his infant son Alexander IV, who governed the empire from 323 BCE to his death during a failed invasion of Egypt in 321 BCE.

11. Actually, Darius III was assassinated in 330 BCE by a conspiracy of Persian nobles headed by Bessus, the satrap of Bactria, who took the throne as Artaxerxes V.

buy the entire royal equipment of Dionysius the tyrant of Sicily,[12] who had been removed from power. It was not only this that strengthened his power, but also the success and goodwill of his subjects, including many who had not previously been under his control. He gave outstanding aid to Antigonus the ruler of Asia[13] when he was besieging Cyprus,[14] and as a reward received Antigonus's nephew Ptolemaeus, the general of the forces by the Hellespont, to be his daughter's husband; this was his daughter from his previous marriage. After achieving such distinction, he disdained the title of tyrant and called himself a king.

Now that he was free from all fear and worry, he gave himself up to a life of continual luxury, so that he grew fat and unnaturally bloated. As a result, not only did he pay less attention to governing the state, but also when he went to sleep he was only with difficulty roused from his soporific state by being pierced with large needles, which was the only remaining way of reviving him from his unconscious torpor. He had three children by Amastris: Clearchus, Oxathres, and a daughter with the same name as her mother. When he was about to die, he left Amastris in charge of the government, acting as guardian along with some others for the children, who were still quite young. He had lived for 55 years, out of which he was ruler for about [30] years. He was, it was said, a very mild ruler and earned the epithet "the Good" from his character; his subjects were deeply saddened by his death.

Even after his departure from this world, the city still flourished, while Antigonus carefully protected the interests of the children of Dionysius and their citizens. But when Antigonus's interest turned elsewhere, Lysimachus[15] again took charge of Heracleia and the children, and even made Amastris his wife. To start with, he was very much in love with her, but when the pressure of events demanded it, he left her at Heracleia and went off to deal with urgent business. When he was free from his many troubles, he soon sent for her to join him at Sardis, where he showed her equal affection. But later he transferred his affection to the [daughter][16] of Ptolemy Philadelphus, who was called Arsinoe, and this caused Amastris to part from him. After leaving him, she took control of Heracleia; she revived the city by her presence, and created the new city of Amastris.[17]

---

12. Dionysius II, tyrant of Syracuse from 367 BCE to 357 BCE.

13. Antigonus the One-Eyed. He had been Alexander's satrap of Phrygia during his campaign, and, after the death of Perdiccas, he spent two decades from 319 BCE to his death in 301 BCE attempting to reunite Alexander's empire under his rule.

14. Cyprus is an error. The reference is probably to Antigonus's siege of Tyre in 315 BCE.

15. A companion and bodyguard of Alexander. He was appointed satrap of Thrace, modern Bulgaria, after Alexander's death in 323 BCE, and, at the time of his death in 281 BCE, his empire included Macedonia and Anatolia in addition to Thrace.

16. Arsinoe was actually the daughter of Ptolemy I Soter and the sister of Ptolemy II Philadelphus.

17. Amastris was located east of Heracleia on the coast of Paphlagonia and formed by the union of four small cities—Tius, Sesamus, Cromna, and Cytorus—which had been conquered by Dionysius.

THE FALL OF THE TYRANNY
(305 BCE TO 281 BCE)

[5] Clearchus had now reached adult age, and became ruler of the city; he fought in many wars, sometimes as an ally of others, and sometimes resisting attacks against himself. In one of these wars, he went as an ally of Lysimachus against the Getae,[18] and was captured along with him. Lysimachus was released from captivity, and later secured Clearchus's release as well. Clearchus and his brother were established as rulers of the city in succession to their father, but the way they treated their subjects was far different from his mild benevolence. They carried out the foulest of crimes; for they caused their mother, who had not particularly interfered in their affairs, to be drowned in the sea when she was on board a ship, by a terrible and evil device.

Lysimachus, whom we have mentioned many times before, was now king of Macedonia, and though his relationship with Arsinoe had caused Amastris to leave him, he still felt some glow of his former passion for her. He was not prepared to ignore her cruel murder; but he hid his feelings very carefully, and pretended to show the same friendship toward Clearchus as before. By many devices and tricks of deception (for he was the cleverest of men at hiding his intentions) he arrived at Heracleia as if to approve the succession. Though he put on a mask of fatherly love toward Clearchus, he killed the matricides, first Clearchus and then Oxathres, making them pay the penalty for the murder of their mother. He put the city under his protection, and carried away much of the treasure which the tyrants had accumulated. After allowing the citizens to establish a democracy, which was what they wanted, he set off back to his own kingdom.

When he arrived there, he was full of praise for Amastris; he marveled at her character and the way she ruled, how she had built up her realm in size and importance and strength. He exalted Heracleia, and included praise for Tius and Amastris, the city which she had founded in her name. By saying all this, he aroused in Arsinoe a desire to be mistress of the places which he was praising, and she asked him to grant her wish. To begin with he refused, saying that it was too much to give, but later as she continued to entreat him, he let her have it; for Arsinoe was not easily put off and old age had made Lysimachus more malleable. When she gained possession of Heracleia she sent there Heracleides of Cyme, a man who was well-disposed toward her, but otherwise ruthless and cunning, a skillful and quick-witted planner. When he arrived at Heracleia, he governed the city strictly, bringing accusations against many of the citizens and handing out punishments, so that they were deprived again of the good fortune which they had just acquired.

---

18. A Thracian people living north of the Danube River, which Lysimachus unsuccessfully attacked in 292 BCE.

Under Arsinoe's influence, Lysimachus killed Agathocles, the oldest and best of his sons, who was the offspring of his previous marriage. First he tried to poison him secretly, but when Agathocles discovered this and spat out the poison, he disposed of him in the most shameless way; he threw him into prison and ordered him to be cut down, on the pretended charge that he was plotting against Lysimachus. Ptolemy, who carried out this outrage, was the brother of Arsinoe,[19] and because of his folly and recklessness was given the name Ceraunus ["thunderbolt"]. By murdering his son, Lysimachus justly earned the hatred of his subjects. So Seleucus,[20] on learning about this and how easily the kingdom could be overthrown, now that the cities had revolted against Lysimachus, joined battle against him. Lysimachus died in this war,[21] after being struck by a spear which was thrown by a man from Heracleia called Malacon, who was fighting for Seleucus. After Lysimachus's death, his kingdom was merged as part of Seleucus's kingdom.

At this point, the 12th book of Memnon finishes.

Books thirteen and fourteen of Memnon's history were devoted to the emergence of Heracleia as a significant power in the Black Sea after the fall of the tyranny. Three themes dominated his account: the return of the exiles and their reconciliation with the rest of the Heracleiotes, Heracleia's import-ant contribution to the struggle against the efforts of the Seleucids to extend their influence in northern Anatolia and the Black Sea, and Heracleia's role as an important Roman ally in the region after the defeat of the Seleucid king Antiochus III at the battle of Magnesia in 190 BCE.

HERACLEIA AS A BLACK SEA POWER (281 BCE TO c. 250 BCE)

[6] In the 13th book Memnon says that the Heracleians, when they heard that Lysimachus had been killed by a man from Heracleia, recovered their confidence, and bravely sought the independence which they had been deprived of for 84 years,

---

19. Actually, he was Arsinoe's half brother, being the son of Ptolemy I by his first wife Eury-dice and living in exile at Lysimachus's court since ca. 287 BCE when Ptolemy I designated the future Ptolemy II, his son by his second wife, as his heir.

20. Seleucus I, satrap of Babylonia since 319 BCE. By the late 280s BCE, his empire included most of the territory of the old Persian Empire, extending from Bactria, modern Afghani-stan, in the east to Syria in the west.

21. Specifically, Lysimachus was killed at the battle of Corupedium in Lydia in February 281 BCE.

first by their native tyrants and then by Lysimachus. First of all, they went to Heracleides and urged him to leave the city, for which they would not only let him go unharmed but would send him on his way with splendid gifts, if only he let them regain their freedom. But far from being persuaded, he became angry and sent some of them off for punishment, so the citizens made a pact with the leaders of the garrison, promising that the garrison would receive equal rights of citizenship and would continue to receive the same pay as before. Then they seized Heracleides and held him as prisoner for a while. This freed them from all fear. They pulled down the acropolis walls to their foundations, appointed Phocritus to be governor of the city, and sent an embassy to Seleucus.

But Zipoetes, the ruler of the Bithynians, who was hostile to Heracleia on account of both Lysimachus and Seleucus (for he was the enemy of both of them), attacked the city's territory and laid it waste. Nor did his own soldiers escape without similar injuries to those they perpetrated, because they suffered almost as much harm as they did to others.

[7] Meanwhile, Seleucus sent Aphrodisius to administer the cities of Phrygia and the upper parts of Pontus. He carried out his business, and on his return he praised the other cities, but accused the Heracleians of being hostile toward Seleucus. Irritated by this, Seleucus used threats to disparage and scare the envoys who came to him, but one of the envoys called Chamaeleon was not frightened by the threats, and said "Heracles is *karron*, Seleucus" ("karron" means "stronger" in the Doric dialect). Seleucus did not understand this, but remained angry, and turned away from them. The envoys could see no advantage either in returning home or in remaining where they were.

When the Heracleians heard about this, among other preparations they gathered allies, sending envoys to Mithridates the king of Pontus and to the cities of Byzantium and Chalcedon. Then Nymphis,[22] who was one of the remaining exiles from Heracleia, urged the others to return home, and said that this could easily be achieved if they did not seem to be pressing for the restoration of the property which was taken away from their parents. He very easily persuaded the other exiles, and their return took place as he predicted. The returning exiles and the city which received them felt equal pleasure and delight, as the people in the city warmly welcomed them and ensured that nothing was missing that might contribute to their welfare. In this way the Heracleians regained their traditional nobility and constitution.

[8] Seleucus, encouraged by his success against Lysimachus, set out to cross over to Macedonia. He longed to return to his fatherland, from which he had set out with Alexander, and he intended to spend the rest of his life there (he was already

---

22. Nymphis was the author of a history of Heracleia entitled *Concerning Heracleia* used by Memnon and a history of Alexander and his successors down to the reign of Ptolemy III (247/46 BCE).

an old man), after handing over the government of Asia to his son Antiochus. But Ptolemy Ceraunus, because the kingdom of Lysimachus had come under Seleucus's control, was himself accompanying Seleucus; he was not despised like a prisoner, but given the honor and consideration due to the son of a king. His hopes were raised by the promises which Seleucus made to establish him back in Egypt as the rightful heir to the kingdom, when his father Ptolemy died. However, though he was honored with so much attention, these favors failed to improve the disposition of an evil man. He formed a plot, fell upon his benefactor and killed him. Then he jumped on a horse and rushed to Lysimacheia, where he put on a diadem, and escorted by a splendid bodyguard went out to meet the army; they were forced to accept him and call him king, though they had previously served under Seleucus.

When he heard what had happened, Antigonus the son of Demetrius[23] tried to cross over to Macedonia with an army and a fleet, in order to forestall Ptolemy; and Ptolemy went to confront him with Lysimachus's fleet. In this fleet were some ships which had been sent from Heracleia, sixes and fives and transports and one eight called the lion-bearer, of extraordinary size and beauty.[24] It had 100 rowers on each line, so there were 800 men on each side, making a total of 1,600 rowers. There were also 1,200 soldiers on the decks, and 2 steersmen. When battle was joined, the victory went to Ptolemy who routed the fleet of Antigonus, with the ships from Heracleia fighting most bravely of all; and of the ships from Heracleia, the prize went to the eight "lion-bearer." After this defeat at sea, Antigonus retreated to Boeotia, and Ptolemy crossed over to Macedonia, which he put securely under his control. Immediately he showed his wickedness by marrying his sister Arsinoe (this was traditional among the Egyptians) and murdering the sons she had by Lysimachus.[25] Then after disposing of them, he banished Arsinoe herself from the kingdom. He committed many other crimes over a period of two years, until a band of Gauls left their country because of famine and invaded Macedonia. He joined battle with these Gauls, and was killed in a manner befitting his own cruelty, being torn apart by the Gauls, who had captured him alive after the elephant on which he was riding was injured and threw him off. Antigonus the son of Demetrius, who had been defeated in the naval battle, became ruler of Macedonia after the death of Ptolemy.

[9] Antiochus the son of Seleucus,[26] who had through many wars recovered his father's kingdom with difficulty and even so not completely, sent his general

---

23. Antigonus Gonatas, who ruled Macedon from 277 BCE to 239 BCE.

24. "Fives" and "sixes" were large war galleys most likely propelled by two banks of sweeps, each worked by five or six men. Such an explanation is not possible, however, for an eight like the "lion-bearer," which probably was a catamaran with two hulls bound together by a platform able to carry soldiers. It would have been a mobile siege weapon instead of a warship designed to ram other similar vessels.

25. Actually, Arsinoe escaped with her eldest son, Ptolemy, and fled to Egypt, where she married her full brother Ptolemy II.

26. Antiochus I Soter, who was king of the Seleucid Empire from 281 BCE to 261 BCE.

Patrocles with a detachment of his army to this side of the Taurus [mountains]. Patrocles appointed Hermogenes, whose family came from Aspendus, to lead attacks against Heracleia and the other cities. When the Heracleians sent an embassy to Hermogenes, he made a pact with them and withdrew from their territory, and instead marched through Phrygia to Bithynia. But Hermogenes was ambushed by the Bithynians, and was killed together with his whole army, though he himself fought bravely against the enemy. As a result of this, Antiochus decided to mount an expedition against the Bithynians, and their king Nicomedes sent envoys to Heracleia to ask for an alliance, which he quickly obtained, promising in return to help the city when it was in a similar plight.

Meanwhile by spending a great deal of money the Heracleians recovered Cierus and Tius and the Thynian territory,[27] but they did not succeed in regaining Amastris (which had been taken away from them along with the other cities), though they tried hard by war and by offering money. Eumenes, who held Amastris, was swayed by an unreasonable anger, and preferred to hand over the city for free to Ariobarzanes the son of Mithridates, rather than to accept payment for it from the Heracleians. At about the same time, the Heracleians entered into a war with Zipoetes the Bithynian,[28] who ruled over Thynia in Thrace. In this war many of the Heracleians were killed after performing acts of true bravery, and Zipoetes utterly defeated them; but when an allied army came to the rescue of the Heracleians, he disgraced his victory by running away. Though defeated, the Heracleians were able to recover and cremate the bodies of their dead without hindrance. Then, having achieved that for which they went to war, they took the bones of their dead back to the city, where they gave them a splendid burial in the monument of the heroes.

[10] At about the same time, a war arose between Antiochus the son of Seleucus and Antigonus the son of Demetrius. Large forces were ranged on either side, and the war lasted for a long time. Nicomedes the king of Bithynia[29] fought as an ally of Antigonus, and many others fought on the side of Antiochus. So after clashing with Antigonus, Antiochus undertook a war against Nicomedes. Nicomedes gathered together forces from various places, and sent envoys to the Heracleians to ask for assistance; they sent 13 triremes to help him. Then Nicomedes went out to oppose Antiochus's fleet, and for a while they remained confronting each other, but neither side started a battle, and they returned without achieving anything.

[11] When the Gauls[30] came to Byzantium and ransacked most of its territory, the Byzantines were worn down by the war and asked their allies for help. All the allies

---

27. Thynias was a territory west of Heracleia on the north coast of Anatolia and not in Thrace as stated later in this paragraph.

28. Ruler of Bithynia from ca. 297 BCE to 280 BCE.

29. Nicomedes I, king of Bithynia from ca. 280 BCE to 255 BCE.

30. The Gauls were a Celtic people, who migrated from Central Europe down the Danube River and crossed into Anatolia ca. 278 BCE after raiding in the Balkans as far south as Delphi in Greece.

provided such help as they could, and the Heracleians gave 4,000 gold pieces (this is what the envoys had asked for). Not long after, Nicomedes made a pact with the Gauls who were attacking Byzantium, and arranged for them to cross over to Asia; the Gauls had tried to cross over many times before, but had always failed, because the Byzantines would not allow it. The terms of the pact were as follows: the barbarians should always support Nicomedes and his children, and should not enter into alliance with any other state which requested it without the permission of Nicomedes. They should be allies of his allies, and enemies of his enemies. They should serve as allies of the Byzantines, if necessary, and of the inhabitants of Tius and Heracleia and Chalcedon and Cierus, and of some other rulers. On these terms, Nicomedes brought the multitude of Gauls over to Asia. The Gauls had 17 eminent leaders, of whom the most important and distinguished were Leonnorius and Luturius.

At first this crossing of the Gauls to Asia seemed to cause only trouble for the inhabitants, but in the end it inclined to their benefit. The kings tried to put an end to the democracies in the cities, but the Gauls strengthened them, by repelling the cities' oppressors. Nicomedes, after arming the Gauls, started by conquering the land of Bithynia and slaughtering the inhabitants, with the assistance of the Heracleians. The Gauls shared the rest of the loot among themselves.

After advancing over much of the country, the Gauls withdrew and chose a section of the land to keep for themselves, which is now called Galatia.[31] They split this land into three parts, for the tribes of the Trogmi, Tolostobogii, and Tectosages. They each founded cities, the Trogmi at Ancyra, the Tolostobogii at Tabia, and the Tectosages at Pessinus.

[12] Nicomedes enjoyed great prosperity, and founded a city named after himself opposite Astacus. Astacus was founded by settlers from Megara at the beginning of the 17th Olympiad [712/11 BCE] and was named as instructed by an oracle after one of the so-called indigenous Spartoi (the descendants of the Theban Spartoi),[32] a noble and high-minded man called Astacus. The city endured many attacks from its neighbors and was worn out by the fighting, but after the Athenians sent settlers there to join the Megarians, it was rid of its troubles and achieved great glory and strength, when Doedalsus was the ruler of the Bithynians.

Doedalsus was succeeded by Boteiras, who lived for 76 years, and was in turn succeeded by his son Bas. Bas defeated Calas the general of Alexander, even though Calas was well equipped for a battle, and kept the Macedonians out of Bithynia.[33] He lived for 71 years, and was king for 50 years. He was succeeded by his son

---

31. Galatia is in central Anatolia near modern Ancyra.

32. The sown men. According to Greek legend, they originated from stones thrown behind him by Cadmus, the mythical founder of Thebes.

33. Bas's victory over Calas occurred ca. 327 BCE. The reigns of his two predecessors, Doedalsus and Boteiras, therefore, must belong to the fifth century BCE and the first half of the fourth century BCE, although their exact dates cannot now be determined.

Zipoetes, an excellent warrior who killed one of the generals of Lysimachus and drove another general far away out of his kingdom. After defeating first Lysimachus, the king of the Macedonians, and then Antiochus the son of Seleucus, the king of Asia, he founded a city under Mount (?) Lyparus, which was named after himself. Zipoetes lived for 76 years and ruled the kingdom for 48 years; he was survived by four children. He was succeeded by the eldest of the children, Nicomedes, who acted not like a brother but like an executioner to his brothers. However, he strengthened the kingdom of the Bithynians, particularly by arranging for the Gauls to cross over to Asia, and as was said before, he founded the city which bears his name.

Not long afterward, a war broke out between the Byzantines and the inhabitants of Callatis (a colony of Heracleia) and of Histria.[34] The war was caused by the trading post at Tomis, which the inhabitants of Callatis wanted to run as a monopoly. Both sides sent envoys to the Heracleians to ask for assistance; the Heracleians gave no military aid to either side, but sent arbitrators to each of them to arrange a truce, though at the time they did not accomplish this. After suffering greatly at the hands of their enemies, the inhabitants of Callatis agreed to a truce, but by that time they were almost incapable of recovering from the disasters which had struck them.

[13] After a short interval of time, Nicomedes the king of Bithynia, who was close to death, named the sons of his second wife Etazeta as his heirs; they were still very young, so he appointed Ptolemy, Antigonus, and the peoples of Byzantium, Heracleia, and Cius to be their guardians. Ziaelas,[35] his son by his previous marriage, had been forced out by the scheming of his step-mother Etazeta and was in exile with the king of the Armenians. But Ziaelas returned to claim the kingdom with a force which was boosted by the Tolostobogian Gauls. The Bithynians wanted to preserve the kingdom for the younger children, and arranged for the brother of Nicomedes to marry the children's mother. The Bithynians collected an army from the guardians who were mentioned above, and withstood Ziaelas's attack though there were many battles and changes of fortune, until the two sides agreed on a truce. The Heracleians fought heroically in the battles, and ensured that there was a favorable treaty. Therefore the Gauls, regarding Heracleia as an enemy, ravaged its territory as far as the river Calles, and returned home with a great quantity of booty.

[14] When the Byzantines were at war with Antiochus,[36] the Heracleians supported them with 40 triremes, but the war did not proceed beyond threats.

---

34. These three Greek colonies were located on the west coast of the Black Sea south of the Danube delta. Histria was the most northerly and was founded by Miletus in the mid-seventh century BCE. The ruins of Callatis, which was founded approximately a century later, are at modern Mangalia in Romania, while Tomis is located between them at modern Costanza.
35. King of Bithynia from 255 BCE to 235 BCE.
36. The reference is probably to Antiochus II Theos (the God), ruler of the Seleucid Empire from 261 BCE to 246 BCE. This is the only reference to this war.

[15] Not long afterward, Ariobarzanes[37] departed from this world, while he was in the middle of a dispute with the Gauls. His son Mithridates was still young; so the Gauls treated the son with disdain and devastated his kingdom. The subjects of Mithridates suffered much hardship, but they were rescued by the Heracleians, who sent grain to Amisus so that they could feed themselves and meet their basic needs. Because of this the Gauls made another expedition against the territory of Heracleia, and laid it waste until the Heracleians sent an embassy to them. The historian Nymphis was the head of the embassy; by paying out 5,000 gold pieces to the Gauls' army as a whole, and 200 pieces each to their leaders, he persuaded them to withdraw from the country.

[16] Ptolemy[38] the king of Egypt had reached the height of prosperity, and decided to favor the cities with magnificent gifts. To the Heracleians he gave 500 artabae[39] of grain, and he built a temple of Heracles, made from Proconnesian marble, on their acropolis.

Heracleia and Rome (c. 200 BCE to 188 BCE)

[17] Having brought his account down to this point, the author makes a digression about the Romans' rise to power: what race they came from, how they settled in Italy, what happened before and during the foundation of Rome. He gives an account of their rulers and the peoples they fought against, the appointment of kings, the change from monarchy to rule by consuls, and how the Romans were defeated by the Gauls and their city would have been captured by the Gauls, if Camillus had not come to its aid and rescued it.[40] Then he describes how Alexander wrote to them, when he crossed over to Asia, that they should either conquer others, if they were capable of ruling over them, or yield to those who were stronger than them; and the Romans sent him a crown, containing many talents of gold.[41] Then he describes their war against the Tarentines and their ally Pyrrhus of Epirus, in which after both suffering reverses and inflicting defeats on their enemies, they forced the Tarentines into subjection and drove Pyrrhus out of

---

37. King of Pontus in northeastern Anatolia ca. 266 BCE. His son Mithridates II ruled from ca. 250 BCE to after 220 BCE.

38. The reference is probably to Ptolemy II Philadelphus, who ruled Egypt from 283 BCE to 246 BCE.

39. An *artaba* was a nonliquid measure used in Egypt. It varied in volume during Egyptian history, but in the Greco-Roman period one *artaba* was equal to slightly more than 27 liters.

40. Actually, Rome was captured and sacked in 387 BCE by the Gauls, who were then, according to Roman legend, defeated and driven off by a hastily collected Roman force led by M. Furius Camillus.

41. There is no other reference to this supposed correspondence with Alexander the Great.

Italy.[42] Then he describes the Romans' wars against the Carthaginians and Hannibal, and their successes in Spain under Scipio and other leaders; how Scipio was proclaimed king by the Spaniards but refused the title, and how Hannibal was finally defeated and fled.[43]

Then he describes how the Romans crossed over the Ionian sea, and how Perseus the son of Philippus when he became king of the Macedonians impetuously broke the treaty which his father had made with the Romans, and was overthrown after being defeated by Paullus.[44] And then he describes how they defeated Antiochus the king of Syria, Commagene, and Judaea in two battles, and drove him out of Europe.[45]

Resuming after this account of the Romans' conquests, the author says that envoys were sent by the Heracleians to the Roman generals who had crossed over to Asia; the Romans welcomed them warmly and treated them with kindness. Publius (?) Aemilius[46] granted them a letter, in which he assured them of the friendship of the senate toward them, and said that they would receive whatever care and attention they needed. Later they sent envoys to Cornelius Scipio, who had conquered Africa for the Romans, in order to confirm the alliance which had previously been agreed. After this, they sent envoys to Scipio again, because they wanted king Antiochus to be reconciled with the Romans; and they also addressed a decree to Antiochus, calling on him to lay aside his enmity toward the Romans. Cornelius wrote back to the Heracleians, beginning as follows: "Scipio, general and proconsul of the Romans, to the senate and people of the Heracleians, greetings." In the letter he confirmed the goodwill of the Romans toward the Heracleians, and that they were willing to put an end to the war with Antiochus. Lucius's brother Publius Cornelius Scipio, who commanded the fleet, gave a similar reply to the envoys of the Heracleians.

Not long afterward, Antiochus renewed the war with the Romans; he was completely defeated, and ended the hostilities by agreeing to a treaty which expelled

---

42. 280 BCE to 276 BCE.

43. The reference is to the First Punic War (264 BCE to 241 BCE) and the Second Punic War (218 BCE to 202 BCE).

44. Perseus, the son of Philip V and king of Macedon from 179 BCE to 168 BCE, was defeated in the Third Macedonian War (171 BCE to 168 BCE) by the Romans under the command of L. Aemilius Paullus.

45. The reference is to the Seleucid king Antiochus III (223 BCE to 188 BCE). Syria, Commagene, and Judaea were only the western provinces of the Seleucid Empire, which still included both Mesopotamia and Iran. The three territories mentioned here would have interested Photius because of their relevance to the Byzantine Empire.

46. There is no known Publius Aemilius in this period. Most likely L. Aemilius Regillus, the commander of the Roman fleet in the war against Antiochus III, is meant.

him from the whole of Asia,[47] and deprived him of his elephants and fleet.[48] Commagene and Judaea were left under his control.

The city of Heracleia sent envoys with a similar message to the next generals who were sent out by the Romans, and these were received with the same goodwill and kindness as before. In the end a treaty came about between the Romans and the Heracleians, in which they agreed not only to remain as friends, but also to fight as allies for or against other states, as either of them required. Identical copies of the treaty were inscribed on two bronze tablets, one of which was set up at Rome in the Capitoline temple of Zeus [Jupiter], and the other at Heracleia, also in the temple of Zeus.

[18] That is what the author relates in the 13th and 14th books of his history.

---

47. Actually, only from Anatolia, which was the original meaning of Asia.
48. Antiochus III was defeated at the battle of Magnesia in 190 BCE. The war with Rome was ended by the Peace of Apameia, which was signed in 188 BCE.

CHAPTER 8

Plutarch, *Life of Alexander*

Preface

Plutarch's Alexander *is one of the longest and most complex of his lives both because of the extraordinary events of Alexander's reign and the richness of the sources available to him. Plutarch cites almost two dozen sources, including accounts of Alexander by his contemporaries and a collection of letters supposedly written by the king. So it is not surprising that Plutarch's work provides important information about the major military and political events of the king's reign. Its special value, however, lies elsewhere. Greek biography was ethical, primarily focusing on the character rather than the deeds of its subjects. Thus, Plutarch's* Life of Alexander *also offers unique information about Alexander's youth, education, and relations with his friends and family.*

[1] I include, in this volume, the life of Alexander the king and that of Caesar, by whom Pompey was deposed. In light of the enormous number of actions involved, I shall make no other preface than to entreat my readers not to object if I fail to present exhaustive descriptions of all their famous actions, but offer, for the most part, abridged accounts of them. For it is not histories I am writing, but lives; and the most glorious deeds do not always reveal the workings of virtue or vice. Frequently, a small thing—a phrase or flash of wit—gives more insight into a man's character than battles where tens of thousands die, or vast arrays of troops, or sieges of cities. Accordingly, just as painters derive their likenesses from a subject's face and the expression of his eyes, where character shows itself, and attach little importance to other parts of the body, so must I be allowed to give more attention to the manifestations of a man's soul, and thereby mold an image of his life, leaving it to others to describe the epic conflicts.[1]

---

1. We are grateful to Dr. Mensch for generously translating this additional passage of Plutarch's *Life of Alexander*.

ALEXANDER'S FAMILY AND YOUTH

[2] That Alexander, on his father's side, was a descendant of Heracles by Caranus, and on his mother's a descendant of Aeacus by Neoptolemus,[2] has never been called into question. It is said that Philip was initiated into the Mysteries in Samothrace at the same time as Olympias. Though he was still a boy and she an orphan child, he is said to have fallen in love with her and betrothed himself to her at once, on persuading her brother Arymbas. The night before they confined her in the bridal chamber, the bride dreamed that thunder was heard and that a thunderbolt fell on her belly and kindled a great fire, which burst into flames that darted everywhere and finally died out.

[3] Alexander was born early in the month of Hecatombaeon (Lous is its Macedonian name), on the sixth[3]—the very day the temple of Ephesian Artemis was burned down. In referring to that event, Hegesias the Magnesian made a witty remark, the coolness of which might have extinguished that blaze. For he said that the temple was probably burned down because Artemis was occupied with Alexander's delivery. All the Magi who were currently residing in Ephesus, believing that the destruction of the temple foreshadowed another disaster, ran through the town striking their faces and shouting that that day had given birth to ruin and dire misery for Asia.

[4] Alexander's physical appearance was best represented by the statues of Lysippus, the only artist Alexander thought worthy to sculpt his likeness. And in fact the traits that many of his successors and friends tried to imitate later on—the tilt of his neck, which inclined slightly to the left, and the moistness of his eyes—have been accurately observed by the artist. . . .

When he was still a boy, his self-control manifested itself in the fact that, though violent and impetuous in other respects, he was unmoved by the pleasures of the body and indulged them very sparingly. His ambition kept his spirit grave and magnanimous beyond his years. For he was not eager for fame of every kind or from every quarter, unlike Philip, who prided himself like a sophist on his eloquence and had his Olympic victories in chariot-racing engraved on his coins. Instead, when the men who attended Alexander asked if he wanted to compete in the footrace at the Olympic Games (for he was swift-footed), he replied, "Only if I can compete with kings."

[5] In Philip's absence, Alexander entertained and became acquainted with envoys from the Persian king, who were won over by his affectionate nature and

---

2. The Argeads, the royal family of Macedon, were supposed to have descended from Heracles, while Alexander's mother's family traced its line back to the son of Achilles. As both lineages ultimately were believed to descend from Zeus, Alexander could and did claim both to be Greek and a descendant of Zeus.

3. About July 20, 356 BCE.

impressed that he asked no childish or trivial question, but inquired about the lengths of the roads and the manner of their journey, and about the King himself, his manner of dealing with enemies, and the Persians' power and prowess. The envoys were so dazzled that they thought nothing of Philip's famed severity as compared with the drive and high ambition of his son. . . . Whenever Philip was reported either to have captured a notable city or to have won a famous battle, Alexander appeared by no means elated, but would say to his comrades, "Boys, my father will get everything first, and will leave no great or glorious deed for *me* to perform with your help."

[6] When Philonicus of Thessaly had brought the horse Bucephalas[4] to Philip and offered to sell him for thirteen talents, they went down to the plain to make trial of him. Bucephalas seemed savage and altogether intractable: he let no rider approach him, and submitted to no one's voice among the men in Philip's suite, but reared up against everyone. In his annoyance, Philip ordered the animal to be led away, thinking him utterly wild and undisciplined, whereupon Alexander, who was present, said, "What a horse they are losing because in their inexperience and softness they cannot manage him!" At first Philip kept silent, but when Alexander continued to interrupt and to murmur indignantly, he said, "Do you criticize your elders in the belief that you are more knowledgeable and better able to manage a horse?" "I would manage this one, at any rate, better than anyone else," replied Alexander. "And if you fail, what penalty will you pay for your indiscretion?" "By Zeus," said he, "I'll pay the price of the horse." This raised a laugh, and they then came to an agreement as to the amount. Thereupon, running right up to the horse and taking hold of the rein, Alexander turned him toward the sun, having apparently guessed that Bucephalas was confused by his own shadow as it fell in front of him and darted about. Alexander ran alongside him for a little way as he trotted, and stroked him with his hand. When he saw that Bucephalas was full of courage and spirit, he quietly flung off his cloak, leaped up, and bestrode him securely. . . . At first there was silence and anguish among the men of Philip's suite. But when Alexander had rounded the turning post properly and rode back to them, elated and swaggering, they all cheered, and his father is said to have wept for joy and to have kissed his son when he dismounted. "Son," said he, "seek a kingdom equal to yourself; for Macedonia cannot contain you."

[7] Observing that his son's nature was uncompromising and that he resisted the use of force but was easily led by reasoned argument to do what was proper, Philip tried to persuade rather than command him; and since he was by no means willing to entrust Alexander's training and discipline to the masters who were instructing him in the arts and general studies, understanding that this was of greater importance—a task for many bits and rudders, as Sophocles says—Philip sent for

---

4. Literally "ox-head" in Greek.

Aristotle,[5] the most celebrated and reputable of the philosophers, and paid him a handsome and suitable fee: though he had destroyed Stagira (Aristotle's native place), Philip resettled it and restored those of its citizens who had fled or been enslaved. As a resort for their leisure and study, Philip gave Aristotle and Alexander the precinct of the temple of the nymphs near Mieza, where to this day they point out the stone seats and shaded walkways of Aristotle.

[9] While Philip was making war on Byzantium,[6] Alexander, who was sixteen years old and had been left behind in Macedonia as regent and master of the seal-ring, subdued the rebelling Maedians, and after seizing their city expelled the barbarians, settled a mixed population there, and named the city Alexandropolis. Present at Chaeronea, Alexander took part in the battle against the Greeks and is said to have been the first to assault the Theban Sacred Band.[7] Even today in Cephisus they point out an ancient oak that is called Alexander's oak; for it stands near the spot where he pitched his tent on that occasion, not far from the Macedonians' common burial-place.

THE DEATH OF PHILIP II

These exploits naturally endeared Alexander to Philip, who rejoiced to hear the Macedonians saying Alexander was their king, Philip their general. But Philip's domestic troubles, which were caused mainly by his marriages and love affairs, and which in some sense infected the kingdom with the concerns of the women's quarters, occasioned many accusations and serious quarrels. These were aggravated by the harshness of Olympias, a jealous and sullen woman, who egged Alexander on. Attalus precipitated a notorious clash at the wedding of Cleopatra, a young girl Philip was taking to wife[8] (he had fallen in love with her when well past his prime). Attalus was the bride's uncle. Having drunk deep at the carousal, he called on the

---

5. Aristotle was a native of Stagira, a Greek city near Macedon that was destroyed by Philip II. His father Nicomachus, a doctor, was physician to Philip's father, Amyntas III (393–370 BCE), so that Aristotle was familiar with the Macedonian court when he became tutor to Alexander and the royal pages in 343 BCE. At that time, he had left Plato's school in Athens and was primarily involved in biological studies in Northwest Anatolia, modern Turkey, traces of which can still be found in his *History of Animals*.

6. In 340 BCE.

7. The Sacred Band was an elite unit of 300 Theban soldiers. The troop was formed in the fourth century BCE and is supposed to have been made up of 150 pairs of lovers. Archaeologists have discovered a mass grave containing 254 bodies, which supports Plutarch's account of the Sacred Band's fate.

8. Olympias was the fifth of Philip's seven wives and Cleopatra the seventh and his only Macedonian wife. She was murdered by Olympias after Philip II's death and may be buried in either Tomb 1 or Tomb 2 of the great tumulus at Vergina.

Macedonians to ask the gods for a legitimate son to be born of Philip and Cleopatra, to be a successor to the throne. Provoked, Alexander cried, "Villain, do you take me for a bastard?" and threw a cup at Attalus. Philip then rose up, his sword drawn, to confront Alexander. But luckily for both, owing to his anger and the wine, Philip slipped and fell. Alexander now insulted him, saying, "This man, gentlemen, was preparing to cross from Europe to Asia, yet he is overturned merely crossing from couch to couch." After this drunken episode, Alexander took Olympias away and settled her in Epirus. He himself took up temporary residence in Illyria.

Meanwhile, Demaratus the Corinthian, a plainspoken friend of the family, paid Philip a visit. After their first affectionate greetings, Philip asked Demaratus how the Greeks were getting along with one another. The latter replied, "How appropriate, Philip, for you to concern yourself about Greece, now that you have filled your own house with such strife and misery." Coming to his senses, Philip sent for Alexander and brought him home, having persuaded him through Demaratus to return.

[10] When Pausanias, who had been affronted through the machinations of Attalus and Cleopatra and had obtained no justice, assassinated Philip,[9] most of the blame was laid on Olympias, on the grounds that she had encouraged and whetted the young man's anger, though Alexander also came in for a share of discredit.

For it is said that when Pausanias encountered him after that affront and lamented it, Alexander quoted the iambic verse from *Medea*:

the giver of the bride, the groom, and the bride.[10]

Nevertheless, after seeking out the accomplices of the plot, Alexander punished them, and was angry with Olympias for treating Cleopatra cruelly in his absence.[11]

ALEXANDER AND THE GREEKS

[11] Thus at twenty years of age Alexander succeeded to a kingship beset by serious jealousies, fearsome hatreds, and dangers from all quarters. . . . He brought a swift end to the barbarians' revolts and wars by overrunning their country with an army as far as the Danube, where he also defeated Syrmus, the king of the Triballians, in

---

9. Plutarch's account of Philip's death has been sanitized. Other sources indicate that Philip and Pausanias, one of Philip's bodyguards, were part of a homosexual triangle. When Pausanias was raped by the servants of Attalus, Cleopatra's uncle, after causing the death of his rival and Philip did not support his demand for vengeance, he assassinated the king in the summer of 336 BCE during the wedding of Alexander's sister, Cleopatra.

10. The reference is to Euripides's *Medea*, line 288, where Medea curses Jason and his new family after he divorced her to take a new Greek wife.

11. See above note 9.

a great battle. On learning that the Thebans had revolted[12] and that the Athenians were conspiring with them, he immediately led his force through Thermopylae. He declared that he wanted Demosthenes, who had called him a boy while he was among the Illyrians and Triballians, and a lad when he had reached Thessaly, to regard him as a man at the walls of Athens.

On reaching Thebes and offering her a chance to repent her actions, he demanded the surrender of Phoenix and Prothytes, and proclaimed an amnesty for those who came over to his side. When the Thebans demanded Philotas and Antipater from him in return,[13] and proclaimed that all who wished to liberate Greece should range themselves on their side, Alexander directed the Macedonians to prepare for combat.

The battle was fought with courage and zeal on the Thebans' part against an enemy many times more numerous. But when the Macedonian guards, after abandoning the Cadmeia,[14] attacked them from the rear, most of the Thebans, finding themselves surrounded, fell in the battle itself, and the city was seized, plundered, and razed to the ground. This was done mainly because Alexander had expected that the Greeks, astonished by such a tragedy, would cower and keep quiet; but he also prided himself on gratifying his allies' complaints, since the Phocians and Plataeans had lodged accusations against the Thebans. Having exempted the priests, all the Macedonians' hosts and guests, the descendants of Pindar,[15] and those who had opposed the citizens who voted for the revolt, he sold the rest, nearly 30,000, into slavery. But the dead numbered upward of 6,000.

THE INVASION OF THE PERSIAN EMPIRE

Having terrorized the Greek cities into submission and stabilized his father's empire, in spring of 334 BCE, Alexander resumed the war against Persia that his father had begun before his death two years earlier. The stated purpose of the war was revenge for the sacrileges the Persians had committed in Greece a century and a half earlier, but, in reality, Alexander treated all subdued territory as his by right of conquest.

---

12. In 335 BCE.

13. Antipater and Philotas's father, Parmenion, were among Alexander's most senior military commanders and had been instrumental in securing the throne for him after Philip's death.

14. The acropolis of Thebes, named after Cadmus, the legendary Phoenician founder of Thebes.

15. Pindar was the most important Theban poet, most famous for his choral odes honoring victors in the major Greek athletic competitions.

[14] The Greeks had assembled at the Isthmus[16] and voted to march against Persia with Alexander, and Alexander was proclaimed commander. Since many statesmen and philosophers had met and congratulated them, Alexander was hoping that Diogenes of Sinope,[17] who was living near Corinth, would do the same. But as Diogenes had very little regard for the king, and remained quietly in Craneion, Alexander went to *him*, and came upon him lying in the sun. Diogenes sat up a little, at the approach of so many men, and squinted at Alexander, who greeted him and asked if there was anything he needed, to which Diogenes replied, "Only for you to move a little out of the sun." It is said that Alexander was so affected by this, and so admired the haughtiness and grandeur of the man who despised him, that when they were departing, and his attendants were laughing and making fun of the philosopher, Alexander said, "Well, had I not been Alexander, I'd have been Diogenes."

[15] As for the size of the expedition, those who give the smallest figures write that it included 30,000 foot soldiers and 4,000 horsemen; those who give the largest, 43,000 foot soldiers and 5,000 horsemen. For provisioning these men, Aristobulus says that Alexander had no more than seventy talents, Duris that he was in possession of only thirty days' sustenance, and Onesicritus that he was also two hundred talents in debt. But though he started out with such small and meager means, he did not board his ship until he had looked into the circumstances of his Companions[18] and distributed to one a farm, to another a village, and to still another the revenue of some hamlet or harbor. And when almost all the royal property had been spent or allocated, Perdiccas said, "But what, sire, do you leave for yourself?" When Alexander replied, "My hopes," Perdiccas said, "then surely we too, who serve with you in the expedition, will share also in these." And when Perdiccas had declined the property that had been allotted to him, some of his other friends did the same. But Alexander eagerly gratified those who accepted or requested allotments, and most of what he possessed in Macedonia was spent in this way. With such ardor, and his mind thus disposed, he crossed the Hellespont.[19]

Ascending to Troy, he sacrificed to Athena and poured a libation to the heroes. And when he had anointed Achilles's gravestone with oil, he and his Companions ran a race around it, naked, as is the custom, and crowned it with a garland.[20]

---

16. The Isthmus of Corinth, the meeting place of the so-called League of Corinth, an alliance of all Greek states except Sparta established by Philip in 338 BCE supposedly to maintain a "common peace in Greece" and prevent the overthrow of existing governments but actually to provide cover for Macedonian domination of Greece and authorize the war against Persia.

17. The most famous Cynic philosopher, best known for his public violation of the norms of civilized life in accordance with the Cynic teaching that one should live "naturally," that is, as an animal such as a dog—a *kunos* in Greek—does.

18. The class of Macedonian aristocrats who had the right to socialize with the king and hunt with him, and who formed the king's cavalry guard.

19. Spring 334 BCE.

20. Alexander claimed that he was avenging the death of his ancestor Achilles.

THE BATTLE AT THE GRANICUS RIVER

The battle at the Granicus River in spring 334 BCE in Northwest Anatolia was of decisive importance for the future of the campaign. Previous Greek invasions of Anatolia had become bogged down and ultimately unsuccessful because of the defensive strategy pursued by the Persians. The result of the Persians' decision to confront Alexander directly instead of adopting the defensive strategy that had worked before and their defeat at the Granicus was the destruction of virtually all Persian forces in Anatolia, thereby enabling Alexander to conquer almost the entire peninsula in less than a year and forcing the Persian king Darius III to fight a defensive war in the heart of his empire.

[16] Meanwhile, since Darius's generals had mustered and arrayed a mighty force at the crossing of the Granicus, it was necessary to fight at the gates of Asia, as it were, for an entrance and dominion there.

Most of the Macedonian officers feared the depth of the river and the unevenness and ruggedness of the farther banks, which they would have to scale during battle. . . . And when Parmenio tried to prevent Alexander from running risks, as it was late in the season, Alexander said that the Hellespont would be ashamed if, now that he had crossed *it*, he feared the Granicus. He then plunged into the stream with thirteen companies of cavalry. Charging toward enemy missiles and steep positions fortified with infantry and cavalry, and across a stream that was surging around his men and sweeping them away, his actions seemed those of a mad and desperate commander, rather than one whose judgment was sound. But he persevered in the crossing, and when he had with difficulty scaled the opposite banks, though these were wet and slippery with mud, he was instantly forced to fight in disorderly, headlong haste, and to engage his attackers man by man, before his men who were crossing could form up in any order. For the enemy assaulted with a roar; and matching horse against horse, they made good use of their spears, and of their swords once the spears were shattered. Many thrust themselves at Alexander, who was easily distinguished by his light shield and the crest of his helmet, on either side of which was fixed a plume of marvelous size and whiteness. Though hit by a javelin at the joint of his breastplate, he was not wounded; and when the generals Rhoesaces and Spithridates rushed at him together, he avoided Spithridates and struck Rhoesaces, who was wearing a breastplate. After his own spear broke, Alexander used his sword. When the two men were engaged at close quarters, Spithridates rode up on one side, raised himself up on his horse, and brought his battle-axe down with main force on Alexander's helmet. His crest was broken off, along with one feather, and his helmet could barely and with difficulty resist the blow: the edge of the axe grazed Alexander's topmost hairs. And when Spithridates was rising up for another blow, Cleitus—the one known as Black Cleitus—anticipated him and ran him through with his spear. At that very moment Rhoesaces fell, struck by Alexander's sword.

While this dangerous cavalry combat was under way, the Macedonian phalanx completed its crossing of the river, and the two infantry forces came to blows. But the enemy infantry did not hold its ground firmly for long; it was routed and put to flight, except for the Greek mercenaries. These men, making a stand on a certain ridge, asked Alexander for quarter. But he, more in anger than by calculation, charged at them ahead of his men and lost his horse, which was struck through the ribs with a sword (this was not Bucephalas, but another). And it was there, as it turned out, that most of the Macedonians who died and were wounded fought and fell, engaging at close quarters with warlike and desperate men.

It is said that twenty thousand barbarian foot soldiers fell, and twenty-five hundred horsemen. On Alexander's side, Aristobulus says that there were thirty-four dead in all, nine of whom were foot soldiers. Alexander ordered that bronze statues of these men be set up. (The statues were sculpted by Lysippus.) Wishing to share the victory with the Greeks, he sent the Athenians in particular three hundred shields taken from his captives; and on all the remaining spoils, grouped together, he ordered that this highly ambitious inscription be engraved: "Alexander, son of Philip, and the Greeks, except for the Spartans, from the barbarians who inhabit Asia."[21] But the drinking cups, purple robes, and any articles of that kind that he took from the Persians were sent, with a few exceptions, to his mother.

THE BATTLE OF ISSUS

The consequences of Alexander's victory at the battle of Granicus were dramatic. In less than a year, Alexander conquered most of Anatolia—modern Turkey—and was poised to invade the heartland of the Persian Empire. Unknown to Alexander, however, Darius III, the Persian Great King, had raised a large army and marched west to intercept him. The two armies met in spring 333 BCE in southeastern Turkey in the plain of the Pinarus River, near the city of Issus. The result was a humiliating defeat for Darius III, who barely escaped from the battle while Alexander captured Darius's family, including the Persian king's mother, wife, and children.

---

21. Although Alexander's official role in the war was commander of the forces of Macedon and the League of Corinth, the dispatch of spoils to Athens highlighted the particular suffering of Athens during the Persian invasion of 480/79 BCE and his desire to win Athenian support for the war. The fact that he kept the Persian luxury goods for himself, however, shows that he viewed all of the spoils as his to do with as he wished by right of conquest.

[20] In Darius's army there was a Macedonian, Amyntas, who had fled from Macedonia and was fairly well acquainted with Alexander's nature. This man, when he saw Darius eager to advance into the narrow passes against Alexander, begged him to stay where he was and contend, with his enormous numbers, against the inferior force of the enemy in plains that were broad and open. When Darius replied that he was afraid the enemy might escape by stealth and Alexander elude him, Amyntas replied, "Rest assured, sire, on that score; for this man will march against you, and indeed will soon be at hand." Despite what he had said, Amyntas failed to persuade the king. Setting forth, Darius marched into Cilicia, and at the same time Alexander advanced into Syria against him. Missing one another overnight, they turned back. Alexander was delighted with this turn of events and eager to encounter Darius near the passes, while Darius was glad to extricate his forces from them and regain his previous encampment. For he now realized that it was not to his advantage to launch himself into a region flanked by the sea and mountains, bisected by a river (the Pinarus), and riddled with broken ground—a setting that favored the small numbers of his enemy. Alexander's good fortune provided the site, though his victory was due more to generalship than luck. For though in numbers he was inferior to the barbarians by so large a multitude, Alexander gave them no chance to surround him, whereas he himself outflanked their left wing with his right, and on getting opposite their flank put the enemy to flight. Through it all he fought in the front ranks, and as a result was wounded in the thigh with a sword while contending with Darius at close quarters, according to Chares, though Alexander himself, in the letters about the battle that he dispatched to Antipater, does not say who wounded him, reporting only that he had been stabbed in the thigh with a dagger, but was not seriously inconvenienced by the wound.

Upon winning a splendid victory and destroying more than 110,000 of his enemies, Alexander nonetheless did not capture Darius, who had got the start in the flight by half a mile or more; but by the time Alexander had turned back he had captured Darius's chariot and bow.

[21] Among the captives were Darius's mother, wife, and two daughters.... But Alexander, considering it more kingly to master himself than to conquer his enemies, laid no hand on these women nor consorted with any other before marriage besides Barsine, who had become a widow after the death of Memnon and was captured near Damascus.[22]

[23] Where wine was concerned he was less susceptible than was generally thought. He came by that reputation because of the time he spent, talking more

---

22. Barsine was a half-Greek, half-Persian noblewoman whom he had met as a child during her father Artabazus's exile in Macedon. She became Alexander's mistress, and their son Heracles was briefly considered as a possible successor to the throne of Macedon after Alexander's death in 323 BCE.

than drinking, over each cup, always engaging in some long discussion when he had nothing else to attend to.[23] . . .

But though in other respects he was the pleasantest of all kings to consort with, and lacked none of the social graces, he had now become unpleasant in his arrogance and very much the rude soldier; not only was he carried away when it came to boasting, but he also allowed himself to be ridden by his flatterers, by whom the more refined among the company were irritated, since they wished neither to compete with these men nor to fall short of them in praising Alexander. For the former course seemed shameful, the latter dangerous. After the carousal, Alexander would bathe and then retire to sleep, often until midday; there were even times when he spent the entire day sleeping.

ALEXANDER IN EGYPT

Following his victory in the battle of Issus, Alexander marched on Egypt. Despite having to conduct difficult sieges at Tyre and Gaza, by the end of 332 BCE, he had conquered most of Syria and Phoenicia as well as Egypt— all without having to fight a single battle. During the almost six months he stayed in Egypt, Alexander founded Alexandria, the first of his city foundations in the territory of the former Persian Empire, and visited the oracle of Ammon in the oasis of Siwah, where he was recognized as the Son of Ammon.

[26] They say that on conquering Egypt Alexander wanted to found a large and populous city and to name it after himself, and on the advice of his architects was just about to measure off a certain site and build a wall around it. Then, one night in his sleep he saw an astonishing vision: a man of majestic appearance, with a great thatch of grey hair, stood beside him and uttered these epic verses:[24]

An island lies in the high-surging sea
Before Egypt; Pharos is what men call it.

As soon as he had risen, he went to Pharos, which at the time was still an island (it lay a short distance off the Canopic mouth), though today it is connected by a pier to the mainland. When he saw a surpassingly fertile spot—a strip of land, nearly

---

23. That Alexander was only a "social drinker" was one of several attempts to mitigate examples of his excessive behavior by the historian Aristobulus of Cassandreia, who seems to have been an engineer and wrote his history of Alexander in old age in the early third century BCE.

24. Homer's *Odyssey* 4.354–55.

equivalent in breadth to an isthmus, that separates a large lagoon and an arm of the ocean that terminates at a large harbor—he declared that Homer was not only admirable in other respects, but also the cleverest of architects, and he gave orders for his builders to trace the city's outline to conform to that site. . . . He ordered his contractors to get the work under way, while he himself set out for Ammon.[25] This was a long journey, one that furnished considerable trouble and hardship.

[27] When Alexander had crossed the desert and reached the site of the oracle, the prophet hailed him with a greeting from the god as from a father, whereupon Alexander inquired whether any of the murderers of his father had escaped him. When the prophet urged him to guard his tongue, as his father was not mortal,[26] Alexander rephrased the question and inquired whether the murderers of Philip had all been punished; he then inquired about his own empire, asking whether the god had granted him supreme power over all mankind. When the god had answered that this too had been granted, and that Philip had been fully avenged, Alexander presented the god with splendid votive offerings, and the priests with gifts of money.

That is what most writers report about the oracles. But Alexander himself, in a letter to his mother, says that he received certain secret prophecies, which on his return he will reveal to her alone. Some say that the prophet, wishing to hail him with the affectionate Greek greeting, "O paidion," misspoke, owing to his barbarian accent, and pronounced the last word with an "s" instead of an "n," saying, "O pai Dios," and that the slip delighted Alexander, whereupon the story spread abroad that the god had addressed him as "son of Zeus."[27]

[28] On the whole, Alexander treated the barbarians haughtily and behaved as if he actually believed in his divine begetting and birth, but to the Greeks he was moderate and restrained when it came to assuming his own divinity. But when writing to the Athenians about Samos[28] he said, "I cannot have given you that free and famous city, for you received it from the man who was then your master and was called my father," meaning Philip. . . .

---

25. For Ammon, see Herodotus, *Histories* 3.25, p. 42 note 49.

26. The prophet's reply implies that Zeus and not Philip was Alexander's true father.

27. That is, the prophet's thick Greek accent caused people to mistake the greeting, *O paidion,* "O, young man," for the phrase *pai Dios,* "son of Zeus." Plutarch is careful, however, to insert the qualification that this is a story that "some say" and not to assert that he believes it is true.

28. In 365 BCE, the Athenians occupied the island of Samos and expelled the local population. They then were able to retain control of Samos with Macedonian support until Alexander issued his exiles decree in 324 BCE ordering the Greek cities to allow the return of all exiles including the Samian exiles. Fear of losing Samos was the principal reason that Athens joined the unsuccessful revolt against Macedonian rule known as the Lamian War (323 BCE–322 BCE) that resulted in the end of Athenian naval power and the overthrow of the democracy.

[29] When Darius sent a letter to Alexander and his friends, requesting him to accept ten thousand talents in return for his captives, to keep all the territory east of the Euphrates, to marry one of his daughters, and to be his friend and ally, Alexander shared the letter's contents with his Companions. When Parmenio said, "Well, if *I* were Alexander, I would accept these terms," Alexander replied, "and so would *I*, by Zeus, if I were Parmenio." He accordingly wrote in reply that if Darius came to him, he would be shown every courtesy; if not, Alexander would march against him at once.

THE BATTLE OF GAUGAMELA

The next two years were decisive for Alexander's campaign. In the fall of 331 BCE, he again defeated Darius III, this time at the battle of Gaugamela in what is now Iraq. Within a year Alexander was master of Persia, and Darius III had been assassinated by Bessus, the satrap of Bactria (modern Afghanistan) who assumed the throne as Artaxerxes V. In the meantime, Alexander had sacked and burned Persepolis, the principal Persian royal residence, thereby signaling the end of the Greek war of revenge that had been the supposed justification for his invasion of Asia. At the same time, his assumption of some aspects of Persian royal protocol to rally Persian support against Bessus had begun to arouse resistance among his closest Macedonian supporters.

[33] And now, after Alexander had addressed the Thessalians and the other Greeks at great length, and they had urged him, with a roar, to lead them against the barbarians, he shifted his spear to his left hand and with his right called on the gods, as Callisthenes[29] says, beseeching them, if he was truly the offspring of Zeus, to defend and strengthen the Greeks. The seer Aristander, wearing a white shawl and a golden crown, rode by and pointed out an eagle soaring over Alexander's head and flying straight toward the enemy, at the sight of which the men grew bold and encouraged one another, the cavalry charged at full speed against the enemy, and the phalanx surged forward like a wave. But before the first ranks had come to blows, the barbarians gave ground and there was a relentless pursuit, Alexander driving the conquered force toward their center, where Darius was. For Alexander saw him from a distance—a tall, handsome man mounted on a high chariot, fenced about with many splendid horsemen, who stood in compact array around the chariot to

---

29. Callisthenes was Aristotle's nephew and the official historian of the campaign. He was imprisoned and probably executed in 327 BCE on the charge of being involved in the so-called Pages' Conspiracy. Nevertheless, despite being incomplete, his history was published and became the ultimate source of all ancient accounts of the first years of the campaign.

resist the enemy's attack. But once Alexander, formidable when seen at close range, had charged after the fugitives toward the ranks who were standing their ground, he astounded and scattered almost all of them. The best and noblest, however, who were slain in front of their king and falling in heaps on one another, hindered the Macedonians' pursuit, struggling convulsively and flinging themselves around the men and horses.

But Darius, faced with all these horrors and seeing his defenders retreating toward him and making it impossible to turn his chariot around and drive through easily, since its wheels were obstructed and jammed by the large numbers of fallen bodies, while his horses, overcome and hidden by the masses of corpses, were rearing up and alarming his charioteer, abandoned his chariot and weapons, mounted a mare that, according to report, had just foaled, and fled. But it is thought that he would not have escaped had other horsemen not come from Parmenio, summoning Alexander with the plea that a large enemy force was still in formation there and would not give ground. In fact, Parmenio is generally criticized for having been sluggish and idle in that battle, either because old age was already impairing his courage, or because he was oppressed by the arrogance and pomp, as Callisthenes phrases it, of Alexander's sovereignty, and regarded it with envy. At the time, though the king was vexed by the summons, he did not tell his men the truth, but signaled retreat, declaring that he would refrain from further slaughter since darkness was falling. And as he drove toward the division that was in danger, he heard on the way that the enemy had been roundly defeated and was fleeing.

[34] The battle having had this outcome, the empire of the Persians appeared to have been utterly destroyed, and Alexander, proclaimed king of Asia,[30] performed splendid sacrifices to the gods and presented his friends with large sums of money, houses, and commands. In his eagerness to be honored by the Greeks, he wrote that all their tyrannies had been abolished and that they might govern themselves autonomously.[31]

ALEXANDER AND THE PERSIANS

[36] On becoming master of Susa, Alexander came into possession, in the palace, of forty thousand talents of coined money and all the other trappings of untold wealth.

[38] After this, when he was about to march against Darius, he chanced to take part in a playful carousal with his Companions that was also attended by women

---

30. "Asia" in this context means the Persian Empire, so Alexander was proclaimed, perhaps by the army, king of the Persian Empire.

31. In 334 BCE, Alexander had ordered the replacement of Persian-supported tyrannies by democracies in the Greek cities of Anatolia to rally support for his invasion.

who came to revel with their lovers.[32] The most popular among them was Thais, an Athenian by birth, and the mistress of Ptolemy, who subsequently became king.[33] Partly wishing to praise Alexander properly, and partly in jest, she was moved during the carousal to make a speech in keeping with the character of her native land, though it was too high-flown for a person of her sort. She said that for all she had suffered wandering about Asia she was on that day receiving her reward, enjoying a luxurious party in the splendid palace of the Persians. But it would be pleasanter still to go on a revel and burn down the house of Xerxes, who had burned Athens,[34] she herself kindling the fire while Alexander looked on, so that a legend might be preserved for mankind that the women of Alexander's entourage imposed a greater punishment on the Persians on behalf of Greece than all her naval and infantry commanders. This speech was received with uproarious applause, and the king's Companions eagerly cheered him on. Captivated, the king leaped up with a garland and a torch and led the way. The other revelers, following with a merry shout, stood around the palace, and other Macedonians who learned of it ran there with torches and were filled with joy. For they were hoping that the burning and destruction of the palace were the acts of a man who had fixed his thoughts on home and would not settle among barbarians. Some say that these events came about in this way, while others say they were planned; but it is agreed that Alexander quickly repented and gave orders for the fire to be extinguished.

[42] Alexander now marched out in the belief that he would again do battle with Darius. But on hearing that the king had been captured by Bessus, Alexander sent the Thessalians home, giving the mercenaries a gift of two thousand talents over and above their pay. And in the course of the pursuit, which proved troublesome and prolonged (in eleven days he covered upward of four hundred miles on horseback), most of his men gave out, mainly from lack of water.

[43] It is said that only sixty rushed together into the enemy's camp, where they actually rode over much silver and gold that had been discarded, passed many wagons of children and women being carried this way and that, bereft of drivers, and pursued the first fugitives, thinking that Darius was among them. They finally found Darius lying in a wagon, his body full of javelins, on the point of death. Yet

---

32. These events took place at Persepolis, the principal residence of the Persian kings in the fourth century BCE, where envoys were received and where the royal tombs were located.
33. Of Egypt. Ptolemy, son of Lagus, governed Egypt from 323 BCE to 282 BCE, first as satrap from 323 BCE to 305 BCE and then as king from 305 BCE until his death in 282 BCE.
34. The sack of the city of Persepolis and the burning of the Persian palaces there in spring, 330 BCE, was, as this passage shows, already controversial in antiquity. Archaeological evidence, which indicates that the palaces were thoroughly looted before being burned and that the fires were confined only to the ceremonial sections of the complex, suggests that the destruction was deliberate and well planned.

he asked for something to drink, and on taking some cool water said to Polystratus, who had given it to him, "This, my good fellow, is the climax of all my bad luck—to be treated well without being able to make a return. But Alexander will thank you for the favor, and the gods will reward Alexander for his kindness to my mother, wife, and children. To him, through you, I give this right hand." So saying, and taking Polystratus's hand, he died. When Alexander arrived, he was visibly grieved by the man's death; loosening his own cloak, he threw it over the body and shrouded it. And later on, when he found Bessus, he had him dismembered. Bending two straight trees toward each other, he attached a part of the man's body to each; then, when the trees were let go, and swung back with a rush, the part attached to each went with it.

[45] From there, after moving the army into Parthian territory, Alexander found himself at leisure, and for the first time donned barbarian attire, either because he wanted to adapt himself to the local customs (in the belief that community of race and custom is a great humanizer of men), or as an attempt to introduce the practice of ritual bowing[35] to the Macedonians by gradually accustoming them to tolerate changes in his way of life and habits. . . . And the sight pained the Macedonians. But since they admired all his other virtues, they supposed they should forgive some of the things he chose to do for the sake of his own pleasure and renown.

[47] Alexander now adapted his way of life more and more to that of the local inhabitants, and encouraged the latter to adopt Macedonian customs, thinking that by means of assimilation and fellowship—by good will rather than by force—he would ground his authority more securely while he himself was far away. That was why, upon selecting thirty thousand boys, he gave orders that they were to study Greek literature and be trained in Macedonian warfare, having assigned them several instructors.[36] As for his union with Roxane,[37] while it is true that, charmed by her youth and beauty, he fell in love when he saw her dancing at a drinking party, the match was also thought to accord well with his immediate aims. For the barbarians were heartened by the fellowship his marriage created, and admired Alexander

---

35. *Proskynesis* involved prostration before the king in recognition of his superiority to his subjects. Although Persians at Alexander's court performed it to him, Greeks and Macedonians mistakenly believed it implied recognition of his divinity and objected strongly when he demanded they also perform it. Callisthenes's refusal to perform it, while popular with Alexander's Greek and Macedonian officers, infuriated the king.

36. His attempt to integrate them into the Macedonian army in 324 BCE was one of the causes of its mutiny at Opis.

37. Alexander married Roxane, "Little Star," 327 BCE, most likely to win the support of her father, an important Bactrian or Sogdian noble named Oxyartes. She and her son Alexander IV were murdered in 310 BCE by Cassander, the son of Antipater, who had seized control of Macedon in 316 BCE.

beyond measure because he had proved so temperate in these matters that he would not even consent to touch, without legal right, the only woman by whom he had been vanquished.

ALEXANDER IN INDIA

The four years from 329 BCE to 325 BCE saw some of the fiercest fighting of the campaign. Once Darius III and Bessus were dead, Alexander was the unchallenged ruler of the former Persian Empire, yet he elected not to stop his campaign. He spent the first two years in Bactria and Sogdiana (modern Afghanistan, Tajikistan, and Uzbekistan) fighting a tough guerilla war before his authority was firmly established in the region. During the next two years, he campaigned in India and fought the last of his major battles against the Indian king Porus. His soldiers confronted war elephants for the first time in this battle. India also proved to be the end of the campaign, as his troops, fearful of rumors of huge armies of elephants ahead of them—homesick, and increasingly suspicious of Alexander's ultimate goals, mutinied and forced him to turn back and lead them home.

[57] When Alexander was about to cross the mountains into India, he saw that his army was overburdened, its mobility impaired by its vast spoils. At dawn, when the wagons had been packed up, he burned his own wagons first, along with those of his Companions, and then commanded that those of the Macedonians be set on fire. And the ambition that prompted this exploit seemed greater and more formidable than the deed itself. For though a few of his soldiers were vexed, most of them, raising an impassioned war cry, shared their necessities with those who needed them, and burned and destroyed their own superfluous goods, thereby filling Alexander with zeal and eagerness. By then he had also become a fearsome and implacable punisher of any who misbehaved. For after appointing Menander, one of his Companions, as chief of a garrison, he had the man killed for declining to remain in office, and personally dispatched Orsodates, one of the barbarians who revolted from him, with a bow shot.

[59] Taxiles is said to have been in possession of a portion of India no smaller in size than Egypt—a region especially rich in pastures and land that bore fine fruit, and to have been, in his own way, a clever man. Welcoming Alexander, he said, "What need have we, Alexander, to fight with one another if you have come intending to deprive us neither of water nor of necessary sustenance, the only things for which sensible men are compelled to fight? As for the other riches and possessions so-called—if I prove the stronger man, I am ready to treat you well, but if the weaker, I do not hesitate to show my gratitude when treated well." Delighted, Alexander clasped Taxiles by the hand and said, "Do you somehow imagine that

after such friendly words our meeting will not lead to a battle? But you will not get the better of me; for I shall contend against you and fight on behalf of the favors I bestow, that you may not surpass me in generosity." Receiving many gifts, and giving more, Alexander finally made Taxiles a present of 1,000 talents of coined money. In doing so, though he greatly pained his friends, he made many of the barbarians regard him more kindly.

But the most warlike of the Indians, who were mercenaries, went about to the various cities, defending them stoutly and doing Alexander great harm. Eventually, after making a truce with them in a certain city, Alexander caught them on the road as they were departing and killed them all. And this adheres like a stain to his military record; in all other instances he waged war lawfully and in a manner worthy of a king. No less than the mercenaries, the philosophers[38] made trouble for him by abusing any kings who allied themselves with him, and by encouraging free peoples to revolt—which was why he had many of these men hanged as well.

[60] Alexander himself, in his letters,[39] has described his campaign against Porus.[40] He says that their two camps were separated by the river Hydaspes, and that Porus, stationing his elephants on the opposite bank, kept constant watch on the crossing. Accordingly, day after day Alexander created plenty of noise and uproar in his camp, and thereby accustomed the barbarians not to be alarmed. And then, one stormy, moonless night, taking a detachment of his infantry and his best horsemen, he marched a distance from the enemy and crossed to a smallish island. Rain poured down furiously there, and many hurricanes and lightning bolts assailed his men. But though he saw some of them perishing and burned to death by the lightning, he nevertheless set forth from the island toward the opposite banks. But the Hydaspes, swollen and agitated by the storm, forced a large breach in its bank, and a large part of the stream surged through it; and the ground between the two channels was too slippery and jagged to provide any secure footing. At that point Alexander is said to have cried, "Athenians, can you believe the dangers I undergo to earn your praise?" ... Alexander himself says that after abandoning their rafts they crossed the breach with their armor on, the water coming up to their chests; and that after getting across he led his horsemen two and a half miles in advance of his

---

38. As the various names Greeks used for Indian ascetics such as Brahmans, gymnosophists, wise men, or philosophers indicate, they confused the ascetics' caste status with their social and intellectual roles.

39. Plutarch quotes numerous alleged letters of Alexander, possibly from a now lost collection. Scholars believe that the authenticity of each letter must be determined separately instead of assuming they are either all authentic or all forgeries.

40. In the case of Porus's and Alexander's ally Taxiles, the Greeks confused the name of the people they ruled, in the case of Porus the Paurava, and the king's city, Taxila, in the case of Taxiles, with that of their ruler.

infantry, calculating that if the enemy attacked with their cavalry, he would prove superior, whereas if they advanced their phalanx, his own infantry would arrive in time. And his expectation was justified. For after routing a thousand horsemen and the sixty chariots that had attacked him, he seized all the chariots and killed four hundred of the horsemen. As Porus now guessed that Alexander himself had crossed the river, he advanced against him with his entire force, except the party he left behind to prevent the Macedonians from crossing. But Alexander, dreading the beasts and the enormous numbers of the enemy, attacked the left wing himself, and ordered Coenus to assault the right. A rout occurring at each wing, Porus's men, forced back, retreated in each case toward the beasts, and crowded in among them. From then on the battle was a scramble until, in the eighth hour, the enemy gave up. This is the account the victor himself gives in his letters.

Most of the historians agree that Porus's height exceeded four cubits by a span,[41] and that because of his stature and the dignity of his physique, his size in relation to his elephant was proportional to that of a horseman's to his horse. Yet his was the largest elephant; and it showed a wonderful understanding and concern for the king, angrily warding off his attackers and repulsing them while the king was still vigorous. But when it sensed that he was wearied by scores of missiles and wounds, and dreaded that he might slip off, it lowered itself gently to its knees; and gently grasping the spears with its proboscis, drew each of them from Porus's body. When Alexander asked the captive Porus how he should treat him, Porus replied, "Like a king"; and when Alexander then asked whether he had anything else to say, Porus answered, "Everything is comprehended in 'like a king.'" Accordingly, Alexander not only allowed Porus to rule the territories over which he had been reigning, appointing him as satrap, but added another territory, having subdued its autonomous tribes, in which there were said to be fifteen peoples, five thousand noteworthy cities, and a great many villages. And he appointed Philip, one of his Companions, as satrap over a territory three times as large.

[62] The battle with Porus sapped the Macedonians' vigor, and discouraged them from advancing farther into India. After barely repelling Porus, who had arrayed twenty thousand infantry and two thousand cavalry against them, they firmly opposed Alexander when he insisted on crossing the river Ganges;[42] for they had learned that it was four miles wide and one hundred fathoms deep, and that the opposite banks were concealed by enormous numbers of infantry, horses, and elephants. For it was said that the kings of the Gandarites and Praesii were awaiting him with 80,000 horsemen, 200,000 foot soldiers, 8,000 war chariots, and 6,000

---

41. Over six feet tall.

42. Actually the Hyphasis River, the modern Beas, in the Punjab region of North India, which is ca. 250 miles west of the upper reaches of the Ganges.

warrior elephants.[43] And this was no idle boast. For Androcottus,[44] who reigned shortly thereafter, made Seleucus a present of 500 elephants, and with any army of 600,000 invaded and subdued all of India.

At first, in his despair and anger, Alexander shut himself up in his tent and lay there, claiming no satisfaction with what he had accomplished unless he crossed the Ganges and regarding retreat as an admission of defeat. But when his friends, who gave him suitable consolation, and his men, who stood weeping and wailing by his door, appealed to him, he relented and broke up camp, fashioning many false and deceptive devices to enhance his renown; for he ordered the manufacture of armor that was larger than usual, taller horse stalls, and heavier bridles, and left these items behind, scattered about, and built altars of the gods, which to this day are held sacred by the kings of the Praesii, who cross the river and perform sacrifices on them in the Greek manner.

RETURN TO THE WEST

The final two years of Alexander's reign were not uneventful. Eager to reach Ocean, the legendary boundary of the world, Alexander led his army down the Indus River to the Indian Ocean, receiving along the way the last and most serious of his many wounds. On reaching the Indian Ocean, he then led his army in what proved to be a catastrophic march through the Gedrosian Desert—modern Baluchistan—in the hope of doing what his ancestors Heracles and Dionysus had failed to accomplish. When he finally reached Babylon in 323 BCE, he was seriously ill, probably from a combination of malaria and complications of the wound, only partially healed, he had received in India. He died on June 10, 323 BCE.

[63] From there, eager to see the outer sea,[45] he built many rafts and ferry boats furnished with oars and was transported down the rivers[46] in a leisurely manner. But the voyage was not free of toil or even of battles: on landing and disembarking

---

43. Plutarch's political geography of the Ganges valley is confused. Praesii was the Greek name for the kingdom of Magadha in the eastern Ganges valley. The location of the Gandarites is unknown, with suggestions ranging from near the Hyphasis to the eastern Ganges valley.
44. Chandragupta Maurya (ca. 321 BCE—ca. 297 BCE), the founder of the Mauryan Empire. Other sources suggest that he was a mercenary commander and may have met Alexander.
45. By "outer sea" Alexander meant our Indian Ocean, which he and his contemporaries believed was part of a single Ocean which surrounded the *oecumene*, the inhabited world known to them, essentially Europe, Asia, and a much reduced Africa.
46. That is, the tributaries of the Indus and the Indus itself.

at the cities, he subdued them all.[47] Against the so-called Malli, whom they say were the most warlike of the Indians, he just missed being cut to pieces. For he dispersed the Indians from their walls with spears, and was the first to mount the wall by a ladder; and when the ladder was shattered, and he was sustaining blows from the barbarians who were resisting from below, he wheeled about, though he had few companions, and leaped down into the midst of his enemies, and luckily landed on his feet. When he brandished his weapons, the barbarians imagined that some flamelike specter hovered before his body, which was why they fled at first and scattered. But when they saw him with two of his shield-bearers, they rushed at him, some of them trying to wound him with their swords and spears as he defended himself; and one, standing a little way off, released from his bow an arrow so forceful and steady that on piercing Alexander's breastplate it lodged in the bones near his chest. He himself yielded to the blow, his body bending double, whereupon his assailant, having hit him, advanced with his scimitar drawn, while Peucestas and Limnaeus[48] stood over the king. When both of these men were struck, Limnaeus perished, but Peucestas held out, and Alexander slew the barbarian.

After sustaining many wounds, Alexander was finally hit on the neck with a cudgel, at which point he planted his body against the wall and merely gazed at his enemies. Thereupon the Macedonians crowded around him, and he was seized, already unconscious, and carried to his tent. And at once there was a rumor in the army that he had died. When with great difficulty and effort they had excised the arrow's shaft, which was made of wood, and succeeded in removing his breastplate, they had to excise the barb that had entered one of his bones. It is said that the barb was three finger breadths wide and four long. That was why, as it was being extracted, he fainted repeatedly and nearly died; but he nonetheless recovered. And when he was out of danger, but still weak and receiving prolonged care and treatment, he became aware, from the disturbance outside, that the Macedonians were longing to see him. He then donned a cloak and went out. After sacrificing to the gods, he again set sail and voyaged along the coast, subjugating great cities and extensive territory.

[66] His voyage down the rivers to the sea took seven months.[49] When he surged into the ocean with his fleet, he sailed out to an island that he called Scillustis, though others call it Psiltucis. Disembarking there, he sacrificed to the gods and observed the natural features of the sea and the points on the coast that were accessible. Then, on praying that no man after him might travel beyond the bounds of his own expedition, he turned back. Appointing Nearchus as admiral,

---

47. The Indus campaign saw some of the hardest fighting of the entire expedition, including the capture of the city of Malli during which he was seriously wounded.

48. The identity of the two men who saved Alexander was controversial in antiquity, with only Peucestas being mentioned in all lists.

49. Roughly, the first half of 325 BCE.

and Onesicritus as chief pilot, he gave orders for the fleet to sail along the coast, keeping India on its right.[50] He himself, advancing on foot through the Oreitans' territory, was led into the direst hardship and lost an enormous number of men, so that not even a fourth of his fighting force was brought back, though his infantry had numbered 120,000, and his cavalry 15,000. Virulent diseases, bad food, the burning heat, and famine destroyed most of them, as they were crossing the untilled country of men who lived poorly and owned only a few miserable sheep whose flesh was inferior and foul-smelling, since the animals had been fed on ocean fish. After crossing the region with great difficulty in sixty days, he reached Gedrosia, where he suddenly had all things in abundance, since the nearest satraps and kings had provided them.

[68] When Nearchus and his men reached him from the coast, Alexander so enjoyed hearing in detail about their voyage that he himself decided to sail down the Euphrates with a large armament, and then, after circumnavigating Arabia and Africa, to pass through the Pillars of Heracles and into the inner sea.[51] He had vessels of all sorts built for him at Thapsacus, and sailors and helmsmen were assembled from all quarters. But his difficult return march, the wound he sustained among the Malli, and the reports of his army's heavy losses raised doubts about his survival, which in turn incited his subject peoples to revolt and occasioned great iniquity, greed, and insolence among his generals and satraps. In short, unrest and revolutionary impulses spread everywhere. . . . For these reasons he sent Nearchus back to the coast (for he was determined to fill the entire seaboard with wars), while he himself proceeded to punish the rogues among his generals. He himself killed one of Abuletes's[52] sons, Oxyartes,[53] by running him through with a spear; and when Abuletes failed to furnish him with the necessary provisions, bringing him three thousand talents of coined money instead, Alexander ordered the money to be thrown to the horses. When they would not touch it, he said, "What use to us are these provisions of yours?" and cast Abuletes into prison.

---

50. Alexander's plan was for Nearchus to explore the coast of Carmania with the fleet while Alexander marched along the coast of the desert region of Gedrosia, modern Baluchistan, with the bulk of the army. The plan failed, however, as geography forced Alexander to divert inland where the army suffered massive losses from hunger and flash floods. Much of Nearchus's account of his voyage survives in a work by the second-century CE historian Arrian titled *Indica*.

51. According to other sources, this was one of several extravagant plans discovered in Alexander's papers after his death that were canceled by a vote of the army at Babylon.

52. Abuletes was the satrap of Susiana, who had surrendered to Alexander and was allowed to retain his office as part of Alexander's effort to encourage high-ranking Persians to support him.

53. Actually Oxathres, the satrap of Paraetacene.

[70] Holding a wedding for his Companions at Susa, he himself married Darius's daughter Stateira and assigned the noblest women to the noblest men;[54] and for the Macedonians who had already married[55] he provided a public wedding feast at which he is said to have given each of the nine thousand invited guests a golden drinking cup for the libations. Distinguishing himself admirably in every way, he even cleared the debts his men had incurred, which amounted to 9,870 talents.

[71] Since the thirty thousand boys[56] he had left behind for training and exercises had acquired manly physiques and handsome looks, and displayed a wonderful ease and lightness in their drills, Alexander was delighted, though the Macedonians grew despondent and feared that he would regard *them* as less valuable. That was why, when he sent the weak and disabled to the coast, they said it was insulting and humiliating that after using men in every capacity he discarded them in disgrace and cast them back to their native cities and parents, no longer the men they had been when he recruited them. They therefore urged him to send them *all* away and to consider all the Macedonians useless, since he now had these young dancers of the war dance with whom he could go forth and conquer the world.

To this Alexander responded harshly, and in his anger showered them with abuse. On driving them away, he gave his guard posts to Persians, out of whom he chose his bodyguards and heralds. When the Macedonians saw him escorted by Persians, while they themselves were excluded and dishonored, they were humbled; and in talking among themselves, they realized that they had been almost mad with envy and rage. Coming to their senses at last, they visited Alexander's tent, unarmed and wearing only their tunics. . . . For two days and nights they persisted in standing at his door, weeping and appealing to him as their master. On the third day, coming forth and seeing them humbled and sobbing pitiably, he wept for a long time; then, after duly scolding them, he addressed them kindly and released the men who were unfit, giving them splendid gifts and writing to Antipater[57] that

---

54. The mass marriage of almost a hundred of Alexander's officers and Iranian aristocratic women occurred in the spring of 324 BCE. In addition to Stateira, Alexander also married Parysatis, daughter of Artaxerxes III, thereby establishing connections with the families of the last two Persian kings. Both women, however, were murdered after Alexander's death, allegedly on the orders of Roxane.

55. During the course of the campaign, Alexander had encouraged his soldiers to marry their Iranian mistresses and other captive women, who together with their children then accompanied the army on its march; in ancient military jargon, they were said to be part of the "baggage." Many of them were killed in a flash flood in Gedrosia.

56. See above Chapter 47 and note 36 on p. 232.

57. Antipater was regent for Alexander in Macedon during the campaign and responsible for management of affairs also in Greece and Thrace.

at all public games and theaters they were to occupy the front seats, crowned with laurel. He also awarded pensions to the children, now orphans, of the men who had died.

BABYLON AND THE DEATH OF ALEXANDER

[73] As he was advancing to Babylon, Nearchus, who had rejoined him after sailing through the ocean to the Euphrates, said that some Chaldaeans[58] had met him and recommended that Alexander keep away from Babylon. But Alexander ignored this advice and proceeded onward. . . . He was also perturbed by many other signs. For example, a tame ass, attacking the largest and most beautiful lion in his menagerie, kicked it to death. And when he had stripped to anoint himself and exercise, and was playing ball, and the young men who were playing went to put on their clothes, they found a fellow sitting silently on the throne, wearing the diadem and cloaked in the royal robe.[59] The man, when asked who he was, was silent for a long time. Then, collecting himself, he said that his name was Dionysius, a Messenian by birth, and that charged with some crime he had been brought there from the coast and kept in chains for a long time; but just now the god Sarapis,[60] standing before him, had removed his chains, led him to that spot, and told him to don the robe and diadem, sit on the throne, and remain silent.

[74] On hearing of this, Alexander obeyed the seers and did away with the man. He himself now lost heart, and grew dubious about divine protection, and suspicious of his friends. He particularly feared Antipater and his sons, one of whom, Iolaus, was his chief cup-bearer; the other, Cassander, had lately arrived.[61] And when Cassander, on catching sight of some barbarians performing

---

58. The Chaldaeans were originally one of several ethnic groups in southern Mesopotamia, who ultimately came to rule Babylon as the Neo-Babylonian dynasty from c. 625 BCE to the Persian conquest of Babylon in 639 BCE. During the Persian and Hellenistic periods, the term "Chaldaean" was used to designate an elite caste of Mesopotamian priests.

59. This story probably refers to an attempt by the Babylonian priests to avert the threats to Alexander by performing a substitute king ritual in which a criminal or slave was made king for a brief period and then killed in the hope that the forecasted evils would be transferred to the substitute king and fulfilled by his death.

60. Sarapis is generally considered a syncretistic Egyptian god created during the reign of Ptolemy I by the identification of the Greek god of the underworld Hades and the Egyptian ruler of the dead Osiris. The reference to Sarapis here and in Chapter 76 suggests that a form of Sarapis may already have existed during Alexander's reign.

61. A document was widely circulated in antiquity that purported to reveal that Alexander was murdered by a conspiracy organized by Antipater, who feared being replaced in his office by Alexander, and carried out by his sons and Aristotle, who prepared the poison, to avenge the execution to Callisthenes.

a ritual bow, could not help laughing, since he had been reared in the Greek manner and had never seen such a thing before, Alexander flew into a rage, grasped Cassander's hair firmly with both hands, and knocked his head against the wall.

[75] Once Alexander had permitted himself to believe in divine influences, his mind grew so troubled and apprehensive that he regarded any odd or unusual occurrence, no matter how trivial, as a sign or portent; and his palace was full of people sacrificing, performing ritual purifications, and prophesying. . . .

After entertaining Nearchus and his men with a brilliant banquet, he bathed, as was his habit before going to bed; but then he joined Medius in a carousal, at the latter's invitation. Then, after drinking all the next day, he fell into a fever.

[76] The royal diaries[62] give the following account of his disease. On the eighteenth of the month of Daesius[63] he slept in the bathhouse because of his fever. On the next day, after bathing, he moved back to his bedroom and spent the day playing at dice with Medius. Then, after bathing late in the day, he performed his sacrifices to the gods, took a little food, and was feverish during the night. On the twentieth, after bathing again, he performed his customary sacrifice; reclining in the bathhouse, he devoted himself to Nearchus, listening to his account of his voyage and of the Great Sea.

On the twenty-first, spending the day in the same way, his fever worsened; he passed a difficult night, and on the next day was in a raging fever. After being carried outside, he lay down beside the great bath, where he talked with his officers about the vacant posts of his realm and how they might be filled by able men. On the twenty-fourth, though in a high fever, he had himself carried out to perform his sacrifices. He gave orders for his most important officers to wait in the courtyard, and for the commanders of 128 men (taxiarchs) and the commanders of 512 men (pentakosiarchs) to pass the night outside. On the twenty-fifth, he was carried to the palace on the other side of the river, where he slept a little, though his fever did not let up. When his officers came to him, he could not speak. His condition was unchanged on the twenty-sixth, which was why the Macedonians, thinking he had died, came shouting to his door, threatened his companions, and forced their way in. And when the doors had been thrown open to them, they all filed past his couch, one by one, wearing only their tunics. . . . And on the twenty-eighth, toward evening, he died.

---

62. It is known that Alexander's secretary, Eumenes of Cardia, kept a diary of the reign. Whether or not the quotations in Plutarch and other sources are actually from this diary is controversial, with most scholars doubting their authenticity.

63. Early June 323 BCE. According to a Babylonian document, Alexander died on June 11, 323 BCE.

[77] Most of these details have been set down here exactly as recorded in the diaries. In the immediate aftermath, no one suspected poisoning; but five years later, they say, when information was given, Olympias had many persons put to death,[64] and cast out the ashes of Iolaus,[65] alleging that he had administered the poison. . . . But most think that the story about the poisoning is a complete fabrication.

---

64. Olympias, Alexander's mother, executed Philip III and his wife, Eurydice, in 317 BCE together with many of their supporters as part of the civil war in Macedon between Cassander and Olympias, who was acting as guardian for Roxane and Alexander's then six-year-old son, Alexander IV.

65. According to the document discussed in note 62, Iolaus was Cassander's brother and Alexander's wine pourer, and he was responsible for serving Alexander the poisoned wine that supposedly killed him.

Suggested Readings

General

Burrow, John. *A History of Histories: Epics, Chronicles, Romances and Inquiries from Herodotus and Thucydides to the Twentieth Century*. New York: Alfred A. Knopf, 2008. A beautifully written history of western historiography from antiquity to the present.

Marincola, John, ed. *A Companion to Greek and Roman Historiography*. 2 vols. Malden, MA: Blackwell Publishing, 2007. A massive compilation of essays by leading scholars on all aspects of Greek and Roman historiography.

Martin, Thomas R. *Herodotus and Sima Qian: The First Great Historians of Greece and China, A Brief History with Documents*. Boston: St. Martins, 2010. A brief but illuminating comparative study of the origin of historiography in Greece and China.

Momigliano, Arnaldo. *The Classical Foundations of Modern Historiography*. Berkeley and Los Angeles: University of California Press, 1990. Important analysis of the significance of the works of Greek and Roman historians for the development of European historiography after the Renaissance.

Greek Historiography

Brown, T. S. *The Greek Historians*. Lexington, MA: D. C. Heath and Company, 1973. Biographical approach to the study of Greek historiography.

Bury, J. B. *The Ancient Greek Historians*. New York: St. Martins Press, 1909. Old study of Greek historiography important for its clear summary of the evidence and the state of scholarship at the beginning of the twentieth century.

Drews, Robert. *The Greek Accounts of Eastern History*. Cambridge, MA: Harvard University Press, 1973. Important analysis of the reaction of Herodotus and his successors to the Persian Wars.

Fornara, Charles William. *The Nature of History in Ancient Greece and Rome*. Berkeley and Los Angeles: University of California Press, 1983. Important discussion of the methodology of Greek and Roman historians.

Luce, T. J. *The Greek Historians*. London: Routledge, 1997. Analysis of the literary aspects of the works of Greek historians from Herodotus to Polybius.

Marincola, John, trans. *On Writing History from Herodotus to Herodian*. New York: Random House, 2017. Comprehensive anthology of Greek and Roman discussions of how to write history.

Scanlon, Thomas F. *Greek Historiography*. Malden, MA: Wiley Blackwell, 2015. Literary analysis of Greek historians from the fifth century BCE to the third century CE.

Starr, Chester G. *The Awakening of the Greek Historical Spirit*. New York: Alfred A. Knopf, 1968. Study of the intellectual preconditions for the emergence of historiography in the fifth century BCE.

HERODOTUS

Blanco, Walter, and Jennifer T. Roberts, eds. *Herodotus The Histories*. 2nd ed. New York: W. W. Norton, 2013. Readable translation accompanied by almost 200 pages of background material, literary criticism, and essays on the historical context of the *Histories*.

Dewald, Carolyn, and Marincola, John, eds. *The Cambridge Companion to Herodotus*. Cambridge: Cambridge University Press, 2006. Twenty articles dealing with a wide range of topics including Herodotus's life, storytelling, religion, politics, and ethnography.

Herodotus. *Histories*. Translated by Pamela Mensch. Edited by James Romm. Indianapolis: Hackett Publishing Company, 2014. A translation for persons who desire a version that is readable but still as literal as possible.

Jenson, Erik. *The Greco-Persian Wars: A Short History with Documents*. Indianapolis: Hackett Publishing Company, 2021. A brief but lucid history of the Persian Wars accompanied by numerous Greek, Egyptian, and Near Eastern documents.

Roberts, Jennifer T. *Herodotus: A Very Short Introduction*. Oxford: Oxford University Press, 2011. An introduction to Herodotus's *Histories* written from the perspective of a Greek historian.

Romm, James. *Herodotus*. New Haven: Yale University Press, 1998. An introduction to the *Histories* emphasizing Herodotus's role as the creator of a new literary genre.

Strassler, Robert B., ed. *The Landmark Herodotus*. New York: Pantheon Books, 2007. A readable translation accompanied by an extensive introduction and notes, numerous maps and diagrams, and over a hundred pages of articles on the historical and geographical context of Herodotus's account of the Persian Wars.

Thucydides

Blanco, Walter, and Jennifer Tolbert Roberts, eds. *Thucydides The Peloponnesian War.* New York: W. W. Norton, 1998. Readable translation accompanied by almost 200 pages of background material, literary criticism, and essays on the historical context of Thucydides's work.

Hornblower, Simon. *Thucydides.* Baltimore: Johns Hopkins University Press, 1987. Lucid introduction to the *History of the Peloponnesian War* by the most important contemporary student of the work.

Kagan, Donald. *Thucydides: The Reinvention of History.* New York: Viking, 2009. Critical evaluation of Thucydides as a historian by the leading historian of the Peloponnesian War.

Roberts, Jennifer T. *The Plague of War: Athens, Sparta, and the Struggle for Ancient Greece.* New York: Oxford University Press, 2017. A vividly written political and cultural history of the Peloponnesian War and its aftermath.

Rusten, Jeffrey S., ed. *Thucydides.* Oxford: Oxford University Press, 2009. Collection of articles by important contemporary scholars dealing various aspects of the *History of the Peloponnesian War* and its ancient and modern reception.

Thucydides. *The Peloponnesian War.* Translated by Steven Lattimore. Indianapolis: Hackett Publishing Company, 1998. A translation that attempts to reproduce as closely as possible in English the effect of Thucydides's austere style.

Zagorin, Perez. *Thucydides: An Introduction for the Common Reader.* Princeton: Princeton University Press, 2005. An introduction that attempts to provide a person reading the *History of the Peloponnesian War* for the first time all that she or he needs to enjoy the work.

Xenophon

Dillery, John. *Xenophon and the History of His Times.* London: Routledge, 1995. Perceptive study of Xenophon as a historian of his own times.

Flower, Michael A. *The Cambridge Companion to Xenophon.* Cambridge: Cambridge University Press, 2017. Valuable collection of twenty-two articles dealing with Xenophon's life, thought, works, and the reception of his works from the Renaissance to the present.

Strassler, Robert B., ed. *The Landmark Xenophon's Hellenika.* New York: Pantheon Books, 2009. Excellent translation of the *Hellenika* accompanied by an extensive introduction, numerous maps, and appendices dealing with the historical context of the *Hellenika*.

ARISTOTLE

Aristotle. *The Constitution of Athens*. Translated by P. J. Rhodes. Harmondsworth, UK: Penguin Books, 1984. Translation of *The Constitution of Athens* with extensive introduction and notes by the leading authority on the work.

Harding, Philip, ed. *The Story of Athens: The Fragments of the Local Chronicles of Athens*. New York: Routledge, 2008. Interesting attempt to reconstruct the content of the local chronicles of Athens that Aristotle used in writing the *Constitution of Athens*.

Stockton, David. *The Classical Athenian Democracy*. Oxford: Oxford University Press, 1990. Lucid account of the history of the Athenian democracy from the reforms of Solon to those of Ephialtes.

THE PARIAN MARBLE

Forsdyke, John. *Greece Before Homer: Ancient Chronology and Mythology*. London: Max Parish, 1956. Basic introduction to the goals and methods of Greek chronologists.

Rotstein, Andrea. *Literary History in the Parian Marble*. Cambridge, MA: Harvard University Press, 2016. Analysis of the *Parian Marble* as a source for the cultural history of Greece.

POLYBIUS

McGing, Brian. *Polybius' Histories*. Oxford: Oxford University Press, 2010. A general introduction to Polybius's *Histories* with emphasis on it as a work of literature.

Polybius. *The Histories*. Translated by Robin Waterfield. Oxford: Oxford University Press, 2010. Readable translation with introduction and notes of the first five books of the *Histories* and the fragments of the sixth book on the Roman constitution and the twelfth book on historiography.

Walbank, F. W. *Polybius*. Berkeley and Los Angeles: University of California Press, 1990. Illuminating study of Polybius as a historian of Rome by the greatest scholar of his work.

Waterfield, Robin. *Taken at the Flood: The Roman Conquest of Greece*. Oxford: Oxford University Press, 2014. Vividly written history of Greece during the period covered by Polybius's *Histories*.

MEMNON

Burstein, Stanley M. *Outpost of Hellenism: The Emergence of Heraclea on the Black Sea*. Berkeley and Los Angeles: University of California Press, 1976. Comprehensive history of Heraclea from its foundation in the sixth century BCE to its liberation from Macedonian rule in 281 BCE.

PLUTARCH

Anson, Edward M. *Alexander the Great: Themes and Issues*. London: Bloomsbury, 2013. Survey of main issues concerning the reign of Alexander the Great in contemporary scholarship.

Beck, Max, ed. *A Companion to Plutarch*. Malden, MA: Wiley Blackwell, 2014. Extensive collection of articles dealing with all aspects of Plutarch's life, his works, and their modern reception.

Duff, Timothy E. *Plutarch's Lives: Exploring Virtue and Vice*. Oxford: Oxford University Press, 1999. Innovative study of the influence of Plutarch's views as a moral philosopher on his work as a biographer.

Jones, C. P. *Plutarch and Rome*. Oxford: Clarendon Press, 1971. Brief but illuminating study of Plutarch's relation to Rome as reflected in his biographies and political essays.

Plutarch. *The Age of Alexander*. Edited and translated by Ian Scott-Kilvert and Timothy E. Duff. London: Penguin Group, 2011. Excellent recent translation of Plutarch's biographies dealing with the fourth and early third centuries BCE.

Russell, D. A. *Plutarch*. 2nd ed. London: Bristol Classical Press, 2001. Standard introduction to Plutarch and his works.

INDEX